D1170588

This book was a gift to the
Bryan College Library
in memory of:

Dr. Ronald Moore
History Professor at
University of Tennessee at Chattanooga
June 2006

EARTHLY NECESSITIES

THE NEW ECONOMIC HISTORY OF BRITAIN

Earthly Necessities

ECONOMIC LIVES IN
EARLY MODERN BRITAIN

KEITH WRIGHTSON

YALE UNIVERSITY PRESS
NEW HAVEN AND LONDON

The New Economic History of Britain
General Editor: David Cannadine

Copyright © 2000 by Keith Wrightson

The right of Keith Wrightson to be identified as the author of this work has been asserted by him in accordance with the Copyright, Designs and Patents Act 1988.

All rights reserved. This book may not be reproduced in whole or in part, in any form (beyond that copying permitted by Sections 107 and 108 of the U.S. Copyright Law and except by reviewers for the public press) without written permission from the publishers.

Set in Sabon MT by Best-set Typesetter Ltd, Hong Kong
Printed in Great Britain by St Edmundsbury Press

Library of Congress Catalog Card Number 00–33557

A catalogue record for this book is available from the British Library.

10 9 8 7 6 5 4 3 2 1

The coins on page 113 are from the reigns of Henry VIII showing the Tudor rose and of William III–George I showing Britannia. Both are from R. Ruding, *Plates to the Annals of the Coinage of Great Britain*, vol. 3 (London, 1840).

For permission to reprint extracts from copyright material the publishers gratefully acknowledge Faber and Faber Ltd and Farrar Straus & Giroux for 'Weighing In' by Seamus Heaney.

For Nicholas and Eliška

Contents

Illustrations

Acknowledgements

My friend Gordon Wardman tells me that this book has 'a particularly middle-aged quality about it'. I am happy to acknowledge that. It is the outcome of some thirty years of trying to understand the dynamics of social change in early modern Britain, and more specifically of twenty-five years of teaching the social, economic and cultural history of the period to students in St Andrews, Cambridge and elsewhere. That experience has involved the contracting of many intellectual debts: to the teachers who introduced me to the period; to the colleagues and students who have discussed its problems with me; to those whose influence has been transmitted only through the printed page.

This book represents my own attempt to make sense of the processes of economic change in Britain between the fifteenth and the eighteenth centuries, to convey something of the distinctive textures of the human experience of that age, and to introduce both in a manner which I hope will explain why they have a continuing claim on our attention. To that extent, it reflects my own preoccupations and perspectives. But of course it is massively dependent upon the work of others. If it has any claims to originality, they rest upon the way that I have tried to blend the ingredients provided by an exceptionally rich historical literature – one which is the collective achievement of generations of scholars and which continues to expand and develop. In the absence of footnotes, I cannot record the source of every piece of information included in the text, or every idea that has influenced my arguments. I have usually named those historians whose opinions and interpretative judgements I have quoted directly. Many more whose work I have found particularly helpful are listed in Further Reading and can be identified there. But behind them stands an army of others whose influence I can acknowledge only in general terms.

The difficult process of writing the book was made easier by the direct involvement of a number of colleagues and friends. Phil Withington and Andy Wood read and commented on the whole of the first draft as it was produced. Geoff Harcourt, Alex Shepard and Jennifer Melville did the same for particular chapters. Rob Colls, Mark Dawson, Craig Muldrew, John Walter and Gordon Wardman all read the penultimate draft and made many suggestions for improvement. David Cannadine and Paul Slack both provided generous encouragement and specific advice which was of great value in preparing the final version. I am grateful to them all and hope that the final product does not disappoint them.

K. W.
18 August 1999

Introduction

Early modern Britain: approaches and interpretations

The study of economic history, as William Cunningham put it in 1882, is 'not so much the study of a special class of facts, as the study of all the facts of a nation's history from a special point of view'. It originated, at a time when historians confined their attention almost exclusively to the political, diplomatic and military spheres, as a form of protest against such an enclosure of the historical imagination. David Hume, in widening the scope of his *History of England* (1754–78) to include, alongside his political narrative, broader discussions of changing patterns of economic, social and cultural life, observed that 'where a just notion is not formed of these particulars, history can be little instructive, and often will not be intelligible'. His contemporary, the political economist Sir James Steuart, noted wearily in his commonplace book that the historians of his day were 'so much taken up in describing battles, that they neglect matters of greater moment and which are of real use to the age they live in'.

In the two and a half centuries since Steuart grumbled by candlelight, the fundamental achievement of economic history has been that its practitioners mounted the first, and for that reason perhaps the most important, of a series of successful challenges to such a narrow vision of the past. And the best of them did so not only by concerning themselves with the fundamental human issues of material existence and the production and distribution of income and wealth, but also by using the study of economic life as a point of entry to an even larger concern with the nature of social organisation and cultural values in past societies – with changes in the manner in which human relationships have been ordered and invested with meaning. If history could once be defined confidently as 'past politics', it is now, as Patrick Collinson observes, 'not so much past politics as past everything'. Its concern embraces the whole life of society. That this should be so is in large part the legacy of those who first engaged themselves in reclaiming, and cultivating an understanding of, the economic past.

Within the study of economic history, the history of the period extending from the later fifteenth to the mid-eighteenth centuries has a special place. From the very beginnings of the subject as an academic discipline in the late nineteenth century, this period was singled out as one which was deemed to have witnessed developments of particular significance. In his *Growth of English Industry and Commerce* (1882) William Cunningham described the fifteenth and sixteenth centuries as 'a period of transition', when 'mediaeval life was breaking up and modern society was slowly rising on its ruins'. George Unwin's 'chief purpose' in writing his *Industrial Organisation in the Sixteenth and Seventeenth Centuries* (1904) was 'to bridge over – however tentatively – the chasm that separates medieval from modern industrial history'. To such founders of the subject, the period from the later fifteenth to the early eighteenth centuries encompassed nothing less than the birth of the modern world, a perception which endures in the conventional application to this period of the general designation 'early modern'.

Such chronological distinctions are always to a degree arbitrary. All historical periods witness continuity as well as change. The conventional reference points of 'periodisation' are imposed upon the past by historians for interpretative purposes – usually to highlight changes deemed to be of particular significance. Once established, they are often challenged and contested, sometimes overthrown. All this is true of the notion of a distinctive 'early modern' period. Yet the perception of these centuries as a period of peculiar importance in the shaping of the modern world has proved singularly enduring. All historians reject the simplistic notions that the course of historical development can be neatly sectionalised, still less that it can be precisely dated, or that the shift from one conventional period to another necessarily involves commensurate change in every dimension of life. Historical change is far too tentative, uneven and muddled a business for that to be true. Yet most historians of 'medieval' and 'early modern' society in Britain would nonetheless see much to agree with in J. H. Clapham's observation that, while ' "History is a seamless garment"; and it is often harder to trace anything like a seam in its economic and social folds than in some others,' it remains the case that 'there is no overlooking the changes – almost suggesting a seam and a new piece – that can be traced early in the sixteenth century'. This is, moreover, a perception that has very deep roots. It was not simply imposed upon the past by modern historians or social theorists, as has sometimes been contended. It was part of the experience of the period itself.

I

Contemporaries knew that they lived in changing times, and some of them were aware of changes that seemed to them of a significance extending beyond the normal range of mutability in human affairs. Close to the beginning of our period, Sir Thomas More reflected in *Utopia* (1515–16) on the nature of the just ordering of economic and social affairs. And in so doing he placed in the mouth of his narrator, Raphael Hythlodaye, a bitter indictment of recent economic change in England, notably the enclosure of plough land for sheep pasture. A generation later, Sir Thomas Smith's *Discourse of the Common Weal of this realm of England* (1549) explored in detail the economic and social ills attending the unprecedented inflation of the mid-sixteenth century, their causation and possible remedies. The passage of another generation saw the publication of William Harrison's *Description of England* (1577), which dwelt in passing – almost as if alluding to what could be taken to be common knowledge among his readers – upon population expansion; the growth of internal trade, of commercial farming and more aggressive estate management by landlords; the rising domestic living standards of some and the growing poverty and insecurity of others. These were just some of the landmarks in a general awareness of disturbing economic and social change, and a complementary sense of the fraying of customary expectations. Such perceptions of the sixteenth century as a time of disruption, challenging conventional values concerning the proper ordering of economic affairs, were characteristic of the age and gave rise to a whole literature of economic complaint, itself a novel phenomenon made possible by another innovation of the day: the printing press.

By the beginning of the seventeenth century, comment on the problems and tensions of the day was giving way among some contemporaries to a more developed sense of longer-term historical change. In his unpublished survey of *The State of England Anno Dom. 1600*, Sir Thomas Wilson revealed a clear sense of the course of change over more than a century, emphasising the growing prosperity of England's yeoman farmers, and a relative decline in the wealth and power of the nobility and gentry, until by learning 'to become good husbands and . . . to improve their lands to the uttermost', landlords had adopted more commercial leasing and rental policies. In his *History of Henry VII* (1622) Sir Francis Bacon similarly, though in less detail, traced the emergence of 'the yeomanry or middle people, of a condition between gentlemen and cottagers or peasants' to the agrarian conditions of the late fifteenth century and to crown policies designed to keep up tenants 'of some substance'.

Wilson and Bacon were primarily concerned with the impact of long-term economic and social change on the structures of power and authority within the English polity. With the crisis of the Civil Wars of the 1640s, the same concern led James Harrington, in his *Oceana* (1656), to develop such a perception into a full-blown model of the interconnections of economic and political change. In Harrington's view, 'Dominion is property, real or personal.' Accordingly, he traced the crisis of royal authority to shifts in the distribution of landed property over almost two centuries. Following Bacon, he attributed the growing independence of 'the yeomanry or middle people' to the agrarian policies of the early Tudors. The power of the traditional nobility was further eroded by the ruinous expenditure on luxuries of landowners whose revenues were inadequate – 'whence followed rackings of rents and at length sale of lands'. Meanwhile, the Dissolution of the Monasteries and sale of church property brought more land to 'the people' (among whom Harrington included the gentry). The balance of power in the commonwealth thus shifted over a century towards 'the popular party'. The decline of the nobility gave rise to the assertiveness of the House of Commons, and ultimately – since 'a monarchy divested of her nobility hath no refuge under heaven but an army' – to civil war.

Much of this was, like the work of Wilson and Bacon, a very lightly sketched, partial and questionable reading of England's economic past. But the essential point is that, like his predecessors, Harrington *attempted* such a reading. R. H. Tawney was not wrong in suggesting that the precursors of economic history in Britain included those who detected an economic and social dimension in the seventeenth-century crisis of the British monarchy and sought to explain its nature. For our purposes, the significance of that search lies in the awareness of reflective contemporaries that sixteenth- and seventeenth-century England had witnessed major changes in the structures of economic life: in population and prices, in the distribution of land and agrarian social relations, in commerce and the enhancement of commercial motivation, in the enjoyment by some of new wealth and the endurance by others of greater poverty. They perceived, sometimes sharply, sometimes dimly and uncertainly, the erosion of an older economic order and the animation of a new. The central themes of the economic history of early modern England have their deepest roots in that perception.

II

Harrington's interpretation of the economic changes underlying political instability and constitutional change in England was not forgotten. His work enjoyed a new vogue following its republication in 1722, and its influence was to be felt long afterwards. In general, however, as R. H. Tawney remarked, 'when the stability of the edifice was assured, speculation as to its foundations fell out of fashion'. In the later seventeenth and early eighteenth centuries writers in both England and Scotland were to have a great deal to say about economic development and the surest routes to national wealth and power. They did not, however, much concern themselves with the origins of these things. That was to come later, in the third quarter of the eighteenth century, when the writers of the Scottish Enlightenment – David Hume, Sir James Steuart, Adam Smith, John Millar and others – took up and significantly developed what D. C. Coleman calls 'the examination of the economic past as an essential element in the understanding of human society'. What did these writers make of the economic experience of the preceding three centuries?

In brief, they saw it as a time of departure and they explained why. To Hume, in his *History of England* (1754), the sixteenth century had seen England's shaking off of the 'habits of indolence' which he regarded as characteristic of traditional agricultural societies. Thereafter the seventeenth century had witnessed 'a more sensible encrease . . . of all the advantages which distinguish a flourishing people' than any preceding period of English history. In his *Inquiry into the Principles of Political Economy* (1767) Sir James Steuart habitually referred to 'Europe four hundred years ago' as if to another era, and was explicit in his characterisation of 'the great alteration in the affairs of Europe within these three centuries': 'From feudal and military, it has become free and commercial.' Adam Smith stated confidently in his *Wealth of Nations* (1776) that 'Since the time of Henry VIII the wealth and revenue of the country have been continually advancing, and in the course of their progress their pace seems rather to have been gradually accelerated than retarded.'

These writers were at one in perceiving the preceding three centuries as a period of quickening in English economic life. England had grown in wealth as English society had become animated by a burgeoning spirit of industriousness and commercialism. They also had much in common in their explanations of how this transformation of fortunes had come to pass.

In his essay 'Of Commerce' (1752), Hume had expounded his view that 'If we consult history, we shall find, that, in most nations, foreign trade has preceded any refinement in home manufactures and given birth to domestic luxury,' a development that 'rouses men from their indolence' and encourages industry through 'a desire for a more splendid way of life'. This argument underlay the analysis scattered across the relevant chapters of his *History of England*. To Hume, a growing desire for luxury consumption among the English nobility, and the pressure of price inflation caused by 'growing demand in the more commercial countries', had stimulated landlords 'to turn their lands to the best account with regard to profit'. They enclosed arable land for sheep pasture, created commercial farms by 'joining many small farms into a few large ones', and raised rents – trends accentuated by the passage of monastic land from the lax stewardship of the monks to 'a different management'. As for the dispossessed and the labouring poor, they were compelled by necessity to shake off the indolence of agrarian custom and to adopt new habits of 'toil and application', an 'encrease of industry' which was 'an effect beneficial to society'. 'By all these means', cities grew and 'the middle rank of men began to be rich and powerful', the resulting superfluity of produce being exchanged with manufacturers 'for those commodities which men's luxury now makes them covet'. An upward spiral of economic growth was under way.

Neither Sir James Steuart nor Adam Smith attempted to write an economic history of Britain as such, though Smith's writing was everywhere informed by the historical knowledge of his day and he drew frequently upon what he knew of the economic past in providing illustrative discussions of his general themes. Both men, however, knew Hume's work well and both used and developed it in their general accounts of the transition in European societies from a feudal agrarian order unconducive to economic improvement to the modern commercial society which they sought to analyse. In particular, they elaborated upon his hints concerning the reciprocal nature of rural and urban development. Steuart's observation that rental income spent on urban manufactures 'began to flow into the hands of the industrious' led him into a discussion of urban growth and of the manner in which the demand generated by expanding urban populations stimulated agricultural improvement and internal trade. Smith identified the 'mutual and reciprocal' gains of town and country as the key to the 'Progress of Opulence in Different Nations'. The division of labour between the rural suppliers of food and raw materials and the urban suppliers of manufactured goods was beneficial to both, and the elaboration of that reciprocal relationship in recent centuries underlay 'a revolution of the greatest importance to the public happiness', one not confined to, but undoubtedly exemplified by, the English case.

With John Millar's *Historical View of the English Government* (1787) the now established themes of English economic and social development were drawn into a new configuration. Unlike Hume, Steuart and Smith, he placed comparatively little emphasis upon aristocratic consumption as a primary causal factor in agrarian change. He focused instead upon the manufacture of woollen cloth. To Millar it was the extension of such manufactures, from the late fifteenth century, which ultimately produced 'an alteration in the whole face of the country'. The growth of manufacturing towns and villages increased market demand for provisions, enhanced farmers' profits, 'gave rise to improvements in husbandry', and enabled prosperous farmers to pay higher rents. The success of woollens also stimulated the development of other manufactures, while England was further enabled, by virtue of its geographical position, long coastline and many navigable rivers, to develop both overseas navigation and the inland trade. By the seventeenth century England had a substantial population 'engaged in various mechanical employments, or in different branches of traffic', most of them dwelling in towns. Urban growth 'proportionably extended' the market for every kind of rural produce and the profits of agriculture, while with closer commercial contact the 'enterprising genius of merchants' was 'naturally communicated to the neighbouring farmers'. Elsewhere, he continued his account of 'diffusing opulence and independence' into his own century, tracing the full emergence of a commercial and industrial society in which 'universally mutual emulation, and mutual intercourse, have diffused habits of industry, have banished idleness . . . and have put it into the power of almost every individual, by the exertion of his own talents, to earn a comfortable subsistence'.

By the late eighteenth century, then, what J. H. Clapham called 'a first, imperfect, reconnaissance' of British economic history had been completed. Whereas their forerunners had wrestled with the economic and social problems of their own day, or suggested the outlines of deeper processes of economic change which might explain shifts in the balance of power in society, the writers of the Scottish Enlightenment had provided the first master narrative of British economic history, the first fully reasoned account of the British economic past. It was a triumphant story. It described, and emphatically endorsed, a revolution in human affairs: the transformation of a sluggish, predominantly agricultural economy, characterised by indolence, widespread poverty and the domination of a predatory aristocracy, into a free commercial society, based upon the satisfaction, through the mechanism of the market, of what Steuart termed 'reciprocal wants'. As Smith put it, 'every man . . . lives by exchanging or becomes in some measure a merchant', a state of things conducive to a highly developed division of labour, to the rational employment of land, labour and capital, to 'improvement', 'opulence', 'independence' and ultimately the public good.

This was the general course and meaning of economic and social change as these writers understood it. In addition, they provided a chronology of gradual transformation. They traced its real beginnings to the changes of the earlier sixteenth century, consolidated and advanced in the late sixteenth and earlier seventeenth centuries and then markedly accelerated after 1660. They established the main themes of change: increased consumption; rising prices; agrarian and agricultural change; urban growth; the expansion of manufactures and commerce; government economic policy (sometimes mistaken in its tenor); the development of financial institutions; the interconnected emergence of widespread wage-labour and of a commercial and agricultural middle class. They identified the principal mechanisms of change: a developing taste for superfluities and the multiplication of 'wants'; the growth of markets, both domestic and overseas; enhancement of the division of labour; competition and the rational employment of accumulated capital 'for the sake of profit'. And finally they isolated the basic motivation of change in the self-interested behaviour of individuals animated, in Hume's words, by 'a spirit of avarice and industry', or engaged, in Smith's gentler phrase, in the 'universal, continual, and uninterrupted effort to better their own condition'.

It was a history for the most part conceived and written by Scotsmen. Yet it focused attention primarily upon the growing wealth of England. Scotland as yet had only a modest place in that triumphant story. Sir James Steuart illustrated a point about prices with a brief depiction of the Scottish economy 'in former times' – a largely rural society, practising agriculture 'solely as a method of subsisting', with few hands employed in manufactures and little demand for grain in the public markets. Yet he did not dwell upon subsequent developments and he regarded Highland society as still 'a pretty just representation of the general state of Europe about four hundred years ago'. Smith had more to say about the improvement of Scottish agriculture since the Union of 1707, but he had a less developed sense of the Scottish than the English economic past beyond the view that 'In England the improvement of agriculture, manufactures and commerce began much earlier than in Scotland.' Millar discussed Scottish political affairs alongside those of England, but in the economic sphere he could observe only that in Scotland 'mercantile and agricultural improvements have been much later'. They had, nonetheless, begun, hitching Scotland's economic fortunes to the English wagon. Perhaps for that very reason, the best intelligences of 'North Britain' had engaged in the task of explaining the roots and nature of an economic momentum in which their own countrymen were now caught up. By doing so, they created the science of political economy, and taught the English how to understand themselves in time.

III

Perhaps the Enlightenment writers did their job too well. In the early nineteenth century the study of political economy underwent a transformation. The Scottish tradition, with its broad historical awareness, combination of inductive and deductive methods in the formation of generalisations, and interest in the genesis of market society, hardened into what would later be termed 'classical economics' – an intellectual discipline which had little interest in either economic history or inductive reasoning. Its best practitioners, with the notable exception of T. R. Malthus, preferred to explore with rigorous deductive logic the dynamics of a commercial economy in being, constructing in the process 'a world stripped of everything but its economic motivations'. Its more numerous camp-followers functioned more as the ideologues of *laissez-faire* capitalism, expounding with an unflinching faith the immutable laws of the market. The perspective afforded by the economic past was not entirely lost – it survived, for example, in the form of histories of particular industries and counties – but it was not a matter of central concern.

Nor did it much concern historians. The celebration of the growth of 'British Liberty' had been initiated by Enlightenment historians who regarded it as both unintelligible without reference to economic and social change and itself one of the conditions of accelerated economic development from the seventeenth century. Their successors ceased to explore that connection, focusing instead upon the elaboration of a more discrete and narrowly conceived account of the emergence of British constitutional genius. The Enlightenment project of enquiry into the nature of human society had itself been subjected to a division of labour, a splitting down into separate specialisms and disciplines.

The consequences of those fissures are only too evident in the work of the most successful of mid-nineteenth-century British historians: Thomas Babington Macaulay. Macaulay's *History of England* (1848) is essentially a vivid account of the Glorious Revolution of 1688, prefaced by an introductory sketch of English constitutional development since the Saxon settlements. Not the least part of its appeal, however, was his celebrated third chapter. In this he attempted 'a description of the state in which England was at the time when the crown passed from Charles the Second to his brother', a survey of society in the 1680s without which, he feared, echoing Hume, his subsequent narrative of events might be 'unintelligible or uninstructive'. The intention was admirable, and the resulting evocation of society and economy remains impressive in many particulars. Yet it also demonstrates his ignorance of much that had been

known by his eighteenth-century predecessors. He had certainly read
Adam Smith as well as Hume. He shared Smith's view that the restless
human desire for betterment was the fundamental cause of advance in
civilisation. His description of how England's national wealth had been
'almost uninterruptedly increasing' for at least six centuries closely followed a passage in *The Wealth of Nations*. But he never took on board
the implications of that statement. Macaulay's prime concern was to
demonstrate that 'the country of which we read was a very different
country from that in which we live'. Accordingly, he concentrated upon
establishing a vivid contrast between the England of the seventeenth and
that of the nineteenth century. In so doing, he primitivised the earlier
period, making no attempt to understand it in its own terms, and ignor-
ing those processes of development over the sixteenth and seventeenth
centuries of which the Enlightenment historians had been acutely aware.
This may have made his history more instructive, but it did nothing for
its intelligibility. The virtues of the third chapter still render it a landmark in the attempt to write social history. For our purposes, however,
it is also a landmark for another reason. It demonstrates the existence of
an early nineteenth-century hiatus, indeed a regression, in the attempt to
understand England's economic past, and the place of the sixteenth and
seventeenth centuries in that history. It illustrates how much had been
lost.

Of historians writing in Britain in the mid-nineteenth century, the one
most closely in touch with the older tradition of approaches to the economic and social history of the sixteenth and seventeenth centuries was
the German political exile Karl Marx. Far from being an alien intruder
upon the interpretation of Britain's economic past, as he is sometimes
represented, Marx's ideas and arguments place him firmly in a line of
descent that can be traced back to the sixteenth century itself. He was
widely read in the printed sources for the period, citing in the first volume
of *Capital* (1867) the works of More, Sir Thomas Smith, Harrison and
Bacon, as well as contemporary legislation on economic issues and
numerous pamphleteers of the seventeenth and early eighteenth centuries. To this extent Marx's view of English economic history was relatively well rooted. And if his concern with class formation and conflict
preceded his long exile in London, it was not, as we have seen, a concept
alien to the indigenous tradition of writing on the Tudor and Stuart
eras. In a very real sense Marx the historian belonged to that tradition.
It influenced him profoundly, and he in turn did much to elaborate and
extend it.

Marx's subject was the nature of the capitalist mode of production,
and he turned to British history as the 'classic ground' on which the capi-

talist system of his day had developed. He knew that various forms of capitalist enterprise and wage-labour had existed in medieval Europe, but regarded 'the modern history of capital' as having commenced with the European commercial expansion of the sixteenth century and three subsequent developments: the 'primitive accumulation' of capital; the creation of a wage-dependent proletariat and a market for labour power as a commodity; and, finally, the development of the division of labour characteristic of capitalism in what he termed 'the manufacturing period', which preceded mechanised factory production and extended 'from the middle of the sixteenth to the last third of the eighteenth century'.

For Marx, these were the essential features of English economic development between the sixteenth and the eighteenth centuries, and 'the basis of the whole process' was 'the expropriation of the agricultural producer, of the peasant, from the soil' – a 'fearful and painful . . . prelude to the history of capital', found in England in its 'classic form'. He described the independent, self-supporting peasantry of the fifteenth century, the long history of its expropriation by ruthless landlords from the sixteenth century onwards and its replacement by a class of large-scale capitalist farmers. Then he traced the consequences. Expropriation created a landless proletariat, harassed by savage vagrancy laws, the poor laws and oppressive labour legislation into 'the discipline necessary for the wage system'. It led also to the creation of a bigger domestic market as self-provisioning gave way to the need to purchase the products of others. Capitalistically structured manufacturing industries spread in town and countryside. Commercial supremacy in overseas markets, assisted by an aggressive colonialism and protective legislation, ensured industrial predominance. The expense of wars fought for commercial and colonial aggrandisement necessitated financial reform, the creation of the national debt and a modern system of taxation which could underpin public credit. By the late eighteenth century, England was dominated by a composite ruling class. The great possessors of land, commercial and industrial capital and the 'new bankocracy' stood in natural alliance, devoted to the ruthless pursuit of their own economic interests – not least by use of the powers of the state – and imposing the 'dull compulsions' of the wage-system upon an exploited proletariat which was gradually being conditioned to accept the conditions of its being as 'self-evident laws of Nature'.

The elements in Marx's history were familiar enough: its chronology and component themes were to a large extent those of his predecessors. In the context of what had gone before, it could be said of Marx that he was *in* the tradition of writing about the economic development of

England between the sixteenth and the eighteenth centuries. But he was certainly not *of* it. What made him different was his interpretative perspective and his tone. Unlike Smith and Millar, he knew what came next. Unlike the political economists of the early nineteenth century, he did not see it as the inevitable outcome of the operation of immutable economic laws. He traced the development not of an essentially benign commercial order based on the neutral mechanisms of the market, the satisfaction of 'reciprocal wants', and 'diffusing opulence and independence', but of a system of exploitation based on the coercive power of capital and the imposition on labouring people of a novel form of servitude. He examined the genesis of that order not only to celebrate its technical achievements, but also to denounce its crimes. In doing so, he combined an economic analysis derived from political economy with the moral indignation and rhetorical hyperbole of the sixteenth-century literature of complaint. The result was an alternative reading of England's economic past, an examination of the underside of the triumphalist teleology of the Enlightenment era, designed to challenge its complacency. He was, in a sense, the heir to two traditions of response to the economic developments of the sixteenth and seventeenth centuries: the shock of disruption and the urge to understand. As an historian, he attempted to explore and to transform the meaning of both. If the landmarks of the territory he traversed were familiar, they were viewed from a radically different perspective, and the voice of the guide was new.

IV

It was not a voice much heard for more than a generation. Marx wrote in German. His work was known to scholars, but the first volume of *Capital* was not translated into English until 1887 and reached a wider audience only slowly. By then, however, the hegemony of political economy which he sought to challenge had already come under fire from a different direction, and an account of English economic development had been created which, if it contained elements sympathetic to Marx's view of the past, owed little to his direct influence.

Marx was not alone in questioning the dogmas of classical political economy. In Germany the mid-nineteenth century had seen the emergence of an historical school of economics, a movement whose leaders advocated a more inductive approach to economic theory, involving in particular the scholarly study of the economic past – not least that of England. In Britain, deep disagreement was emerging over the legacy of political economy and its policy implications in a darkening economic climate in which British economic supremacy could no longer be confidently assumed. Heterodox views, for example, were vigorously expressed by James Thorold Rogers and by the young William Cunningham, as well as by overseas delegates, at the 1876 meeting of the Political Economy Club. Marx was even less alone in his revulsion at the impact of industrialisation on the labouring classes. A long tradition of vigorous protest at the social evils which flowed from the measurement of all human relations by the yardstick of the economic already existed in England, and it was taking a new form in the 'condition of England' question which agitated late-Victorian society.

Both influences found embodiment in the school of historical economists which emerged in the English universities in the 1880s. Of these the most charismatic figure was Arnold Toynbee, whose Oxford lectures on the industrial revolution (published after his premature death in 1883) inspired a generation of students. To Toynbee, the classical conception of self-interested 'economic man' was a morally repugnant travesty, and the industrial revolution a cataclysmic demonstration of the degradation and social dislocation resulting from an unbridled acquisitive individualism. Like Marx, he was 'an inspired historian of alienation'. His critique of contemporary capitalism, however, was expressed in a more familiar idiom of social responsibility and Christian morality, and he was an impassioned advocate not of revolution but of social reform guided by an ethical and historically informed economics. Toynbee's stature as an inspirational figure was unique, and he established the industrial revolution of the late eighteenth and early nineteenth centuries as the critical turning point of British economic history. In other respects, however, he was not alone, and for our purposes he was of less significance than those of his contemporaries and successors who concerned themselves with the deep context and long-term preconditions of that cataclysm, notably William Cunningham and W. J. Ashley.

In the context of the struggle over the future direction of British economics, the historical economists took an embattled stance. They were very much aware of the German historical school and frequently cited those works of its leading figures which addressed English history. Nevertheless, they were by no means pale imitators of the German model. While highly critical of the timeless assumptions of orthodox economics, and influenced by notions of social evolution, they were not themselves engaged in a search, by other means, for general laws of economic development. Their interest was more in the limits of theory, and their central belief was that the validity of any economic theory is relative to the circumstances and values of a particular time and place.

Cunningham insisted that past economic systems should not be judged by the anachronistic standards of modern theory. All economic behaviour must be understood as occurring 'in a definite political society and . . . influenced by the current views of right and wrong'. Thorold Rogers attacked political economy as 'a hard and dry system, which . . . only proposes to suffering humanity a bundle of unwelcome truths which it affirms to be natural laws', yet which 'are neither truths nor laws . . . but at the best are doubtful tendencies elevated to the rank of principles'. Ashley repeatedly declared his belief that political economy was not 'a body of absolutely true doctrines', but rather 'a number of more or less useful theories and generalisations', that 'economic conclusions are relative to given conditions' and that they 'possess only hypothetical validity'.

Accordingly, the historical economists concerned themselves with past economic cultures in the round, with their institutional frameworks, characteristic relationships and central ideas. They were acutely aware that economic change involved a myriad of factors other than the strictly economic. Economic history should be concerned 'not only with the production of wealth, but also with the evolution of social organisation', a process, as Ashley put it, not to be represented as a teleological 'sketch of continuing change in any one direction – say of increasing human freedom – but of the growth and subsequent decay of a series of different economic organisms, as they were in turn affected by political, moral or physical conditions'.

This was a scholarly project of considerable moment. It would transcend what had previously passed for economic history in its range and rigour. It involved the task of exploring, according to the emerging standards of 'scientific history', the considerable corpus of documentary evidence of economic and social affairs already being made available by editors of the public records and by local record societies but as yet little employed by professional historians. But it was not just a scholarly initiative. The historical economists were also prepared to pronounce judgement on the course of change. They used their knowledge of the past to inform their views on contemporary policy. Though they varied in their politics and in their positions on specific issues, they were social and economic reformers, committed in the main to the promotion of a regulated capitalism as an alternative to both *laissez-faire* indifference to prevailing social conditions and socialist rejection of the market economy. As historians, they sympathised profoundly with the casualties of economic change. As reformers, they attacked the continued dominance of economic doctrines which tended, in Ashley's words, 'not only to assume, but also to inculcate, the pursuit of material self-interest'. But they were also aware, as L. L. Price put it in an aside directed at Marx, that economic history could provide 'a salutary corrective' of other 'exaggerations of the role of economic forces in the drama of mankind'.

Economic history as an academic discipline thus emerged as what has been called 'a study of actualities, a revolt against abstract economic dogma'. At the same time, it was created in a context which meant that 'the notion of economic history as a path to social reform was for a long time to permeate its study and exposition in Britain'. Its leading practitioners were keenly aware of the complexities, contingencies and ironies of historical change, and advocated with some passion that the past must be understood in its own terms. Yet they were also 'present-minded' to the extent that they were aware of the bearing of historical experience on the problems of their own day. This inevitably coloured their approach to the sixteenth and seventeenth centuries – a period of central significance in Cunningham and Ashley's overviews of English economic history and of particular interest to the younger scholars who consolidated their achievement in the years before 1914 with more specialised studies of industry, trade, finance and agriculture under the Tudors and Stuarts.

As we have seen, they regarded those centuries as having witnessed the birth of the modern era, as a period of gradual transition towards the world of *laissez-faire* capitalism, originating in the disruption of a medieval economic order which they perceived as in some respects its antithesis. The medieval economy was portrayed as distinctive in both its structures and its values. It was corporate, highly regulated and hostile to the expression of an economic individualism disruptive of the common good. It was not a world innocent of the power of capital, but one in which capitalist enterprise was peripheral to the main structures of economic life and permitted to operate only within strict limits. Economic relationships, as Cunningham put it, were conducted with 'constant regard to the *relations of persons*', which gave them a certain moral character, rather than involving merely 'the *exchange of things*' in a morally neutral market, which he took to be characteristic of the modern economy.

Cunningham and Ashley were both aware that the transition which they sought to trace was a complex and uneven process. They wrote sensitively of the relationships of continuity and change in time, and of the difficulties of the adjustments of mind and habit involved. But they also tried to highlight what Ashley called 'the dominating or preponderating forces' of the period, and these were on the side of change. In their work and those of their immediate successors, the principal themes emerged clearly. Economic life became increasingly complex and differentiated in response to expanding markets, both domestic and overseas. A national economy emerged, subject to nationally conceived economic policy. There was an expansion of the role of capital in production and of capitalist modes of organisation in both agriculture and industry, heralding that 'predominance of capital' which Cunningham regarded as 'the leading feature which distinguishes modern economic conditions from those of the Middle Ages'. There was the growth of what Ashley called a spirit of 'individual initiative and enterprise', and a shift in economic values and aspirations which gave greater recognition to the legitimacy of pursuing personal gain. Private interest, once subordinated to the public good, came gradually to be identified with the public good, leaving no room for 'authoritative insistence on moral as distinct from legal obligations'. Older economic institutions, relationships and expectations were dislocated. The structure of society was transformed and simplified around the three fundamental divisions of land, capital and labour in which 'men arrange themselves according to the things they own and exchange'.

These central themes were deployed to guide the reader through a detailed account of gradual adjustment to changing circumstances in particular economic spheres. There were differences of emphasis. Ashley stressed the erosion in the sixteenth century of the older structures of urban and rural economy under 'the sheer force of self-interest', no longer adequately contained or 'ashamed to use its strength'. Thorold Rogers concentrated on 'the degradation of labour'. Cunningham prioritised policy and the 'effort to promote economic progress by government action'. He traced with approval the gradual emergence, in the wake of the 'social disorganisation' of the earlier sixteenth century, of the regulatory 'mercantile system' of the seventeenth and early eighteenth centuries. Nor were they united in their interpretations. Thorold Rogers and Cunningham disagreed profoundly on the purpose and consequences of Tudor labour legislation. Despite these and other differences, however, their collective achievement was immensely impressive. Where their predecessors had conducted a reconnaissance of the period, the historical economists provided the first thoroughly documented survey of the territory, placed it in full perspective, and pronounced authoritatively on what it meant.

In their larger professional aims as economists they were unsuccessful. Under the influence of W. S. Jevons and Alfred Marshall, political economy metamorphosed into a less dogmatic 'neo-classical' economics. But it retained at its heart a narrow conception of 'economic man', and remained an essentially theoretical discipline, preoccupied with equilibrium and showing little interest in change over time. The historical economists exerted little influence on the future of their discipline. Instead, they founded a new one: economic history.

V

To the founders of English economic history the early modern period mattered profoundly. It was the pivot on which their whole conception of England's economic past turned, and as such it attracted many of their immediate successors. George Unwin, for example, explored the world of early industrial organisation; W. R. Scott that of trade and finance; R. H. Tawney the agrarian changes of the sixteenth and early seventeenth centuries; R. B. Westerfield and N. S. B. Gras the evolution of markets and marketing. Alice Clark added a previously unconsidered dimension with her interpretation of the impact of capitalist organisation on women's work. Moreover, the broad interpretation of the period which the founders had established was to endure for half a century. It was not uncontested. Unwin, for instance, shared neither Cunningham's assessment of the role of the mercantilist state in economic progress nor Ashley's suspicion of individualism, and took a far more positive view of 'the emancipation of the economic forces of society.' Eileen Power, in 1933, felt it necessary to counter any implied idealisation of medieval society, stressing that 'the capitalistic spirit was at work on all sides in the Middle Ages', though the sixteenth century 'allowed the old spirit more scope'. Nevertheless, the textbooks of Cunningham and Ashley continued to be reprinted and the most widely used new general account of the period to appear between the wars, Ephraim Lipson's *Economic History of England* (1913–43), was very much in their tradition. Lipson's major interpretative innovation was his argument that the industrial revolution should not be viewed as a violent break with the past, but as a further development of a complex capitalist order which was already well established by the eighteenth century. In tracing the emergence of that order, however, his work can be said to have constituted in the main a further elaboration of the existing agenda.

Real change in the interpretation of the early modern period came only after the Second World War. It was in some ways heralded, however, by the posthumous publication of J. H. Clapham's *Concise Economic History of Britain* (1949), a work based on lectures delivered in Cambridge in the years 1908–35.

Clapham represented a different tradition. He was a protégé of Alfred Marshall, who had consciously distanced himself from the legacy of the historical economists. In addition, he was an advocate of more precise, quantitative research into economic change. He has been described as the leading figure in a 'neutralist' approach to the economic past, as opposed to the dominant 'reformist' school of the early twentieth century. In fact there was nothing neutral about his views. Politically he was sympathetic to gradualist social reform, but 'left no doubt of his enthusiastic support for a capitalist system driven by competition'. Above all, however, he was an academic, with an austere view of the scholar's role, which, as G. N. Clark observed, led some readers of Clapham's *Economic History of Modern Britain* to complain that his approach showed 'little of the sympathy with economic misery or the indignation against economic oppression which inspired many of those who wrote on the same period'. Nor was his own research devoted to the early modern period. It was through the accident of death that his *Concise Economic History* culminated in 1750 and thereby became an influential text in the teaching of the periods before industrialisation.

As we have seen, Clapham viewed the sixteenth century as a major turning point. In his account of developments over the next two centuries he touched most of the familiar bases. Yet he did so in a manner which contrasts markedly with that of his predecessors. The changes which had animated the period were described in a cool, sometimes sardonic tone. He was aware of the inequities of economic change, but reported them dispassionately. He offered no explicit interpretation of the relative significance of the economic variables discussed, still less a characterisation of the essential meaning of change, beyond the implication that it was triggered by the impact of inflation and population growth on what was already a substantially commercialised economy. The role of the state was marginalised. There was none of the discussion of contemporary economic ideas that had characterised the historical economists. Indeed, human motivation was very rarely touched upon, and, on the rare occasions when it was discussed, Clapham tended to assume the existence of maximising commercial attitudes on the part of actors in the economy. Of his general influence on economic history, it was said by one of his admirers that he found 'a mass of half-knowledge, overgrown with picturesque and stubborn weeds' and began the task of clearing it. Of his account of early modern England, it might be closer to the mark to say that his 'weeding' extended virtually to interpretative defoliation. He provided a narrowly defined, one-dimensional account of economic change, and in doing so he drained the historical processes involved of part of their meaning.

They were shortly to acquire an alternative meaning. In the optimistic climate of the post-war decades the central problematic was that of economic growth. And in an expanding historical profession the analysis of past economic growth gradually came to replace the triumph of capitalism and individualism at the heart of the economic historian's enterprise. Among early modernists, F. J. Fisher used his inaugural lecture at the London School of Economics in 1956 to emphasise the question of the extent to which the sixteenth and seventeenth centuries had witnessed economic growth, in the sense of rising per-capita income, and to demonstrate, in a brilliant survey of the field, how hard it was to answer that question in the current state of knowledge. The familiar territory of Lipson had become in Fisher's memorable phrase 'The Dark Ages of English Economic History'.

If that was the case, however, the task of illuminating them was already under way and it was to continue for the next two decades in the form of a steady stream of thoroughly researched theses, articles and monographs, most of them based on previously little-explored archival evidence, which would collectively provide some of the answers to Fisher's questions. The cumulative achievement was formidable. Indeed, it can be said to have transformed the historical landscape. It provided the richly detailed, quantitatively precise and chronologically more exact account of change in sector after sector of English economic life between the sixteenth and the eighteenth centuries – in trade, prices and wages, agriculture, industry and population – which is the inheritance of all students of the period. If the achievement was great, however, it was also won at some cost. For the historical landscape was transformed in another sense too, not least in the range of the subject and the relative significance of the early modern period within it.

Economic history was becoming more narrowly defined, restricted for the most part to the territory which Clapham would have regarded as the proper sphere of the economic historian. There was diminishing interest in the social, cultural and political contexts of economic activity. 'Non-economic' influences were less likely to figure in a style of analysis, which maintained, in D. C. Coleman's words, a certain 'detachment' from 'theoretical constructions claiming to explain the "rise of capitalism" or the like'. Indeed, the general political climate of the cold-war era rendered embarrassing the very conceptual vocabulary employed by earlier generations of scholars. Responses to population and price trends replaced the rise of capitalism and individualism as the central dynamic of the age – a source of many new insights, but in itself an equally partial approach to the problem of change. Explanation of those responses tended to assume the general applicability of neo-classical market mechanisms, though this was rarely made explicit. Increased professional specialisation meant that debate regarding the course and causes of change tended to be largely confined to the problems of discrete sectors of economic activity, rather than extending to the characterisation and interpretation of change in the structures of economy and society as a whole. And within the histories of particular sectors, the preoccupation with growth could foster an element of 'whiggish' teleology in the manner in which economic progress was charted up to the eve of the industrial revolution. At worst, the story could be reduced to a catalogue of historical tape-breasting which involved sprinting past decades of inertia or failure in the anxiety to emphasise eventual success, and in which economic success became its own justification.

Taken as a whole, the portrayal of the economic history of early modern England in the post-war decades presented something of a paradox. More was known about the course of economic development in the period, and in more detail, than ever before. Yet the subject had contracted in range and diminished in significance. The old central problematic of change had gone. With it had gone the more composite conception of the subject. Economic history had abdicated its role as the champion of a larger vision of the past, and tightened its discursive boundaries. The new problematic of growth had proved impressively fertile in its empirical and technical achievements. Yet it begged, or ignored, some important questions about the nature and causation of change. Moreover, its very successes tended to involve a diminution of the significance of the period. If no fundamental change had taken place in the economic structures and culture of the period, then it became essentially a long, slow run-up to the industrialisation of the late eighteenth century, less a dividing range in historical experience than a landscape of gently rising foothills. The fashionable use of the term 'pre-industrial' to characterise the period encapsulated this reduced significance, and compounded it by substituting chronological vagueness where once there had been a sharp sense of the distinctiveness of the times.

VI

By the mid-1970s, economic history as it had been recast in the post-war decades was also losing its momentum and its audience. This was partly because a great part of the job which a generation of economic historians had undertaken had been done – and done well. It was also a consequence of two shifts of attention which Fisher had presciently identified in 1956.

He observed, first, that the economic history of modern Britain was dividing, from a point in the eighteenth century, 'not merely into two periods, but almost into two separate disciplines'. It became even more so with the rise of 'cliometrics' and the 'new economic history' – a mode of analysis involving the theoretical modelling of historical problems, often in algebraic form, and 'testing' them against the 'reality' of quantitative data assembled for the purpose. The early modern period offered limited opportunity for the exercise of such technical bravura. Models derived from contemporary economics contained too many inappropriate assumptions about economic behaviour in the past. The documentary evidence for the period did not lend itself readily to more sophisticated forms of quantification. Its investigation required other, more traditional skills and qualities of imagination. Such humanist traditionalism, however, was less valued in the prevailing climate of deference to the current best practice of economics. The period was being by-passed by the new brand leaders of economic history.

Fisher's second observation concerned the emergence of social history as a separate area of specialisation: one which in his view seemed 'designed . . . to take over the field from which the economic historian is retreating'. He was right. By the 1970s a 'new social history' of the early modern period had not only thoroughly occupied that field but was expanding well beyond it. This movement resulted in the creation of a bundle of new histories of social relationships and of the cultures that inform them. It represented a massive expansion of the historical agenda of the period, and as such constituted the dominant historical initiative of the late twentieth century. Yet it was a movement from which economic historians, for the most part, stood aside.

As a result, by the late 1980s, the economic history of much of the early modern period appeared relatively dormant – in marked contrast to the continuing vigour of the historiography of the industrial-revolution era. Research continued along established lines, and individual work of distinction continued to appear. But the field as a whole seemed marked by a loss of self-confidence and a contraction of interest. Apparently unwilling or unable to redefine itself, it was becoming marginalised both within economic history and within the history of the early modern period as a whole.

VII

Among some of its practitioners, the diminished standing of the economic history of the early modern period is a matter for lament. Yet the situation can also be viewed more positively, as one which presents exceptional opportunities. First, the subject remains the territory of historians fundamentally committed to a humanistic conception of their discipline and its range of concern. They have not been unresponsive to the methodologies of 'cliometrics' where these seem appropriate. But the field has escaped the withering effects of a methodological fad which, in its attempt to achieve credibility with an economics profession little interested in the social and cultural complexities of past societies, has reduced the discussion of some problems in modern economic history to what E. P. Thompson likened to a landscape blasted by ten years of drought.

Secondly, the rise of social history has much to offer the economic historian. It has provided a vastly enriched sense of the context of economic change in early modern England. It also touches directly upon matters of economic concern in a myriad of ways. In its studies of specific regions, of rural and urban communities and of particular social groups, it has explored ways of restoring a sense of the relatedness of economic, social, political and cultural change. As yet all this may have had only a limited impact, but its potential is obvious.

We have, then, every opportunity to take a fresh approach to the economic history of the early modern period as the study 'not so much of a special class of facts as . . . of all the facts of a nation's history from a special point of view'. That task involves three interconnected things. In the first place it requires an appreciation of the empirical and interpretative legacy of the subject which I have tried to outline in this introductory chapter. That legacy has developed as different historians have approached the period animated by a variety of preoccupations and priorities. It constitutes a resource which can be drawn upon eclectically to provide fresh perspectives for our own time on the processes of continuity and change within the period. Achieving such a perspective further requires an effort to re-emphasise the significance of the period, and an attempt to 'reproblematise' the course of development within it.

Central to the argument of this book is the view that the early modern period was indeed a turning point in British economic and social development. Its significance can be summed up in the assertion that it witnessed the fuller emergence and increasing dominance of the structures and culture characteristic of a 'market society'. These developments did not come from nowhere. Medieval society was not some kind of primitive inversion of modernity, untouched by the commercial spirit. But the period from the sixteenth to the eighteenth centuries did witness the gradual creation of an integrated national economy in which market relationships were the central mechanism – and which was itself closely linked to a nascent world economy. In the course of this development, market relationships grew in scale, pervasiveness and power. The market became not just a means of exchanging goods, but 'a mechanism for sustaining and maintaining an entire society'. Moreover, the market economy, as it emerged, became increasingly a capitalist economy. The period saw the growth of opportunities for the accumulation and productive investment of capital; the extension and ideological sanctification of exclusive rights of private property; the expansion of forms of enterprise in agriculture, manufacturing and commerce in which capital and capitalist forms of organisation were essential for the exploitation of market opportunities; a massive expansion of the market for labour power as a commodity to be bought and sold; and a redistribution of economic power into the hands of those who embraced the productive ideal and were able thereby to exercise leverage on the development of society as a whole. All this involved a quickening of economic activity, significant increases in agricultural and industrial output and rising percapita income and consumption for at least a substantial part of the population, at least some of the time. Those were the gains. It also involved social and cultural changes, shifts in individual and collective behaviour, a recasting of power relationships and transformations of expectations and life-chances which could be intensely traumatic in their particular impact. Those were the costs.

Taken together, these developments gave the early modern period its particular texture as lived experience and its significance in the development of British society. They are not unfamiliar. Elements of what I have briefly summarised can be found in the views of reflective contemporaries; of the political economists of the eighteenth century; of Marx; of the historical economists of the nineteenth and the economic historians of the twentieth centuries. The perception of the early modern period as one of gradual but fundamental transition is not one which has been foisted upon us by misguided social theorists, as has sometimes been alleged. It was there from the beginning. Each subsequent generation has elaborated our understanding of the nature and course of that transition. As a result we are able to see more of the whole, to identify the central features of change over twelve generations. It is time to re-emphasise firmly why it mattered.

'Reproblematising' the period means in part an explicit emphasis upon these central themes. It also means that in approaching them it is necessary to look critically at the element of predictability which has sometimes tended to characterise their exposition by historians, at the kind of *a priori* reasoning in which our accounts of the course and causation of change are too heavily influenced by our prior knowledge of the eventual outcome. The recasting of the economic world that took place in early modern Britain was a confused business, a halting, messy accumulation of discontinuities, spread unevenly over time and space. If the cumulative consequences seem clear with the benefit of hindsight, the lived experience was by no means so clear-cut or predictable. There were always alternative options for the actors involved. There was always the possibility that different outcomes might flow from their actions. Consequences were frequently unforeseen and unintended. Motives could be various and contradictory. Change was often hard fought as people struggled 'to create, oppose, defend and legitimise new circumstances', and it was by no means universally accomplished.

Devising ways of conveying a sense of the uncertainty and unevenness of change and the complexity of its causation is not an easy matter. The traditional approach has been to examine in turn the problems of development in each individual sector of the economy. This certainly has its virtues, but it also runs the risk of fragmenting the reader's sense of the overall context and of slipping unwittingly into a kind of sectoral teleology. It can obscure some of those conjunctures of circumstance which generated a momentum of development in one direction rather than another. It can conceal the extent to which societies at any one point in time contain, in Perry Anderson's words, 'a mixture of forms', and the manner in which change commonly involves 'an expansion of one of them at the expense of others, so that historical development proceeds not by stages but by overlaps'.

In what follows the problems of continuity and change will be approached by adopting a different form of analytical narrative, one which will try to pay close attention to the nature of changing contexts and options in economic life. Part One will attempt to introduce some of the essential structures of economic life in the late-fifteenth and earlier sixteenth centuries. Part Two will focus on the dynamics of change between the early sixteenth and early eighteenth centuries, unfolding the story of change in a group of chapters each of which will examine the principal developments within a particular sub-period. In this way I hope to provide a more integrated account of the problems faced by particular generations: how the contexts of economic life were changing; how people responded; the circumstances and contingencies influencing their responses; the modified situations encountered by their successors. The prominence given to particular aspects of change will necessarily vary for each of these sub-periods, for each had its own priorities and dynamics. But in each case the objective will be that of providing an analytical narrative which can highlight the critical developments and place them within a coherent explanatory context. Finally, Part Three will explore the structures of economic life in the later seventeenth and early eighteenth centuries, as a means of bringing out in more detail the cumulative outcomes of the processes of change discussed in Part Two, and the new 'mixture of forms' prevailing in 'Augustan' Britain.

In all of this the work of social historians of the early modern period will be drawn upon freely to incorporate aspects of economic life which have not figured prominently in earlier accounts of the period, and to indicate the ways in which economic practices and priorities were embedded in social relationships. More prominence will also be given to the question of economic culture than has been customary in recent economic histories of the period. Both are essential if we are to appreciate contemporaries' priorities and motivations, their perceptions and understandings of the processes in which they were involved, and the contemporary meanings of their experiences and responses. Both are also essential as a means of grasping that, as the historical economists appreciated, economic relationships, ideas and motivations are relative things, that the familiar values of 'rational economic man' cannot simply be assumed, and that change in this sphere was itself a vital element in the making of market society.

Finally, this book will attempt to provide an economic history of early modern Britain, as distinct from early modern England. This has not previously been attempted and it presents real difficulties. The economic history of Wales has for the most part been silently incorporated into that of England – just as the principality was politically and legally incorporated in the reign of Henry VIII. There is some justification for that perspective, as we shall see, but more can be done to acknowledge both the distinctive features of Welsh society and economy and the Welsh dimension of a shared history. Scotland's economic history, in contrast, has been effectively excluded from that story, not least by the insistence of earlier generations of Scottish historians upon the exceptionalism and backwardness of the northern kingdom prior to the eighteenth century. I. F. Grant's pioneering *Social and Economic Development of Scotland before 1603* (1930) stressed that Scotland was 'markedly exceptional in the static nature of her economic development' between the fourteenth and the seventeenth centuries, and until the 1980s most accounts of early modern Scotland still stressed the backward and peripheral nature of its economic life before its sudden quickening at the turn of the seventeenth and eighteenth centuries. Scotland seemed to have no part to play in the dominant narrative of economic change in Tudor and Stuart England and Wales, save as an envious observer. Its entrance on to the stage of British economic history came later, with the era of industrialisation.

There are nonetheless real benefits to be gained by extending the scope of this study to include, where possible, the Scottish dimension. In the first place, consideration of the distinctive structures of Scottish economic life and its different chronologies of change can illuminate powerfully the alternative possibilities which the period contained. This is particularly so since a new generation of Scottish historians have focused their attention upon the central problem of how an apparently 'impoverished country with essentially medieval trading patterns and an underdeveloped economy at the end of the seventeenth century . . . rapidly caught up with her southern neighbour in the eighteenth century'. If the dynamics of Scottish economic life in the sixteenth and earlier seventeenth centuries still remain in some ways frustratingly obscure, we now have at least a clearer understanding of Scotland's economy and society in the later seventeenth century, and a better appreciation of the formative developments which preceded the 'triumph of commercial forces and relationships' in the subsequent century. Awareness of this can be as instructive in considering the more familiar story of English and Welsh developments as the arguments of those Scottish thinkers who reflected upon and provided the first thoroughgoing analysis of those forces and relationships.

A fresh approach to the economic history of early modern Britain, then, is possible if we combine the cumulative achievements of earlier historians of the period with more recent shifts in knowledge of and perspective on its history. It is also needed. It is needed to restate emphatically the significance of a period of change just as momentous as the later era of industrialisation. The early modern period saw the creation of a capitalist market economy and society: the commercial civilisation of the political economists. This was not a process of change confined to Britain, but it was one in which Britain had a major part to play and one which in Britain took its own peculiar forms. This, in itself, did not render inevitable the subsequent process of industrialisation. But, without it, that later development would have been unthinkable. For that reason alone, the nature of economic change in early modern Britain has a claim on our attention. Its relevance is all the greater because the impact of those changes raised issues concerning the conduct of economic affairs which continue to resonate in our own time. In examining how they arose and the different ways in which the people of the time confronted and resolved them, we enter into a dialogue with their ghosts which is of more than merely historical interest.

PART ONE

Households in a landscape, c.1470–c.1550

In the year 1509, Edmund Dudley lay imprisoned in the Tower of London, awaiting execution on trumped-up charges of treason. In the time-honoured manner of public men whose careers have come badly unstuck, he wrote a book – *The Tree of Commonwealth* – in which he attempted, as a loyal subject, to define the conditions for the flourishing of the realm of England under its new king, the young Henry VIII.

The term 'commonwealth' or 'commonweal' was a keyword of the sixteenth century. By it Dudley meant both the common good, or common interest, and the social and political structures responsible for achieving that condition of public welfare. His book took the form of an elaborate allegory, depicting commonwealth as a great tree – sustained by the roots of love of God, justice, trust, concord and peace and bearing the fruits of 'tranquilitie', 'good example', 'worldly prosperitie' and 'honour of god'. Its health was to be ensured by the collective endeavours of a plurality of social groups acting under the guidance of the king as the fountain of justice, arbiter of conflict and guarantor of good order. Each of these groups had interests potentially in conflict with those of others. Yet, if each performed its proper duties, the realm would be welded into a prosperous and harmonious whole in which all would share proportionately in the fruits of commonwealth.

Dudley's vision of commonwealth was characteristic of medieval Christian social morality. His ideal was communitarian, but it was not egalitarian. Each member of the whole was to contribute 'in his degree' and to enjoy the benefits of commonwealth only 'after his degree'. The subjects of the realm were divided into three 'orders' or 'estates', each with its God-given role to play and each with its characteristic 'defections' or failings to be reproved. First came the clergy, whose part was to pray for all, to sustain Christian values by their pastoral ministry and to eschew the temptations of worldly advancement. Next came what Dudley termed the 'Chivalrie' of the realm: the lay elite, comprising the titular nobility and the larger body of knights, esquires and 'other gentlemen by office or auctoritie'. Their duty was to defend the realm in time of war, and to govern justly under the king. They were to avoid 'vaine delectation' in their styles of life, to refrain from abusing their social power to oppress, and to be 'the helpers and relevers of poor tenantes' and 'the maynteynors of all poore folkes'.

Third, and lastly, came 'the commynaltie of this realm': the common people. Their general duty was to work to get a living for their families, 'for the god lyfe of all the commynaltie in substance standith in trew labor and lawfull busynes'. 'The chief of theis folkes', namely 'the substantiall marchauntes, the wealthie graziers and farmers', were to avoid covetousness and fraudulence in their dealings. The remainder were enjoined to labour with 'honestie and trew diligence', to 'sett' their children, while young, 'to some trew labor or busynes', and to keep their servants from idleness – 'the verie mother of all vice in man and whoman, both noble and unnoble'. They were not to 'presume above their owne degree', nor to 'grudge nor murmur' against the fact that they were born 'to lyve in labor and pain, and the most part of their tyme with the swete of ther face'.

If all this was achieved, with the vital assistance of good government, then commonwealth would be evident in a society distinguished by moral health, concord, material prosperity and full employment:

> How kyndly and how loveingly will merchaunts and craftysmen of the realme by and sell together and exchange and bargain one thing for another. How diligently and busyly will the artificer and husbandman occupie ther Labor and Busynes and how well content men will be from the highest degre to the lowest, to encrease ther howshold servauntes and laborers, whereby all idle people and vagaboundes shalbe sett a worke.

Edmund Dudley was utterly traditional in his perception of society. The model of the three estates as a blueprint for a harmonious Christian social order dated back to the early middle ages. In adopting its conventions, he was concerned to articulate well-established ideals of social and economic morality, not to examine economic processes as a distinct field of enquiry. Yet, in doing so, he placed economic prosperity and material well-being close to the heart of his definition of commonwealth, and he alluded both explicitly and implicitly to the characteristics of a complex social and economic order. This was no simple world of priests, a warrior aristocracy and a myriad of self-supporting peasant communities whose labour and surpluses directly sustained the others. On the contrary, Dudley assumed a highly differentiated economic and social structure. It was one in which the division of labour and economic specialisation were already relatively advanced, and in which a substantial non-agricultural sector was employed in manufactures and in trade. Moreover, it was already a significantly commercialised economy. Many economic transactions were of a less personal nature than those between family members or neighbours; a complex network of economic interdependence existed; the value of goods was assessed by monetary means, and they were bought and sold for profit. Markets existed for most commodities, for land, and for labour. Both local and regional exchange and long-distance commerce were well established, served by specialist occupations, and smoothed by commercial institutions and laws.

If we are to place the developments of the sixteenth and seventeenth centuries in their proper perspective, it is essential that we do not oversimplify the nature of economic life at the turn of the sixteenth century. The market order has a long history, and, as R. H. Britnell has insisted, a vital part of that history is medieval. Yet it is equally essential that we appreciate the limits of the commercialisation of the late-medieval economy. For if this was an economic culture familiar with markets, it was also one which lacked the concept of a market order as a self-regulating system of economic relationships. To a very considerable degree, it was hostile to the notions of untrammelled individual freedom in economic affairs and material gain as an end in itself. Contemporaries regarded economic activity as being subordinated to ethical ends. They assessed its legitimacy in terms of moral imperatives and their attitudes were both enshrined in their economic institutions and expressed in practice. We need to grasp both dimensions of that *status quo ante* if we are to appreciate the nature and the dynamics of the changes which took place over the succeeding two and a half centuries. Part One of this book will attempt to introduce them more fully by exploring the structures of economic life in the various spheres of human association identified by Edmund Dudley. In elaborating his ideal of commonwealth he wrote not only of the three great orders or estates of society, but also of 'towns' and 'cities', 'companies' and 'fellowships' as constituent parts of the realm. Chapters Three and Four will examine the rural and urban communities to which he was alluding, and their regional and national interconnections. First, however, we must consider the sphere of association which he regarded as the most fundamental of all: the household.

CHAPTER ONE

Household economies: structures and roles

When sixteenth-century people used the term 'oeconomy', they employed the word in its original Greek sense to mean the management of household affairs. The notion of *an* economy or *the* economy in the modern sense can scarcely be said to have existed in England, Scotland or Wales, let alone for Britain as a whole. Nor would it have been appropriate. If we wish to envisage the whole, then, it is best imagined as a mosaic of loosely interrelated but partly autonomous units: local, regional and national. Of those units the most basic was the household, and for this reason an account of the economic life of the sixteenth century must begin with an examination of household economies – their variation; their demands; the relationships and the values that sustained them and gave them meaning.

i. *Household size and composition*

The household of the sixteenth century – and for long afterwards – can be defined in the first instance as a unit of residence and of authority: a group of people living under the same roof and under the authority of the household head – usually, though not always, an adult male. In addition it was an institution 'geared for work': work directed towards the satisfaction of the household's needs as a unit not only of consumption and reproduction but also of production. This much most households had in common. Yet they could also vary enormously in terms of their size, their composition and their functional complexity.

At the top of the social scale, the households of the nobility could be vast institutions, organised not only for the maintenance of a noble family at their expected level of magnificence, but also for the administration of great landed estates, the conduct of local government and the pursuit of social and political power. Lord Darcy, the leading magnate of the West Riding of Yorkshire, for example, maintained a household of eighty persons in 1521, which included, alongside his immediate family, household and estate officers and numerous menial servants, the sons of his clients among the regional gentry, engaged in 'honourable' service in return for an education in the skills and accomplishments appropriate to their status. Twenty-four of them accompanied him to war against the Scots in 1523. Such regional courts, for that is what they were, were of course rare. But even a country gentleman of less commanding status, like Sir Thomas Lestrange of Hunstanton, Norfolk, could keep a household of seventeen persons in the 1530s. Members of the social and political elite had a certain 'port' or style of life to maintain which elaborated the complexity of their domestic establishments. These were the great households. Those of less elevated personages were, of course, both smaller and less elaborate in their internal structures. Nevertheless, they varied a good deal, and this point deserves some emphasis, since it has become conventional to stress the structural homogeneity of English households in the early modern period.

Below the level of the gentry, it is now commonly insisted, English households were overwhelmingly 'nuclear' in structure, consisting of a married couple (or the widowed survivor of such a couple) and their children. English households were rarely 'extended' by the inclusion of one or more co-resident kinsfolk beyond the conjugal core. 'Multiple' family households, in which two or more related couples and their offspring co-resided, were rarer still. This is undoubtedly the picture which emerges from the analysis of early census-type listings of particular local communities which survive for England from the sixteenth century. At Coventry in 1523, for example, the average household size (3.8) was small, and only a handful of over 1,300 listed households deviated from the 'nuclear' norm. In the parishes of Clackclose Hundred, Norfolk, in 1557, average household size was 4.85. At Ealing, Middlesex, in 1599, it was 4.75 and some 78 per cent of the households of the parish were nuclear in structure.

This predominance of the nuclear-family household is very much what might be expected in a society in which the evidence of marriage practices indicates that newly married couples were usually expected to establish independent households of their own. They were not usually cushioned by cohabitation with the parental generation and unmarried siblings, as in the large and complex households which certainly existed in the peasant communities of some parts of central, southern and eastern Europe. That most new households were expected to be economically independent units is, of course, a matter of considerable significance. It implies that marriage would be relatively late and not universally attainable, delayed until the partners to a match were economically and socially mature, and preceded by the necessary accumulation of the resources to establish and support a household. This in turn has implications about the proportion of the population able to marry, the fertility of marriages and the length of time between generations – all matters of signal importance for the stability or growth of local populations.

Nevertheless, to insist too emphatically upon the nuclearity of English households in the early modern period can be seriously misleading. It focuses attention upon a single criterion for the classification of household structure – the kinship connections which existed among core household members. And in emphasising this dimension of household composition, it threatens to divert attention from the equally important fact that many households in the early modern period included persons linked to the household head by ties other than those of kinship. As we have seen, average household size was relatively small. But a substantial minority of households were significantly larger than that average. Moreover, in many places the majority of the population actually lived in that minority of larger households. Occasionally this was because such households included co-resident kin of the householder: an aged parent, an unmarried brother or sister. Far more often, however, it was because these households included people affiliated to the householder not by blood or marriage, but by contract.

Such additional household members were generally of two types: servants or apprentices. Servants were for the most part young people hired into the families of their employers, to whom they were rarely related, in return for board, lodging and a money wage. They had generally left home to enter service in their early or mid-teens and were employed on annual contracts. Some might renew these contracts and remain with a master for several years. Most changed master annually, moving from household to household and place to place, until eventually marrying and settling in their mid- to late twenties. Their duties varied. In towns they might be largely domestic, and the majority of servants were young women. In rural areas, both men and women servants were most often 'servants in husbandry', engaged in all forms of farm labour as well as in domestic tasks. But, whichever was the case, they constituted a large and distinctive part of the labour force. Servants made up almost a quarter of the entire population of Coventry in 1523: two-fifths of households there contained servants, as did a similar proportion of the households of Romford, Essex, in 1562. It has been estimated that perhaps 60 per cent of the English population aged between fifteen and twenty-four lived as servants in the minority of wealthier households which could afford them and needed their labour, and, though we have no comparable figures for Scotland or Wales, the institution of service was also familiar in both those countries.

Servants, both male and female, were to be found in town and country alike. Apprentices were more commonly to be found in urban households, or in those of rural craftsmen, and were usually male. For the most part, they were youths in their late teens or early twenties whose parents had bound them by formal indenture to masters who undertook to teach them a trade and to provide them with 'meat, drink, apparel, lodging and all other necessaries'. They were also usually migrants to the towns, like John Bird, the son of a husbandman of Bulkington in the Forest of Arden, who travelled the hundred miles to London in 1523 and became bound for twelve years to Peter Cave, a draper. Apprentices differed from servants in that each was expected to remain in the household of a single master for the duration of his 'term', in that they were not paid wages, and in their relative status and prospects – which were usually superior. Like servants, however, they were numerous, especially in the major cities. In 1550 there were an estimated 7,250 apprentices living in the City of London – roughly a tenth of the entire population.

Servants and apprentices were of major importance to the nature of the sixteenth-century household as a unit of residence and as a social and economic institution. Their presence in so many rural and urban households differentiates the domestic life of the period markedly from that of more recent centuries. And much the same might be said of other employees who sometimes also dwelt in their masters' households, or lived out but took their main meals at their masters' table. These realities provide a sharp reminder that the conventional classification of household types in terms of the kinship bonds of household members *other* than servants and apprentices can be seriously anachronistic. Early modern households may well have been predominantly nuclear family households in terms of their kinship structures. But many of them differed markedly from the modern nuclear family structurally, conceptually and as functional units. Structurally, they included members affiliated by contract. Conceptually, such persons were regarded as full members of their master's 'family' – a word which contemporaries used to describe the entire household, rather than to refer only to relatives by blood or marriage in the modern sense. Functionally, these additional members were taken on for purposes which exceeded the range of most modern households, with their primary focus on consumption, child-rearing and emotional support. In the households of the great their purpose might be partly ornamental – the 'idle serving-men' of whom the moralists of the time complained. But most were there, as Anne Kussmaul puts it, 'not to maintain a style of life, but a style of work; the household economy'. Their presence or absence depended ultimately on the labour requirements of the domestic economy as a productive unit.

ii. *'Honest and worldly lyvings'*

For most households, that meant agricultural production, or its ancillary crafts. England in 1520 had a population of around 2.4 million, of which it has been estimated that only 5.25 per cent lived in the largest towns with more than 5,000 inhabitants, and probably as many again in cor-porate towns of smaller size. Wales in 1540 had a total population of perhaps 250,000 at most, of whom around 3 per cent lived in the four major towns with some 2,000 inhabitants each. Scotland in 1560 had a total population of around 700,000, with perhaps 1.7 per cent dwelling in Edinburgh, the sole town with more than 5,000 inhabitants, and a further 2.5 per cent in towns of more than 2,000. The figures are educated guesses. But the fact remains that demographically these were overwhelmingly rural societies.

Beneath the level of the landed gentry – who were resident in only a minority of the rural communities from which they drew their rental incomes – English rural society, and that of the anglicised regions of Wales, was conventionally divided into yeomen, husbandmen, craftsmen, cottagers and labourers. Yeomen were sometimes defined as owner-occupiers possessing freehold land to the value of at least forty shillings a year. In practice, however, a yeoman was simply a substantial farmer, whatever his mode of tenure, one who was in a position to produce a considerable marketable surplus over and above the needs of his family, and usually a regular employer of non-family labour. Yeomen were the 'cocks of the parish'. Husbandmen were small farmers, generally with a holding capable of supporting a family and producing a modest surplus in most years, and relying for the most part on family labour. Village craftsmen and tradesmen, who were to be found in most communities save the smallest, varied in their relative prosperity. Some, like millers, blacksmiths or butchers, were often men of substance. Others, like weavers, tailors or alehousekeepers, were often relatively poor. Most fell in between. Most also combined their trade with farming to a greater or lesser extent, like Richard Redley of Wigston Magna, Leicestershire, whose inventory, taken in 1539, included his blacksmith's forge and tools, valued at sixteen shillings, and farm goods to the value of over five pounds.

Cottagers and labourers held only a few acres of land at best. Some plied a trade, and many enjoyed rights of pasture on the common lands of their villages, which enabled them to keep a beast or two, but most relied on wages for a significant part of their living. Nevertheless, as W. J. Ashley observed, 'we are not to conceive of these labourers as a body of men in regular employment at fixed wages'. Relatively few permanent labourers were employed even on the substantial farms of the time – which relied for their regular labour needs on resident servants. Waged employment for the cottager or labourer tended to mean a scattering of casual paid jobs, with a peak of activity at certain seasons. The situation can be exemplified from the records of the labour hired by the Capell family on their 300-acre home farm at Stebbing, Essex, in 1483/4. They employed eleven resident servants as the core of their labour force. Fifty-two others were hired episodically for between one and thirty days each. Two-thirds of the days worked by these labourers fell in harvest time, while the remainder involved seasonal tasks like sowing and harrowing the fields and the intermittent hiring of extra hands to thresh grain when need arose. Such paid work constituted a crucial element in the living of those who performed it, a vital cash supplement to a subsistence based on their cottage gardens, small plots of land and common rights.

The proportions of local populations falling into these broad socioeconomic categories varied in accordance with the patterns of local agriculture and the contingencies which had shaped the distribution of land within particular communities. The taxpaying householders of the arable parish of Terling, Essex, in 1524/5, for example, can be categorised into nine very large farmers (11.8 per cent); twenty-eight lesser yeomen, substantial husbandmen and prosperous craftsmen (36.8 per cent); eighteen smaller husbandmen and craftsmen (23.7 per cent); and twenty-one cottagers and labourers (27.6 per cent). In the pastoral and cloth-working parishes of the Kentish Weald, on the other hand, yeoman accumulations of over sixty acres of land were few, but small farms of around twenty to thirty acres were numerous and tiny cottage holdings very common. Considerable attention has been paid to the size of labouring population with little or no land in the early sixteenth century – in particular through attempts to interpret the records of the 'Great Subsidy' tax of 1524/5, which included men taxed on wages. Such men were numerous, including approximately a fifth of all taxpayers in Leicestershire, a quarter in parts of Norfolk, a third in Lincolnshire and Devon, and still more in parts of Essex. To conclude on the basis of such evidence that perhaps a fifth to a quarter of the rural population were already

landless labourers, however, is premature. Some of those included were
certainly servants rather than independent householders. Even more can
be shown to have held small parcels of land, as in Kibworth Harcourt,
Leicestershire, where three of the ten listed wage-earners held land and
a further four were sons of landed families who may well have been
earning a living as labourers as a temporary stage of the life cycle, with
the expectation of eventually achieving smallholdings of their own. On
the other hand it is entirely possible that some of the rural poor were
omitted from the tax assessment altogether.

Given these variations and uncertainties, it is safest to conclude that
at the opening of the sixteenth century English rural society was already
highly differentiated, containing a large minority of households of considerable substance, a broad middling band who could enjoy a modest
but relatively secure living as small farmers or craftsmen, and a further
large minority who pieced together a bare living as best they could. Taken
as a whole, however, it is also the case that access to land, or to the use
of land (in the form of common rights) remained very widely distributed. Even the labouring poor enjoyed such access to a considerable
extent and complete dependence upon agricultural wages was still exceptional in most areas. They were not, in the full sense of the word, a rural
proletariat of the type that was to characterise English rural society by
the later eighteenth century.

This was even less the case in the rural societies of Scotland and of
much of Wales, which lacked, it has been said, 'a labourer class as
opposed to labouring individuals'. In the areas subject to Welsh customary law, co-heirs to the traditional clan lands retained powerful rights of
hereditary proprietorship and to the use of the pastures and waste crucial
to an essentially pastoral economy. In Scotland the 'fermes' into which the
estates of the great proprietors were divided were let out either to single
tenants or to joint tenants who farmed them co-operatively. Whichever
was the case, these men of substance sub-let parcels of land to the
'cottars' who made up the majority of the rural population and who
were provided with a cottage, enough land for subsistence, a 'kailyard'
vegetable plot and grazing rights, in return for their labour on the tenants'
lands when it was required. Rural craftsmen were frequently cottars
too. Given such a system, there were few landless labourers in rural
Scotland. It was a grievously poor rural society in which most households
scraped a hard living from an unrewarding soil. But in the northern
kingdom, as in Wales, it was almost universally the case that most people,
in Clapham's words, had 'if not a foot, at least a toe on the land'.

As we have seen, the inhabitants of the towns were a small minority
of the population of early-sixteenth-century Britain. They were, none-

theless, a very significant minority. The towns of the period ranged in size and importance from small market towns, some of which were little more than large villages galvanised by commercial activity on their market days, to the capital cities of Edinburgh (pop. c.10,000 in 1560) and London (pop. c.55,000 in 1520) which dwarfed all competitors in their respective kingdoms. But even the smallest had occupational structures and economic roles considerably more diversified than those of rural settlements, and the larger cities displayed economic structures of dazzling sophistication by the standards of the time. Indeed urban communities could be defined by virtue of their concentration of highly variegated economic activities within one densely settled location.

Surveys of the occupational structures of the major towns in the late fifteenth and early sixteenth centuries tend to stress the prevalence of five broad occupational categories. These were: the entrepreneurial and distributive trades (including merchants, mercers, grocers, clothiers and drapers); manufacturing (notably the production of textiles, clothing, leather, wood and metal goods); the production and retailing of food and drink (including butchers, bakers, fishmongers and the keepers of inns, taverns and alehouses); the building trades (masons, carpenters, tilers, plumbers and so on); and finally the small but prestigious bodies of professional practitioners (notably lawyers, physicians, apothecaries and clergymen). In addition every town contained substantial numbers of semi-skilled or unskilled labourers whose particular tasks might vary from day to day.

Within this general pattern the component occupational groups varied in their significance from town to town. Norwich and Worcester were major centres of textile production. The leather trades were prominent in Leicester and Chester; the wood and metal trades in Bristol; the distributive trades in ports like Hull or Lynn. It has been suggested that in Scotland's leading burghs manufacturing was generally less important than was the case in English towns. In the main, however, the degree of local specialisation in urban economies was limited and relative. Most towns of any size exhibited the same broad range of occupations – those, in Ashley's words, 'needed to supply the ordinary wants of the townsmen and the country round'. The markets for most urban producers were as yet too contained in size and extent for it to be otherwise. And for the same reason, specialisation was also limited in a second sense: it was by product rather than by process. Most urban craftsmen produced a single type of product – hats, gloves, pewter tableware and so on – and were engaged in every stage of its manufacture. Given the limits of demand in the markets they served, there was little incentive to enhance the division of labour so as to raise individual productivity and the scale of production. Only in the textile trades, which enjoyed much larger markets than was usual, was the division of labour much advanced.

Among the numerous urban occupations there existed a distinctive pattern of differentiation by wealth and status. An anonymous 'Apologie' for the city of London, probably written around 1580, divided the people of the city into three 'parts' or 'sorts': first, the merchants and 'chief retailers'; second, 'the most part of retailers and all artificers'; and third, those termed 'hirelings'. Of these groups, the second – 'they of the middle place' – was deemed the most numerous. As a crude guide to the essential distinctions within urban society it is one which also has relevance a century earlier.

The mercantile and entrepreneurial elite of the towns have been described as men 'of mixed enterprise, who primarily represented wholesale trade but combined it with one or more of a number of other interests'. Their primary interest was usually in a single staple commodity, but they also traded in anything else that provided an opportunity to turn a profit. These were men like William Mucklowe, sometime mayor of Worcester. He was primarily an exporter of cloth, but in 1511 he also imported from the Netherlands goods as varied as canvas, velvet, damask, sugar, bells, swans' feathers, spectacles and paper. Such men enjoyed a distinctive economic position, through their control of the wholesale trade, and a distinctive social and political position, through their dominance of municipal government. Some of them were prodigiously rich by the standards of the time. In 1523, for example, the personal wealth of Robert Jannys, grocer and alderman of Norwich, was assessed at £1,100, a sum equal to the tax paid by the entire city of Rochester.

Beneath the mercantile elite there was usually something of a pecking order of trades in terms of their relative wealth, social standing and prominence within particular urban economies. This was reflected in the fees charged to enter a given trade, access to positions of honour and authority in urban institutions, and the orders of precedence adopted in the rich ritual and ceremonial life of the late-medieval city. Taken as a whole, however, 'the most part of retailers and artificers' constituted the core of the urban community. The principal distinction among them was between those who plied their trades as independent masters and those who served as 'journeymen' – skilled men who had completed an apprenticeship, but served as employees in the workshops of master craftsmen and did not engage in trade on their own account. Of the latter, some lived in the households of their masters. Most, however, did not: they were married and had families of their own, but came to work each day in their employers' shops. Estimates of the proportions of urban householders falling into these different broad categories are difficult, given the available sources. In Coventry, however, it seems likely that around 1520 the mercantile elite constituted some 6 per cent of the city's householders. Other independent tradesmen and craftsmen made up 35 per cent of households, journeymen a further 32 per cent. The remaining 27 per cent of householders were those regarded by contemporaries as 'the poor': labouring people and poor widows.

Such figures provide a preliminary sense of the urban social order and of how its constituent householders gained their living. In considering the economic structures of the towns, however, three further distinctions need to be made regarding the organisation of the crafts and trades, distinctions which had major implications for the domestic economies of those who lived by them.

Most of the processing and manufacturing trades were organised in accordance with what Unwin termed the 'handicrafts system'. In this the independent master was a man of modest capital, in the form of premises, tools and equipment, and sufficient circulating capital to finance the regular purchase of raw materials and to maintain a stock of finished goods for sale. He worked at his trade with his own hands, assisted by an apprentice or journeyman, and dealt directly with the consumers of his products. This was a system which depended for its health upon the ready availability of raw materials, relatively simple manufacturing processes which could be conducted in the master's workshop, and a local market in which goods could be sold directly to the consumer.

Some trades, however, were more differentiated in their organisation. These included those in which contractors might take on many workmen, skilled and unskilled, as was sometimes the case in the building trades. Of greater overall significance, however, were those in which the possibility of exploiting bigger, non-local markets for particular products had encouraged merchant capitalists to involve themselves in the large-scale organisation of manufacturing.

Such involvement took two forms. In what later became known as the 'domestic system', the small master continued to purchase his own raw materials and to undertake most stages of the production of the finished goods. His products, however, were sold not to local consumers, but to the merchant who had the capital to maintain a substantial stock of goods and the commercial expertise to see to their transportation for sale in distant markets. Under the domestic system, the individual master retained a considerable measure of immediate independence in the conduct of his trade, and he gained the advantage of access to larger markets for his products. Nevertheless, he also became fundamentally dependent on the merchant who controlled the marketing of the finished goods.

In a second variant, usually described as the 'putting-out' system, the role of the merchant capitalist was more elaborate. He purchased the raw materials and financed the entire manufacturing process by putting out each stage of the work to specialist workers who were paid by him at piece-rates. This system of production was best attuned to situations in which raw materials were less readily accessible, and the manufacturing process involved several stages which could not easily be conducted in a single workshop. It involved a more elaborate division of labour and is best exemplified by the textile industry, of which it was observed that 'the making of a broadcloth consisteth not in the travail of one or two persons, but in a number as of xxx or xl persons at the least, of men, women and children'. In the putting-out system the merchant capitalist was master of the whole process from first to last. He owned the raw materials, co-ordinated the manufacturing process, sold the finished product and supplied the circulating capital which sustained the whole system. His employees worked for the most part in their own households, and direct supervision was exerted over only part of the manufacturing process (the preliminary cleaning and dyeing of wool in the clothier's workshop, for example, or the fulling of woven cloth in his fulling mill). As a result, journeymen, who lacked the capital to set up independently, could operate in practice like small masters, working with their own (or hired) tools in their own homes. Some were able to work both for a capitalist employer and on their own account. In the putting-out system, however, they retained little real independence. They were essentially wage-workers.

Of these three systems of organisation the handicrafts system remained predominant in the miscellany of crafts and trades that characterised most urban economies. In Scotland, which had no major long-distance trade in manufactured goods, it was virtually universal. By 1500, however, its continued vitality in the urban context was in part a result of the removal of manufactures organised on the domestic and putting-out systems to alternative locations in the countryside. This remains in many ways an obscure process, and will be explored more fully in Chapter Four. For present purposes it is enough to say that many small country towns in particular regions had become centres of specialised manufacturing, which had also come to permeate the economies of their rural hinterlands. These industries in the countryside were sometimes organised on the domestic system, as in the woollen districts of south-east Lancashire, the West Riding of Yorkshire and north Wales (where small masters wove their own wool into rough 'Welsh cottons' sold via

Oswestry to the drapers of Shrewsbury). In the textile districts of Suffolk
and Essex, the Kentish Weald and the west country, however, an initial
pattern of this kind had largely given way by 1500 to the putting-out
system in small cloth towns like Lavenham, Cranbrook or Malmesbury
and their satellite villages. In the metal trades of the Sheffield and
Rotherham area, both systems could be observed: independent small
masters produced the finer goods, but simpler products were made from
iron put out to the 'many smiths and cutlers' described in 1540 as inhabiting rural Hallamshire.

By 1500 this geographical expansion of manufacturing had produced
a variety of rural economies in which agriculture and manufacturing
existed side by side as components of the inhabitants' household
economies. A great many of the metalworkers of Hallamshire held
small farms, usually of less than ten acres, and also enjoyed common
rights on the moors of the area. In the Kentish Weald many of the men
engaged in the textile trades also held at least a cottage holding and
possessed agricultural goods. Nevertheless, the penetration of manufacturing employment in many areas was already formidable. If, as has
been estimated, there were 1,300 weavers active in the Kentish Weald in
the mid-sixteenth century, then weaving alone must have involved around
16 per cent of the male population over the age of fifteen. The process
of spinning would have involved an even larger proportion of local
households. It has been suggested that 5,000 spinners were required to
support the cloth output of the area. This would mean the employment
of some 35 per cent of the total of children aged from five to fourteen
and women aged fifteen and above in the local population. The prevalence of such manufacturing employment in the countryside was already
such that E. A. Wrigley has estimated that in 1520 perhaps 20 per cent
of the English population living outside the towns of more than 5,000
inhabitants were already engaged in non-agricultural employments. This
is no more than a reasoned guess and to describe such people as the 'rural
non-agricultural' population is somewhat misleading, since they would
include the inhabitants of the many towns which had populations smaller
than 5,000. Nevertheless, even if we make allowance for the populations
of such lesser cities, the recalculated figures suggest that around 15 per
cent of the truly rural population of England lived, in part at least, from
profits and wages earned in manufacturing employments. In the areas
where those industries were concentrated, of course, the figure would
have been much higher.

The vast majority of people in early sixteenth-century Britain, then,
gained their livings from agriculture; a large minority, especially in

England, from the processing of agricultural products and minerals into manufactured goods and from retail and wholesale trade; and some from various combinations of these forms of employment. Most did so relatively independently, by virtue of their tenure of land, or possession of a domestic workshop. Others relied to a greater or lesser extent upon the sale of their labour to others. Throughout this already relatively complex occupational structure, however, the household remained the principal locus of production and the most characteristic unit of labour organisation. To a very large extent economic organisation *was* domestic organisation. And, this being the case, differences in the occupations of, and resources available to, individual households shaped the patterns of their existence and the roles of their members. It is to these patterns and roles that we must now turn.

iii. *Roles in the domestic economy: gender and age*

As working units, all households were spheres of interdependence. Their maintenance and survival depended on the contributions of all their members. Yet households were spheres not only of reciprocal obligation, but also of authority. Their functioning as economic units was inevitably coloured by what have been termed principles of 'hierarchical differentiation', the prevailing assumptions regarding the roles and standing of household members according to gender, age and 'place'.

This was a patriarchal society in the sense that authority was conventionally located in the persons of adult males generally and male household heads specifically. Contemporary moralists laboured the fact in their prescriptive writings on household government. The husband was 'the highest in the family and hath authority over all, and the charge of all is committed to his charge'. The wife was his 'associate' or 'yokefellow', but also his 'subordinate' or 'deputie', her duty being to 'walk jointly with him under the conduct and government of her head'. Together, the master and mistress of the family were 'they which have power and authority over children', and further exercised a quasi-parental jurisdiction over servants and apprentices. In practice, domestic relations were shot through with ambiguities and inconsistencies. Yet the ubiquity of patriarchal assumptions can never be ignored. Moreover, they were firmly embodied in law, most fundamentally in the law of property.

Property was for the most part vested in male household heads. In English common law, which applied also to Wales after 1540, a man was able to acquire and hold property, contract debts, make a will and engage independently in economic activity. These rights extended also to an unmarried woman, or 'femme sole', be she maiden or widow. Married women, however, were subject to the doctrine of 'coverture'. The rights of a married woman, or 'femme covert', were seriously curtailed. Though a wife retained her title to any freehold lands of her own (unless these were formally transferred), her husband acquired a life interest in the rents and profits of her lands even if she predeceased him, provided there was 'live issue' of the marriage. In addition, all her moveable goods and chattels became his. She was unable to enter contracts on her own behalf, and her husband was held liable for her debts. Her rights were limited to those of her 'dower', whereby as a widow she was entitled to one-third of her late husband's lands for the term of her life. In Scottish law the situation was somewhat different. Scottish law recognised 'community of property'. Neither partner to a marriage could dispose of land without the other's consent and, if a wife predeceased her husband, her 'third' reverted to her kin. Moveable goods, however, came under the control of the husband, and, though a wife could make a will, she could do so only with her husband's consent.

These rigidities of the law were qualified in various respects. In England, the developing law of equity provided for the creation of trusts by which married women were able to retain control of property which would otherwise have passed to their husbands. Ecclesiastical law, which governed the inheritance of moveables, recognised the rights of widows and children to particular shares of family property and restricted the husband's right to dispose of it by will. Local customary law might also permit more flexible property rights. On the manor of Sonning in Berkshire, for example, women could hold customary land in their own right, or as joint tenants with their husbands, and widows had the right to hold their former husbands' land until death or remarriage. (To allow a widow a third of the holding was common elsewhere.) By the custom of London, married women could be treated as 'femmes soles' in certain circumstances – permitting them to hold property, to establish retail businesses and to plead in the city's courts – though they were not permitted to practise crafts independently. Again, some individuals could choose to recognise moral rights unprovided for in law. Thomas Pyrkyne of Chislet, for example, did so when in 1549 he willed to his wife 'all her own household stuff which she brought with her when I married . . . all her bedding, brass and pewter, brewing vesell, paire of almayne rivetts, a great cupboard and all her chests'. And some individual women can be found acting as if in ignorance of the laws of coverture, perhaps with their husbands' compliance.

Women's property rights, then, varied in accordance with the provisions of different systems of law, their place of residence and their access to legal assistance. They varied above all, however, with their marital status. Throughout Britain, widows of substance could enjoy rights comparable – though rarely wholly identical – to those of men. They were householders. At other stages of the life-cycle, women's legal identities derived from those of their menfolk. Adult men were accorded independent occupational identity. Women were identified as the daughters, spouses or widows of particular men. Prior to marriage the main occupational identity recognised for a woman was that of servant. Once married, she might be the mistress of the house, but she was not the householder. She was, as William Perkins put it, 'the other married person'.

Despite these constraints, women's economic contribution was indispensable. The duty of the householder was to maintain his family by his labour according to his degree, to exercise authority in the management of its affairs, and to play a part in the training of his sons, servants and apprentices. That of the mistress of the household was to display skill in the arts of 'huswifery'. By that term contemporaries understood a range of activity rather different from that implied by its modern derivative 'housewife'. In the first place, it was far less concerned with the maintenance of the domestic environment. Housing was simple. The homestead of even a prosperous farmer consisted of a large 'hall', earth-floored, open to the rafters, and containing a central hearth, with a screened-off 'parlour' at one end, a service area at the other, and perhaps a separate kitchen in the yard. The merchant houses of the towns were also focused on a hall, with service rooms behind, private chambers above and cellars or storerooms. Craftsmen generally had a small workshop and a single living room. The poor inhabited tiny cottages or tenement rooms in congested alleys and yards.

Within such dwellings, furnishings were few, consisting for the most part of cooking and eating implements, bedding and provision for seating and storage. The domestic furnishings of the Worcestershire husbandman Richard Sclatter, for example, consisted of the simplest kitchen equipment, notably a large brass pan, tubs and buckets, some bedding, three 'boards for a bed', additional boards and trestles for a table, one chair, one form and three chests. John Smith, a Leicestershire tanner, had a board, two forms, a cupboard and three chairs in his hall; three chests and bedding in his parlour; and three cupboards and various utensils in the kitchen. The furnishings of merchants and gentlemen were costlier and rather more elaborate (including, for example, bedsteads and joined tables) but they were not essentially different in range and type. A domestic setting of such bare simplicity made relatively few demands. Floors needed to be swept or periodically strewn with fresh rushes. Pots needed to be washed and scoured. There was tidying to be done and the periodic washing of sheets and personal linen – a heavy though infrequent task – but little more.

The art of 'huswifery' was rather more concerned with the general management of the household's daily consumption needs. Food preparation would, of course, have been central. The wealthy, according to one observer, exceeded in 'number of dishes and change of meat', and a principal daily duty of the mistress of a household of substance was to 'take order' for the provision of the day's meals with her kitchen servants. At times of festival, humbler people could also 'exceed after their manner'. But most people, most of the time, lived on bread or oatcakes, pottage or porridge, 'white meats' (cheese, butter and eggs), bacon, and occasional poultry and butchers' meat, washed down with weak ale. Few kitchens had spits on which to roast meat. Most had pots and pans. Larger households baked their own bread and brewed their own ale. Most probably did not, carrying their prepared dough to a communal oven, or relying on bakers and alehousekeepers. All this took time; the fetching and carrying of water alone could expend a good deal of time and energy. And then there was the perennial making and mending of clothes and bedding. This might often include the spinning of one's own wool and linen yarn to be worked up by a local weaver, a reminder that the management of domestic consumption also extended into the provision of essential resources for the household. And in considering this, the basic distinction to be made is between those households which functioned as units of production, as well as of residence and consumption, and those which did not.

The notion that a woman was economically supported by her husband was not alien to early modern society, as is sometimes alleged. There are references enough to the husband's duty to 'provide for', 'maintain' or 'keep' his wife, indicating a privileging of the male role in resource provision. But the practical reality, nonetheless, was of mutual interdependence in the joint endeavour of sustaining their family. As Sir Anthony Fitzherbert tells us in his *Booke of Husbandrye* (1523), it was already 'an olde common saying, that seldom doth the husbande thrive without leve of his wyf'. Fitzherbert described the daily duties of the mistress of a substantial rural household as a constant round of activity in which domestic tasks – sweeping, tidying, providing for meals and directing the labour of servants – paled into insignificance beside her direct productive role in providing resources for the household. This included numerous self-provisioning activities: the keeping of pigs and poultry, the dairy and a garden; growing flax and hemp, and spinning yarn for linen; preparing part of the wool clip for the household's clothes; malting, brewing, the taking of grain to the mill and the baking of bread. It also involved labour in field and barn: haymaking, reaping, winnowing, or anything else required 'in tyme of nede to helpe her husbande'. And it involved marketing too. It was the woman of the house who went to market most often, to sell not only the surplus milk, eggs, poultry and pigs which she had produced, but also the grain she had helped to reap and winnow, and to buy 'al maner of necessary thinges belonging to a household'. As this, and other evidence, implies, there was hardly any sphere of farmwork, save the heaviest tasks like ploughing, from which women were excluded.

The households of craftsmen and tradesmen presented a different set of circumstances. Whereas most peasant women would have been familiar with some agricultural tasks from childhood and trained in others as servants in husbandry, most trades were formally closed to women. The tiny numbers of female apprentices enrolled in the towns were generally apprenticed to learn 'huswifery' in general, or as seamstresses, or in the retail and food trades. Some would have brought a knowledge of appropriate skills to the businesses of their husbands. Some might be permitted by borough customs, such as those of Lincoln and London, to carry on a business other than that of their spouses, like Margaret Purcell, a skinner's wife, who maintained the 'trade of victualling'. Most tradesmen's wives, however, lacked formal training in the 'mystery' of a craft.

Nevertheless, a good many of them acquired the relevant skills informally. In Coventry, most craft fellowships forbade masters to teach their skills to persons other than their apprentices *and wives*. Others might forbid the participation of wives too; but, if so, such prohibitions were often more honoured in the breach than in the observance, for many women combined their domestic duties with engagement in productive work. Women were engaged in every branch of textile production in town and country alike, and not just as spinners. An act of 1554 remarks of the task of wool sorting and grading that 'the experience thereof consisteth only in women, as clothiers wives and their women servants'. They were also active as weavers in Bristol, York, Hull, Norwich and London, where unsuccessful attempts were made to restrict them. Women were also involved either in ancillary roles, or directly, in many other trades. A deposition of 1514 shows us Thomas Simons, a stationer, at 7.15 one morning, standing 'at his stall . . . and the wife of the said Simons was by him'. In 1547 and 1554, the London Carpenters' Company became exercised about women going to the riverside to choose and buy timber on behalf of their husbands. Harry Weller, a master bricklayer of Chester, was paid eight pence a day for a job in 1556, while his wife got a further two pence a day 'for carrying water and sand'. Similar instances occur of women working alongside their husbands as bakers, butchers and brewers. The clearest indication that such practice was general is that widows were commonly permitted to continue to exercise a dead husband's trade while they remained unmarried. At York, it was confirmed for all trades in 1529 that widows of freemen who were 'disposed to live sole and without any other husband' could not only 'occupy their husband's craft', but also 'take journeymen and apprentices into their service'. Some plied their trades for many years. At Chester in 1574 as many as five of the active smiths were widows – a remarkable proportion, given that many younger widows were in an excellent position to remarry swiftly if they chose, and many did (not infrequently, to an aspirant senior apprentice or journeyman).

In manor house, farmyard and workshop, women were heavily engaged in providing, as well as managing, the resources for their households' living. Among the wives of labouring men, such opportunities for participation in household-based productive activity were rarer. But this is not to say that they were wholly dependent upon their husbands' wages. In the countryside the tiny holdings and common rights of cottagers, the poultry, pigs, 'milch kine' and small flocks which they sustained, and the supplies of vegetables, fuel, wild fruits and small game which they provided, enabled many of the 'poorer sort' to engage in forms of self-provisioning which fell largely to the women. Moreover, women also worked as agricultural labourers, especially in seasons of peak labour demand. Women, most of them married, provided a third of all hired day-labour on one large farm in Essex in 1483/4. On another in 1539/40 they were similarly engaged, sometimes alongside their husbands. Thomas Magott and his wife worked fairly regularly during seven months of the year. William Lene was employed during the summer, grossing almost £3 in wages altogether, while his wife earned nearly three shillings more at harvest time. Perhaps, like most poor women, she also gleaned the fields after harvest, gathering for domestic use grain overlooked by the reapers. Such agricultural wage work was intermittent. Involvement in putting-out industries, however, could provide a small but regular income. The numerous poor women spinning for the clothiers of Kent could earn two or three pence for spinning a pound of wool – a day's work. This was equivalent to half a day-labourer's usual wage. They would have known the truth of Fitzherbert's remark that 'a woman cannot get her living . . . with spinning on the distaff, but it stoppeth a gap'.

The wives of urban wage workers spun at home too, and for the same reason. In a survey of the poor of Norwich, conducted in 1570, almost three-quarters of the married women listed were engaged in the preliminary processes of textile manufacture. Some, whose husbands were sick or otherwise unemployed, were the chief sustainers of their families. In Retford, Nottinghamshire, the linen trade played the same role. Others took in sewing, or knitting, or washing, or made lace. Many of the lodgings of urban journeymen and labourers, however, were in all likelihood deserted for much of the day by men and women alike. Women were very much part of the 'reserve army' of casual labour in the towns. They can be found outside their homes in a variety of public, semi-public and private workspaces, fetching and carrying, washing and scrubbing, doing any one of the tasks described in the Norwich survey as 'helpe others'. They cleaned streets. They powered the treadmill of the iron crane that served the quayside at Chester. And they were ubiquitous as small-scale dealers, principally in foodstuffs, like the wife of Thomas Hunt of Witham, Essex, who 'buyeth butter and selleth [it]', or Rose Hearse of Maldon, who walked each week to Chelmsford market to sell fish and oysters.

The role of the wife within the household economies of the sixteenth century, then, was complex and varied. It extended beyond immediate domestic tasks to include a variety of self-provisioning activities, the supervision of servants, assisting her husband in farmwork or trade, wage-earning in or out of the domestic environment, and independent engagement in small business. The mix would have varied with the circumstances of particular households, but throughout society the central characteristic of the gender division of labour was the flexibility and adaptability of the female role.

Moreover, this constant round of productive activity took place in the context of women's further role in what can be termed reproductive labour. Most couples married and established independent households in their mid- to late twenties (though among the wealthy it was not uncommon for women to marry younger). Demographic research indicates that in this pre-contraceptive age a woman could expect to bear her first child within eighteen months of marriage, and thereafter to have further children at average intervals of two to three years for the remainder of her fertile life – if indeed she lived to the age of menopause. In other words, the married women whose working lives we have been surveying were pregnant for a quarter to a third of their adult lives and were perennially besieged by young children. (About a third of the population was under fifteen years of age in 1541.) As regards the rearing of young children, the gender division of labour appears to have been fairly clear. This was deemed women's work, the fulfilment of their natural function. And even though she might be able to call on the assistance of older children, or servants and (among the gentry and many urban households) employ a wetnurse to care for infants, it seems likely that, as Patricia Crawford puts it, the lives of women were 'structured around the rhythms of their pregnancies, childbearing and childrearing'. That endless cycle was central to their role as the principal carers of the household. Theirs were the hands that bound wounds, prepared medicinal herbs, wiped sick or soiled bodies and stilled distress. There was little need for Fitzherbert to advise any woman of the house to 'alway be doyng of some good worke that the devil may fynde the[e] alway occupied'. He was nearer the mark when he recognised that 'it may fortune sometime that thou shalte have so many thinges to do that thou shalte not wel know where is best to begyn', and to recommend prioritising tasks by asking 'what thinge should be the greatest losse if it were not done'. Thomas Tusser agreed that 'Huswives affaires have never none ende'.

In the agriculturally dominated, labour-intensive, low-productivity, pre-mechanised, pre-contraceptive environment of the period, with its high-dependency ratio of children to adults, it could scarcely be otherwise. And for the same reasons, children were also expected to play their part in the household economy. Childhood, writes Keith Thomas, was lived 'under the tyranny of time' in the early modern world. It could not be prolonged. Only a small minority experienced formal schooling in the early sixteenth century. Most children began early on the acquisition of the work skills which would maintain them as adults and were expected to participate in the gaining of the family's living from the earliest point at which they could be useful.

The extent to which child-labour was exploited, however, should not be exaggerated. Children were numerous, to be sure, but their lack of physical strength and appropriate skills made it unlikely that they were extensively employed in early childhood. Barbara Hanawalt's analysis of the records of late-medieval coroners' inquests provides illuminating evidence of the activities in which children were engaged at the moment that they met untimely deaths. Before the age of seven they were already undergoing a process of role differentiation: boys were often with their fathers and girls with their mothers when they suffered mortal injuries arising from such activities as wood cutting, brewing or fetching water. But they were not usually engaged in such work themselves: they were playing near by. The age of seven or eight, however, heralded a 'striking change'. Boys were now employed as shepherds, cowherds, mill hands or reapers; girls also helped with the harvest, gathered fuel or tended younger children. In short, they had become part of the productive life of their families.

Other evidence suggests that children were gradually introduced to tasks deemed to be within their capabilities. These might be in and around the house – fetching water; cleaning and mending; tending pigs and poultry; picking fruit – or in the fields – herding; assisting with the plough-team; bird-scaring; weeding; binding corn or gleaning. Such tasks, however, were intermittent and they were still unlikely to be fully employed or involved with heavier or more skilled work before their early teens. More sustained use of child-labour was more likely to be found in households engaged in domestic manufactures. It was certainly so among the poor of Norwich in 1570, where, for example, the widow Ann Bucke had two children aged nine and five 'that worke lace', and Edmund and Tamizin Harrison had 'five children, the oldest of the age of 10 yeres, and 2 of them spinne and the rest be yunge'.

In such ways children contributed to their own keep, but they were unlikely to earn it in full. Some endured already the drudgery which was to become characteristic of child-labour in the early industrial era. The chores of most were perhaps more an introduction to the skills and disciplines of adult life than a full role in domestic production, and they are more likely to have been a charge on, than a significant asset to, the family economy. By their early teens they may have acquired a fair proficiency at many tasks. By then, however, few could have found full employment in a small farm or workshop, and they were transferred as servants or apprentices into households with more sustained and extensive labour requirements. There, under the direction of a master and mistress, young women learned the numerous skills of housewifery, and young men the care of draught animals, the handling of plough, cart or harrow, or the mysteries of a trade – completing the training, as full, though subordinate, members of a productive household unit, which fitted them eventually to establish households of their own.

CHAPTER TWO

Household economies: priorities and strategies

The household, as we have seen, was a unit geared for work, within which its members' roles were allocated in accordance with basic contemporary assumptions regarding the proper place of men, women, children and youths. The particular patterns of work obtaining within individual households, however, varied widely. Such differences were partly structural in nature – governed by the basic economic circumstances of particular social groups, and to that extent predictable. They were partly contingent – influenced by the accidents of fertility and mortality, and differences of personality, aptitude and luck. Household economies shared certain general characteristics, but also evidenced a host of different working strategies, each representing a response to specific configurations of needs, resources and capabilities. Much of this inevitably remains obscure. Enough, however, is accessible to the historian to permit a characterisation of the dominant priorities of the household economy and an exploration, in part at least, of the strategies by which their realisation was pursued.

i. Survival

The first of these priorities was fundamental: the survival of the household. This required above all the maintenance of the flow of resources upon which the household most immediately depended by combinations of direct self-provisioning and of engagement in the market as producer and consumer. In urban society it was the latter which dominated. Most urban households were dependent on the market in a double sense. On the one hand, most were obliged to purchase the bulk of their foodstuffs, raw materials and other day-to-day requirements. On the other hand, the incomes with which they did this depended upon market demand for either the goods they manufactured or their labour. For some, as we have seen, this might mean a dependence on the vicissitudes of large, long-distance markets, as was the case with great merchants, or people involved in manufacturing in the domestic or putting-out systems. To the majority of independent masters it meant a more limited, localised, but relatively predictable demand, principally that of their fellow citizens and the rural population of their immediate hinterland. To labouring people it meant whatever work they could get.

Some of these realities extended also into the countryside in those regions where manufacturing had become established as a major plank in the local economy. The balance of most rural household economies, however, was still heavily weighted towards the provision of their own consumption requirements. This was still essentially a subsistence economy of small producers, relying primarily on family labour, consuming most of the produce of their holdings and providing for most of their own domestic needs. Such a situation is not to be confused with self-sufficiency. Few, if any, rural households would have been wholly self-sufficient. Some essential commodities could not be produced on even a large and well-stocked holding – salt, for example, or metal goods. Many families would also have needed to buy foodstuffs and other agricultural products which were temporarily or permanently beyond their own productive resources. Moreover, they needed to generate a cash income for particular purposes, such as the payment of rents, dues and taxes, or providing their children's 'portions'. They might need to hire labour to pay for specialist services. Nevertheless, most needs could be met by participation in localised markets or engaging in by-employments. The economies of most households remained subsistence-oriented in the sense that they were not producing *primarily* for the purpose of market exchange. In much of England and Wales money played only a marginal part in their day-to-day dealings, which were often conducted on credit between known and trusted individuals: it was a unit of reckoning, rather than a regular means of exchange. In Scotland, where both rents and labour were usually paid in kind, its role was negligible for most of the peasantry. Moreover, the prevailing economic climate at the opening of the sixteenth century would have reinforced these characteristics. Land was relatively available. Rents were relatively low. There was limited need to engage with the market either to provide for subsistence needs or to generate income. Such realities, of course, varied regionally. Those parts of Hertfordshire, Kent and Essex which served the London food market, for example, were much more commercialised. But in general it was probably the case that, as an Italian visitor to England remarked c.1500, agriculture seemed 'not to be practised beyond what is needed for the consumption of the people'.

Extensive self-provisioning was also typical of more substantial yeoman and gentry households. On the 200-acre farm of Thomas Willoughby of Chiddingstone, Kent, in 1518/19 much of the wheat and oats grown would have been required for household consumption, and the sheep flock was almost wholly dedicated to that purpose. The principal business of the farm was cattle production for urban markets, yet even here the Willoughby household consumed nine oxen, six steers and fourteen kine, while selling only eighteen, fourteen and twenty-five respectively. Much the same would have been true of most yeoman households. Unlike the modest husbandman, however, a gentleman like Willoughby needed to acquire a substantial cash income if he was to maintain his status. That income came partly from rents and partly from commercial production on some scale – in 1519 he made £60 from livestock sales, his most important source of income after rents. A similar commercial orientation was to be found among the large farmers who produced far more than they could possibly consume or even sell to neighbours. Their enterprise was directed at the supplying of food and agricultural raw materials to medium- to long-distance markets in the towns and manufacturing districts. The presence and the entrepreneurial ambition of such farmers were to be of the first significance for the future of the rural economy. But in 1500 it was still the case that, as Tawney argued, 'to the mass of the peasantry . . . the commercial side of agriculture offered no problem, because for the mass of the peasantry it did not exist'. Professor Overton suggests that probably 80 per cent of English farming was oriented primarily towards subsistence in the sixteenth century. The proportion in Scotland, where most landlords took their rents in kind and themselves supplied the urban sector, was even higher.

Whether the flow of household resources depended upon self-provisioning or upon the market, it provided for most people a fairly bare living. Professor Overton estimates that in a year of 'normal' harvest (with a yield/seed ratio of 4 : 1) a yeoman farmer with 100 acres of wheat could produce – after reserving grain for his household's bread and the next year's seed – a marketable surplus worth £70. This was a substantial income by the standards of the day, when £1 was equivalent to forty days' wages for a skilled craftsman in the building trades, or sixty days' wages for an unskilled labourer. And it would remain significant even after deductions for the payment of rents, tithes and the wages of the servants or labourers needed to help till a farm of this size. A husbandman with only ten acres of wheat, however, would have a marketable surplus worth only £2.5. In a year of 'abundant' harvest (with a yield/seed ratio of 6:1) prices would fall. To the larger farmer this would mean a reduction of the market value of his surplus to £48. For the small man, however, a greater yield more than compensated for lower prices and the value of his surplus could rise modestly to £3.

Dr Howell has attempted a more elaborate calculation, based on the actual cropping patterns in Kibworth Harcourt, Leicestershire, at the end of the fifteenth century, and including allowances not only for the domestic consumption of crops but also for the payment of rents and tithe obligations. She estimates that the husbandman with a traditional 'virgate' holding (twenty-four acres) would end the year with a surplus worth £2.2 at the prices of the day. A 'half-virgate' holding (twelve acres) could have a net surplus of only £0.4. Such were the modest margins from which most peasant households had to provide for any other than their most immediate needs. Little wonder that their inventories of domestic goods were so sparse.

In the case of urban society, such calculations are rarer, given the paucity of information on the actual earnings and expenditure patterns of most townspeople. Professor Woodward, however, estimates that at the rates of payment prevailing in the early sixteenth century a master craftsman in the building trades in Hull and Lincoln would have had to have been fully employed for 142 out of a maximum of 313 working days in order to feed himself, his wife and two children in the 1540s. If he had two more children (or a couple of apprentices) he would need 186 full days' work to cover his household's dietary needs. The comparable figures for a building labourer with two or four children would have been 214 and 279 days' work respectively. Given the facts that the work available to such townsmen, and to many of their fellows in other trades, would have been intermittent, and that these calculations do not include allowances for the costs of clothing, fuel and rent, their livings can scarcely have been princely – even when supplemented by the further earnings of their wives and older children.

These figures, moreover, relate to relatively good times, and as such they do not convey a full appreciation of the insecurity of the household economy. Harvest failure brought 'dearth' – the rapid and drastic escalation of food prices occasioned by scarcity. In such circumstances, Overton's hypothetical yeoman would see his cash income soar to £110.6, since his gross yield still afforded a substantial surplus which could be sold at vastly inflated prices. But such men were few. The gross yield of the husbandman's ten acres would be reduced to the grain he needed to feed his family, with no surplus to provide for next year's seed, let alone to sell. The alternatives were stark. Did he reserve the seed and accept either short rations for his household, or the need to buy in bread corn at high prices? Did he consume part of the seed corn and hope to provide later for next year's needs? Overton estimates a net loss on the year's farming of £13.6 – a catastrophe which could leave a lingering legacy of debt or force the sale of stock and land. The consequences for those with smaller holdings, the landless and those dependent on the market in all years were even worse. In one area of rural Norfolk in 1557, a survey of 985 households revealed that 465 (46 per cent) had no stocks of grain in hand. In the towns the living costs of craftsmen and labourers soared, while demand for their products and labour slumped as potential customers and employers cut back expenditure on all but their most essential consumption needs. Some of the poor of town and country starved, or succumbed to diseases of malnutrition.

Such years were relatively rare, but they could occur with devastating unpredictability. Between 1480 and 1520 there was only one truly disastrous harvest year: 1482/3. But there were two catastrophes of this kind in the 1520s. And the variability of the harvest was not the only source of insecurity. Trade interruptions could seriously disrupt the economies of both the towns and rural industrial districts. In 1527 a stoppage in the cloth trade led London merchants to cease buying cloth, and 'when the clothiers lacked sale, then they put from them their spinners, carders, tuckers etc., and such other which live by clothmaking'. Such instant disinvestment on the part of the clothiers could have drastic consequences for hundreds of households.

Then there were the perennial insecurities occasioned by high mortality rates. Epidemic diseases – notably the bubonic plague – could cull whole communities from top to bottom in a few weeks, bringing their economic life to a temporary standstill and leaving in their wake scores of broken families. The towns were worst hit – York suffered seven major mortality crises between 1485 and 1550 – but some rural areas suffered badly enough too, albeit less frequently. And epidemics were only the sharpest reminders of a constant threat of infectious disease which meant that average life expectancy at birth in the late fifteenth and early sixteenth centuries was in the order of only 32–34 years. Infants and young children were the most vulnerable, but of those who reached adulthood few could expect to live beyond their fifties. Young adult women faced the additional hazard of premature death in childbed. For all these reasons, historical demographers have stressed the fragility and impermanence of the households of the time, above all in the urban environment where congestion and squalor fostered disease and facilitated its transmission. Many households were thinned by the early deaths of children, broken by those of spouses and reconstituted by remarriage,

sometimes repeatedly, leading the historian of late-medieval Coventry
to observe that 'while the household surely was the basic unit of society,
we should never underestimate the impermanence of its membership
nor exaggerate the stability of the relationships it engendered'.

Such cold realities, to which could be added a host of other less dramatic occasions of misfortune, constituted an environment of risk,
threatening the precarious viability of the household economy. This in
turn engendered a mentality which valued security and stability over
growth and change; a preference for the tried and reasonably true over
innovations which might promise much but might also threaten to
increase vulnerability; economic strategies which were essentially defensive, designed to minimise risks rather than to maximise gain.

For the urban craftsman this meant the production of familiar wares
for which there was an established market, rather than 'product diversification'. It also meant control of the numbers permitted to participate
in the supplying of that market. To the husbandman, it meant patterns
of production determined in the first instance by utility to the household,
rather than exchange value, and the maintenance of those customary
practices which were most likely – in the light of experience – to achieve
subsistence needs and sustain an existing way of life. This commonly
involved a diversification of activity in the interests of security, rather
than a specialisation which might enhance productivity but at the cost
of exposing the household to the vicissitudes of the market for a
particular crop. Hence the preference for varieties of mixed farming,
wherever this was viable, and the relative homogeneity of farming over
large areas. In the Lutterworth area of Leicestershire, for example, four-
fifths of farming inventories for the years 1530–50 reveal a familiar combination of cereals, cattle, sheep, pigs and poultry, horses, flax and fodder
crops (peas and beans). Richer and poorer farmers differed in the scale
of their operations, but not in the basic pattern of diversified husbandry.
Regional patterns of agriculture naturally varied in accordance with
differences of soil, topography and climate. But a preference for mixed
husbandry wherever possible was a general characteristic, one evident
even in the constraining physical environment of the Scottish Highlands.

Some of this farm produce was intended for sale. Some was primarily
for domestic use. But all could be marketed or retained for home consumption as occasion demanded. Moreover, such diversity had the
further advantage of securing a flow of resources and potential income
across the agricultural year. It might peak at particular seasons – the
grain harvest, or the cattle fairs – but it was not dependent on a single
staple commodity yielding a block of income at a single point. This was
an economic strategy of diversification in the interests of domestic

security, and it could be augmented by engagement in by-employments or occasional wage-labour. It was not an option available to all. For the poor, it might be closer to the mark to speak of an economy of makeshifts and expedients, rather than of a strategy of diversification. But it was a common ideal. From the perspective of the modern agricultural economist it might well appear perverse in its diffusion of effort, waste of energy and lack of attention to economies of scale or comparative advantage. But it had its own logic. As Tawney wrote, 'We should be false to the spirit of our period if we did not recognise that the economic ideal of most, an ideal often implied though not often formulated, was less the opening of avenues to enterprise than the maintenance of groups and communities at their customary level of prosperity.'

It was sometimes formulated. Conventional Christian doctrine taught that economic gain to maintain one's household in its appropriate station was both legitimate and laudable. The pursuit of wealth as an end in itself, however, was tainted with the sins of covetousness and avarice. The sturdy independent ploughman who pursued the former and eschewed the latter was a familiar and approved figure in the moralistic literature of the time – the more so when early translations of classical works on household management reinforced the ideal of a domestic sufficiency. Few householders can have read such literature, but most were exposed to the pervasive influence of the church's teachings. Furthermore, the values which underpinned such household strategies were very much formulated in the many vernacular proverbs which represented the collective wisdom of a predominantly oral culture; not so much learned, as the collector Oswald Dykes later observed, as sucked in 'with our Mother's milk'. Proverbs often endorsed customary agricultural practice, sometimes in a form adapted to specific localities, as in 'when Westwood Wood is motley, then 'tis time to sow barley'. They cautioned against poor bargains – 'hee hath sold a beane and bought a peaze'. They stressed the virtue of experience – 'the burnt child dreads the fire'. And above all they counselled prudence: 'a stitch in time may save nine'; 'enough is as good as all'; 'better a bit than no bread'. These were the cardinal virtues informing the strategies of good husbandry and good housewifery. As they well knew, 'a great housekeeper is sure of nothinge for his good cheere, save a great Turd at his gate'.

ii. *Dispersal*

The second major priority of the household economy was provision for the future well-being of its members, and in particular their capacity to form and sustain independent households of their own. In this there were three crucial moments: the 'putting forth' of adolescent children into the larger world; marriage; and the transmission of property by inheritance. These moments of transition might occur in any order. They could be concentrated or dispersed in time. But whatever the case, all required the intermeshing and reconciliation of the needs and expectations of the household as a whole with those of its individual members. As such, they involved what Tamara Harevan terms 'collective family timing strategies'.

Such calculations were an inevitable part of the 'dispersal process' of the family, by which young people left their households of origin to enter the households of others as servants or apprentices, or to establish households of their own at marriage. In the case of servants it has been suggested that the institution of service was well attuned to accommodating the interests of different families in a world of small producers, while at the same time providing for the needs of adolescents and young adults. At any one point in time, some households would have had children approaching an age at which they were capable of a fuller working role, but could no longer be usefully employed at home. Others would have required additional labour, either temporarily (while their own children were too young to work, perhaps, or after a spouse's death) or permanently (on larger farms or in households engaged in multiple employments which stretched their labour capacity). In a society of small property-holders, in which labour was not always available for hire, annual service contracts provided an elegant means of transferring the labour of the young between households. All that was required in the case of those households which hired servants was that, in Dr Kussmaul's words, 'the marginal cost of a servant's labour was equal to the cost of maintaining the servant'.

Such was the basic logic of the system. But there was more to service than just the balancing out of labour needs between households. Some families not only put their own adolescent children into service, but also took in servants themselves. Such cases alert us to the fact that service was also perceived as a means of advancing, perhaps of advantaging, a child in the process of transition into the adult world. As servants, young people acquired skills and work experience in a variety of households, sometimes of a kind not available at home. In addition, servants earned wages as well as their keep. These were initially small, but graduated towards regular quarterly or annual payments, and could be saved towards the eventual establishment of an independent household. One Essex eighteen-year-old, for example, was hired for £1 a year and the pasture of two sheep; he was already accumulating his own flock. In addition, service moved the young to and fro across the countryside and from country to town. It familiarised them with areas of economic opportunity. It advanced the process of individual maturation by confronting them repeatedly and increasingly with situations in which they had to exercise choice and judgement: whether to take service with a particular master; what wages to ask for or accept; how to relate to masters, mistresses and peers; when to leave service, marry and set up independently.

Much of this was relevant to apprenticeship too. In the case of apprenticeship, however, the advantaging mechanism was perhaps most prominent in a family's expectations. Apprenticeship involved financial investment in a child's future in the form of the premium paid to a master when the indentures were sealed. Among the great merchant companies of the major cities, to which even the sons of gentlemen might be apprenticed, this could be a formidable sum of money. Among the clothiers of Kent it was still around ten pounds, and even a weaver in that county might ask several pounds to take on a youth.

Such circumstances meant that a modicum of wealth in the previous generation was a necessary condition for apprenticeship to all but the poorest trades. Nor did the family's investment necessarily end there, for on completion of an apprenticeship, after perhaps seven years, the young craftsman or tradesman also needed to find the wherewithal to set up shop if he was ever to become an independent master. In some trades this might require very little in the way of working capital, but it was rarely negligible. Among the lesser trades of London it was around five pounds, but it could rise to several hundreds in the highest echelons of the urban occupational hierarchy. On completion of an apprentice's term it was common for his master to pay the fee for his enrolment as a freeman, to provide a suit of clothes, money and a set of tools, and perhaps future employment as a journeyman. Journeymen might be able to save enough from their earnings to set up independently in the lesser trades, especially if they married prudently. But the prospects of many would have depended upon further assistance from their families of origin, in the forms of inheritance, gift or loan. All in all it has been suggested that in mid-Tudor London 'becoming a householder and thus having a shop of one's own was a reasonable expectation for most men' who completed their training. But many did not. The drop-out rate among apprentices was high in every major town. Some died young. Others abandoned their apprenticeship at one stage or another. Their fate was partly of their own making, of course, but it was also profoundly influenced by the extent to which families were able and willing to put their resources into securing a child's future. As a strategy of advancement, apprenticeship depended heavily for its success upon an ongoing interrelationship of individual and familial needs.

Both service and apprenticeship, then, were means of preparing the young for their future assumption of adult responsibilities as house-holders. For most, marriage was the point at which those responsibilities were fully assumed. And like the leaving of home, it was a point of tran-sition at which individual desires and ambitions had to be reconciled with larger familial goals.

The making of a match was a complex process. Outside the most socially elevated and politically significant circles it was rare for parents simply to arrange the marriages of their children. Most young people exercised a considerable degree of choice in the selection of a marriage partner. They were, nonetheless, expected to choose within a pool of eli-gibles of appropriate social and economic standing. And whether they initiated their own courtships or responded to the promptings of parents and guardians, their choices were subject to what has been termed the 'multilateral consent' of all interested parties – a process exemplified by a dying Berwick man who envisaged his daughter marrying 'when that god shall send her ane partner that she cane be contented withall, by the advisement of hir mother, her brother William and all other my frends and heyrs'. There was a collective element in making a match, and within that process economic matters had a considerable bearing on the winning of general consent and goodwill. As one observer of a bethrothal put it, 'the yong folk be come together for love, but parents must cast how they shall live'.

The extent to which the economic security of a marriage was a parental matter inevitably varied. In families with little or no property, the young were obliged to provide for themselves and to delay their mar-riages accordingly. One youth, on asking his master's goodwill to marry a fellow servant, was 'advised . . . for that he was but poore and litell worthe that he wold tarry so long tyme and gather somewhat togither in the meane time wherewith they might better stay themselfs and be able to lyve when they shuld marry'. Most did so, gradually accumulating savings from wages, legacies and gifts from masters and kin which would enable them to marry. This was true of men and women alike. Isabel Fowler, a servant who died unwed, had amassed a good stock of move-able goods by the time of her death, including chests, clothing, almost three pounds in back wages held by a former master's executors and three cows worth five pounds.

Among the propertied, from husbandman to lord, economic arrange-ments involving both families were often critical to the making or marring of a prospective match, and negotiations were begun as soon as a serious 'motion of marriage' was entertained. Essentially, these concerned the establishment of a 'conjugal fund' adequate for the maintenance of an independent household. The prospective groom was expected to provide at the least a house and a means of living. The bride brought her 'portion', generally in the form of goods or money, but sometimes including land or other real estate. The resources concerned might partly have been accumulated by the young couple themselves, but they also depended crucially upon parental assistance in the form of either inheritance or transfers which were, in effect, advances on their future inheritances.

The sums involved, of course, varied with social station. In the late fifteenth and early sixteenth centuries, the portions provided for daughters of the English peerage averaged £750. Those of the daughters of knights averaged around £280. Among Kentish villagers they averaged £5 (ranging from a few shillings to over £20). But whatever the level, marriage negotiations involved hard bargaining over the respective contributions and also frequently included arrangements for the security of the bride in the event of her widowhood. The decisions made represented assessments of what a family could reasonably provide in order to secure a desirable match and endow a new household – calculations which also had to consider the implications for any younger children yet to be provided for. If all was resolved satisfactorily, a new household was established. If not, the denial of parental consent and assistance could mean denial of the opportunity to enter safely into independent adulthood.

Both the 'putting forth' of children and provision for their eventual marriages were closely connected to the question of inheritance. Given the relatively late age of marriage and the likelihood of death before the age of sixty, it was commonly the case that only some, if any, children had been 'advanced' before a householder's death. Provision therefore needed to be made for the continuance of the household as an economic unit and for the future needs of its remaining members. Dying householders carried a heavy burden of responsibility, and their wills, which survive in abundance, give insight into the strategies by which they tried to discharge it.

Such strategies were partly governed by the demands of the law. The inheritance of real property (land and houses) was governed by a variety of legal systems: the common law or local customary laws of England; Scottish law; or Welsh customary law. In most of England and Scotland, land law favoured impartible inheritance – the descent of such property to a single male heir, usually by primogeniture to the eldest son. Welsh custom, however, favoured division between male heirs (partible inheritance or 'gavelkind') until its abolition in 1542, and this remained customary in parts of England, notably Kent. In the absence of sons, equal division between daughters was usual, and in all systems the widow's dower was reserved to her for the term of her life. All this, however, could be modified by the right to devise land by will, according to the testator's personal preference, a right secured in England and Wales by the Statute of Wills of 1540. The inheritance of moveable goods was governed by ecclesiastical law, which favoured an equitable distribution: one-third passing to the widow; one-third being divided among the children; the remainder being the 'dead man's part' to be bequeathed as he chose. The law, then, imposed certain constraints and enshrined certain expectations, while also permitting areas within which discretion could be exercised. It was the exercise of that discretion which most engaged the attention of householders as they attempted, within the limitations of the resources at their disposal, to attune their decisions to the particular circumstances of their own families.

The result was what appears at first sight a bewildering variety of individual inheritance strategies. But certain dominant themes emerge. Noblemen and gentlemen were inevitably preoccupied with the preservation of the ancestral patrimony on which the name, power and standing of their houses depended. Accordingly male primogeniture was the norm, buttressed by forms of legal trusteeship, such as the 'entail' or the 'use', designed to protect its integrity and to secure its transmission in the male line. More generally, there was an assumption that the eldest son should be privileged by passing on to him the principal source of a household's living. In England this usually meant the core land-holding, or the premises and equipment necessary to pursue his father's trade. Among Scottish farm tenants, who lacked the right to pass on their holdings to heirs, it meant the lion's share of the farm stock and efforts to secure a new tenancy from the laird.

All this might be expected, given the economic realities and social values of the time. What is perhaps more striking is the effort also made to provide for younger children at all social levels. Land and houses might be acquired in addition to a family's main holding for the future purpose of endowing younger children with a small estate, or at least a dwelling place and toehold on the land. If an eldest son had already been set up independently with parental help, then a reduced core holding might pass to a younger sibling. If some children had already been 'advanced' during a parent's lifetime by the provision of marriage portions, apprenticeship premiums or the like, then preferential treatment might be given to those remaining. Thus Ann Colyer, a Durham woman, gave a larger share of her goods to her daughter Alice, who 'had remained with hir and ayded hir in hir old age, whereas all the rest of hir daughters were married and forth with their portions'. Inheriting sons might be charged with the responsibility of generating the income necessary to pay for their siblings' portions. Robert Fisseleden, a Kent yeoman, willed his land in 1546 to his eldest son (thereby preserving it from division by the custom of 'gavelkind') but required him to pay an annual sum to each of his brothers for eight years. Nicholas Wake, of Norfolk, received a transfer of his parents' land in 1505 on condition that he paid each of his brothers seven marks and ten shillings (over £5).

In sum, as one historian of inheritance puts it, 'while the custom of primogeniture was influential, it is a wholly inadequate description of the "grid of inheritance" among ordinary people'. The ideal was rather that, as one lawyer advised, 'a good and naturall and loving father' would exercise 'a faithfull care and providence to advance everye of his children according to his Abilitie with some small porcion of lyvinge or substaunce'. This was a matter which preoccupied householders as their children grew. The Durham yeoman Richard Shawter, for example, discussed 'the bestowing and bringing upp of his two sonnes' with a neighbour in the fields. He was advised 'to put one of his said children to be prentice to some good occupation, whereby he might be able to earne his leavinge in tyme to come, and thereby he mighte be more liberall to that childe which he ment to traine and bringe up in husbandrie'. Such provision was the principal end towards which resources were accumulated. And it imposed obligations on dying men which could extend even to the unborn. Richard Coles, a Stourbridge scythe-maker, was not alone in the care he exercised when in 1552 he left his 'best anvil to the child that is in my wife's womb'.

Nor was it a matter for fathers only. Male householders dominated the formal enunciation of the terms of wills. Yet it is equally apparent that the successful completion of most strategies of advancement depended ultimately upon the future sustaining of the household economy by widows. Few widows retired immediately, or at all, to enjoy the maintenance provided for them by their 'dowers' or 'thirds'. On the contrary, it was usual for them to be named as executors of their husbands' wills and most were also granted full control of the family property at least until the eldest son came of age, and very commonly for life. Their principal inheritance was a set of responsibilities, to be discharged as they saw best, whether within the context of a further marriage or by assuming the role of household head. The tacit assumption of their capacity to do so brings us to a final set of issues regarding strategies and priorities in the household economy: those of authority and power.

iii. *Authority and power*

The various household economic strategies which we have considered have in common a certain quality of 'jointness': they affected the interests of the household as a whole, and involved the accommodation of that collective interest to those of the individuals who comprised it. To speak of 'household strategies' or 'family strategies', however, can beg the important question of the extent to which decision-making in the household economy was truly collective. Households, as we have seen, were organised on the principle of 'hierarchical differentiation'. If their domestic economies involved interdependence and complementarity of effort, the contributions of their members were not necessarily regarded as of equal importance or value. If the conjugal families at their core were in a sense spheres of altruism, they were not necessarily free from competition over resources and clashes of personality. The members of the household might inhabit the same hall-house, but it was a space demarcated by place and role: parlour and servery, chair and stool, featherbeds and straw mattresses. Some dipped first into the dish, and the words of some carried greater power.

Neither law nor domestic ideology left much room for doubt about the ultimate location of authority in the household. It lay with the master and, by delegation, with the mistress of the household, who would herself become household head in the event of widowhood. (At least 12 per cent of the householders of Clackclose Hundred, Norfolk, in 1557 were women.) Nor can it be doubted that it could be exercised with crushing force to exert control over both resources and individuals. 'Thou filth and harlot,' screamed one Yorkshire woman at her daughter in 1490, 'Why art thow handfast with John Wistow? When thy fadre knowys it, he wyll dynge the[e].' Yet it is equally apparent that the personal dynamics of households were far more varied and the subjectivities of their members far more complex than the neat prescriptions of contemporary ideology could admit. Within the structure of domestic authority, each member of the household was accorded certain responsibilities and permitted certain privileges. These varied in their range, and in the extent to which they were recognised. But they provided a basis for the individual interpretation of roles and for the exercise of influence upon the decisions which determined the strategies of the household.

Wives were not only their husbands' 'helpmeets'. They were also 'yokefellows'. The collective subordination of women did not preclude recognition of their individual competence and self-reliance in economic affairs. Such qualities were expected, and marriage provided the opportunity to display them more fully. Outside the context of the household few women could exercise authority in economic affairs. Within it, however, they had a role in the daily provision and management of resources which could, and often did, confer a right to be informed and to be heard. Fitzherbert advised the wife who had been to market 'to make a true rekening . . . to her husband what she hath receyved and what she hath payed'. But he also went on to advise the husband 'to show his wife in lyke maner. For if one of them should use to disceive the other, he disceyveth him selfe, and he is not lyke to thryve, and therefore they must be true eyther to other.'

To 'be true eyther to other', to 'hold together', to 'agree quietly together as man and wife should do' were the vernacular ideals of marital mutuality which had their most immediate expression in the conduct of the household economy. That did not necessarily mean that they transformed it into a sphere of 'rough and ready equality'. But it did involve the development, within the context of the prevailing definition of gender roles, of a flexible working relationship in the pursuit of shared priorities. This being the case, it stretches credibility to imagine that wives were simply passive enactors of their husbands' directions or mute spectators of decisions affecting the well-being of their families. We know all too little of how these matters were conducted on a day-to-day basis, but it is certainly apparent that wives had a part to play in some of the most significant – and therefore most often recorded – decisions of the family cycle. They had a voice in the approval of prospective matches and the negotiation of their terms. They were present at the deathbeds of their husbands, advising upon, and on occasion openly disputing, the terms of the wills which they subsequently administered as executrixes. And they appear elsewhere, now supporting, now checking, like the woman who, when her husband was about to obey a legal injunction, 'came to him and did stand with him', following which hasty discussion 'he changed his former speaking and said that hee would pay no money'. Such acknowledged participation in the guidance of the domestic economy was a source of independent identity, confidence and self-esteem for women which could be robustly expressed in word and deed. 'As the goodman saies, so let it be,' ran the ambiguous proverb. 'But as the good wife saies, so it must be.' The strategies which governed the household economy were hers too.

Both the responsibilities and the privileges of the young were more constrained. Children, servants and apprentices lived under the immediate and sometimes heavy-handed directive authority of both father and mother, master and mistress. Yet the process of socialisation in the household involved not only the reproduction of authority structures and the inculcation of skills, but also a gradually developing participation in decisions affecting their own lives which constituted a process of maturation, leading eventually to adult autonomy. Children were given a voice in their choice of future occupation, where this was an option, as when a Leicestershire smith left a share in his 'forge and shoppe' to his son Richard in 1539 'yf Ryc be mynded to that occupacon'. Once placed outside their households of origin they learned as servants and apprentices how to relate to the ways and demands of the masters and mistresses of the households in which they served. This did not mean that they were likely to be accorded any voice in the central decision-making of those families. But they could certainly influence the terms and conditions of their own subordinate place, by contractual negotiation, by their mode of conduct in the performance of their work, and on occasion – especially when legitimate expectations had been betrayed – by open insubordination. Servants could dispute the appropriateness of the tasks allocated them, or protest at failure to pay them as promised. Apprentices could and did lay complaints against their masters and mistresses for maltreatment or neglect of their proper training. They were not necessarily much younger than their masters and could behave as much like truculent younger brothers as dutiful sons.

Such accumulating experience of individual self-direction meant that, as young adults, children could erupt into the decision-making of their families of origin, above all in the interrelated strategies of marriage and inheritance. They were permitted at least a voice, and sometimes considerable personal initiative, in the matter of their own marriages, and could sometimes determinedly insist upon it, as when Elena Couper, kneeling before her irate father, declared of her suitor, 'I wyll have him whosoever say nay to it. And I desire no more of your goodes but your blessyng.' They could assert their interest also in the marriages of their siblings, as when John Paston's mother ruefully commented of her other children that 'some be of that age, that they can tell me well enough that I deal not evenly with them to give John Paston so large and them so little'. Inheritance, and the disputes which it sometimes occasioned, could reveal equally powerful feelings of entitlement, hard-fought rivalries over the sharing of the resources of the household and bitter resentment at real or imagined failures to recognise individual needs and deserts. Awareness of the disruptive potential of ill-conceived family strategies undoubtedly played a major part in shaping the decisions that were made.

The household economy was a sphere of authority within which decision-making power was unequally distributed. In the conduct of its affairs there was much to encourage both women and the young to conform to the prescriptive pattern of household roles, and to counsel self-restraint in coping with the limitations imposed upon their personal autonomy. Yet, as has been observed in another context, 'power is a relationship, and a relationship which, while shaped by economic and social structures and cultures, is experienced through individuals', and subject to the 'difference arising from personality'. The glimpses that we have of the actualities of domestic decision-making in our period reveal that it could be subject to all the tensions deriving from such a situation and could be shaped by a domestic politics of conflicting desires and expectations, reproach and concession, rupture and reconciliation. The fact that this was so did not alter, or even pose an explicit challenge to, the basic structures of economic and social power in the household. But it demonstrates the ingenuity and determination with which those in subordinate positions worked to ease the chafings of what could be a massively restrictive system. Success or failure in the management of the domestic economy could depend crucially upon the extent to which these claims and counter claims could be satisfactorily resolved. Such 'jointness' as the strategies of the household possessed often arose from the multilateral reconciliation of competing demands for consideration in the deployment of resources. How well that difficult task was achieved influenced the vicissitudes of the household in the present. The manner of its achievement shaped both the opportunities and the personalities of those who would govern the households of the future.

The economy and society of the early modern period has been described by David Rollison as 'a culture of households in a landscape'. Those households differed in their size and structure, their means of living, their wealth and status, capacities to provide for themselves securely in the present and to afford opportunities in the future to those born, trained and socialised within them. They had in common a fundamental role in the organisation of production in agriculture and in manufacturing, and in the reproduction of economic structures through the transmission of skills and resources to the next generation. Their consumption needs, and the manner in which they met them, determined the size and structures of markets for goods and services. Their production needs exercised a similar influence over the markets for land, capital and labour. Moreover, the priorities, values and strategies of households gave meaning and purpose to economic activity. Their characteristic attitudes and objectives shaped the nature of economic ambitions, be they centred on endurance or on the aspiration to thrive.

For all these reasons, the household was fundamental to the economic history of early modern Britain. Much of what has been described in this and the preceding chapter was to endure throughout the period. But much was to change as well. Where continuities are observable, they very commonly represent the perdurance of particular characteristics of organisation and mentality within a context of changing circumstances over which the members of individual households had only limited control. There were new challenges to the viability of the domestic economy which required adaptation, a reactive process of change in order to preserve. There were also new opportunities, ways of pursuing traditional objectives by innovative means, which could make some households more assertive participants in the furtherance of change. The family, it has been said, is invariably 'both a custodian of tradition and an agent of change'. In sixteenth- and seventeenth-century Britain this dual role was the more significant because of the very centrality of the household to the structuring of the economy, society and culture of the time. The course and outcomes of the economic dynamic of the age depended ultimately upon the aggregate response of tens of thousands of households, and of *all* their members, to pressures and opportunities partly beyond and partly within their control. This chapter has attempted to introduce some of the context necessary for understanding why this was so. But it has explored the structures of the household economies of the late fifteenth and early sixteenth centuries in relative isolation. A fuller appreciation of the context of economic change requires that we now attempt to place them in the larger economic and social landscapes within which they had their existence.

CHAPTER THREE

Beyond the household: economic institutions and relationships

The household economy has provided our point of entry to some of the basic structures and priorities of economic life in the later fifteenth and early sixteenth centuries. As will already be apparent, however, households did not exist in isolation. On the contrary, every family pursued its living within a larger context of economic institutions and relationships.

Richard Lowson, for example, was a small tenant farmer of Whickham, Co. Durham. His will and inventory suggest that he lived principally from the corn and cattle produced on his manorial holding. His list of debts and credits, however, reveals that at the time of his death he was engaged in uncompleted transactions with seventeen other persons: small sums of money borrowed or lent; payments due for the purchase of cattle, malt, a flitch of bacon; wages as yet unpaid. One of those named was a local gentleman, termed by Lowson 'my master'. Another was his own servant. Most are identifiable as his neighbours among the manorial tenantry of Whickham, one of whom was also his father-in-law. But he also had dealings with men from three nearby villages, and with a tradesman in the city of Newcastle. And he was owed money 'for carryche' of coal from local pits to the River Tyne, whence it was shipped to provide fuel for the hearths of London.

Odonell Selbye, a contemporary of Lowson's, was a man of much greater substance. He was a leading burgess of Berwick-upon-Tweed who served three times as mayor in the 1530s. Most of the dealings recorded in his probate documents were centred on Berwick and its environs, where he dealt in salmon, canvas, linen and agricultural produce. But his activities also extended throughout north-east Northumberland. He had kinsmen among the minor gentry of the area – two of whom assisted a fellow burgess in supervising his will – and he owned land himself, deriving part of his income from his tenants' rents. Moreover,

Selbye was also linked, via the coastal trade, to suppliers and customers in Newcastle, Lynn in Norfolk, and the city of London.

Each of these men conducted his affairs within a mesh of relationships of economic and social obligation, reciprocity and exchange. These varied in their nature. Some were hierarchically structured, extending up and down the social scale. Others were more horizontally aligned, expressing interaction among effective equals. Some were concentrated within particular localities, constituting dense complexes of regular interaction. Others were more loosely distributed in space and time, more geographically extensive. Some involved powerful ties of personal obligation, others more neutral, less emotionally charged transactions. Some were relatively stable, patterned or institutionalised, others less formally structured. Taken as a whole, however, they demonstrate how each household was the focal point of a set of overlapping, intersecting networks of association, which linked it into larger systems of economic and social relations.

This chapter and the next are concerned with exploring that connectedness. Chapter Three will introduce some of the more localised relationships and institutions that shaped the economic affairs of men like Lowson and Selbye: lordship and tenancy; neighbourhood; the fraternity of urban companies; kinship. Chapter Four will explore the further networks of exchange in which they were also involved, extending outwards from the local community into the broader entities of the district, the region, the nation and the arenas of international trade, and examining these interconnected spheres of activity as a system of economic relations in motion, shaping the fortunes of Britain's constituent communities and regions at the turn of the sixteenth century.

i. *Lordship and tenancy*

In the rural economy, the basic defining relationship was that of lordship and tenancy. Rural Britain can be imagined as a myriad of settlements scattered unevenly over a landscape of great diversity: the dispersed farmsteads and hamlets of much of Scotland and Wales; the nucleated villages of lowland England. It was a landscape that in 1500 had not yet been formally mapped. Yet it had long been mapped and structured in a different sense. Medieval social organisation was inscribed on the land through lordship: the possession of the soil and the authority which sprang from that possession.

Lordship derived ultimately from the monarch. Medieval law had no concept of *absolute* property in land save that of the crown. In strict theory, landlords held their estates conditionally, in return for the services which they rendered either to the crown or to intermediary superiors in the hierarchy of lordship. In practice, however, the gradual accretion of rights not only to hold land, but also to alienate it to others, to transmit it by inheritance, and to be free from arbitrary confiscation, had led to the development of powerful notions of individual proprietorship. For most practical purposes, Britain was owned by a tiny minority of the population: the monarchs of the day, the nobility, the gentry and such corporate institutions as the church or universities. In the early sixteenth century almost nine-tenths of Devonshire was owned by the crown, four noblemen, some 350 knights, esquires and 'mere' gentlemen and fifty ecclesiastical institutions. The West Riding of Yorkshire had around 20,000 households, of which only 350 were those of landowners. In 1550 the vast county of Aberdeenshire was divided among 500 landlords, of whom fifty held two-thirds of the whole.

The land was divided into units of lordship of uneven size and distribution: the manors and 'honours' of England and Wales; the baronies and 'regalities' of Scotland. Some lords held only a single estate, or a group of small estates within a particular area. Some had extensive interests scattered across several counties like archipelagos of power and influence. A few dominated large and compact territories, like the marcher lords of Wales, the Highland chieftains of Scotland who combined tribal with feudal authority, or such English nobles as Lord Berkeley, who consolidated his Gloucestershire lands out of a desire 'of being imbowelled into the soil of that country'. Whatever the case, the fact of lordship was fundamental to the structuring of rural economy and society. Access to land was crucial to the livelihood of most people, and that access was controlled by historically developed structures of power over the most basic of economic resources.

Those who cultivated the land did so, for the most part, as tenants, and on terms which set the basic parameters of their individual domestic economies. Crucial to their position were the interconnected issues of the forms and relative security of tenure by which they stood 'seized' of their holdings, the rents and services which they owed to their lords, and the nature of the 'customs' which governed their relationships both to their lords and to one another.

Modes of tenure varied enormously, as did their associated degrees of security, but some general patterns can be discerned. Forms of peasant proprietorship existed – for example, the 'odal' tenures of the Northern Isles, English tenancies in 'free socage', or the individual freeholds of the former Welsh clan lands. Tenant rights, however, were generally far more qualified. In Scotland they were particularly limited. The lands of

Scottish baronies were divided between the 'mains' (the laird's home farm) and the tenant lands let out in 'fermes' to either single or joint tenants. Some tenants had written leases or 'tacks' granting tenancy for periods which might extend to life, but were more commonly for short periods of years (usually five) in return for a down payment, or 'grassum', and an annual rent. Most were 'tenants at will', holding their land only on a year-to-year basis at the will of the lord. In practice the insecurity of Scottish tenants was moderated by the willingness of lords to renew tenancies on their expiry, or even to grant them to a former tenant's heirs. On the Paisley Abbey estates in 1526–55, almost two-thirds of new tenants were related to the preceding occupier, and elsewhere the fifteenth century had seen the emergence of so-called 'kindly' tenancies, whereby tenants were permitted unhindered occupation and the succession of heirs by 'kindness'. This, however, was an act of goodwill. So long as tenants remained in short supply, the lord had an interest in 'kindness'. But few tenants had any legal guarantee of their position, and it must be remembered also that most of the Scottish peasantry were 'cottars' whose access to land depended on their own informal agreements with tenants or tacksmen. Their rights were minimal.

In England and the anglicised areas of eastern and south Wales, the basic unit of lordship was the manor, comprising 'demesne' lands, 'anciently and time out of mind' reserved to the lord's use, freehold tenancies and 'customary' land. Freeholders enjoyed a secure title, the rights to sell, lease and bequeath their land, and the protection of the common law. They held around a fifth of the land in many areas, and still more in some. The lord's demesne had formerly been cultivated by serf labour. By 1500, it was usually leased out to tenants for periods of years or lives in return for an initial 'entry fine' and an annual rent negotiated at the time of the granting of tenancy. Customary lands, in contrast, passed by 'admission' and 'surrender' in the manor court, on terms which were subject to the 'custom of the manor'. In the central middle ages, such land had been held by unfree serfs or 'villeins' – 'at the will of the lord and according to the customs of the manor' – in return for the performance of labour services on the demesne and the payment of various customary dues. By 1500 serfdom was largely, though not entirely, extinct as a legal status. Some customary tenants remained tenants at will, holding from year to year, with no legal rights beyond that of harvesting a growing crop if required to relinquish their tenancy. Most, however, were 'copyholders', holding land by virtue of a copy of the entry on the manor court roll recording their admission to the tenancy. Their common designation covered a bewildering profusion of actual terms and conditions, which varied according to the customs of individual manors. All copyholders paid an entry fine and an annual rent. But some manors accorded rights of inheritance, while others granted land only for years or lives. On some, entry fines or rents had become fixed. On others they remained 'arbitrary' and renegotiable when the present tenancy expired. The extent of the proprietary rights enjoyed by such tenants thus differed greatly. A copyholder of inheritance with a fixed fine and rent was virtually as secure as a freeholder. Others might be much more exposed to the estate-management policies of their landlords – though rarely to the extent that was prevalent in Scotland.

The rents and obligations owed by tenants were as variegated as their forms of tenure. For freeholders they were negligible, involving only a small payment in 'recognition' of a lord's jurisdiction and the obligation of 'suit' at his court. English leaseholders paid money rents based on an assessment of the current value of the land. In the late fifteenth and early sixteenth centuries leases were generally long and their terms were generous. In Scotland, however, 'tacks' were shorter and their terms more onerous. Money rents, or 'maill', were of minor significance in the rental incomes of most Scottish lords – only 16 per cent of the rental value of the barony of Lochleven in 1548–53, for example. Most rents came in kind, often in the form of a third of the grain crop, as in the customary rhyme 'ane to saw [sow], ane to gnaw, and ane to pay the laird witha'. In addition tenants might owe further renders of produce or fuel; the obligation to use the laird's mill and smithy ('thirlage'); labour services on the 'mains'; and the duty of carrying produce to the 'caput' of the barony where rents were paid. One tenant of Coupar Angus Abbey in 1472, for example, was granted his tack for a small cash payment, eight 'bolls' of barley and malt, five bolls of oats, nine hens, twenty-five loads of peat and further carriage services when required.

Copyhold rents in England and lowland Wales varied enormously. What can be said in general is that they bore no necessary relationship to the current value of the land. They tended to cluster around certain conventional figures, often related to locally prevalent units of land-holding – the 'yardland', or the 'oxgang', for example. These units had an ancient rationale, representing so much ploughing, or the land deemed necessary to support a peasant family. But they had no fixed acreage equivalents, and the rents paid for them were the haphazard product of the commutation of obligations once owed to the lord into money rents. Nor were they closely linked to changing market conditions, often persisting for generations even when they were not fixed. Rather, they tended to reflect the general balance between the subsistence needs of the population and the land resources of an area. In the conditions of population stagnation and tenant shortage around 1500 they were generally low, save where unusual circumstances stimulated the local demand for land.

Throughout Britain, then, lordship and tenancy was a defining relationship. It created a matrix of rights and obligations crucial to the respective household economies of lord and tenant alike. Its particular forms were shaped not by absolute property rights, or by maximising 'economically rational' estate management, but by a variety of historically developed accommodations between the interests of lords and tenants which produced particular outcomes in specific local contexts. Those outcomes were enshrined in custom.

Custom was one of the keywords of economic and social relations: one which carried both practical significance and legitimising power. Custom has been described by Susan Reynolds as 'an accumulation of rules about what was right and wrong and about the right procedures for enforcing [them]'. It was a code of practice which had grown up in a particular place, creating an environment of assumptions and expectations which had powerful moral, and indeed legal, force.

In the view of lawyers, custom derived its authority from antiquity, continuance 'time out of mind of man', certainty and reason. Yet despite its patina of antiquity, custom was in fact malleable. Some customs were maintained. Others were cancelled or gradually eroded. New customs evolved and acquired legitimacy. Custom was subject to change because it was not only a code of practice, but also a field of contest, 'an area in which opposing interests made conflicting claims', in E. P. Thompson's words. On the Bishop of Worcester's west-midlands estates some tenant dues and services lapsed in the fifteenth century because the tenantry rejected them and their lord acquiesced. Copyhold tenure in its many forms had emerged from numerous localised reworkings of the relationships of lords and tenants.

Operative custom at any one time was thus the outcome of cumulative adjustment, in response to initiatives from either party. On the manor of Bushey, for example, a 'customary' listing prevailing usages laid down on the one hand the dues payable to the lord on the deaths of tenants, or when a tenant sub-let land, and on the other hand the rights of widows, the tenants' entitlement to timber from the lord's woods and the maximum fine which could be demanded on the renewal of a copyhold. Custom was created by, and binding on, both lords and tenants. It was enforced by both in courts in which the lord's steward sat as judge and the principal tenants as jurymen. It represented what Professor Kerridge terms 'an equilibrium of interests', or in Tawney's striking phrase, 'a sort of great collective bargain'.

As a result, custom set the patterns of expectations which provided the criteria for judging whether the relationships of lords and tenants were deemed equitable and legitimate ('reasonable') or exploitative. Its evolution was central to the late-medieval transition from a rural society of lords and villeins to one of landlords and tenants; and its vulnerability or sustainability was equally vital to the subsequent development of landlord–tenant relationships in the face of changing circumstances. Conflict over custom thus provides moments of disclosure, revealing the pressures of economic change, the manner in which they were responded to by both the possessors of the land and those who worked it, and the shifting balance of power between landlords and a set of larger entities: tenant communities of neighbours.

ii. *Neighbourhood*

'Neighbourliness' was another keyword of sixteenth-century social relations, expressing a critically important social ideal. The relationship which it defined was based upon residential propinquity, interaction of a regular kind, and a degree of consensus regarding proper conduct among neighbours within local communities which were, as one contemporary put it, 'the first societyes after propagation of familyes wherein people are united . . . in . . . the mutuall comforts of neighbourhood and intercourse one with another'. Such focused interaction and normative consensus were created partly by institutions, not least those of lordship. The sense of collective identity of rural communities was derived in part from the inhabitants' common relationship to a lord, and it was further elaborated in the formulation of local custom. Custom, it has been said, 'presupposes a group or community within which it is practised'. More, it helped to constitute such groups, expressing a community of interest among neighbours, defining their relationships not only to the lord but also to one another, and contributing to the formulation of a sense of place and of selfhood within that place.

All this was evident in the ways in which the institutions of lordship and tenancy were also institutions of self-regulation within the tenurial communities to which most people still belonged. It was perhaps most visible in the organisation of common-field agriculture. In this system each tenant held parcels of land scattered in strips across great open fields, while further enjoying access to certain collective 'use rights' – to common pasture on the fields after harvest and on areas of permanent common grazing land, or to the resources of food, fuel and materials provided by the woods, common and 'waste'. The system had many variants. In the predominantly arable and relatively densely settled English lowlands, the tenants of open-field manors generally held their lands in two, three or four large fields, with associated shares of the meadow land and rights to use relatively limited, and jealously guarded, areas of common. In the pastorally oriented and more thinly settled districts of the upland north and west, there were often rather more fields on the best land, while each township claimed a share of the extensive upland pastures which lay between them. In Scotland the tenants of a 'ferme' might hold strips of land in the permanently cultivated 'infield', while enjoying large areas of 'commonty', from which an 'outfield' might periodically be taken in for the cultivation of a crop or two of oats. A similar system probably prevailed in the uplands and mountains of Wales, which further shared with Scotland the practice of transhumance, whereby herds were removed to highland pastures for the summer and tended from temporary dwellings, known in Scotland as 'shielings'.

What all these systems had in common was a need for the co-operative organisation of husbandry. They entailed a good deal of collective activity – ploughing, sowing, harvesting, haymaking, the folding of sheep on the stubble after harvest, and the supervision of herds on the common – and all this required decision-making about timing and good tenant practice. In England and manorialised Wales this usually involved decisions of the manor courts which all tenants were obliged to attend. The authority of such courts derived ultimately from the manorial lord, but it was to a considerable extent exercised by the tenants gathered in what was in effect a village meeting. Such gatherings were principally concerned with the making of by-laws and with the presentment of offences by officers elected to enforce them. These included rules of cultivation, established 'for the common profit and with the assent of all', regulations regarding the use of the common and waste, and a variety of matters of dispute among the tenant body. The court of Hunstanton, Norfolk, in the early sixteenth century, for example, synchronised ploughing and harvest and organised common grazing, while fining individual tenants for such offences as ploughing up a neighbour's boundary stone, refusing to share the use of a cart, failing to ring pigs' noses, allowing a cow to graze on a neighbour's holding, or exceeding the 'stint' of beasts permitted on the common. In Scotland, tenants were similarly expected to attend periodically the 'head courts' of their barony, where they acted as jurymen in the settlement of disputes, while at the level of the individual 'fermetoun' they held their own 'Birlaw courts' which determined the 'settings' of land among joint tenants, and enjoined them 'to concur in keeping of good neighbourhood one with another, in tilling, labouring, sowing, shearing, pasturing and dyking, and in all other things pertaining to good and thrifty neighbourhood'.

Such statements might imply an idyll of peasant co-operation. It was much less so in reality, as we have seen. But, as Jeanette Neeson has argued, if common-field agriculture was 'riven with dispute and noisy with argument', it is also the case that such arguments were often resolved, for 'negotiation was as vital to common-field agriculture as pasture'. Engagement in the same arguments was an indicator of the shared life of the manor or fermetoun, and the cultural stress upon the ethic of neighbourliness was one way of ensuring that they were settled in the interests of the individual and collective well-being of the tenantry. There was a strong expectation of conformity to a system of agriculture governed by customs determined, as William Harrison put it, 'upon good ground and reasonable considerations'. This might be inhibiting to some, but its essential purpose was the maintenance of a sustainable system of husbandry aimed at ensuring the subsistence of a community of neigh-bours whose interdependence was palpable in the intermingled holdings of the common fields.

If communal agricultural organisation presents a particularly visible example of neighbourhood, however, it was far from being the whole story. Many settlements were not coterminous with units of lordship, and their manorial structures were weaker. Moreover, there were large areas of England – perhaps 45 per cent of the cultivable area by 1500 – in which the common-field system was not the prevailing mode of agricultural organisation. In much of East Anglia, in Kent and in many parts of northern and western England, agriculture was practised in 'severalty': that is, tenants held their land in separate fields enclosed by hedges or walls. In Scotland also the arable lands of many fermetouns were divided into consolidated fields for which each tenant paid a share of the rent. Where such 'enclosure' was the norm, working association among neighbours was more limited and there was less need for collective decision-making. It might still be required for the management of common pasture, as was often the case. But in some areas pasture too was held in severalty – as in most of Essex and Kent, where manor courts functioned more as land registries than as institutions for the regulation of husbandry.

In such circumstances the ecclesiastical parish might provide an alter-native framework for the conduct of neighbourly relations. It was in all areas at the least an additional source of local identity, and in England the fifteenth century had seen a flowering of what has been termed parish 'communalism' – expressed in the rebuilding and beautification of churches, the fraternity and commensality of parish religious guilds, and the elaboration of the ritual and festive life of the parish as a Christian community. But, whatever the institutional framework, neighbourhood was also expressed informally, in the perennial personal contact of the inhabitants of small-scale, face-to-face communities. In this sense the neighbourhood was itself a 'primary group'. Its component households were interlocked in all manner of ways: rendering practical assistance and support; proffering advice or reproof; borrowing and lending; engaging in small-scale buying and selling; arbitrating quarrels; visiting the sick; celebrating the rites of birth, marriage and death.

All this added up to a tangled skein of interpersonal connection, evidenced, for example, in the 'close web of friendship, mutual regard and responsibility' revealed by Professor Dyer's analysis of the wills of fifteen families in the Worcestershire village of Claines in the years 1513–40. It could also constitute what Craig Muldrew terms an 'economy of obligation', vital to the well-being of individual households. This was most evident in moments of particular need, as when neighbours organised 'bride ales' to assist in the endowment of a new household, or supported 'help ales' like that held by a Wiltshire villager who had lost his only cow and was advised by a neighbour 'to provide a stand of [ale] and he would bring him company to help him towardes his losses'. But it was also of continuing significance. Access to the resources of neighbourly help and co-operation could be vital to the functioning of the household economy, especially during the most burdensome phases of life. And sustaining such access depended above all upon the maintenance of 'credit' in the neighbourhood: the reputation of individuals and households as honourers of their obligations.

'Credit' is defined by Muldrew as 'the cultural formation of the household as an economically reliable unit'. Its meaning extended far beyond mere financial capacity. Householders of credit were 'industrious in their husbandry', 'friendly and neighbourly', 'ready to assist each other upon occasion', people of 'good, honest and quiett behavior', who gave 'good will for good will and one goode toorne for another', and found their neighbours ready, in return, to 'pleasure' them 'with purse, pastime, creditte and councell'. A person's credit as a neighbour was established by long experience in small-scale societies in which the behaviour of individuals and families was subject to constant scrutiny and in which sanctions of exclusion could be invoked against the delinquent. The sustaining of one's credit was a vital form of social insurance in an insecure world in which, as Roy Porter observes, 'the warp of self-preservation had to be interwoven with the weft of neighbourliness'. The price of that modicum of security was conformity to the standards of the neighbourhood and the acceptance of limits upon both personal autonomy and economic individualism. It was a price that many were willing and some were constrained to pay.

iii. *Citizenship and fraternity*

Lordship and neighbourhood were also of relevance to urban society. The more significant English cities and the Royal Burghs of Scotland paid to the crown an annual 'fee farm' of consolidated rents and tolls in recognition of crown lordship, though they had long enjoyed effective autonomy by virtue of their charters of liberties and privileges. Lesser towns were often 'seigneurial boroughs' (in Scotland 'burghs of barony') governed by seigneurial courts and owing their fee farm to their lord. Neighbourhood was as characteristic of urban streets and parishes as of rural communities, as one Joanne Harewood learned when, as a young bride, she arrived in Folkestone to be greeted by 'divers of the towne . . . And some said that knew her not, whiche is she shalbe our neighbour? . . . Whereupon they drannke to her.'

Towns, however, were also distinguished by their relative independence and distinctive institutions. Urban autonomy had developed from the basic right to hold markets and to possess institutions of self-government by a process of slow accretion. Inevitably, it varied in its extent. But it could produce a strong sense of civic independence, especially if a town had achieved the accolade of incorporation, which conferred legal identity as a corporate body – as expressed in Chester's charter of 1506, which declared that 'the said mayor and commonalty be one community by themselves and under the name of the mayor and citizens of the city of Chester'.

Within that collective identity, the urban community was comprised of a variety of component groups. Its core members were the citizens or burgesses who possessed the freedom of the city, and the members of the craft fellowships, companies or guilds (in Scotland 'incorporations') which had evolved from loose associations of men with a common occupation into 'organised communities with exclusive rights', controlling the affairs of particular trades. These two categories overlapped. Citizenship was the prerequisite for full participation in the economic and political life of the town. It could be acquired by various means – including patrimony, marriage, purchase or 'redemption' and apprenticeship – but it was unusual for it to be accorded to more than a minority of townsmen: around half the householders of York; a quarter of those of Exeter; a third in the larger Scottish burghs. Citizenship, however, was usually contingent upon membership of a guild. Variations in the size of citizen bodies tended to depend upon whether the franchise was available only to independent masters (as at Exeter) or was extended also to journeymen who had completed their apprenticeship (as in York, London and most Scottish burghs).

Citizens, then, were a privileged group. But, as we have seen, even within the body of freemen there were marked differentials of economic and political power. Overall control of the urban economy and society usually lay in the hands of an elite of leading merchants. This was sometimes formally constituted in the recognition of a dominant merchant company: the 'merchant guilds' of Scottish burghs, or the Merchant Adventurers of Newcastle-upon-Tyne, for example. More often it was an informal, but nonetheless distinct, oligarchy comprising the members of the principal councils in municipal government. New members were co-opted from among those deemed 'the most sad and sufficient', 'the able and discreet', or 'the graver sort' of citizen, a process in which the ordinary citizen rarely had much voice beyond the proposal of candidates. In practice the civic aristocracy was composed of senior 'liverymen' from the most significant (that is, wealthiest) urban companies. York's aldermen represented only eighteen of over ninety trades; London's were drawn from the twelve 'Great Companies' of the city. Their essential functions were to defend vigorously the privileges and liberties of their city – above all the monopoly of freemen over all wholesale and retail trade within their jurisdiction; to manage corporate property; to regulate the markets and fairs which permitted the participation of outsiders subject to conditions regarding time and place; to exercise a general control over the price and quality of goods traded; to maintain law and order and to settle disputes.

These councilmen were also leading figures in the guilds – institutions described by Unwin as the 'social embodiment' of the handicrafts system. The number of these organisations varied from place to place. In the early sixteenth century Coventry had thirty-three, Salisbury twenty-six, Carlisle only eight. Sometimes they were composite bodies amalgamating related trades, like the York Carpenters' Company, which also included wrights, sawyers, carvers and joiners. Sometimes they were more finely differentiated as particular specialisations sought to assert their separate identities. (Edinburgh witnessed fourteen new incorporations in the years 1474–1536.) Internally they also varied in structure. The large and powerful London companies, for example, consisted of the 'liverymen' from whom were chosen their Masters, Wardens and Courts of Assistants, and the 'yeomanry', the body of lesser masters and journeymen who had their own subordinate officers and organisation. Promotion to the livery was reserved for the most successful only. Elsewhere, however, guilds were often small – with perhaps twenty to forty masters and as many journeymen – and the degree of internal differentiation among members was less pronounced, though always subject to the hierarchical distinction between masters and journeymen.

The guild system was in essence a system of control. Its basic purpose was to regulate competition within limited local markets in a manner which would ensure the livelihood of guild members. This was attempted in the first instance by controlling entry to the trade. Rules were laid down restricting the numbers of apprentices permitted, the fees to be charged for taking them, and the length of time they must serve. Admissions to the freedom and to independent mastership were also controlled by fees and property qualifications, while efforts were made to exclude all 'forreiner' craftsmen (that is, non-members). Secondly, the conduct of masters was regulated. Standards of manufacture were enforced by 'searchers' with power of entry. Prices were determined, to ensure 'a reasonable rate' for work done. Members were disciplined for such offences as 'prowling other men's bargains', 'procuring away' customers, or 'meddelling' in other trades. Thirdly, attempts were made to control labour and labour relations. On the one hand, this included efforts to secure stable employment for journeymen – as when the York carpenters ruled in 1482 that preference in hiring should be given to any 'brodir of the said fraternitie' who lacked work – and a willingness to hear journeymen's grievances. On the other, it involved the setting of wages and conditions of labour and the placing of restrictions upon labour mobility. When the Coventry Cappers lengthened the hours of the working day in 1520 and their journeymen protested, the men were ordered to obey and masters were empowered to dock their wages if they left work early. Leaving one master's service for another could be subject to licence, and to 'entice or lure away' journeymen was forbidden – both means of minimising competition among employers. All this was achieved by 'ordinances' which were approved or modified by town councils and provided collectively a matrix of control for the urban economy.

It is important not to exaggerate the dominance of the guilds. Most townspeople were not directly involved with them. Nor were the regulative intentions of guild ordinances always successful. Nevertheless, they could be very effective indeed, and the attitudes fostered by the guild system were of larger significance in the conduct of the economic life of the towns. They kept alive a set of values embodied in guild ordinances which emphasised competent workmanship, honest dealing, fair treatment of apprentices and journeymen, payment of one's dues, regular attendance at meetings, brotherly regard for one another, and obedience to proper authority. It would be naive to suppose that these ideals were everywhere adhered to. But it would be equally naive to think that they could be flouted with impunity. Those who contravened them could be fined, admonished, forced to acknowledge their errors publicly or to reconcile their differences – like the two London pewterers ordered by their company to drink together like 'lovers and friends'. These were expressions of an economic culture in which the premium was placed not upon initiative, enterprise and competition, but upon order, regularity, stability and security; in which, as Cunningham expressed it, 'the ordinary object of ambition was not so much that of rising out of one's grade, but of standing well in that grade'. And it extended into the broader social and economic activities of the fellowships: the levying of dues to provide relief for members reduced to poverty by sickness or misfortune; provision for orphans, widows and the aged; the pre-wedding perambulations of the town 'to gather the good will of the yeomanry'; compulsory attendance at the funerals of brothers and sisters of the guild and the maintenance of prayers for their souls.

All in all the guilds promoted a powerful spirit of fraternity and mutual responsibility which reflected medieval ideals of association. Such values were shared by the rulers of the towns whose exercise of authority was informed by notions of stewardship and obligation to the wider community, and who sought to harmonise the economic interests of potentially hostile groups in the general interests of 'amity, love and quietness'. Nor were they alien to the poor. In Susan Reynolds' words, late-medieval urban society 'while undoubtedly stratified, resembled a trifle rather than a cake: its layers were blurred and the sherry of accepted values soaked through them'.

iv. *Kinship*

Throughout this discussion of local economic institutions and relationships a particular idiom recurs in the terminology of the records: one of 'kindness', 'friendship' and 'fraternity'. Neighbours were enjoined to live in 'kindly intercourse' and 'friendly unity', guild members to be 'brothers', 'sisters' and 'friends'. This was in fact an idiom of kinship, invoking the affective bonds of family relationships. Forms of economic association thus overlapped conceptually with those of kinship, and this fact inevitably raises the question of the significance of kinship in the economic relations of the time.

In one respect, as we have seen, kinship was of fundamental significance – in transmitting property between the generations and facilitating the entry of the young into independent adulthood. But what of the broader roles of kinship, and in particular those of the networks of kinfolk which extended beyond the nuclear family household?

In some parts of Britain there are good reasons to regard kinship relations as central to the structuring of economic life. In the Welsh clan lands prior to 1542, title to land depended upon co-ownership among descent groups (though this system was gradually giving way to the recognition of individual freeholds). In Highland Scotland, the clans were bonded by what was termed in 1587 'pretense of blude' and the 'place of their dwelling': a mixture of kinship and lordship. The clan chief and his principal 'tacksmen' – who were usually junior relatives – controlled access to the land and therefore subsistence, among clansmen who were either genuinely of common descent from distant ancestors or who had become attached to the clan and had taken its name. In times of dearth chieftains recognised the quasi-paternal responsibility to sustain them by providing relief from the stored food 'renders' of their tenants.

Throughout Britain, bonds of kinship also had a significant role in the 'social uplands' of the aristocracy and gentry. In provincial society both intermarriage among the landed families of a county or region and the establishment of cadet branches created series of overlapping networks of connection which were bound together not only by neighbourhood, but also by blood. In both political and economic affairs, gentlemen turned first to those whom one Scottish lord termed his 'surname and frendes'. The nineteen men who witnessed deeds for Richard Clervaux of Croft, Co. Durham, in the years 1440–73, for example, were closely intermeshed by ties of kinship, some to as many as six of the others. Sir John Conyers of Hornby had ten kinsmen by blood or marriage among the gentlemen retainers of the Nevilles of Middleham in the 1470s – all of whom enjoyed the economic fruits of the Nevilles' lordship. Such networks could involve extensive mutual co-operation in the acquisition, management and defence of property, providing a trusted core of 'friends' within the gentry community who acted as patrons, go-betweens, executors, arbitrators, witnesses, trustees and, if necessary, armed supporters.

Among urban elites too, kinship could provide a bond of solidarity in both political and economic affairs. Leading citizens were frequently closely interlinked by blood and marriage. Of the twenty-four men who served as sheriffs in Coventry between 1517 and 1547, for example, six were fathers, sons or brothers of others, at least seven were connected by marriage, and a further four acted as godparents for one another's children. In trade, relatives provided an 'operational extended family' of trusted individuals with shared commercial interests, who provided credit, advice, support and contacts. Much the same could be said of the leading members of the professions, for example lawyers. Of the six Londoners who held land in Cheshunt, Hertfordshire in 1484, five were legal officials in the employ of the Duchy of Lancaster. They were further interconnected by marriage and they acted together in the acquisition, disposal and mortgaging of land.

Among the population at large, however, the role of kinship was more qualified. In practice, it depended upon the extent to which kin were locally available, and the degree to which they recognised special obligations to one another. The accessibility of kinfolk within a particular locality is not to be taken for granted. Prevailing levels of fertility and mortality could profoundly influence the numbers of living kin available in any given generation. Geographical mobility, especially among young adults seeking land or work outside their villages of origin, could scatter the members of a family across a substantial area. Studies of particular communities suggest that many contained a core of 'dynastic families', with several branches, which had been resident for generations – their local persistence often being attributable to their possession of significant land-holdings. Local marriage alliances could further elaborate such family networks, as in the matches between the sons and daughters of three clothiers of Cranbrook, Kent, which produced four closely connected households in the younger generation. But most households were not embedded in such dense clusters of locally resident kin. They had one or two relatives living near by at best. Nor were local kinship networks necessarily stable over time. They could build up and disperse in the course of any individual's life-cycle. In most English settlements a minority of closely related households formed little webs of connectedness within the context of a neighbourhood composed mostly of unrelated families. Beyond that, kinsfolk were scattered across a broader area – a lateral extension of family ties which meant that, though the immediate neighbourhood was not usually structured by kinship ties, such connections could, if occasion arose, provide points of access to a more extensive social area.

The degree of practical obligation recognised among kinfolk was also subject to considerable variation. In Scotland, kinship was recognised through shared descent from a common ancestor in the male line. The surname was the key: so much so that on marriage a wife was 'brought into juxtaposition' with her husband's kin, but retained her own surname. Such a system facilitated a strong awareness of bonding within a surname group: kinsfolk were readily identifiable and could be drawn upon. In England, however, descent was traced through both father and mother. Outside the aristocracy and gentry, whose titles and estates passed in the male line, people's sense of kinship was more diffuse and variable. Distant relatives might be recognised as 'cousins' or as 'friends', or they might not; and as a result the acknowledgement of binding obligations to such relatives was more optional.

The available evidence suggests that in England groups of *genealogically* close kinfolk – for example, members of the same nuclear family of origin; siblings; the closest affines – were of considerable practical importance for certain purposes, whether or not they lived near by. Such kin were commonly called upon to act as the executors or 'supervisors' of wills, or to look to the interests of young children. They were ready to accept such obligations, and in return might exert their own claims upon a household – above all claims to inheritance in the absence of heirs. *Residentially* close kin were also commonly drawn upon for aid and support – some families, it has been plausibly suggested, were in effect 'functionally extended' by virtue of the perennial interconnectedness of their domestic economies. But such ties were not necessarily more significant than those maintained with unrelated neighbours. Those kin who were more distant either genealogically or residentially constituted a more dispersed resource. They might be called upon periodically for particular purposes, and there was a reasonable expectation that, if a request was not too burdensome, they would respond. In sum, there were certain critical areas of family affairs in which the claims and obligations of kinship were of major significance: notably those concerning family property and its disposal. Here kinsfolk constituted a community of interest. For the rest, kinship was part of 'a distributive economy of assistance and services' which was by no means exclusively, or even primarily, an area of kinship activity. The situation is encapsulated in the situation of a Staffordshire man of whom it was complained that he was 'allied, acquainted, frended, or near kynne' to many of the jurors hearing his case in a land dispute. He was in a position to activate any or all of a variety of support networks, of which kinship was one.

'The most fundamental of all bonds in medieval society', writes Professor Clanchy, 'was that of mutual obligation.' The institutions and relationships which have been surveyed here demonstrate the continuing vitality of such bonds at the turn of the sixteenth century. They provided the co-ordinates of identity for individual actors in economic life. They bound people together within particular localities in a manner which gave a strong 'local particularity' to the economic culture of the time: a particularity of place and custom, and a concrete personalisation of general assumptions about values and conduct. In such contexts, economic dealings were so much bound up with direct personal relationships as to acquire an implicit, and sometimes explicit, moral character.

This was a vital aspect of the economic realities of the age. At the same time, it is necessary to remain aware of the limits to this web of mutual obligation, and the boundaries that were placed on the various

communities described here. For these institutions and relationships
could exclude as well as include. Tenancy was a socially bounded identity. It might include most inhabitants of a manor, and often did. Yet there
were also places with a substantial landless population which enjoyed
few if any of the privileges of tenancy. Non-tenants were 'forreners'
or 'outintoun dwellers': a distinction usually invoked against non-
inhabitants, but one which could also be a basis for social differentiation
within particular communities. Neighbourhood was an attractive ideal.
Yet it could mask the existence of a hierarchy of belonging within which
distinctions of rank, wealth, gender and age could limit the extension of
neighbourliness. Fraternity was an exclusive identity by definition. Craft
fellowships usually excluded women, save by right of their husbands, and
the exclusion of 'alien', 'stranger' or 'foreigner' craftsmen was central to
their very being. Kinship obligations varied in significance and could fade
with social and geographical distance. Moreover, each of these relationships could be inflected by the realities of power or disrupted by conflicts
of interest which could be structural as well as personal. It was perhaps
for this very reason that such a cultural stress was laid upon the
excitement and reinforcement of a sense of mutual obligation. Hence the
considerable expenditure of the great on the open-hall hospitality and
'good housekeeping' which demonstrated the magnanimity of good lordship; the commensality of the guild feasts and drinkings; the great feast-
day processions in which the constituent groups of urban society
paraded, ranked in precedence yet of one body; the rural wakes, ales and
festivals said to promote 'mutual amity, acquaintance and love . . . and
allaying of strife, discords and debates between neighbour and neighbour'; the elaborate funerals in which whole communities of place or
occupation brought their members 'honestly' to the grave.

   This was not an idyllic traditional world. It knew conflict and self-
interest well enough. But it was also a world which gave emphasis to
the needs of the community as well as to those of individual households,
and in which the restraining bonds of mutual obligation could powerfully influence the conduct of economic affairs. Perhaps it was easier to
do so at the turn of the sixteenth century. Most villagers still had access
to the land. Landlord–tenant relations were relatively stable. Life-cycle
advancement was still a reasonable expectation for journeymen. Wage-
dependency and permanent poverty were still limited in extent. Part of
the drama of economic change would derive from the manner in which
these relationships and values fared when put to a sharper set of tests.

CHAPTER FOUR

Beyond the household: economic networks and dynamics

The particularity of local communities derived in part from the distinctiveness of their customs, institutions, expectations and patterns of relationships. But it was also shaped by the manner in which they were linked into larger worlds. As Charles Phythian-Adams puts it, the myriad of local communities constituted 'a dense complex of places which at one and the same time were entities in and of themselves . . . and integral parts, both socially and economically, of sequentially *larger* places'. It is to those larger places, and their interconnectedness, that we must now turn.

i. *'Countries'*

Prominent among such places were what contemporaries throughout Britain called 'countries', a term which in this context denoted not a territorial state, but rather 'a landscape, a society, an economy, and in some respects a culture'. A 'country' could be quite localised – as in the case of Gowrie, Teviotdale or the Vale of Berkeley. It could be more extensive – as in the 'north country' or 'west country'. But, whatever the case, to speak of a 'country' implied an area with a distinctive economic and social identity.

Such countries are customarily discussed by historians as a means of establishing a taxonomy of the rural economy, based upon varying patterns of physical geography and economic activity. England's agrarian structure, for example, has been variously categorised by landscape and by agricultural type. The predominantly mixed farming zone of the lowland south and east is contrasted with the more pastorally oriented highland zone to the north and west of a line extending from Teesmouth to Weymouth. 'Fielden' areas, with an emphasis on arable production, are distinguished from a variety of types of pastoral husbandry associated with the woodlands, fens or moorlands. Alternatively, a larger range of distinctive 'pays' has been suggested: the wolds and downlands of Yorkshire, Lincolnshire and the south; the heathlands of Norfolk and Dorset; the vales of the south midlands; the forests of the west and south-east, moorlands of the north and south-west, fens of the east, coastal marshlands and so on. Each of these is associated with particular patterns of agricultural practice – the sheep-corn husbandry of the open fields in the wolds and heathlands, the predominantly arable farming of the south-midland vales, the extensive pasture of the north, or the intensive pasture of the dairying and stock-fattening areas of the western and southern vales and woodlands. Scotland and Wales were far less variegated. A single English county might contain several distinguishable 'pays'. Lincolnshire, for example, had four: the wolds, the fens, the western clay vales and the coastal marshlands. In contrast, two-thirds of Scotland consisted of rough grazing country. The principal distinction to be made there was between the essentially pastoral systems of the cattle-rearing Highlands and southern uplands, and the arable areas of the central and eastern Lowlands, which focused on oats and barley production. Wales was similarly dominated by the central Cambrian massif and a pastoral agriculture pursued on open common grazing land, though arable production and dairying were more characteristic of the lowland vales and coastal areas.

The distribution of industrial activity is less subject to such categorisation, but it was already sufficiently widespread to give a very distinctive complexion to particular areas. Various forms of mining and quarrying had long been established in parts of the highland zone. Lead was mined in Derbyshire, the Mendip Hills, and the north Pennine dales; iron in Eskdale, the Forest of Dean and the Sussex Weald. Coal deposits were widely exploited, albeit usually on a relatively small scale – notably on Tyneside and in Co. Durham, in Glamorgan and around Holywell in north Wales, around the Firth of Forth in Scotland, and to a lesser extent in parts of Yorkshire, Lancashire and the north and west midlands. On a much larger scale, the spread of manufacturing industries organised on the domestic or putting-out systems had already created distinctive local economies within a variety of geographical 'pays'. Woollen cloth was manufactured in wood-pasture districts in Suffolk and Essex, Kent, Wiltshire, Somerset and Devon, in the uplands of west Yorkshire, south-east Lancashire, Westmorland and north Wales, and in fielden north Norfolk. Linen was produced in south-west Lancashire and in the Lincolnshire fens, metal wares in the hills of Hallamshire around Sheffield and in the vales and heathlands of the west midlands.

All this is useful as a guide to the range of variation to be observed in Britain's rural economies. But it is of limited analytical value in interpreting the economic geography of early modern Britain. Physical geography provides only a partial explanation of the patterns of agricultural variation and the peculiarities of regional identity. In some areas it proved a determining factor for the simple reason that it permitted few options in husbandry – as in the fells of the Forest of Pendle, Lancashire, described as 'extremely barren and unprofitable and . . . capable of no other corn, but only oats, and that only in dry years'. This was grazing country. Most areas, however, did permit alternatives, and human responses to the facts of landscape and climate varied. Again, particular farming countries were often far less homogeneous in detail than is allowed for in conventional descriptive generalisations. Close analysis of farming inventories can reveal a considerable variety of 'farm types' within a single 'pays', and varying degrees of conformity to the predominant regional norm. Nor can the location of rural industries be explained simply in terms of the presence of mineral deposits, the local production of other raw materials, or the existence of fast-flowing streams to drive mill wheels. Rather, the distinctive 'countries' perceived by contemporaries were often shaped not so much by the visible attributes of an area as by its invisible ones – by patterns of economic and social interaction and flows of goods and people. They were created, sustained and modified by particular patterns of interconnection established over time and space. The early primacy of Tyneside in coal production, for example, was not simply the result of the existence of coal deposits accessible to the relatively simple technology of the time. It depended also upon the closeness of those deposits to the River Tyne, the ease with which coal could be shipped thence by coastal traffic to distant urban markets – above all, London – the high costs of alternative fuels in those markets and the entrepreneurship and mercantile connections of the Newcastle 'Hostmen' who established and dominated the trade.

Awareness of such factors is vital to a proper understanding of the distinctive patterns of particular local economies, their articulation into larger economic systems, and the dynamics of their establishment, reproduction and modification over time. This requires, in effect, an analysis of systems of exchange, of markets and the flows of internal trade which bound them together into Phythian-Adams' 'sequentially larger' entities.

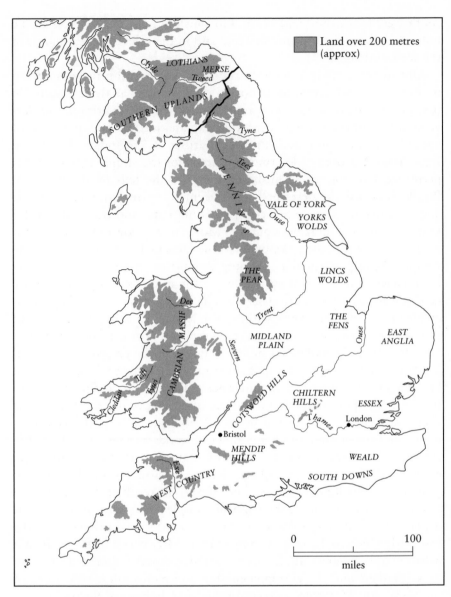

Map 1. England and Wales: principal geographical zones

Map 2. *England and Wales: principal towns, river systems and areas of rural industry in the sixteenth century*

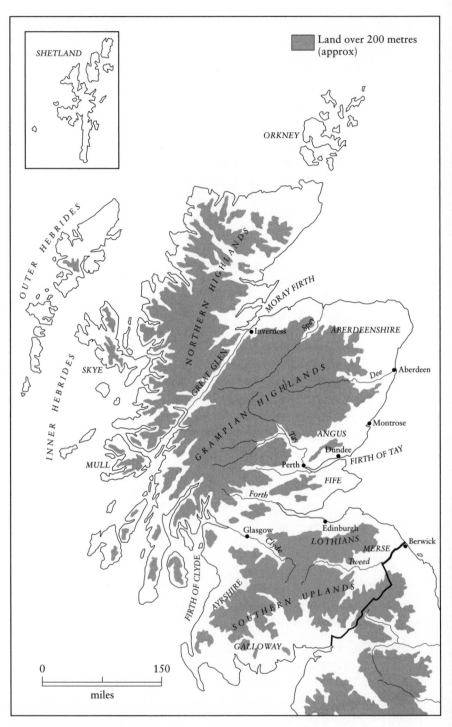

Map 3. Scotland: physical regions and principal towns

ii. Markets

For analytical purposes, four overlapping spheres of commercial activity can be distinguished. The most basic of these involved the intensive small-scale dealing which took place among the inhabitants of an immediate locality. In rural society this commonly involved a kind of quasi-commercial extension of neighbourliness, well documented in those numerous minor transactions – often involving credit – which we have seen recorded in wills and inventories. It might also be structured by local patterns of lordship and social differentiation. In Hunstanton, Norfolk, for example, the household of the resident lords, the Lestranges, 'functioned virtually as a local market for the small producers of the locality'. In the years 1518–21 the Lestrange accounts recorded 655 minor transactions with seventy-nine individual suppliers of fish, pigs, poultry, butter and the like, most of whom lived within two or three miles of Hunstanton and many of whom were tenants. Conversely, landlords or substantial farmers frequently supplied local needs in a manner which rendered recourse to formal markets unnecessary. Scottish lairds commonly sold back to tenants parts of the grain delivered to them as rent-in-kind. In Essex in 1538–40 the Tyrell estate rarely sent wheat or oats to market – these crops were sold locally in small quantities, not infrequently to estate workers. In the towns too, a good deal of the business of small tradesmen was conducted with fellow townspeople within what remained highly localised markets. And, as in the countryside, urban inventories and court records indicate that many of these transactions were conducted on credit or 'trust' in a manner that created a complex web of economic interdependence among known individuals extending up, down and across local societies which were more diverse but no less intimate than their rural counterparts.

In all likelihood most small husbandmen and tradesmen conducted the greater part of their commercial dealings within such contexts. A second sphere of activity, however, was that comprising rural–urban and inter-urban trade at the level of the district, 'country' or sub-region. Despite their elements of autonomy, rural and urban economies were in no sense separate spheres. As John Patten writes, 'it is helpful to think not of town and country . . . but rather of interconnected socio-economic areas that were centred on a town'. All towns depended on the countryside for supplies of food and raw materials and for much of their custom. Country-dwellers needed the towns as trading forums for their produce and as suppliers of specialist manufactures and services. Moreover, similar reciprocities existed between urban economies – or rather between those town-centred socio-economic areas. In both instances, the vital unit of analysis is that of the country town and its hinterland, or 'market area'.

All market towns were, in Julian Cornwall's words, 'essentially part of the countryside which [they] served and from which [they] gained most of [their] living'. They varied nonetheless in both their size and their significance in the structuring of commercial activity within their 'countries'. The smallest have been aptly described as 'market villages' – villages 'with an overlay of urban activities' – and as 'foci in time', briefly galvanised into activity on their market days. Nevertheless, they performed a vital role in binding the settlements around them into larger economic units. The inhabitants of the Leicestershire village of Kibworth Harcourt, for example, had the option of attending markets which lay within walking distance on most days of the week. Regular use of those markets for the exchange of small surpluses provided them with several points of entry into the larger economy of the district. Moreover, such periodic influx from surrounding villages meant that even small towns were able to sustain a range of specialist activities somewhat greater than that represented in the average rural settlement. In a survey of occupations in the Babergh Hundred of Suffolk in 1522, for example, the twenty-seven villages had between two and fourteen male occupations each. The small towns of Boxford, Nayland, Lavenham and Long Melford, however, had between eighteen and twenty-seven. Sudbury, the most significant market town of the district, had forty-nine.

Sudbury provides an example of what have been termed 'district market towns': places with a more extensive role in articulating the patterns of exchange of an area. Some simply provided more services than any rival. Some had developed a degree of specialisation in addition to their general trading functions, as in Retford, Nottinghamshire, where two-fifths of the recorded trades of the town were related to leatherwork. And where such elements of specialisation existed, they were often linked to the enjoyment of a particularly significant place in local patterns of communications. Darlington's position on the Great North Road, for example, helped it become the principal livestock market for the Teesside area, and drew in custom from throughout north-east England to its annual cattle fair. It is scarcely surprising that butchers, skinners, tanners and leather-workers were unusually prominent in the town's occupational structure and that it was also a major supplier of leather to other northern towns – notably York. Indeed, some market towns enjoyed a position so strategically significant that they have been termed 'cardinal markets', places which helped to link adjacent 'countries' into sub-regional systems of exchange. Richmond, north Yorkshire, stands where the Pennine dales descend into the Vale of York and channelled the exchange of the wool and dairy produce of the one for the grain of the other. Lewes in Sussex performed a similar role in articulating the distinctive economies of the Wealden forest and the Sussex downs.

Market towns of varying size and significance thus connected villages into localities, localities into districts or countries and countries into sub-regions. Their intersecting areas of influence constituted what Phythian-Adams calls 'the most concentrated form of local society' beyond the individual settlement. In Scotland this found formal expression in the 'liberties' of the Royal Burghs; the districts within which trading was permitted only in the burgh market. In England market areas were less formally structured, but their influence is discernible in local patterns of population mobility and of economic and social connection. Where evidence permits the reconstruction of the distances over which people moved in the course of a lifetime, or over which they maintained economic and social contacts of various kinds, it commonly emerges that they operated principally within some five to ten miles of their settlements of origin or residence. In Kent, for example, one survey of 'marriage horizons' reveals that around half the villagers concerned found marriage partners within their parishes; 70 per cent married within five miles distance; 84 per cent within ten miles; 93 per cent within fifteen miles. Such distances reflected their areas of regular economic and social interaction: the 'social areas' constructed primarily from intersecting patterns of marketing activity and the small towns which shaped them. They serve to remind us that 'countries' owed their identities not simply to the landscape, but also to patterned flows of goods and people.

Such flows were for the most part locally contained. In considering them, however, we have already touched upon the existence of some larger-scale trading networks which tied particular 'countries' into regional and interregional systems of interdependence, and on occasion connected them further with international networks of exchange. The key commodities traded in this third level of interconnection were foodstuffs, raw materials, manufactured goods and luxury products. Foodstuffs were required by the greater cities, and by densely populated 'dependent areas' of the countryside, on a scale which could not be supplied by their immediate hinterlands. Hence the longer-distance trade in grain and malt, and the droving trade in livestock, herded together at the fairs of the pastoral north and west and then driven south and east. Raw materials like coal, lead, iron, leather, wood and above all wool were also traded over long distances: Newcastle coal fuelled the hearths and forges of London; wool from Leicestershire and Lincolnshire supplied the spinning wheels and looms of Wiltshire and East Anglia. Manufactured goods like Sheffield knives or Chester gloves found their way to markets throughout England, while textiles were both extensively distributed to serve domestic markets and intensively channelled along the routes to the major ports which served the export trade. Luxury goods such as wines, spices, dried fruits and fine fabrics were imported and then distributed inland via the major towns.

Any town could have a hand in the gathering and distribution of such goods. Some, however, had a particularly prominent role, over and above their more localised marketing functions, in the stimulation and articulation of these long-distance flows. Worcester, for example, held three markets a week to serve a marketing area which stretched some twenty-five miles east to west and some fifteen miles north to south: the core area of its regular trade. But it also stood at the intersection of road systems linking England and Wales, the south-west and the north, and London and the west midlands, while its position on the Severn made it a significant inland port. Its four annual livestock fairs made it prominent in the droving trade from Wales to the south-east. Its cloth manufacturing involved strong commercial ties to London and the Netherlands. The Severn linked it to numerous lading places and ultimately to Bristol and the sea through a barge trade in cloth, leather, coal, luxury goods and miscellaneous manufactures. Similarly, Hull drew in cloth from the West Riding and lead from Derbyshire for export. It supplied Spanish iron to the cutlers of Sheffield via the rivers Trent and Idle, and in return distributed knives and edge-tools along the east coast and to London. Haverfordwest articulated the land routes of southern Wales, the river traffic of the western Cleddau and the barge trade of Milford Haven. It supplied corn, cloth, wool and hides to Bristol and was also the principal distribution centre for luxury goods throughout south-western Wales.

The greatest of such towns – places with populations in excess of 6,000 in the 1520s – have been termed the 'provincial capitals' of the time. Newcastle-upon-Tyne was the principal trading centre of England's four northernmost counties, dominating both land and coastal traffic. It was also the main staple for the export of northern wool, a major supplier of grindstones quarried in the area and, of course, the principal centre of the coastal coal trade. York was both the principal ecclesiastical and administrative centre of the north of England and a natural point of exchange for the whole region. It dominated the marketing networks of the Vale of York, supplied specialist services like bell-casting, clock-making and book-binding for the entire northern region, and was a focal point for both overland and river traffic in Lincolnshire grain, East Riding wool, the dairy produce of the dales, Kendal cloth and the lead and iron of the Pennines and the north Yorkshire moors. The navigable River Ouse linked the city upriver to Boroughbridge, downstream to Hull and thence to London and overseas.

Variants of the same story could be told for Norwich in the east, Bristol in the west, Coventry in the midlands, and such similarly commanding Scottish provincial centres as Perth, Dundee and Aberdeen. And just as patterns of local mobility reveal the integration of local social areas, so also the migration flows of the major cities reveal their regional and interregional significance. Norwich drew in apprentices from all over East Anglia and sometimes from further afield. Bristol had an even larger catchment area. Half its apprentices in the earlier sixteenth century came from more than fifty miles away, a fifth from as far afield as Yorkshire, the north-west and East Anglia, and many from south Wales. Families from thirty-seven towns and villages in the midlands sent apprentices to Bristol, and twenty-five of those places, significantly, lay close to the River Severn, the vital artery of contact with the city.

Such provincial capitals were already places of national significance: integrating regional economies internally and channelling interregional flows of goods and people. The final level of articulation at the national level, however, was provided by Britain's capital cities. In both England and Scotland in the early sixteenth century, the urban systems were already somewhat polarised. Edinburgh, with its population of around 10,000 in 1550, was the only Scottish city of more than 5,000 inhabitants. London, with 55,000 people in 1520, as compared with Norwich's 12,000 or Bristol's 10,000, was even more dominant. The capitals provided the biggest markets by far for food, fuel and raw materials, already drawing heavily upon both their immediate hinterlands and more distant sources of supply. They were the largest suppliers of both manufactured goods and specialist services to provincial customers and clients. Above all, they were the principal centres of international trade.

Edinburgh was the major player in Scotland's admittedly limited overseas trade – exporting skins, wool and fish (mostly to the Netherlands) and importing wine and salt from France, grain, timber and pitch from the Baltic, and miscellaneous manufactures from the Low Countries. London enjoyed complete dominance in English overseas trade, based upon its proximity to the Netherlands – the largest market for English cloth – and the monopolistic control of the Netherlands trade enjoyed by the Merchant Adventurers' Company. In 1500 woollen cloth constituted some two-thirds of the total value of English exports and most of that cloth passed through London, having traversed the country by pack-horse from its regions of origin. In return for this, and for such minor export commodities as lead and hides, came high-quality fabrics (silks, damasks and fine linens), miscellaneous manufactured goods not produced in England (for example, pins, paper and starch) and such luxury groceries as wine, oils, spices, dried fruit and sugar. Most of these goods came from the Netherlands, above all via the city of Antwerp – the great European entrepot of the day, and England's principal point of contact with the trading systems of the Mediterranean, northern Europe, the Atlantic seaboard and the transoceanic possessions of Spain and Portugal, which were being drawn in the early decades of the sixteenth century into a 'loosely articulated world economy'.

Not surprisingly, London's dominant position in England's internal and external trade was reflected in the city's truly national migration field. Of a thousand new freemen admitted in the years 1551–3, only a fifth had originated in the metropolitan area itself. A quarter came from the south-east and East Anglia, a quarter from the midlands and a quarter from the northern counties, with smaller contingents from the south-west (where Bristol provided alternative opportunities), Wales, and Ireland. Interestingly, only a single individual came from Scotland. The two national capitals gave a degree of articulation to the economies of England and Scotland respectively, and yet the economic lives of the two kingdoms were surprisingly little connected. As yet they remained two essentially separate economic and social spheres, distanced by ancient enmity.

iii. *A system in motion*

The distinctive features of particular 'countries' were thus moulded not only by local and regional geography, but also by established patterns of economic and social interaction. Hitherto both these and the economic institutions and relationships of the period have been introduced in an essentially 'synchronic' manner, as a set of relatively enduring realities. Yet this was not simply a set of static structures. It was also a system of economic relationships in motion, subject not only to the mutability of short-term fluctuations of fortune, but also to longer-term influences on the prevailing patterns of economic activity. Each of its characteristic structures had been historically developed. They contained layers of time. And some of those developments had been relatively recent. This being the case, no account of the contexts of economic life at the beginning of the early modern period can be complete without a complementary discussion of the economic dynamics of the late fifteenth and early sixteenth centuries, an introduction to processes of change which were of profound significance in shaping the economic world 'in being' in the early decades of the sixteenth century.

Four aspects of change deserve particular attention: first, the emergence of the English yeomanry; second, the enclosure of the open fields in large areas of England and their conversion to pasture; third, the spread of manufacturing industry in the countryside; and, fourth, the restructuring of parts of the urban system. None of these processes was general or all encompassing. They were more salient – or at least better documented – in England than in Scotland and much of Wales, and even within England they affected some areas much more than others. Nevertheless, they were sufficiently marked to give a particular character to the economic and social experience of the late-medieval period, and in important respects created the preconditions for subsequent economic change.

In the early sixteenth century Britain remained an overwhelmingly rural society. Access to the land was widespread. Yet at the same time there was great diversity in the size of the holdings farmed by individual tenants. To this extent, the tenant population was already highly differentiated. The fact of peasant inequality was not in itself a novelty; it had existed from the earliest times. The *degree* of differentiation observable by 1500, however, was a relatively recent development, and one of considerable significance.

In the mid-fourteenth century, the demographic disaster of the Black Death had ushered in a long period of demographic stagnation, which by 1520 had reduced the population of England to around 2.4 million – half the level prevailing in 1300. Demographic contraction on this scale had profound consequences for the whole of society, and most immediately for the rural economy. On the one hand, population decline entailed a marked reduction of demand for agricultural produce in the market-dependent sectors of society. Prices fell. Internal trade shrank. On the other hand, land was more available, and the general shortage of labour meant that, where it was still required, wage levels rose. Taken together, these developments opened up new possibilities for the adjustment of relationships between landlords and tenants and for the restructuring of rural society in general.

From the perspective of the landlords, large-scale production on their demesne farms utilising the labour services of servile tenants was no longer an attractive option. It made more sense to let out their demesne lands to substantial tenants, if such could be found, and to convert servile tenures into rent-paying copyholds. From the perspective of the tenants, there was much less competition for the available land. Tenants were now

sought and even cherished by their lords. Conditions were no longer conducive to the heavy-handed exploitation of seigneurial rights, and the
result was a gradual shift in the balance of power between lords and
tenants. Serfdom slowly bled to death. Better terms of tenure were established and consolidated. The landless, or near-landless, population
declined. Basic living standards rose, for it was easier to obtain at least
a foothold on the land, and often enough a holding of sufficient size
to provide fairly securely for a household's self-provisioning. Within
this general context of tenant prosperity, however, there also emerged a
more pronounced degree of economic differentiation among the rural
population.

In part this was a consequence of the leasing of manorial demesnes.
On some manors, the demesne was parcelled out piecemeal among
numerous tenants and used to supplement customary holdings. At
Kempsey, Worcestershire, in 1471, some thirty-seven tenants took
parcels of the demesne, and at Hunstanton, Norfolk, the demesne was
let in small units of eight to twenty-five acres each. Elsewhere, however,
demesne farms were let as single units, or in very substantial blocks,
to small numbers of tenants – as was the case at Upwood and Warboys
in Huntingdonshire, or at Ledston, Yorkshire, where one Brian Bewley
leased the entire 180-acre demesne from Pontefract Priory. Different
patterns of demesne leasing could thus produce very different results:
at one extreme, a broad-based expansion of holdings among the
participating tenantry; at the other, a radical differentiation between
large-scale demesne farmers and the tenants of conventional customary
holdings.

A further influence was the gradual redistribution of customary land
through the operation of peasant land markets. Such markets in small
parcels of land among the tenants of a manor had long existed. In the
course of the fifteenth century, however, manorial land markets underwent subtle change. Lords who no longer had an interest in preserving
standardised holdings for the purposes of exacting labour services and
seigneurial dues no longer opposed accumulation. Land no longer
burdened with servile obligations became more attractive to potential
buyers. High mortality rates and the extinction of tenant families
brought land on to the market more frequently. The general availability
of land made peasant families less reluctant to alienate parts of their
holdings. Land transfers grew in both size and frequency and were less
defensively contained within particular family and kinship groups.

Altogether, the fifteenth century provided greater opportunities to
acquire land, and a disproportionate share of the land available tended
to pass to those of the peasantry who combined ambition with relatively

deep purses. On many manors *average* holding sizes increased, but so too did the *range* of holding sizes, above all in the more commercialised areas, such as at Cheshunt, Hertfordshire, where by 1484 one-third of the manorial tenantry held 70 per cent of the land. The English 'yeomen' had emerged. How far such processes were paralleled elsewhere in Britain is less certain. But manorialised Wales appears to have followed the English pattern in most respects, while in the 'Welshries' there is some evidence that smallholdings were being accumulated and converted into freeholds by the adoption of English law. The word 'iwman' (yeoman) entered the Welsh language in the fifteenth century. Scotland, in contrast, had no tenant land market. But serfdom disappeared there too, and it seems likely that lords were willing both to grant larger tenancies and to renew them more readily. 'Kindly' tenancy was a product of late-medieval conditions.

All this helps to explain how land was accumulated; but it does not in itself explain the motivation for such accumulation. It is easy enough to imagine why small peasant farmers might have wished to acquire more land. It enabled them to provide better for their households and extended their margins of security. Accumulation beyond what could comfortably be farmed with family labour, however, is less readily explicable. This was not, after all, a generally propitious climate for commercial agriculture, with its contracted markets, low prices and high labour costs. Nevertheless, the accumulation of land by ambitious farmers was not irrational. Up to a point there was still scope for successful commercial farming. Some established markets remained to be served, notably those of the major towns. The spread of rural industry also created new concentrations of population. To a considerable extent the climate of opportunity must have depended upon location and access to those markets which remained relatively buoyant – a crucial factor, perhaps, in explaining why in some areas men were willing to take leases of substantial demesne farms, while in others they were not. Again, the withdrawal of manorial lords from large-scale production involved, in R. H. Britnell's words, 'a significant change in the locus of commercial decision-taking'. Yeoman farmers may have been content with lower profit margins than were acceptable to demesne-farming lords. If the terms of their tenancies were generous, they could do well enough according to their own lights.

Moreover, given such opportunities, there was something to be gained in other respects, for the demand for land was not simply a reflection of its immediate utility for agricultural production. Land was the securest form of investment for surplus wealth. It could be sub-let. It could be used to advance children by the generation of income to fund dowries and portions, or by direct endowment. William Goodgraine, for example, had accumulated nine parcels of land in addition to his inherited holding by the time of his death in 1528: one went to the eldest son, who also received the patrimonial holding; four to a second son; two to a third son; and one each to his fourth and fifth sons. Such dispersal of one generation's acquisitions to establish the next was commonplace. Finally, land gave status. Its possession raised the standing of a family. If accumulated holdings were retained and passed on intact to a principal heir, they could both perpetuate that standing and lay the foundation for future advancement. The accumulation of land and the emergence of the yeomanry, then, were not necessarily indicative of a burgeoning spirit of agrarian capitalism. Its motivation could be a curious mixture of economic individualism and familial collectivism. If it sometimes involved the adoption of a more commercial orientation, it could also be contained within the values of the peasant system. Its overall effect, nevertheless, was a gradual modification of the agrarian social structure of many communities, a process of differentiation which was to be of profound significance for the development of rural society in the sixteenth century.

Similar ambiguities surround the issue of the enclosure of the open fields, and the conversion of former plough land to pasture. As we have seen, in 1500 an estimated 45 per cent of the cultivable area of England was already enclosed and farmed 'in severalty'. Much of this land had probably never been cultivated in open fields. A good deal, however, had been enclosed and converted to pasture in the late middle ages – an early enclosure movement which was particularly evident in the late fifteenth century and continued up to the 1520s.

In the course of the fifteenth century, most landlords had abandoned direct demesne farming and adopted the role of rentiers. Maintenance of their rental incomes, however, depended on the tenanting of their lands, and in a period of demographic contraction tenants were sometimes in very short supply. As a result, some of the poorest land previously brought into cultivation was allowed to revert to waste for lack of tenants, and the margins of settlement gradually contracted. Newsham-on-Tees, for example, which had supported eleven tenant families and an uncertain number of cottagers in the late fourteenth century, had been virtually deserted by the early sixteenth century. In such circumstances, the enclosure of the open fields and their conversion to pasture provided an answer to the landlord's problems. Pastoral farming was more extensive in its nature, and fewer tenants were required. Prices for livestock and in particular for wool were holding up better than those for grain crops. Lettings to one or two graziers could at the least provide some income from land which might otherwise lie untenanted. At best it might significantly enhance the estate income of landlords whose rent returns were stagnant or declining.

Such circumstances underlay a general shift in land use from arable to pasture, save in those areas – like Norfolk – where markets for arable produce remained unusually good. In the most extreme cases, it led to the final extinction of former settlements and their replacement by enclosed sheep-walks and cattle granges. Hence the many deserted medieval village sites which have been revealed by aerial photography – 67 of them in Gloucestershire; 40 in Worcestershire; 165 in Northumberland. More commonly, enclosure was partial and its consequences less drastic. But it made a major impact nonetheless upon the landscape of substantial areas of England. Of the thirty-six townships in the Lutterworth area of south Leicestershire, six were enclosed and depopulated between 1480 and 1507, while others were partially enclosed – the overall outcome being the conversion into estate pasture farms of 17 per cent of the area.

This, then, was the 'depopulating enclosure' observed with alarm by contemporaries like Thomas More. In truth it was a far less dramatic process than he and others imagined. It was not, as yet, a major source of grievance to the manorial tenantry. For the most part, the land affected had already fallen untenanted into the hands of manorial lords. Depopulation was as likely to have preceded conversion to pasture as to have been precipitated by it. Landlord intervention often came in the form of a final *coup de grâce* – as when Sir John Conyers evicted the last inhabitants of South Cowton in 1489, pulled down the four remaining cottages, and converted 120 acres to pasture.

Nor was early enclosure very impressive evidence of the advancement of capitalist agriculture in England. To be sure, it depended for its success upon the entrepreneurship of large-scale graziers like Michael Pulteney of Misterton Hall, Leicestershire, who fattened Welsh cattle bought in Coventry for resale via the fairs of Northampton, supplied mutton to local markets, and sold the wool clip of his 1,800 sheep to the clothiers of Gloucestershire and elsewhere. But it rarely involved investment in the improvement of grazing land for intensive use. For the most part, it was a matter of grazing sheep on low-grade permanent pasture, the most extensive of all forms of husbandry. To the landlords involved, enclosure was less a strategy of improvement, inspired by commercial ambition, than a low-cost, second-best solution to the problem of tenanting their lands. It was less the harbinger of agrarian revolution than a response to the depressed conditions of the fifteenth century. Nevertheless, like the differentiation of the peasantry – which it also served to enhance – enclosure and its associated shifts in land use helped to create the context of response to the very different conditions which were to develop from the second quarter of the sixteenth century.

The third and fourth aspects of change – the 'ruralisation' of manufacturing industries and restructuring within the urban system – can be considered together, for they were closely connected, and indeed linked in turn to the changing complexion of the rural economy.

As has already been emphasised, the principal economic roles of the towns in this period were the provision of specialist manufactures and services, and the co-ordination, at different levels, of the flows of internal trade. These roles gave the urban system its *raison d'être*, and its overall structural coherence. Within that structure, the fortunes of individual towns depended first upon the demand for the goods and services which they provided within their immediate hinterlands, and secondly upon their relative place within larger systems of exchange – inter-urban, interregional or international.

In a predominantly rural society in which many households were primarily self-provisioning, there were obvious limits to the demand for goods and services which sustained most urban economies. This being the case, it is scarcely surprising that the long period of population contraction after 1350 posed threats to the towns in the form of reduced rural demand and diminishing marketing activity. Such adverse developments could, however, be offset, at least in part, if certain favourable circumstances were also operative. Rising levels of prosperity among some country folk could help to sustain demand for urban goods and services despite the general contraction of the rural population. Again, if labour shortages raised the wages of the urban poor, this might provide an internally generated source of demand within urban economies. And if members of the social elite retained their purchasing power, this too could stabilise the core demand for luxury products traded over long distances.

To some degree it seems likely that these compensating factors were indeed operative. In addition, the fifteenth century witnessed the emergence of a major new source of demand for urban products, in the form of overseas demand for English woollen cloth. Whereas in the 1350s under 5,000 cloths had been exported each year, by the 1440s annual exports had reached the level of 57,000 cloths. A period of relative stagnation thereafter was succeeded by new growth from the 1470s, and by

1500 some 80,000 cloths were being exported annually to the cities of the Netherlands, where they were dyed, finished and sold on to markets in northern and central Europe.

All this had the potential to sustain the vitality of urban economies. Nevertheless, it does not appear to have been sufficient to support the whole of the urban system which had emerged by the fourteenth century. Some small towns which relied solely on localised exchange were rendered redundant in this period, and ceased to hold markets. Larger towns appear to have held up better, yet the period also echoed loudly with complaints of urban economic decay. Indeed, the frequency of these complaints was such that Charles Phythian-Adams has characterised the late fifteenth century as 'an unparalleled period of urban contraction', extending into the early decades of the sixteenth century, while others have written of this period as undergoing a 'late-medieval urban crisis'.

Part of the problem was almost certainly that the general context of demographic decline and commercial contraction was not sufficiently alleviated by the compensating factors outlined above. Those major towns which succeeded in holding their own may have done so partly at the expense of the trade of weaker competitors. In addition, new sources of demand for traditional urban products like woollen cloth did not necessarily provide direct benefits to the urban economy. Initially, the growing demand for English cloth certainly had that effect. In the 1390s cloth production was still substantially urban in location: west-country production was dominated by cities like Salisbury, Bristol, Bath and Wells; that of the north by York, Ripon and Kendal. By the mid- to late fifteenth century, however, cloth production was shifting rapidly into the countryside. At first, this took the form of the establishment of offshoots of parts of the productive process in rural areas adjacent to established urban centres of production. Gradually, however, the older centres of production became eclipsed by the sheer volume of activity which had been transferred to the small towns and villages of, for example, eastern Somerset and western Wiltshire, south-east Lancashire and the West Riding of Yorkshire, the Kentish Weald, the uplands of north-central Wales, or the Stour Valley on the borders of Suffolk and Essex, where it was organised by merchant clothiers on either the 'putting out' or the 'domestic' systems.

Such shifts of location can be explained in part by the local availability of raw materials, or of swift-running streams to drive the wheels of fulling mills. But such factors were of minor significance. Many clothing districts acquired their wool from relatively far afield. Mill-races could be constructed where they were required. Of far greater significance was a combination of two critical factors: first, men of commercial experience and capital seeking to produce cheaply for distant markets and therefore anxious to minimise their costs; secondly, the availability of relatively cheap, under-employed, rural labour.

The merchant capitalists whose expertise and capital were necessary to expand production, to co-ordinate the various stages of an elaborate productive process and to market the finished product were usually located in the towns. But the towns did not necessarily provide the best environment for expansion. The principal cost of production was labour, and skilled urban labour was in short supply, relatively expensive, and controlled and defended by the guilds. In the rural areas, in contrast, labour was available through the part-time employment of the agricultural population during the slack periods of the agricultural year. Moreover, rural producers were both unorganised and only partially dependent on the wages earned in manufacturing employment. Their labour came relatively cheap and they could be paid long in arrears – in effect extending credit to the merchant capitalist who paid them only when he had sold his cloth.

The most attractive areas for industrial expansion appear to have been those of predominantly pastoral agriculture where under-employment during parts of the agricultural year was particularly marked, and the inhabitants were likely to welcome supplementary employments. As a result there is a generally good fit between the presence of rural manufacturing and predominantly pastoral districts – be it the wood-pasture areas of the south-east and south-west, or the upland pasture of the north and Wales. But it was not necessarily so. Some predominantly arable areas were also involved – as in Norfolk. And conversely there were substantial pastoral areas which were uninvolved – as in Durham and Northumberland, or the Cambridgeshire fens. What really mattered was the availability of labour at low cost, ideally within convenient distance of the merchant capitalist's established commercial networks. If these conditions were present, then rural manufacturing could be relatively easily established. Many of the skills involved were relatively simple, perhaps already quite familiar, and no worker needed to master more than part of the productive process. And, once established, the manufacturing districts had a propensity to grow. Migrants were attracted (sometimes from the towns) and local infrastructures were built up which encouraged further expansion within a district.

All this represented in part the growth of a new industry in response to new sources of overseas demand, rather than simply the relocation of older-established manufactures. But the recasting of the geographical division of labour inevitably impacted upon the established urban system. Some towns lost their textile industries to the countryside.

Others were affected by the reorientation of trading flows that accompanied the rise of rural industries. The growth of the cloth trade was complemented by the decline of the export of raw wool, a severe blow to some of the wool-exporting ports of the north and east coasts. The cloth trade was primarily focused on the ports of the south and west, and over time was increasingly funnelled through London, to the detriment of the 'outports'. London alone handled 70 per cent of England's cloth exports in the 1480s, and 80 per cent by the 1530s.

The economic fortunes of England's towns, then, were shaken by a conjunction of factors in the later fifteenth and early sixteenth centuries: a general context of weakened demand for urban products; the relocation of the most buoyant manufacturing industry to the countryside; a rearticulation of some long-distance trading networks and therefore of the place of some towns within them. These factors account for the marked similarity in the complaints of urban decay which characterised the period: loss of population; diminishing market tolls; declining staple industries; loss of trade; the removal of substantial citizens.

Within this general litany of complaint, there were some particularly traumatic experiences. York, which had been at its peak of prosperity and influence at the turn of the fifteenth century, saw its population decline by more than a third in the course of the century before 1540. The trade of its markets contracted. Its cloth production fell by three-quarters between the 1390s and the 1480s, by which time it had been eclipsed by the developing cloth towns of the West Riding. Its overseas trade also declined in value as a result of its inability to compete with Hull and with London. In the early sixteenth century it was still a major city, still the home of wealthy citizens and still distinguished by the splendour of its civic and ecclesiastical buildings; but it was fundamentally reduced in circumstances. Coventry had also held its own in the early fifteenth century. Between 1434 and 1520, however, its population fell from 10,000 to 6,600. The number of master weavers fell by a third between 1450 and 1520. Some substantial citizens relocated to the countryside. By 1523, after a series of short-term crises which exacerbated its structural problems, a quarter of the houses stood derelict in some parts of the city.

Few towns suffered quite so badly. But few English towns escaped entirely, and, though less is known of urban developments in Wales and Scotland, there are some indications of comparable processes of contraction and restructuring within the urban system. Those towns which best withstood the pressures of the times were those which proved able to stave off the most damaging threats to their prosperity. Norwich and Worcester proved able to control rural competition and remained major centres of cloth production. Gloucester lost its cloth industry, but compensated by developing a large-scale capping industry. Those towns which did well were those which proved to be the beneficiaries of changes which sapped the economic vitality of others. Small towns like Lavenham, Suffolk, grew into prominence through industrial development. Ports with industrial hinterlands like Colchester, Exeter, Southampton, Newcastle or Hull achieved greater significance in reoriented trading networks. And then, of course, there was London, steadily enhancing its multi-faceted domination of the English urban system.

Many towns faced problems in the late fifteenth and early sixteenth centuries. Yet the notion of a general 'urban crisis' is exaggerated. Some towns suffered acutely, yet few remained completely mired in their difficulties, and some did well. In the final analysis, what the period witnessed was less an 'urban crisis' than what has been termed 'a transfer of weight within the urban system', a reshuffling of the existing urban hierarchy and a decisive shift of some forms of manufacturing outside it. That was a painful process for many towns, but the essential urban infrastructure remained intact. Moreover, in some respects the urban network was tightened, and extended in its reach – notably by the penetration into the countryside of large-scale manufacturing industries and with them the essentially urban economic relations involved in their processes of production and distribution.

iv. *The limits of commercial integration*

Taken as a whole, this account of commercial networks and their dynamics at the turn of the sixteenth century may well convey an impression of an integrated system of exchange encompassing most of England and Wales, if not Scotland. And so, to an extent, it was. It is not difficult to imagine fish caught off Anglesey, salted with Cheshire salt, and packed in barrels made of Irish barrel staves, being eaten by a Bristol merchant clothed in a gown of Norwich cloth and a shirt of Dutch linen. He might well have cut his food with a Sheffield blade and accompanied it with a French wine drunk from a pewter goblet made locally from Cornish tin and Mendip lead. All this mattered a great deal. Yet at the same time it is important to appreciate the limits of these currents of trade and of the market integration and commercial penetration that they exemplify.

In the first place, it remained the case that the proportion of total national output that was actually traded was limited, and the proportion that was traded over long distances was severely limited. This was still a primarily rural economy aimed in the first instance at forms of household subsistence which rarely involved commercial dealings of any greater sophistication than relatively localised exchange. Most of the population therefore had limited involvement with larger markets as either producers or consumers. They consumed most of their own produce and such income as they derived from the sale of the remainder was unlikely to be devoted principally to the consumption of manufactured goods or imported luxuries. Those who were more heavily involved were a minority. They included townspeople; the inhabitants of 'dependent areas' of the countryside, who were employed in rural industries producing for distant markets; the larger commercial farmers who supplied the towns and such areas; a variety of middlemen trading in food and raw materials, usually from urban bases; and of course those members of the social elite who were the principal consumers of luxury goods. Any attempt at putting an overall figure on this segment of the population inevitably involves reasoned guesswork, but it can be instructive.

We might assume, for example, that in England in the 1520s around 10 per cent of the population was urban; perhaps 15 per cent was engaged in 'rural non-agricultural' occupations; and the rural social elite made up a further 2 per cent. Numbers of substantial commercial farmers are much harder to estimate, but an attempt can be made. According to a survey conducted in 1520, the city of Coventry required 1,056 bushels of wheat each week to supply its bread needs. In a year, then, the city would have needed almost 55,000 bushels. Professor Overton estimates that in a 'normal' year in the sixteenth century a substantial farmer with 100 acres of wheat would produce a marketable surplus of around 700 bushels. Coventry, then, would have consumed the marketable output of seventy-eight such farmers. In 1520 the population of Coventry was around 6,600. The combined urban and 'rural non-agricultural' populations of England numbered around 600,000. Supplying that total would have required the surplus of some 7,090 large farmers. If we assume that such farmers maintained large households of servants, with an average household size of ten persons, they and their households would still have constituted only 3 per cent of the English population. We might double that figure to allow for other commercial farmers supplying not bread corn, but meat, malting barley and dairy produce. But even so it would still seem unlikely that the total of 'market-oriented' producers and consumers constituted much more than a third of the English population. Indeed, many of those included in that total would have been partially self-provisioning or otherwise engaged to only a limited extent in commercially oriented activity. In Scotland and Wales, with their smaller urban and rural-industrial populations, the comparable figures would have been much smaller.

All this considered, it seems likely that both the density of market integration and the intensity of commercial involvement varied enormously. Some areas were perhaps already relatively commercialised. The counties of East Anglia, and the south-east, for example, were densely populated, economically variegated in terms of both agriculture and rural industry, thickly sprinkled with small towns, well served by roads, navigable rivers and coastal communications and economically focused by the major cities of Norwich, Colchester, Canterbury and above all London. In Scotland, similar advantages were enjoyed in Fife and the Lothians. Yet in much of Britain at this time longer-distance marketing connections are perhaps best thought of as significant but limited commercial currents flowing across local economies which for the most part retained a considerable degree of effective autonomy. Cattle from the north and west, for example, traversed the midland plain, yet that region remained a zone of mixed farming which supplied most of its needs locally. Moreover, even within the more commercialised zones, there were many whose domestic economies still followed a different logic.

Given such realities, historians seeking to conceptualise the whole have struggled to find ways of expressing both the fact of commercial interconnection and its limitations. This was 'an elaborate mosaic' of interlocking rural economies, but also a highly 'territorial economy'. It was 'an aggregate of local and regional economies', rather than a fully integrated whole; 'a loose bundle of mainly self-sufficient economic entities'; 'an amalgam of different societies all at varying stages in their evolution, all influencing each other, yet all developing in their own way . . . at different paces, so that one finds older societies co-existing, often with equal vigour, alongside the new'.

All of these formulations have validity. As we have seen, market relationships had a vital place. This was not a world innocent of commercialisation. Yet at the same time local and regional economies did retain a high degree of autonomy. Price regions were relatively localised and failed to exhibit a consistent relationship to one another. Wage levels were also highly variable. Considerable differences existed in the weights and measures employed in different areas – despite medieval efforts at standardisation – and the variant sizes of bushels and bolls, pounds and stones suggest an inward-looking world governed by locally specific notions of proper dealing. Moreover, attitudes towards market relationships themselves were ambivalent. Their necessity was universally recognised. Yet people were acutely conscious of their potential for abuse, and this anxiety was reflected in the close regulation of many markets – above all those in foodstuffs.

The rules governing the marketing of grain provide an apt example. In order to prevent its interception by middlemen and the 'forestalling' of the market, no grain was to be transported save on market day. Before market the magistrates and officers met those with grain to sell to 'confer together for some reasonable price for their grain to be sold there'. Actual prices were determined not by the free play of supply and demand, but by bargaining around that publicly announced norm. No grain was to be sold before 9 a.m. It was sold first to those requiring it 'for the necessary provision of their own houses' and in quantities not larger than two bushels. Commercial dealers like brewers, bakers and 'corn badgers' were not permitted to buy before 11 a.m. All dealing was to take place in open market. 'Engrossing' (the amassing of goods) and 'regrating' (buying for resale at the same or another market) were forbidden. Such regulations were widely observed throughout Britain as a means of preventing the cornering of the market in a vital commodity which was all too real a threat in locally circumscribed markets. Of course, they were often evaded. But to do so was a punishable offence. And their very existence, like that of the guilds' regulation of other trades, is significant. They expressed the values of an economic culture in which the benefits of commercial exchange were fully recognised, but regarded nonetheless as subordinate to the need to exercise control in the interests of the well-being of the immediate community.

All in all, then, this was not so much a commercialised economy as a largely traditional, fundamentally agrarian economic order with a limited commercial sector primarily engaged in the supply of limited long-distance markets for foodstuffs, raw materials, some manufactured goods and luxury products. That sector was larger and more complex in England, much more contained in Scotland and Wales. Within it, the predominant flows of goods appear to have been from the north and west towards the more heavily populated, richer, more urbanised south and east. Yet it would be inappropriate to characterise these flows simply in terms of a more economically developed and commercially dynamic geographical core served by a relatively backward northern and western periphery. Such a model might have some applicability to Wales. There the majority of fairs and markets were located in towns which 'lay in an arc facing outwards to England' along the south coast and in the marches. The principal roads ran west to east, and the dominant commercial centres lay outside Wales, in Chester, Shrewsbury and Bristol. It would certainly apply to the relationship between Highland and Lowland Scotland. But in general it is probably closer to the mark to think less in terms of a single geographical core area than of a set of economically sophisticated core activities which by 1500 had dispersed outposts all over Britain. Many localities had commercially oriented inhabitants who were directly involved with distant markets and whose dealings differed markedly from those of their neighbours in scale and complexity. Some strategically placed districts had knots of such people, binding them more systematically into larger economic networks.

Such outposts of commerce were perhaps rarer in Scotland and Wales, but they existed in some form all over Britain and they could exercise a powerful leverage on the direction of local economies. The limits on their development were not primarily set by the inadequacies of the commercial infrastructure or the transportation networks of the day – for both, as we have seen, contained considerable potential. Rather, they derived from the limited demand exerted, both within Britain and from overseas markets, for the goods and services which they supplied. They were, nonetheless, of considerable potential significance, and their presence made possible many of the changes in the pace of economic activity which were to characterise the sixteenth century – some of them already stirring in the decades around 1500.

PART TWO

Transitions

CHAPTER FIVE

Prices and people, c.1520–c.1580

In 1509, as he composed his *Tree of Commonwealth*, Edmund Dudley was only too aware of the vicissitudes of political fortune. He assumed, however, the relative stability of the social and economic order. It was not one without change, as we have seen. But it was one in which change proceeded at a pace which rendered it scarcely perceptible to most contemporaries, and on a scale which posed no fundamental threat to the established structures of economic and social relationships, or to the values that informed them. Within two generations, such certainties were to dissolve. In the second quarter of the sixteenth century the pace of change quickened markedly in response to a series of challenges which not only galvanised economic activity in unanticipated ways, but also seemed to threaten the very assumptions that underpinned the security of the prevailing economic and social order. In Scotland, Sir David Lyndesey represented 'Jhone the common weill' as clothed in 'raiment all raggit', with 'visage lean' and 'richt melancollous countenance'. In England, Hugh Latimer demanded rhetorically from the pulpit, 'What man will let go or diminish his private commodity for a common wealth?' To such moralists the disorienting economic dynamic of the sixteenth century could be attributed directly to human failure, to rejection of the ideal of commonwealth extolled by Dudley. Most contemporaries, however, were more immediately preoccupied with the central economic fact that seemed to epitomise the disturbing experience of their age – rising prices. And some also noted another: 'such increase of people . . . that the land was never so full', as William Harrison put it – demographic growth.

i. *Prices*

'Nothing makes history, exalts and debases classes and kingdoms,' wrote Clapham, 'like changes in the value of money.' Sixteenth-century people knew the truth of that adage only too well. They lived in a world in which the prices of basic necessities could fluctuate wildly from year to year, above all in accordance with the state of the harvest. Such years of 'dearth' were feared but expected. The truly distinctive feature of sixteenth-century experience, however, was the novel phenomenon of long-term inflation. Price indices constructed from the records of purchases of foodstuffs and manufactured goods indicate that throughout the later fifteenth century prices had remained relatively stable. From around the second decade of the sixteenth century, however, they began to rise, modestly at first, but gathering momentum in the 1520s and 1530s. In the 1540s and 1550s they rose rapidly, before settling back to a slower, though still continuing, growth in the 1560s and 1570s. By the 1570s, the price of a hypothetical 'basket of consumables' constructed to reflect most of the basic needs of a typical household was more than three times what it had been at the turn of the century.

Within this general trend, the most striking characteristic of the price rise was the different pace of price inflation observable between different commodities, a set of differentials illustrated in Table 1. The price of wheat, the most expensive bread corn, rose more slowly than did that of cheaper grains like rye or oats. Between the 1490s and the 1570s, for example, the decadal average wheat prices rose 3.7-fold, as compared to a 4.6-fold rise in the price of rye. Again, dairy products rose in price more slowly than did grains, achieving a 2.2-fold increase over the same period, and only really moving upwards from the 1540s. The prices of industrial products also rose at a more modest pace, becoming significant only from the 1540s and amounting to a 2.3-fold increase by the 1570s.

Such differentials are further complicated by the existence of considerable local variation in price levels and trends. This was, of course, a highly regionalised economy, with marked local variations in the conditions of supply and demand. Moreover our best evidence of continuous price series comes from only a small number of urban centres in the south of England, that are aggregated to produce 'national' price indices that are inevitably somewhat artificial. A price index for London alone, based upon the recorded prices for twelve basic consumption items (including foodstuffs, drink and fuel) indicates an overall 2.5-fold increase in the prices paid by London consumers between the 1490s and the 1570s. In London, as is shown in Table 2, prices rose modestly from the 1510s to the 1530s (at about 6 per cent per decade), increased rapidly in the 1540s

Table 1: *Index of Prices, Southern England (Decennial Averages)*

	Wheat	Rye	Cattle	Dairy Products	Industrial Products	'Basket of Consumables'
				(1450–99 = 100)		(1451–75 = 100)
1490–99	91	99	90	102	97	101
1500–09	109	123	103	93	98	104
1510–19	114	112	119	93	102	111
1520–29	144	195	143	94	110	148
1530–39	140	190	147	109	110	155
1540–49	171	–	174	139	127	192
1550–59	285	–	266	216	186	289
1560–69	293	338	290	225	218	278
1570–79	336	459	358	223	223	315

Commodity Prices from: P. Bowden, 'Statistical Appendix', in J. Thirsk, ed., *The Agrarian History of England and Wales Vol. IV. 1500–1640* (Cambridge, 1967), pp. 857–862.

'Basket of Consumables' calculated from: E. H. Phelps-Brown and S. V. Hopkins, 'Seven Centuries of the Prices of Consumables Compared with Builders' Wage-Rates', *Economica* (1956), reprinted in E. M. Carus-Wilson, ed., *Essays in Economic History Vol. 2* (London, 1962), p. 194

Table 2: Composite Price Index, London (twelve consumption items)

	Decennial Average (1457–71 = 100)	% Change
1490–99	98	–
1500–09	101	3.1
1510–19	108	6.9
1520–29	115	6.5
1530–39	122	6.1
1540–49	145	18.9
1550–59	212	46.2
1560–69	224	5.7
1570–79	241	7.6
1580–89	257	6.6

Source: S. Rappaport, *Worlds Within Worlds: Structures of Life in sixteenth-century London* (Cambridge, 1989), p. 131

and 1550s (which saw rises of 18.9 and 46.2 per cent respectively) and then settled back to growth of 6–7 per cent per decade in the 1560s and 1570s. The inflation suffered by London consumers was thus somewhat less dramatic than that indicated by 'national' figures, and it is doubtless the case that many local and regional variations of this kind are yet to be explored. Nevertheless, the broad general picture remains the same: prices were rising from the second decade of the sixteenth century, they rose sharply in the 1540s and 1550s, and the upward trend continued at a slower pace thereafter.

Why? Contemporaries had a ready enough explanation: human greed. They blamed the covetousness of farmers and dealers in the victuals trades demanding higher prices and allegedly willing to manipulate the supply of the markets in order to achieve them. They castigated the covetousness of landlords seeking to enhance their rental incomes and thereby forcing farmers to raise their prices in order to meet those demands. More specifically, and more guardedly, they blamed the covetousness of rulers willing to manipulate the quality of the silver coinage in order to boost the revenues of the state.

The latter allegation had a very specific justification. Between 1542 and 1551 the governments of Henry VIII and of the young Edward VI were confronted by the need to raise vast sums of money in order to finance wars with France and Scotland. One expedient adopted repeatedly was that of reducing the silver content of the coinage, while retaining its face value. In 1551, for example, the mint reduced the silver content of the coin produced by a quarter, thereby minting more coins from a given quantity of silver and enabling the crown to retain the difference. Such windfalls, however, were not long retained. The money was rapidly spent on military costs, with the result that the overall face value of the coinage in circulation increased dramatically – from an estimated £1.19 million in 1542 to around £2.6 million in 1551. Such manipulations met the short-term needs of government, but rapidly undermined confidence in the currency. People demanded more coins for goods sold, and prices escalated rapidly, eventually forcing the administration of the Duke of Northumberland to order a revaluation later in 1551, which attempted to restore confidence by calling down the face value of the coinage. Public faith in the coinage, however, was not fully restored until the early years of the reign of Elizabeth I, when the crown undertook, boldly and successfully, a complete recoinage.

This 'monetary' explanation of the rapid inflation of the 1540s and 1550s was subsequently supplemented by a further attempt to explain inflation in essentially monetary terms, originating with the French thinker Jean Bodin and introduced to English audiences by Sir Thomas Smith in 1581. Bodin held that the underlying cause of the price rise throughout Europe was the influx of silver from the recently acquired Spanish possessions in the New World. Such silver, disbursed by the Spanish crown to meet the costs of its imperial commitments and gradually dispersed through the trading networks of Europe, was held to have vastly increased the supply of money. With more money chasing the goods available, prices inevitably rose – an apparently convincing explanation of the longer-term European inflationary trend to place alongside short-term factors peculiar to the English polity.

Explanations focusing upon such monetary factors long held the field in historical discussions of the Tudor price rise. Growing knowledge of sixteenth-century economic trends, however, has brought greater awareness of the problems inherent in these arguments. That there must have been some increase in the money supply in the sixteenth century, all are agreed. Without it, the price rise could scarcely have occurred. Yet in itself this factor appears not to have been a sufficient cause of the inflation of the period for a variety of reasons. First, an increase in the supply of money does not necessarily cause prices to rise. Unless accompanied by an increase in economic activity which requires a larger quantity of money to oil the wheels of commerce, it can mean that the circulation of the coinage merely slows down, or that surplus coin is hoarded. If, on the other hand, there is a shortage of currency to meet existing economic needs, then a good deal of additional coin can be absorbed without raising prices significantly. There is, in fact, abundant evidence that ready money was in short supply throughout the period: hence the very extensive use of sales credit, and the practice of only periodically 'reckoning' up the balance of debts and credits between tradespeople and customers as a preliminary to the settlement of the difference in coin. Growth in the available coinage could simply have had the effect of monetarising more transactions of this type.

Secondly, there is a lack of chronological fit between the course of the price rise and the points at which monetary factors can be said to have had a significant impact. It is considered highly unlikely that much Spanish silver had entered England before the 1540s, when bullion from the New World began to arrive in Europe in large quantities and may have found its way to England through international trading networks. Debasement of the coinage was a phenomenon peculiar to the later 1540s and early 1550s. Yet the upward trend in prices, as we have seen, began several decades before that time, and it continued after the stabilisation of the coinage. Moreover, prices appear to have been rising not only earlier, but also faster than can be accounted for by any available estimate of the increase in the money supply (save during the maelstrom of mid-century debasement). And, finally, inflation which was essentially monetary in origin should have made all prices rise at much the same rate. In fact, as we have seen, they did not. There were marked differentials in the timing and extent of the inflation of prices for different commodities.

In short, monetary factors have to be part of any explanation of the price rise, but they cannot fully explain its particular chronology and characteristics. The way forward in broadening the range of explanation of this vital phenomenon was signalled as early as 1767 by Sir James Steuart. He went against received wisdom by suggesting that a critical further factor in determining prices was not so much the issue of money supply as that of changes in the numbers of consumers obliged to buy goods and in their capacity to do so. In other words, he directed attention to the changing state of demand for both goods and labour. It took many years for historians to catch up with that insight. But they began to do so when they first realised that in the early sixteenth century the population had started to grow.

ii. Population

It is hard to appreciate how ignorant historians were of population trends in early modern Britain as recently as the 1950s. Since then, however, enormous energy has been expended on the reconstruction of the demographic record – so much so that an awareness of its nature has become vital to any understanding of economic and social development in the period. In the case of England, evidence in the form of taxation listings and parish registers of baptisms, marriages and burials permit the reconstruction of population dynamics from the early sixteenth century. Some of the results of this research are set out in Table 3. We can concentrate initially upon the evidence presented in the first two columns of that table.

Analysis of taxation lists of the adult male population suggests that in the early 1520s the total English population was in the order of 2.4 million. This figure is in fact remarkably close to that estimated from the records of the Poll Tax of 1377, a finding which confirms the long late-medieval demographic stagnation. By 1541, however, estimates based upon the analysis of the entries in parish registers – which recorded baptisms, marriages and burials from 1538 – suggest that the population had reached almost 2.8 million. By 1551 it was in the order of 3 million. By 1571, after a dip in the late 1550s, it was close to 3.3 million and by 1581 some 3.6 million. Between the 1520s and 1581, then, the English population had risen by approximately one-third – and it was still growing. Indeed, its growth was accelerating. Calculations of the annual percentage rate of increase from the 1540s to the 1580s suggest that in the 1540s the population was growing at a rate of 0.64 per cent per annum. This rate of growth was reduced to 0.17 per cent per annum in the 1550s – for reasons to be explained later – but in the 1560s it quickened to 0.94 per cent and in the 1570s and 1580s it reached 1.1 per cent per annum. These were exceptional rates of growth for any pre-modern population. In particular, rates of growth in excess of 1 per cent per annum were quite extraordinary, and were not to be matched again in England until the late eighteenth century.

In seeking to explain this remarkable demographic upsurge, it is helpful to begin by considering a simple model of the components of demographic change in the early modern period and their relationship to the economic and social environment of the time. Such a model is presented in Figure 1. As Figure 1 indicates in diagrammatic form, population size at any one time depends in the first instance upon the relationship existing between the primary demographic variables of fertility and mortality. Levels of fertility in turn were profoundly influenced by the social conventions surrounding the institution of marriage. As we have seen, eligibility for marriage was regarded as dependent upon the economic and social maturity of each prospective married couple, and in particular upon their capacity to sustain an economically independent

Table 3: *Population growth in England, 1520–1591*

	Total Population	% Annual Rate of Natural Increase		Mortality (e_0)		Fertility (GRR)
1520	c.2,400,000					
1541	2,773,851			1541	33.75	2.869
1551	3,011,030	1540–49	0.64	1551	37.99	2.795
1561	2,984,576	1550–59	0.17	1561	27.77	2.322
1571	3,270,903	1560–69	0.94	1571	38.22	2.130
1581	3,597,670	1570–79	1.11	1581	41.68	2.322
1591	3,899,190	1580–89	1.10	1591	35.51	2.358

e_0 = average life expectation at birth.
GRR = gross rate of reproduction.
Source: E. A. Wrigley and R. S. Schofield, *The Population History of England, 1541–1871, A Reconstruction* (London, 1981), pp. 183, 528
Figures in columns 3 and 4 refer to 5-year periods centring on the dates shown

Figure 1: Population and Economy: a simple model

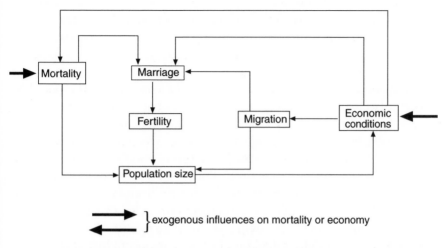

Source: Adapted from more complex models presented in E.A. Wrigley and R.S. Schofield, *The Population History of England, 1541–1871. A reconstruction* (London, 1981), pp. 457–69

household. This in turn influenced both the age at first marriage – which was generally delayed long after puberty, usually falling in the mid- to late twenties – and the proportions of the population able to marry. In a pre-contraceptive era, the prevailing age at first marriage was the principal determinant of the fertility of individual couples. Variations in the proportion of the population able to marry, and therefore of the number of reproductive units formed, was a further determinant of the general reproductive capacity of the population.

This discussion already alerts us to the significance of a further variable of fundamental importance: economic circumstances and the prevailing level of living standards. Those conditions were themselves heavily influenced by population size and the balance obtaining, within a given social system, between the level of population and the available economic resources for its sustenance. They determined marital opportunities, as we have seen. They could exert a direct influence upon levels of mortality: most dramatically when famine conditions precipitated a 'crisis of subsistence'; more generally through their influence upon the physical well-being and resilience of the population. They could also influence patterns of migration, whereby population was redistributed in response to the push and pull of economic opportunity – a factor which affected both levels of population in particular districts and local marital chances.

This is an exceedingly simple model of the 'pre-industrial'

demographic regime, and could be greatly elaborated. But it has the virtue of drawing attention to the principal factors involved in the demographic equation and to the relationships between them. Taken as a whole, it could constitute a self-adjusting system, a 'homeostatic demographic regime' functioning to produce, through a set of interrelated compensatory mechanisms, a general balance between population and economic resources. But it was not wholly self-contained, for it could be subject also to the destabilising effects of two further 'exogenous' factors. First, there might be independent influences upon economic conditions introduced from outside the system. Secondly, there might be independent influences upon prevailing levels of mortality, notably those shifts in the virulence of infectious disease which, it has been argued, gave an element of autonomy to the death rate. Both factors, as we shall see, could be of vital importance in precipitating demographic change.

This simple model can help us to understand the population dynamics of early modern England. But we must begin by going back to the long demographic stagnation of the later middle ages which, as has been indicated, appears to have continued until the second quarter of the sixteenth century. It is well established that the initial demographic contraction was occasioned by the disastrous plagues of the mid-fourteenth century – the Black Death, an outstanding example of the 'autonomous death rate' in action. More puzzling is the question of why the population took so long to recover from that catastrophe. In the aftermath of the plague, economic circumstances were favourable. Land was more readily available. Wage rates were high. In principle, opportunities should have been good to marry and to bring up the families which, in the course of a generation or two, might have repaired population losses. Yet, clearly, this did not occur. Instead, population stabilised in the fifteenth century at something like half its previous level.

In confronting this paradox, some have argued that we perhaps exaggerate the extent to which the fifteenth century was a golden age of prosperity for the common people and that the enhanced marital opportunities which might be predicted were in fact more apparent than real. The available land was not equally distributed among potential householders. Wage *rates* were good, but the general contraction of economic activity might have meant that paid work was not necessarily regularly available to those who sought it. Opportunities to enter the urban crafts and trades were reduced. Labour shortages may have enhanced the significance of service as an institution and kept the young tied up in service contracts while they slowly accumulated the wherewithal to set up their own households. Where land was available, improved expectations of *eventual* independence may even have encouraged the young to wait in hope, rather than marry to scrape an uncertain living as cottagers. For any or all of these reasons, marriage in the fifteenth century may have been relatively late, and less than universal, and fertility relatively constrained. We are obliged to speculate, since we have little direct evidence of the actualities of marriage or fertility in the period. Nevertheless, the numbers of children listed in the wills of late-fifteenth- and early-sixteenth-century testators do not suggest that the population was doing much more than merely replacing itself.

To argue thus may be to paint too sombre a picture. But even if marital opportunities and levels of fertility were better, as others would argue, we must consider a further factor: the exceptionally severe mortality rates of late-medieval England. Whether or not the fifteenth century should be regarded as the golden age of the peasant and the labourer, it was, in Sylvia Thrupp's famous phrase, the 'golden age of bacteria'. There is considerable evidence that mortality from epidemic disease remained high in both the towns and villages of fifteenth-century England. Mortality crises occurred relatively frequently, culling local populations, sapping their demographic vitality and inhibiting their potential for recovery. Dr Poos has estimated that average life expectation at birth in fifteenth-century Essex was in the order of 32–34 years, and, if this was so, then mortality at such a level could dampen the effects of modestly buoyant levels of fertility. If fertility was itself rather less than buoyant, then the severe mortality of the period can easily account for the long failure of demographic recovery. As E. A. Wrigley and R. S. Schofield put it, England in 1500 had 'a population with a great potential for growth', but that potential could only be realised 'if higher rates of mortality did not intervene'.

What caused the change so evident from the second quarter of the sixteenth century? Any answer must inevitably be speculative, since the decisive shift towards renewed population growth took place in the obscure decades before the advent of parish registration in 1538. Nevertheless, a number of possible explanations can be suggested. In the first place it is important to remember that renewed population growth was initially a largely rural phenomenon. Most towns did not begin to grow again until later in the sixteenth century. The dominant explanation of this shift is that it was occasioned by an autonomous fall in rural death rates. At the turn of the sixteenth century, it is argued, the virulence of epidemic disease diminished – for bacteriological reasons beyond the sphere of human action. Thereafter, the plague gradually withdrew from the countryside to become a largely urban phenomenon, only occasionally spilling over into those rural areas which maintained the closest contact with the major towns.

This is a powerful argument, but in its baldest form it does not account fully for the available evidence. Professor Dyer, for example, has shown that mortality crises occasioned by epidemic disease were still far from uncommon in the rural west midlands in the early sixteenth century. Yet in that area the average number of children recorded in lists of manorial tenants was rising. One implication of such evidence might be that fertility was rising despite continued high mortality. Nor is it difficult to suggest circumstances which might have stimulated marital opportunity and enhanced fertility in at least parts of rural England around the turn of the sixteenth century. One factor may have been the stimulation of rural economies by the growth of manufacturing industry in the countryside. Overseas demand for English cloth rose continuously between the 1470s and the 1540s, with a particularly notable surge in the decades 1490–1510 – another largely 'autonomous' factor exerting influence upon the English situation. One estimate suggests that between 1500 and 1540 overall cloth production may have risen by a third. If this was indeed so, it would have occasioned a commensurate increase in the numbers of those partly or fully employed in cloth manufacture, an enhancement of the incomes of their households, the build-up of greater population densities in the manufacturing districts, and a quickening of economic activity both within those districts themselves and in the areas which supplied their needs. All this might prove conducive to marital opportunities and to enhanced fertility.

Such considerations, however, are not necessarily incompatible with the view that an autonomous decline in mortality levels was a crucial factor in triggering population growth. Rather, it adds to the complexity of the situation. It underlines Wrigley and Schofield's point that this was a population with a high potential for growth if that potential was not checked by excessive mortality. Larger numbers of surviving children – a phenomenon also visible in the wills of men dying in the 1530s in the industrial areas of Kent – depended not only on their being born, but also upon their survival to succeed the parental generation and to expand the size of the next generation. Mortality crises could indeed remain severe in the early sixteenth century. There were some violent upsurges of mortality in the 1520s and 1540s, associated with the 'sweating sickness' or the plague, and the years 1557–9 witnessed a catastrophic nation-wide epidemic – probably of influenza – which temporarily reversed the trend of population growth. Nevertheless, such eruptions do appear to have been a less regular hazard to life than had been the case in the fifteenth century. They were more spaced in time:

occasional calamities rather than the regular culling which could smother the potential for demographic growth.

From the 1540s the evidence of the parish registers at last permits historical demographers to attempt more sophisticated estimates of the prevailing demographic rates, and the results – set out in the third and fourth columns of Table 3 – are intriguing. Between the 1540s and the 1580s, average life expectation at birth rose from around 32–34 to around 38–41 years: a marked decline in the level of mortality which was interrupted only by the catastrophic epidemics of the later 1550s. Calculations of the gross rate of reproduction over the same period indicate that levels of fertility were relatively high, but gradually declining, especially from the 1550s. In sum, these figures suggest that population growth was taking place in a situation in which both fertility and mortality were declining, the former modestly, the latter somewhat more significantly.

In the light of our earlier discussion, a possible interpretation of these figures is that fertility had indeed been relatively buoyant in the early sixteenth century (though perhaps more sluggish in the fifteenth century). If that was the case then an improvement in mortality could have quite marked consequences. Larger generations would survive to adulthood. As population began to grow, however, fertility slowly began to adjust downwards – in all likelihood through the mechanism of later or fewer marriages. But, despite that slow adjustment, larger generations were still surviving to marry and to reproduce, albeit at a lower level of fertility. In consequence, the population grew. Demographic recovery was under way and it was sustained. Indeed it quickened from the 1560s when the crisis of 1557–9 was succeeded by a whole generation of relative freedom from the spectre of epidemic mortality.

One final argument in favour of the view that the renewal of population growth was primarily triggered by declining levels of mortality can be provided by comparison with Scotland. England was not alone in experiencing demographic expansion. The population rise of the sixteenth century, like the price rise, was a European phenomenon, and neither can be explained in terms of factors peculiar to the English situation. Though the demographic evidence for Scotland is flimsy and does not permit the calculation of demographic rates comparable to those available for England, there is little doubt that population was also rising in the northern kingdom. By the mid-sixteenth century, new settlements were being founded and old ones divided to accommodate greater numbers. The cultivated area was being extended for the same reason. Yet we have no reason to suppose that at the turn of the sixteenth century Scotland had experienced an economic stimulus comparable to the expansion of the English cloth industry. This suggests that in Scotland population growth was occasioned by an 'autonomous' decline in the prevailing rates of mortality. On present evidence the same appears to have been largely true of England, though with the vitally important caveat that the stirrings of economic expansion in England contributed to a potential for growth which was greater than that elsewhere in Britain.

iii. *Prices and people*

After this lengthy demographic excursus, we can now return to the problem of the price rise and attempt a composite explanation of the whole process which takes account of both long-term and short-term influences upon price trends. To begin with long-term factors: it seems likely that there was indeed a gradual increase in the money supply in early-sixteenth-century England. New World silver, however, is unlikely to have made a significant impact before the 1540s. Any earlier increase in the quantity of silver coin in circulation is more likely to have originated in the silver mines which were developed in central Europe in the later fifteenth century, or in the coining of bullion previously hoarded as silver plate. The former may have entered England via the cloth trade. The latter may have been stimulated by the need to meet the requirements of a quickening internal trade. Any increase in the supply of money prior to the 1540s, however, is unlikely to have exerted a strong inflationary influence because the pre-existing coinage was in all likelihood inadequate to meet the needs of existing levels of economic activity. New silver was probably absorbed fairly easily in the monetarisation of some of the many transactions routinely conducted on credit and it seems improbable that there was a significant surplus of money. It is, however, possible that the quickening of economic activity increased the velocity of circulation of the existing coinage, thereby assisting prices to rise.

That quickening of activity derived from rising market demand for basic items of consumption, above all for foodstuffs. But it is unlikely that in the first instance this was the result of a growing national population pressing upon available food resources. As we have seen, there is no reason to suppose that the overall population was growing before the 1520s, yet prices were already edging upwards by that decade. The initial source of increased market demand may have lain less in population growth *per se* than in a shift in the distribution of the population between those households which were primarily self-provisioning and those which had greater occasion to purchase their needs in the market. In a society in which many households were essentially self-provisioning and a relatively small proportion of total agricultural production was marketed, market prices were determined by a limited number of purchasers exerting demand for a limited marketed surplus. Nevertheless, that limited number of purchasers must have been growing. The involvement of larger numbers of people in rural industries and the growing population density of the manufacturing districts, for example, may possibly have occasioned a shift in the distribution of the population between those who remained primarily self-provisioning and those who had both occasion and the capacity – as a result of their wages or other cash earnings – to buy. A larger population of consumers may therefore have been exerting demand in an economy – or rather a loosely linked collection of regional economies – with a limited capacity to respond quickly by increased production. In consequence prices began to edge upwards.

Population growth from the 1520s would have exacerbated this situation by creating an even larger market-dependent sector of the population pressing upon relatively inelastic resources. The price rise continued and accelerated. Moreover, rising prices for basic necessities had the effect of bringing about shifts in the structure of demand. The differentials observable in the upward course of grain prices – evident by the 1530s and increasingly marked by the 1550s – are probably attributable to hard-pressed consumers switching from more expensive to cheaper grains, causing the prices of the latter to rise more rapidly than the former. Dairy produce, meat and manufactured goods, which rose in price later or less severely, may have been subject to less intensive demand, or alternatively capable of expanding production more quickly. The emergence of these differentials may well be our best indicator of the point at which overall population growth became the principal force propelling the continued inflationary trend.

All this may help to explain the gradual long-term inflation of prices from the early decades of the sixteenth century and the distinctive characteristics of the price rise. At the same time, however, there were factors which operated to contain, or dampen down, inflationary forces. Some constraints were economic, notably the ability of consumers to buy. Prices cannot rise beyond the capacity of at least a sufficient number of consumers to continue purchasing. Others were institutional. Early-sixteenth-century England did not constitute a 'perfect market' governed by the untrammelled forces of supply and demand. Contemporaries remained attached to the notion of the 'just price'. Prices in the open markets were subject to the regulative authority of market officials. Both prices and wages were regulated by urban magistrates and the guilds. This was, in Cunningham's words, an economic world in which 'utility determined whether any exchange took place, but considerations of fairness regulated the terms of the exchange'. The role of short-term factors in the price rise may well have been that of periodically smashing through such constraints. Short-term causes such as the debasements of 1542–51, the heavy government expenditure of the 1540s or the harvest failures of 1549–51 and 1557 are the immediate explanation of the exceptional violence of the price rises of the 1540s and 1550s. They drove up prices to unprecedented levels. They also forced the upward adjustments in wages which were necessary if wage-earners were to be able to continue to subsist. And once such breakthroughs had taken place, prices seem never to have fallen back to their preceding levels. Rather, they settled at a plateau somewhat higher than before and then proceeded to rise again at a gentler pace. In this, short- and long-term factors met to shape the course of the price rise, the former fuelling its sudden spurts, the latter sustaining its upward trajectory.

In sum, it seems probable that in England monetary causes of inflation, though significant, were in the main less decisive than shifts in demand occasioned by a changing balance between producers and consumers within local economies, which was consolidated and advanced by population growth. But no single model of change is applicable to the whole of Britain. In Edinburgh and Stirling the prices of grain and ale roughly doubled between 1525 and 1550, much as was the case in London. Between the 1550s and the 1570s, however, they rose precipitately at a time when, after the crisis of the 1550s, the pace of inflation was slowing in England. By the early 1580s the price of oatmeal in Scottish urban markets had grown five-fold since the mid-1550s, an escalation of prices far worse than anything experienced in England. Inflation in Scotland may have been partly occasioned by the demand exerted by a rising population, yet very few of the Scottish population purchased their foodstuffs outside the towns. Nor is Scotland, with its limited overseas trade, likely to have witnessed a significant influx of Spanish silver. Rather, the peculiarly severe nature of Scotland's inflationary experience is attributable largely to the fact that its coinage was becoming the most drastically debased in Europe, as the monarchs of the period repeatedly reduced its silver content to meet their short-term needs.

In Scotland, then, the course and causes of the price rise were very different from those in England. Nevertheless, in the central decades of the sixteenth century both kingdoms were beset by population growth and by inflation. We must turn now to consideration of the consequences, to the complex of responses which led some contemporaries to see the commonwealth drowning in a rising tide of covetousness, its ideals and obligations submerged in the pursuit of what they termed 'commodity': material self-interest.

CHAPTER SIX

Commodity and commonwealth, c.1520–c.1580

That demographic growth and inflation were the principal underlying causes of economic change in sixteenth-century Britain seems beyond dispute. The outcome, however, was far from predictable. It depended upon the manner in which different individuals and groups sought to cope with, adjust to or take advantage of the changing contexts of their economic lives. This meant, in the first instance, shifts in the conduct of household economies and in the relationships within which they were embedded. The nature of those adjustments varied in accordance with the problems faced by specific social groups, the options perceivable by their members, and their differing capacities to advance or defend their interests within the prevailing structures of economic power. As might be expected in a predominantly rural society, both the pressures of the times and the opportunities which they afforded first became visible in the relationships of landlords and tenants.

i. Lands and rents

The household economies of landlords were only partially exposed to the threats posed by inflation. Most possessed home farms for the supply of the immediate needs of their households. Moreover, as large-scale producers – or, in Scotland, as the recipients of rents paid in kind – they could benefit from the sale of substantial marketable surpluses at rising prices. Indeed in Scotland the principal influence of inflation upon landlord–tenant relations was probably to encourage the continued taking of rents in kind and to inhibit their conversion to money. Most English and Welsh landlords, however, already derived the bulk of their income from rents paid in cash by their tenants. They depended upon that income to sustain the more expansive patterns of consumption which were the visible sign of the status of their families. As prices rose, slowly eroding their purchasing power, they came under pressure to adopt different policies. And their main problem in doing so was the legacy of the relatively generous tenancies which had been granted in the very different conditions of the late fifteenth and very early sixteenth centuries. At worst, the fines and rents which could be expected from their tenants had become fixed. At best, the tenancies conceded tended to be relatively inflexible, granted for long periods and subject to customs highly favourable to the tenants.

This situation bred a variety of responses. Some sought to expand their direct farming and to engage in the supply of increasingly profitable markets. The Lestranges of Hunstanton, for example, were typical of many Norfolk and Suffolk landlords in resuming the direct use of some pasture formerly let to tenants, and exploiting more vigorously their right to graze sheep over their tenants' fields after harvest (the 'fold-course'), thus achieving a larger wool clip for sale to the clothing districts. They also became involved in cattle fattening for urban markets and engaged directly in the coastal grain trade, maintaining a small ship for that purpose. Such enterprising landlords could learn, as Sir Thomas Wilson later put it, 'to become good husbands' of those parts of their estates kept 'in hand'. But all landlords also needed to address the problem of how to maintain the value of their income from tenanted lands.

Several possible courses of action were open to them. One was to revise the terms of leasehold tenancies when they fell in for renewal, raising fines and rents and shortening the lengths of leases to facilitate their more frequent adjustment thereafter. The major obstacle to the implementation of such a policy was that leases might take decades, even generations, to fall in. A ninety-nine-year lease granted in 1470 was not capable of improvement before 1569. A lease for three lives might fall in quickly, or it might last for half a century. Another expedient was the raising of the rents of tenants-at-will. This could easily be achieved in Scotland, where by the 1540s there were complaints of significant increases in rents either in money or in kind, and of the abrogation of the legally unprotected rights of 'kindly' tenants. In England, however, tenants-at-will were a small minority.

Much more difficult was the problem posed by customary land held by copyhold tenure. As we have seen, copyhold tenants held their land on a bewildering variety of terms and were protected by the prevailing manorial custom, which could greatly inhibit the lord of the manor's freedom of action. Prior to the 1570s, the efforts of landlords appear to have been focused upon the improvement of their income from copyhold land by the raising of the fines payable on the granting or renewal of tenancies. These generally constituted a bigger component of the annual revenue of a manor than the small rents paid for copyholds, and they could be enhanced in several ways. In the case of 'copyholds of inheritance', fines were required in law to be 'reasonable' in the specific sense of not being set at a rate which would defeat the custom of inheritance by being beyond the heir's capacity to pay. But they could be edged up gradually. If fines had become fixed in the recent past, a lord might challenge the validity of the prevailing custom by using the court rolls of the manor to demonstrate that it had not existed 'time out of mind of man'. If fines were neither fixed nor limited by the custom of inheritance, lords had a freer hand: they could grant holdings to whomsoever they pleased in return for the best fines they could get. And where possible, of course, enhanced levels of fines could be accompanied by increases in the annual rents.

Some landlords went still further and attempted to transform the structures of tenure on their estates by converting customary tenures into more flexible forms of leasehold. Copyholds falling vacant could be taken into the lord's hand and relet as leasehold. They could be bought up. Copyholders could be tempted to accept leases by offering them initially favourable terms, or pressured into relinquishing their holdings by demands for exceptionally high fines. As a result a good deal of land passed from the customary to the leasehold sector, as on the Earl of Northumberland's estates in west Yorkshire where a strategy of conversion was successfully pursued between 1536 and 1570.

In the central decades of the sixteenth century many lords and their stewards engaged in efforts to enhance their estate incomes by any or all of these means. In Cheshunt, Hertfordshire, leasehold rents grew sharply from the 1540s. On the estates of the Bishop of Worcester copyhold fines were rising from the 1530s. On the Herbert estates in Wiltshire they doubled on new takings between 1500 and 1550, and on a sample of East Anglian manors a similar increase occurred between 1540 and 1578. The annual rental value of the Bures estate in Essex crept upwards from around £170 in the 1530s to £200 in 1547 and £225 in 1560.

For the most part the process of change was gradual and uneven. Landlords proceeded piecemeal, revising the terms of individual tenancies as and when an opportunity presented itself. Predictably, the fines and rents paid for new tenancies led the way. Average rents lagged well behind, restrained by the various forms of protection sheltering existing tenants and their heirs. Some lords also conducted themselves with discretion, in a manner reflecting their own respect for custom and the canons of 'good lordship'. Sir Nicholas Bacon contented himself with modest improvements in the terms of leases granted on his Norfolk and Suffolk manors, and exerted only moderate pressure to obtain higher fines and rents. Others had fewer inhibitions, like Sir John Yorke, who more than doubled the rents of his tenants at Whitby in the 1540s, by 'extort power and might and by great and sore threatenings of the said tenants'. But, whatever its pace and manner, the trend in rents was upward. It was continuous and cumulative. And, as it proceeded, what may have begun as a defensive strategy among landlords anxious to secure their own real incomes could become in the hands of some a more aggressive determination to carve for themselves a bigger share of the income to be derived from the land.

All this was rendered possible by the fact that with a rising rural population land was in demand to an extent scarcely known since the earlier fourteenth century. As larger generations came to adulthood, the tenant shortage characteristic of the fifteenth century was emphatically reversed – the more swiftly because the intervening process of differentiation in holding size rendered the absorption of increased numbers more difficult. Untenanted land was now rapidly taken up. Squatters nibbled at the extensive tracts of waste land in areas of fell and forest, as in the Forest of Inglewood in Cumbria where a survey of 1578 detailed 178 such illegal encroachments. Tightening local land markets also affected family strategies. At Hanbury in Worcestershire, where in 1480–99 only 13 per cent of manorial land transfers had taken place within the family, the comparable figure for the years 1520–40 was 70 per cent – a shift also observable in manors throughout East Anglia. Families were becoming more cautious about parting with the land they held. Some responded to the need to provide for larger numbers of surviving sons by dividing their holdings among them. But this was a perilous strategy now that land was less available. It made sense only where the presence of rural industries or generous common rights provided additional means of generating income and resources – as in Rossendale, Lancashire, an upland area involved in woollen manufacturing, where many copyholds were so divided. More generally, successful tenants became reluctant to shed land which they had accumulated, beyond the hiving off to younger children of small parcels acquired specifically for that purpose. They provided for their younger children in cash or goods. Core holdings increasingly remained intact, with the result that in most areas the numbers of tenants on the land did not rise as the population grew. Inevitably, this meant that the population of largely or wholly landless people increased.

These gradually changing circumstances also help to explain a shift in

attitudes towards enclosure in the early sixteenth century. As we have
seen, early enclosure had been primarily a response of landlords to the
problem of tenanting their lands in a period of demographic contraction. It aroused relatively little controversy and occasioned the concern
of government only insofar as the 'decay of tillage' was deemed to have
fiscal and military implications, or to have been conducted in an oppressive manner. Cardinal Wolsey's great enquiry of 1517–18 into the extent
of enclosure since 1488 was principally motivated by such concerns, and
was not intended to restrain all forms of enclosure. 'Where a man doth
enclose and take in his own proper ground where no man hath
commons', enclosure was deemed not only permissible, but also 'beneficial to the common wealth'. Prosecutions were to be made only 'where
any man has taken away and enclosed any other man's grounds, or hath
pulled down houses of husbandry and converted land from tillage to
pasture'.

By the 1520s this early enclosure movement was largely over. Various
estimates suggest that in the course of the sixteenth century no more
than 2 to 3 per cent of the cultivable area of England was subject to enclosure. In some particular areas the proportion of land enclosed was
higher, but as a general phenomenon 'depopulating enclosure' had faded
with the circumstances which had originally occasioned it. Moreover,
where enclosure still occurred, it tended to be of a somewhat different
nature. In the midland counties, some landlords still enclosed in response
to the continuing demand for wool and meat, often enclosing their own
demesne lands. But after 1520 most sixteenth-century enclosure involved
neither conversion of tillage to pasture nor encroachment upon the open
fields. Rather, it was directed at the taking in and enclosing of areas of
waste and common, as for example in the uplands of Yorkshire and
Lancashire. It was often conducted piecemeal, and not infrequently by
agreement with the tenants of the manors concerned.

Paradoxically, however, it was in the second quarter of the sixteenth
century that enclosure emerged as the most rancorous source of
grievance on the land, and enclosers were demonised as enemies of the
commonwealth. Fewer small tenancies were available to would-be
husbandmen. Yet they could see around them the physical evidence
of former plough land, with its distinctive ridge and furrow patterns,
now given over to graze sheep. Common rights were now more vital
than ever to the viability of household economies. Yet they were diminished as tracts were taken in, enclosed and given over to exclusive use
in 'severalty'. The conversion of demesne farms to pasture reduced
employment opportunities for the cottager and the landless. Such cir-

cumstances gave enclosure a new meaning and a highly charged symbolic significance.

> Gret men makithe now a dayes
> A shepecote in the Church
> Commons to close and kepe
> Poor folk for bread to cry and weepe
> Towns pulled down to pastur shepe
> Thys ys the newe gyse

So ran the *Ballad of Nowadays*. It was rarely literally true, but it presented a powerful image of change on the land.

By 1550 the 'new guise' lamented by the balladeer included not only enclosures, but also increases in fines and rents and threats to prevailing forms of tenure. In part it was a story of landlords acting, under the pressure of inflation and in response to the opportunities created by demographic growth and land-hunger, to reverse the balance of power established in the late middle ages between those who owned the land and those who farmed it. The policies of landlords, however, were only the most visible part of a more complex process of change in rural society, one in which yeomen and husbandmen also played their part.

ii. *Yeomen and husbandmen*

As we have seen, the situation of tenants varied enormously in terms of the size of their holdings, the security of their tenancies and the terms on which they held them. Their experience was far from uniform, and they were neither helpless in the face of their landlords' initiatives nor passive in response to the economic trends of the time.

Initially at least, and sometimes for decades or even generations, many were relatively sheltered from the consequences of the inflationary trend. They produced much of their own food and household needs. Their tenures and customs often protected them from rent rises for considerable periods of time. The rising costs of what they were obliged to buy in the market (metal wares, for example, or cloth) were for many more than compensated for by a more rapidly rising income from what they had to sell (notably grain and livestock). Indeed, for many the early years of the price rise may have brought rising cash incomes. It was certainly so for the tenants of Kibworth Harcourt, Leicestershire. There the absentee landlord's complaisance allowed rents to remain stable throughout the early sixteenth century. Assuming that agricultural yields also remained stable, Dr Howell calculates that the rising local prices for produce would have meant that between the 1480s and the 1550s the net income of a husbandman holding twelve acres of land would have risen by around nineteen shillings a year, and that yielded by a twenty-four-acre holding by some sixty-two shillings a year. For such people the margin above subsistence was expanding, and the surplus income could be utilised in whatever manner they chose.

If this was the case for most tenants in some fortunate areas, then some could do even better, notably the substantial yeomen, who were already more commercially oriented than their neighbours. They too enjoyed the protection of self-provisioning and of established tenancies on terms which changed slowly if at all. Many also held freehold land immune from any landlord's policies. Their larger holdings gave them the added advantage of potential economies of scale, the lower production costs per acre which translated into higher profits per acre. And though they also needed to employ more labour, population growth meant that the shortage of readily available labour that had inhibited some commercial farmers in the past was gradually being reversed. They were therefore in an excellent position to reap the benefits of dealing in bulk in both local and more distant markets. Indeed, some used their commercial experience and favourable locations to extend their activities from simply producing for the market to engaging as middlemen in the supply of urban markets. The farmers of the Liberty of Havering provide a telling example. They owed only small annual rents to the crown and their renewal fines were fixed by custom at one year's rent. They were there-fore able to enjoy virtually the entire profits of their husbandry. And they had ample opportunity to do so in a highly commercialised area of south-west Essex which was heavily engaged in supplying London via the important marketing centre of Romford.

All this considered, the well-documented trend among substantial farmers towards retaining accumulated holdings intact, and the gener-ally growing determination of tenants to keep land in the family where possible, can be seen as involving more than just defensive caution in a period of developing land hunger. It could also reflect the fact that the powerful combination of population growth, increasing demand for agri-cultural produce and rising prices was creating a novel degree of com-mercial opportunity. The possession of land had always been the basic guarantee of a household's subsistence. Now it also provided expanding opportunities to enhance a household's income, living standards and status. Taken together, these were powerful incentives not only to retain land-holdings, but also, if possible, to expand them.

These are relatively neglected dimensions of the situation of the English peasantry in the early to mid-sixteenth century – which is more commonly described in terms of a defensive struggle against mounting seigneurial demands. But they deserve close consideration. For it is entirely possible that for a considerable time there was a significant redistribution of a rising national income towards agricultural producers at the expense of both market-dependent consumers and rentier landlords who had to struggle to find ways of expanding their own share of the profits to be made in agriculture.

This situation would begin to change only as and when landlords were able to edge upwards the fines and rents paid by their tenants. At that point the surplus income of the tenant would begin to be eroded – as was exemplified in 1549 when Hugh Latimer compared the expansive lifestyle of his yeoman father, who had paid a rent of three to four pounds, with the more constrained situation of his successor on a rent of sixteen pounds a year. Such a shift might place tenants in difficulty – the familiar picture of the peasant scraped to the bone by a grasping landlord. But it is equally likely that it exerted pressure on tenant households to engage more fully in production for the market, focusing upon whatever found the readiest sale in a particular locality in order to expand the cash incomes necessary to pay higher rents. In short, it could stimulate a rearticulation of household economies towards an enhanced commercial involvement. This might necessitate risk, but it was a risk that many husbandman households were gradually constrained to face.

Larger farmers, whose household economies were already more commercially oriented, were probably for the most part well able to afford higher rents for their land without any serious threat to their prosperity – though this, of course, did not prevent them from resenting and resisting such encroachments on their surplus income. Many of them were also more than willing to expand the scale of their activities when the chance arose. Their competition for the tenancy of more land was certainly one of the reasons why the price of small parcels of land rose in the inter-tenant land market of many manors – at Hevingham, Norfolk, it quadrupled between the 1530s and the 1580s. And doubtless it also made a substantial contribution to the ability of landlords to achieve higher rents when holdings fell vacant or tenancies were renewed. William Harrison observed in 1577 that farmers were well advised to apply early for renewal of their leases 'sith it is now growen almost to a custome that if he come not to his lord so long before, another shall step in for a reversion'. As a result, the differentiation of the tenant population which had begun in the fifteenth century was both consolidated and advanced. The large proto-capitalist farmer was becoming even more a feature of the English social landscape by the 1560s than had been the case half a century earlier.

All this helps to explain the evidence of rising domestic living standards among yeoman and husbandman households in the second and third quarters of the sixteenth century. Looking back in the 1570s, William Harrison asked the old men of his Essex parish what had most changed in their day. They pointed to three things 'marvellouslie altered': 'the multitude of chimnies latelie erected', to secure a smoke-free domestic environment; 'the great amendment of lodging', by which they meant the acquisition of superior bedding; and 'the exchange of vessell' from wood and horn eating utensils to pewter. A decade later, in revising his *Description of England*, the scrupulous Harrison added that these improvements were not universal and that his informants also noted certain 'verie grievous' things 'too too much increased' – notably 'the inhansing of rents' and 'the dailie oppression of copiholders' by increased fines. But he still held that they extended at least to 'artificers and many farmers' in the south of England. And he retained the view that, despite the fact that 'all things are growen to most excessive prices', farmers were able to enjoy such novel comforts while still having 'six or seven yeares rent lieng by . . . therewith to purchase a new lease' (though he added in 1587 that such prosperity was achieved 'by vertue of their old and not of their new leases').

The testimony of Harrison and his parishioners is amply confirmed by the documentary and archaeological evidence of improved rural housing – the first phase of what W. G. Hoskins called 'the great rebuilding of rural England' – and by the analysis of inventories of domestic goods. This period did indeed witness a marked increase in both the quantity and quality of domestic goods listed in the inventories of yeomen and husbandmen: bedsteads, joined tables, cupboards and chairs, pots and pans, as well as the feather beds, sheets, pillows and shows of pewter which so impressed Harrison's greybeards. The very fact that inventories themselves multiply in the probate records from the 1530s onwards may in itself be indicative of the elaboration of domestic possessions. The tenant prosperity which they catalogue must have contributed to the general vitality of local economies, providing custom for local craftsmen, urban artificers and tradesmen, and the inhabitants of the manufacturing districts. It was all part of the general economic quickening of the age.

The period between the 1530s and the 1570s, then, witnessed a developing tension and instability in the relationships of landlords and tenants, fraught with actual or potential conflicts of interest. Yet for both groups it could also be a period of expanding economic opportunity, reflected in an enhanced material prosperity which, if not general, was at least widely shared. This paints a somewhat less pessimistic picture of change in rural society during much of the sixteenth century than is usual: an alternative perspective on the nature and consequences of the initial response to inflation and demographic growth. But of course it was not all buoyancy; no process of economic and social change ever is. There were those groups in society for whom the economic experience of the second and third quarters of the sixteenth century was emphatically one of loss. Most prominent among them was the church.

iii. *The disendowment of the church*

Between the 1530s and 1560s the medieval church in Britain was to a large extent disendowed – in England and Wales by the dissolution of the monasteries and chantries, and in Scotland by the 'feuing' movement. This immense economic change was not in itself a direct consequence of inflationary or demographic pressure. Its immediate causes lay in the religious and political turmoil of the Reformation era. But it was certainly related to the financial needs of the English and Scottish crowns, and it sharply illustrates the acquisitive ambition unleashed in those best placed to exploit the contingencies of the times.

The 1540s have been called 'the predatory phase of Tudor financial policy'. In that decade, it has been estimated, the governments of Henry VIII and the young Edward VI enjoyed a 'fiscal capacity' which was not to be matched again until the 1650s, and took a larger proportion of national income than was to be the case until the 1690s. This revenue was required above all for war, the increasingly expensive sport of kings. And it was achieved in the main by two 'non-sustainable expedients'. One, as we have seen, was the debasement of the coinage. The other was the seizure and disposal of church property.

Prior to the Henrician Reformation of the 1530s, the church in England and Wales possessed massive landed endowments. In 1535, for example, between a quarter and a third of the land area of Essex, and over two-fifths of the landed income of the West Riding of Yorkshire, belonged to the church. In 1536 and 1539–40, some 60 per cent of this church land was transferred to the crown by the dissolution of first the lesser and then the greater monasteries of the kingdom. This prodigious seizure of property was ostensibly justified by monastic corruption and the reforming intentions of Henry VIII as Supreme Head of the newly established Church of England. In 1545 and 1547, it was supplemented by the dissolution of a further range of religious foundations, notably the chantries and religious guilds endowed with smaller properties to celebrate masses for their founders' souls, a practice no longer deemed theologically justified in a more doctrinally Protestant church.

The dissolution was probably initially intended to provide a vast and permanent enhancement of the crown estate. The pressing needs of royal expenditure in the 1540s, however, meant that much of the confiscated property was rapidly transferred to third parties. By Henry VIII's death in 1547, around two-thirds of the monastic land had been disposed of, and still more was to follow before the accession of Mary I in 1553 brought England's temporary reconciliation to the Roman Church. Some was distributed in the form of gifts, or granted on highly advantageous terms to influential political figures. But by far the greater part was sold, usually at the prevailing market rate of 'twenty years' purchase' (that is, twenty times the annual rental value). As a result the land market was galvanised throughout the kingdom. Prior to the dissolution it had been rare for whole manors to become available for purchase. Most aristocratic and gentry estates were safeguarded by entails, and were transferred only by inheritance or marriage. Monastic lands had previously been inalienable, but they had frequently been administered by or leased to laymen and in every locality such men knew the pickings to be had. Now they were up for grabs and the result was something of a feeding frenzy among potential purchasers which was especially vigorous in the 1540s. In Essex alone, more than 200 manors changed hands between 1536 and 1560, some of them frequently.

The sheer scale of the bonanza was such that the demand for land among those able to raise the capital to buy appears not to have exceeded supply. Those known to have bought, however, provide something of a rollcall of the principal beneficiaries of economic change in mid-Tudor England and Wales. Most were the heads of established landowning families, usually gentlemen anxious to seize the opportunity to extend their existing estates, and sometimes to rationalise them by selling outlying properties to finance the purchase of monastic land nearer their seats. Sir Thomas Tresham pursued such a policy to consolidate his estate at Rushton, Northamptonshire, purchasing both monastic and chantry land, despite his own continued allegiance to the old faith. Some were younger sons of gentry families who established cadet branches of their lines.

A significant minority, however, were 'new men' in landed society. They were most numerous within the hinterlands of major cities or where industry was well established. Merchants from Lynn and Norwich bought in Norfolk, rich clothiers in Suffolk and west Yorkshire. London wealth was particularly prominent among purchasers in Essex and Hertfordshire. Nicholas Bacon provides an outstanding example. A son of the sheep-reeve of Bury St Edmunds Abbey, he rose to prominence as a successful lawyer and crown officer. In 1540–8 and 1560–2, he spent 10,000 pounds on church property and died in 1578 a knight and the founder of a landed family in his native region. At the other end of the spectrum of purchasers were prosperous yeoman farmers. Many simply bought their own farms. Some crowned careers of piecemeal accumulation with acquisitions which secured a place among the lesser gentry of their counties.

The upheaval was not confined to the countryside. Many religious houses were located in urban centres and had formerly controlled a vast amount of urban property. Those of York, for example, had owned more than 400 houses within the city. Chantries, religious guilds, hospitals and almshouses were also particularly common in the towns. Some struggling urban economies were hard hit by the loss of the custom generated by their abbeys. Many urban authorities were further alarmed by the transfer of property occasioned by the dissolution – above all when it enhanced the influence of purchasers among the local gentry – and by the threatened loss of charitable institutions. They were particularly resentful of the seizure of the assets of religious guilds which were generally administered by their lay members and regarded as the property of the community.

One response to the threat of confiscation was the pre-emptive seizure of guild and chantry property, as in Boston, Lincolnshire, in 1545 and in Carmarthen in 1546. At Walsall both the lands of the Guild of St John (worth £100 per annum) and the Guildhall were concealed from the crown's commissioners and quietly appropriated by the town. In the longer term many civic authorities undertook and doggedly pursued a strategy of acquiring former ecclesiastical property from its original purchasers. This might be done through the agency of individual townsmen, by the creation of self-perpetuating bodies of 'feoffees' empowered to hold particular properties in trust, or by the acquisition from the crown (for a price) of charters of incorporation which rendered the civic body capable of holding property in its own right. (The circumstances created by the dissolution were a principal reason for the wave of new incorporations which took place in England and Wales in the generations after 1540.) As a result, a substantial amount of former church property gradually came into the hands of urban authorities, enabling them to re-endow charitable institutions and substantially boosting the revenues which they were able to raise and disburse for civic purposes.

The cumulative effect of the whole process was the greatest transfer of property in England and Wales since the aftermath of the Norman Conquest. The most obvious consequence of this cataclysm was a spectacular increase in both the numbers and the collective wealth of the gentry. In Norfolk, gentry families held half the county's manors in 1530, three-quarters in 1565. In Essex the nobility's share of manorial properties rose from 12 to 17 per cent over the same period, the gentry's from 52 to 70 per cent. And in both counties, as elsewhere, there was a significant expansion in the numbers of families claiming gentle status. Less immediately apparent, but of no less significance in the long term, was the massive reduction of the economic role and influence of the church. Vast resources had passed into the full control of the laity. Henceforward the management of most of those resources, and the deployment of the income derived from them, would be subject to the priorities not of ecclesiastical institutions but of propertied households.

Much the same might be said of the comparable transfer of church land into lay proprietorship in Scotland. This, however, was achieved not by single acts of confiscation, but by the more gradual process of the 'feuing' movement. Feuing involved the purchase by the tenants of church lands of a 'feu ferme': an hereditary tenure. It was not an alienation as such, for the alienation of church land was forbidden in canon law. The feuar paid a substantial down payment for the security of a feu ferme and an annual 'feu duty' which was, initially at least, an economic rent. It was the rapid Scottish inflation of the third quarter of the sixteenth century that rendered the feu duty negligible and the feu ferme, in effect, a freehold tenure.

Feuing had been known since the twelfth century as a means of raising capital from church estates. It became more common in the late fifteenth and early sixteenth centuries: seventy-six feu charters are known to have been granted in the period 1500–36. Between the 1530s and the 1570s, however, the trickle of feu charters became a flood. Some 2,800 are known to have been granted, with the peak of activity falling in the 1560s. The causes of the escalation of feuing lay in the exceptional financial pressures placed upon the church in the central decades of the sixteenth century. Royal taxation of the church was heavy under James V and the regent Mary of Guise. Capital was also needed to repair the devastation wrought by English armies in the 1540s. By the 1560s the triumph of the Scottish Reformation led many abbots, or the lay 'commendators' who often administered church estates, to engage in feuing as a means of anticipating eventual confiscation under a Protestant regime, some of them feuing to their own kin, or pocketing the revenues raised. But, whatever the immediate motivation, by 1570 many abbeys had feued most of their land, and much of the best farmland in Scotland had passed irrevocably into lay control.

As in the case of the dissolution, the beneficiaries of the feuing movement were socially varied, but in Scotland their social composition was more broadly based. Feuars included noblemen (3 per cent) and lairds (29 per cent) bent on extending their estates or establishing cadet branches. They included members of the professions (3 per cent) and burgesses of the towns (8 per cent) setting themselves up on the land. But a very high proportion (at least 44 per cent) were of lower social standing. Many were sitting tenants of the lands they feued, with the result that some townships were transformed by feuing into communities of owner-occupiers. Others used their feu charters to create a single heritable unit out of several tacks which they already held and thereby transformed themselves into petty lairds. Still others took feus over the heads of existing tenants, with the same end in view. Thomas Niven was a joint tenant of Monkredding, Ayrshire, prior to 1540. He subsequently took a feu of the whole township. By 1560 the other tenants were *his* tenants and the elevation of his family was under way. The process varied, but the overall outcome is not in question. The disendowment of the church in Scotland, as in England and Wales, both consolidated the existing landlord class and expanded the numbers of lay proprietors, enhancing the economic power of those with both the means and the will to seize the day, and strengthening their capacity to reap the benefits of economic change.

iv. *Wages and poverty*

The economic stripping of the church was both catastrophic and highly visible. Other victims of economic change were less immediately obvious and the deterioration of their fortunes proceeded slowly and insidiously, but they were increasingly numerous as the century advanced. Among them were those husbandmen in England and Wales who were unable to meet demands for increased fines and rents and were forced to relinquish their holdings; Scottish tenants facing higher rents or threatened with eviction when feus were taken over their heads; or the many would-be husbandmen among the young who were no longer able to secure an initial toehold on the land in the face of rising fines and competition from those able to outbid them for available holdings.

Most numerous of all, however, was that growing body of people in both town and countryside whose living derived wholly or principally from wage-earning.

In their *Population History of England*, Wrigley and Schofield established the existence of a striking relationship between population growth and the purchasing power of wages in early modern England. If population grew at a rate of more than 0.5 per cent per annum, real wages fell. The reasons for this phenomenon are clear. When population growth exceeded this level, the supply of the basic necessities of life could not be expanded sufficiently rapidly to meet increased demand. Prices rose. At the same time, there was too little demand for the growing supply of labour to ensure that wages kept pace with rising prices. Real wages fell. As we have seen, the English population was growing at a rate of 0.6 per cent per annum from at least the 1540s, and at a substantially higher rate in the 1560s and 1570s, and there is much evidence to support Wrigley and Schofield's assessment of the consequences.

Despite rising prices, wage rates rose only slowly. Employers appear to have experienced no difficulty in securing labour at customary rates of pay, and the statutory wage maxima established in England in 1495 and 1514 – at a time of relative labour shortage – were long observed. Wage rates rose significantly only after the drastic price inflation of the 1540s and 1550s and even then they lagged behind prices. Agricultural wage rates in southern England rose by two-thirds between the periods 1490–1509 and 1550–69. But they did so only after 1550. Meanwhile average grain prices had trebled. The real wages of building craftsmen in the towns of southern England fell by almost 40 per cent between the 1500s and the 1540s, and by close to 50 per cent by the 1550s. They recovered only modestly in the 1560s and 1570s to something like two-thirds their previous level. In the cities of Scotland, meanwhile, real wages also pursued a downward course, though one which cannot be measured with comparable precision for this period.

The shocking nature of these figures make it important not to exaggerate either the extent or the consequences of the decline. Where demand for labour was more buoyant, real wages held up better. Among skilled and semi-skilled workers in London, for example, they fell by only 25–30 per cent between the 1500s and the 1550s, and after the drastic mortalities of the late 1550s and early 1560s had recovered to 80 per cent or more of their earlier value by the 1570s. Again, wages were well above subsistence level in 1500. They had some way to fall before misery ensued, and the fact that prices continued to rise suggests that most wage-earners retained the capacity to buy the basics of existence. Even in the 1540s, a building craftsman in Hull could earn enough to feed himself, a wife and three children if he obtained 164 days' work a year. The comparable figure for a labourer was 246 days – a much more difficult proposition – but allowance should be made also for the probable earnings of wives and older children. As for agricultural labourers and workers in rural industries, many had cottage holdings and access to common rights which meant that they were not wholly dependent upon the purchasing power of their wages. And in town and country alike, falling real wages might be compensated for by working more days or longer hours.

Nevertheless, it would be perverse to minimise the effects of declining real wages. That London journeymen of the 1570s earned real wages *only* a fifth lower than those of their grandfathers was scarcely a cause for celebration among those concerned. That Hull building workers who enjoyed regular employment, never fell sick, lived soberly and had industrious wives and children could just about feed their families is comforting. But families needed housing, clothes and fuel as well as bread. Employment was frequently intermittent. Working longer and harder was more an option for the independent craftsman than for the labourer. And over-stocked labour markets could mean that work was less available for women and children as well as for men. Nor were common rights a universal safety net in the countryside. On some manors they extended to all inhabitants. On others they belonged to tenants only and were denied to the growing numbers of the landless. In areas of enclosure they were severely attenuated.

Despite all qualifications, these were hard times. And the evidence that consumers were trading downwards in terms of foodstuffs provides ample confirmation of the scraping existence endured by labouring people. William Harrison, the celebrant of enhanced domestic living standards among farm tenants, also observed that the price of the staple foodstuffs of the 'inferior sort' of people was 'never so deare as in my time'. Rye and barley was often beyond the reach of 'the artificer and poore labouring man'. In times of dearth such people ate peas, beans, oats – 'for hunger setteth his foot first into the horse manger' – and even acorns. 'I will not saie that this extremitie is oft so well to be observed in time of plentie as of dearth,' he added, 'but if I should, I could easilie bring my triall.'

This deterioration of dietary standards among the 'inferior sort' was indicative of the emergence of poverty on a new scale. Poverty, of course, was in itself no novelty. But widespread poverty in the sense of the inability of householders to sustain an independent living at a level of material well-being deemed decent by the standards of the day had not been a major source of concern in the fifteenth and early sixteenth

centuries. The poor had been for the most part victims of individual misfortune or of crises in the domestic life-cycle – the aged, propertyless
widows, orphans, the sick and the maimed – rather than members of a
large and permanent class. They were relatively few in number and their
needs were provided for by their kin, by neighbourly charity and by the
alms dispensed by monasteries and religious fraternities or from the
parish 'poor man's box'.

As the sixteenth century advanced, however, there was a growing
awareness that the problem of poverty was changing in both its scale
and its nature. On the one hand, those deemed by contemporaries to be
poor 'by impotencie', or 'by casualtie' – the deserving poor – were
increasing in their numbers. Estimates based on surveys of London
parishes suggest that, whereas in 1518 around 6 per cent of the city's
inhabitants fell into these categories, by 1552 the proportion had grown
to almost 11 per cent of a significantly larger population. On the other
hand, poverty was also increasingly apparent in what seemed to be two
disturbingly novel forms.

The most visible and alarming symptom of change was the growth of
vagrancy. To contemporaries the streets of the towns and the highways
which linked them seemed littered with 'rogues and vagabonds', 'masterless men' and 'wanderers': able-bodied, often young, idle, rootless and
outside the disciplines of household and community. Some were on the
tramp in search of work, like the man who told Montgomeryshire magistrates in 1568 that he 'dwells nowhere nor has no abiding but there as
he may have work'. Others led an entirely marginal existence, like the
woman taken in Cheshire in 1574, who confessed that 'she has used the
art of begging from her cradle'. Whatever sympathy or kindness they
might encounter on an individual level, they were collectively denigrated
as the 'thriftless poore', and conventionally associated with filth, disease,
crime and sedition. It was no accident that in Tudor translations of the
New Testament the phrase chosen to describe the street idlers who
mobbed St Paul in Thessalonica (Acts 17:5) was 'evyll men which were
vagabondes'.

Less obvious and less remarked upon, but far more numerous, were
those 'poor labouring people' who worked, but whose domestic
economies were ones of constant makeshifts and expedients, fraught
with the perennial risk of tumbling into severe poverty in the event of
any misfortune. The fragility of their livings was sharply revealed in any
year of harvest crisis or trading slump. In Worcester, a city of around
4,000 inhabitants, a normal year like 1563 saw eighty-eight 'impotent
poor' receiving relief from the city, most of them aged people living
alone. In the dearth of 1556–7 a municipal survey listed 761 persons –

close to a fifth of the city's population – deemed unable to subsist without relief, and almost two-thirds of them were married couples with children. Such 'crisis poverty' was of course exceptional. Usually the labouring poor scraped by, little observed, but they constituted a large and growing background presence in local society. They were most numerous in the towns, where the wholly wage-dependent population was most concentrated, and in those areas of rural industry where the workforce was effectively proletarianised. But they were present also in agricultural parishes, characterised by Harrison as 'not often above fortie or fiftie households . . . whereof the greater part nevertlelesse are verie poore folkes, oftentimes without all maner of occupieng, sith the ground of the parish is gotten up into a few men's hands . . . whereby the rest are compelled either to be hired servants unto the other, or else to beg their bread in miserie from doore to doore'.

The growth of poverty was the most telling evidence of the conse-quences of demographic and economic change: greater numbers; more children and elderly people to be supported; more young adults who could not permanently achieve an independent living; growing landless-ness; a larger proportion of the population dependent on the vicissitudes of wage-labour. The poor were more numerous, more visible, in some respects more threatening to the 'better sort' of inhabitants. They were the living evidence of changing times, and, in a society in which the living standards of many were improving, their exclusion was a standing reproach.

v. *Protest and resistance*

By the 1540s, contemporaries were acutely aware of the symptoms of eco-nomic change, but it was not easy for them to comprehend the nature of the dynamic in which they were embroiled. They had no clear knowledge of the actual extent of change. Nor did they possess the analytical tools for the conceptualisation of economic change in itself. Their perception was shaped by the inherited categories of medieval moral philosophy, in which economic behaviour was treated not as a phenomenon to be analysed in its own terms, but rather as a branch of personal and social morality – the morality expressed in the ideal of commonwealth.

Such ideals not only persisted, they were also passionately re-emphasised and widely disseminated in a powerful literature of moral complaint. In Scotland its authors included the satirists Sir David Lynde-say and Sir Richard Maitland. In Wales vernacular bards depicted a harsh and acquisitive society in which, in Glanmor Williams' words, 'gain had become the mainspring of human existence'. In England, protest reached its apogee in the works of the Protestant moralists patronised by Protector Somerset in the early years of the reign of Edward VI – men like Henry Brinkelow, Robert Crowley, Thomas Becon, John Hales and Hugh Latimer, known collectively as the 'commonwealthsmen'.

To the commonwealthsmen, most of whom were clerics, the Reformation represented not simply the jurisdictional independence of the Church of England from Rome, or doctrinal change, but a spiritual awakening which demanded the remoralising of social relationships. They espoused the ideal of a Christian commonwealth, governed by distributive justice, in which the members of each estate should enjoy an appropriate share in return for performing their duties according to their degree. Yet they saw all around them the evidence of the corruption of social and economic relationships by the sin of covetousness, the 'insatiable thurst of gredynes of men', the pursuit of 'commodity' by 'such as passe more on the world then god, more on ther pryvat profett then on the common welthe'.

Whether the period was indeed witnessing a novel outpouring of ruthless economic individualism is hardly a matter that can be determined with certainty. Self-interested economic behaviour was scarcely an innovation of the sixteenth century, and its less scrupulous manifestations had been the object of moralistic condemnation since time immemorial. The commonwealthsmen were certainly mistaken when they imagined an earlier golden age of harmony and social responsibility unblemished by such practices. Yet, despite their rhetorical excess, they were perhaps right to detect a shift of standards in economic life and an erosion of constraints on the manner of its conduct. Neither established economic relationships nor the values informing them were simply swept away by a tidal wave of greed. But there is evidence enough of how the pressures and the opportunities of the times could combine to bring about a rearticulation of both. Expediency could encourage a hardening of the notion of individual property rights and place greater emphasis upon the necessity of enhancing income. Deeper involvement in commercial markets could increase the willingness to take risks and to pursue advantages. The prospect of personal and familial betterment could stimulate the appetite for gain. Both shifts of conduct and the unease it bred among those who bent with the prevailing winds are strongly implied in the defensiveness with which they allegedly justified themselves by twisting to their purpose the scriptural warrant that it was lawful 'for every man to use his owne as hym lysteth', or 'do as he will with his own' (Matthew 20:15).

Orthodox moral opinion disagreed, and in this regard the authors of the complaint literature were profoundly orthodox. Their social vision was conservative. Yet it took on potentially subversive implications when they turned from general denunciation of the moral chaos of the times to address the specific failings of particular social groups. No one was exempt from this. Ploughmen and craftsmen were reproved for idleness, shoddy work and excessive consumption of resources through gluttony and drunkenness. The poverty of the 'thriftless poore' was largely attributed to their 'owne defaults'. But the fiercest criticism was reserved for those 'caterpillars of the commonwealth' whose greed and oppression occasioned the sufferings of others, above all those 'ungentle gentlemen' who neglected their duty of stewardship. 'The erth is the poor mannys as wel as the rych,' declared Brinkelow, characteristically, and the abuse of economic power by the latter was represented in starkly binary terms, and denounced with prophetic vehemence. 'The earth O Lord is thine,' ran a barbed prayer for landlords:

We heartily pray thee to send thy Holy Spirit into the hearts of them that possess the grounds, pastures and dwelling places of the earth; that they, remembering themselves to be Thy tenants, may not rack and stretch out the rents of their houses and lands, nor yet take unreasonable fines and incomes after the manner of covetous worldlings; but so let them out to other that the inhabitants thereof may both be able to pay the rents and also honestly to live, to nourish their families and to relieve the poor.

Such conceptions of Christian stewardship, as F. J. Fisher remarked, involved a perception of divine grace as 'an instrument for perpetuating the uneconomic allocation of resources'. But that was precisely the point. 'If there were no God,' thundered Robert Crowley in 1548, ' then would I think it lawfull for men to use their possessions as they lyste . . . But forasmuch as we have a God, and he hath declared unto us by the scripturs that he hath made the possessioners but Stuards of his ryches . . . I think no Christian ears can abyde to heare that more than Turkysh opinion.'

The pamphlets and sermons of the 1540s and early 1550s constitute a magnificent literature of protest, vibrating with the righteous indignation of what Tawney called 'an age that has rediscovered the Bible'. But the response to damaging economic change also took more direct forms. It has been suggested that in English towns the partial recovery of wage rates in the 1560s may have been influenced by the refusals of craftsmen to accept any further reduction of their living standards. These matters are obscure, but it seems significant that legislation in 1548 forbade 'artificers, workmen or labourers' to 'conspire, covenant or promise together or make any oaths that they shall not make or do their works but at a certain price and rate'. And in 1562 the rarely heard voice of the urban craftsman spoke clearly when the leaders of the York building crafts rejected an attempt to reimpose archaic wage ceilings and suggested instead that wages be settled by agreement with individual employers. They added, lest the firmness of their purpose be underestimated, 'for the truth is, do with us what so ever shall please you, for we will not work for that wage that will not find [provide for] us'.

Far better known is the history of resistance to agrarian change in England. From the 1530s the countryside was pockmarked with minor disorders as the tenantry of particular manors resisted changes in their customs, or attempts by landlords to encroach upon, or enclose, their commons. Their actions varied from legal challenges to rent strikes (as at Henbury, Worcestershire, in 1533), the occupation of disputed land (as at Pitstone Common Wood, Buckinghamshire, in 1569) and the systematic destruction of new enclosures. They were purposeful and highly organised affairs, often conducted in alliance with other interested parties such as members of the clergy or neighbouring gentlemen, and remarkably orderly, rarely involving bloodshed. They represented not the desperate spasms of an oppressed and immiserated peasantry, but the truculent resistance of self-confident manorial communities determined to fend off any encroachment upon the customary rights which secured their relatively advantageous position. The apparent absence of comparable actions in Scotland suggests either that landlord–tenant relationships changed less in the northern kingdom or that the tenurial weakness of the Scottish peasantry gave them few such rights to defend.

In general these conflicts were confined to individual communities and were essentially reactive in nature. But the anxieties and grievances which they expressed were widespread. Evidence of tenant protest survives for thirty of the 600 townships of the West Riding of Yorkshire between 1520 and 1546, which may well be merely the tip of the iceberg. And on two occasions it escalated beyond such local incidents to involve whole regions and to include demands calculated both to enhance tenant rights in general and to arrest future change.

In 1536 the north of England was convulsed by the Pilgrimage of Grace. This 'revolt for the commonwealth' had multiple causes, notably hostility to the Reformation and the dissolution of the monasteries and fears of new forms of royal taxation. But in Cumbria and the dales the rising of the commons was fuelled by resentment of agrarian change –

above all the levying of excessive entry fines. One of the rebels' principal demands was that henceforth 'the commonalty be used as they should be' in matters of rents and tenures, which meant in effect the future tying of their landlords' hands. In 1549, Protector Somerset's commission on enclosure provided the catalyst for widespread action against enclosures in Somerset and Wiltshire, the midlands and the south. In East Anglia, where enclosure was less of an issue than rising rents and the abuse of 'foldcourse' commoning rights by landlords, it led to 'the campyng time', a co-ordinated protest involving the gathering of the commons in camps to petition for redress of their grievances. The Norfolk rebels, encamped at Mousehold Heath near Norwich under the leadership of Robert Kett, confidently presented to the king's representatives a catalogue of demands both great and small. Some were essentially conservative – for example, the restoration of copyhold rents to the levels of 1485. As with the northern rebels, however, others involved innovatory restrictions upon the future actions of their landlords, notably the demands 'that no lord of no mannor shall comon uppon the Comons' and – in response to the Duke of Norfolk's attempt to exploit the remaining vestiges of serfdom – 'thatt all bonde men may be made ffre, for god made all ffre with his precious blode sheddyng'.

These peasant rebels were people whose political ideas had been formed in the environment of manorial and parish custom, and it has been said of them that 'their idea of good government [was] the enforcement of an ideal customary'. This was so. But their struggle to defend themselves against innovations damaging to their households and communities involved more than the recapturing of an idealised past. If the commonwealthsmen sought to recall gentlemen to their Christian duties, the peasantry, in Diarmid MacCulloch's words, 'were determined to create a world in which gentlemen were kept at arm's length'.

vi. *Commodity* and *commonwealth?*

The rebels failed. Local resistance was not infrequently able to slow the pace or mitigate the consequences of agrarian change. But the more ambitious programmes of 1536 and 1549, which might have redirected its course, ended in bloody suppression. Moreover, the alarm occasioned by the events of 1549 in England's governors had the further effect of discrediting the commonwealthsmen. They had never advocated rebellion, but their rhetoric was held to have encouraged it.

The idea of the commonwealth, however, did not vanish. The impassioned mid-century literature of complaint subsided (though it left a residual influence long detectable in radical Christian discussions of economic justice). The larger discourse of commonwealth, however, continued, less as a medium of moral prescription or condemnation than as a vehicle for the discussion of policy, for cooler and more constructive reflection on the problem of how the elusive common interest and the good of the polity might best be secured in a more complex and less stable economic world.

Sir Thomas Smith's *Discourse of the Commonweal of England* – initially composed for private circulation at the height of the turmoil of 1549, and subsequently revised before its anonymous publication in 1581 – exemplified this continuing potential. Smith was the son of an Essex farmer. He had risen to become Professor of Civil Law at Cambridge, served as principal secretary of state in 1547–9 and, after a hiatus in the 1550s, re-entered state service under Elizabeth I. He was a public man, and a realist, with little sympathy for those he termed 'hotlings', who 'devise commonwealths as they list'. He was no less concerned with the economic problems of the day; his book was squarely focused upon them. But he approached them not to denounce departures from the ideal, but rather to seek to understand the complexities of economic relationships, to explore the motivations of different groups of actors in the economy, and to draw out policy implications.

This was achieved by means of a dialogue between a gentleman, a husbandman, a craftsman and a 'doctor' (scholar). The representatives of the different social groups offered their opinions and rehearsed their discontents. The doctor provided a distanced analytical authority, exploring the underlying causes of their problems and suggesting solutions. In this way Smith achieved a multivocal, socially complex perspective on the difficulties of the times. He exploded the simplicities of the commonwealthsmen's conception of economic relationships. And through the voice of the doctor he proposed means of accommodating conflicts of interest which differed significantly from those of the moralists in that they sought to work with the grain of the times. Enclosures could be beneficial if conducted by agreement and with a fair distribution of the former common land. Tillage might best be encouraged by permitting corn exports. In response to the view that men cannot be prevented from making 'their most advantage of that which is their own', he responded not with the conventional denunciation of covetousness, but with qualified agreement. 'Yes, marry,' *but* 'men may not *abuse* their own things to the damage of the commonweal'. Limits must be set on the legitimate pursuit of economic advantage. In short, Smith accepted the widespread reality of self-interested economic behaviour. He was also aware of its potential benefits. But he sought to prevent the socially destabilising consequences of unrestrained surrender to that impulse and to channel its energy for the benefit of the commonwealth. Both ends could be achieved by good laws.

Smith was an exceptionally perceptive analyst of the problems of the commonwealth. But he was not the only public man obliged to come to terms with the realities of the times, to accept that it was neither possible nor expedient to reverse the economic dynamic of the day, and to place his faith in the positive effects of good laws. From the 1530s onwards a stream of 'penal' statutes and royal proclamations had attempted to stem, guide or respond to the pressures of economic change. By mid-century the need for intervention by the magistrate seemed all the more pressing and it came in two phases.

The first of these was essentially a response to the manifold economic crisis of 1549–51. Rebellion in 1549 was followed by further debasement of the coinage, accelerated inflation and in 1551 a disastrous slump in the cloth trade. The long upward trend in cloth exports had quickened in the 1540s as the price of English cloth fell in overseas markets. In 1549–50, however, it peaked and then collapsed as the market became glutted, precipitating widespread distress in the export-oriented clothing districts. Measures taken by the governments of Edward VI and Mary I between 1551 and 1555 were intended primarily to stabilise this deteriorating situation. In late 1551 the coinage was revalued. In 1552 laws were passed ordering the return to tillage of land converted to pasture since 1509, and against abuses in marketing 'iniurious to the whole commonwealth'. Corn dealers ('badgers') were required to be licensed by local magistrates. The same year saw an act for the more systematic collection and disbursal of alms for the poor by parish officers. Records were to be kept and compulsion was authorised against those who refused to contribute voluntarily. Between 1552 and 1555 a further series of acts sought to stabilise the distressed cloth industry. To enforce quality, statutory descriptions of particular types of cloth were provided, and the system of 'searchers' was revised and extended. 'Gig mills' were prohibited to protect employment. Restrictions were placed on the ownership of looms, the taking of apprentices and the spread of the industry outside corporate and market towns and areas where it had been established for ten years.

The second phase began with the accession of Elizabeth I and owed much to the guiding influence of her secretary of state Sir William Cecil, later Lord Burghley. It is likely that it was for Cecil that Sir Thomas Smith had originally composed his *Discourse* in 1549, and the two men provide a link between the debates of the later 1540s and the measures introduced in the 1560s and 1570s. Cecil gave close personal attention to economic affairs. He was a man of notes and memoranda, a collector of expert opinions and a drafter of papers meticulously listing the pros and cons of particular policy options. He came to power with a definite programme of measures to be introduced after the settlement of the more pressing issues of religion and foreign affairs which occupied the first years of the reign. And he developed it thereafter in a manner which suggests a dual strategy. On the one hand, he sought stability – a reknitting of the frayed social fabric of the commonwealth. On the other hand, he encouraged expansion – the orderly development of economic activity within a stable social environment.

The first step was the recoinage of 1560–1, which was overseen by Cecil and Smith. In 1563 the great 'Statute of Artificers' was enacted, a comprehensive framework of regulation for labour relations which also extended the seven-year apprenticeship system into the countryside and provided for the annual assessment of maximum wage levels by county magistrates. Smith had a hand in that too, as did numerous members of parliament who grafted on clauses reflecting their preoccupations in this area. The same parliament brought a revision of the statutes relating to enclosure and tillage, which avoided the prohibition of enclosure in itself, but forbade further conversion of tillage to pasture and required the restoration of some formerly arable land. Agrarian grievances were further recognised and forms of redress provided by decisions of the prerogative courts and Chancery relating to tenures and fines, and by the extension to copyholders of the protection of the common law courts – both developments which had begun in the 1550s and were now consolidated.

Subsequent parliaments added to the growing corpus of legislation. The Usury Act of 1571 embodied the controversial decision to permit lending at interest up to a statutory rate of 10 per cent. This measure was hotly debated and Cecil himself agonised over the question of whether or not lending at interest was contrary to the law of God before reaching a decision that was characteristically both principled (usury was wrong) and pragmatic (some lending at interest could be permitted to prevent a greater evil). The following year brought a major step forward in the evolution of the poor laws. Justices of the Peace were empowered to survey the poor and to 'tax and assess' all inhabitants to provide for them, appointing local collectors and overseers to administer the relief funds – a policy of compulsory rating already pioneered by some cities, but now extended nationally. The vagrant poor, in contrast, were subjected to a revised catalogue of punitive measures, of which whipping was the least.

Meanwhile the privy council, under Cecil's guidance, adopted a variety of measures intended to promote both national security and the development of national resources. It encouraged iron production and the manufacture of munitions, shipping and fisheries, overseas trading initiatives and the settlement of skilled Protestant refugees in English cities. It also proved highly receptive to projects for the establishment of new manufactures, above all those aimed at import substitution, which promised the double benefit of improving an adverse balance of trade and at the same time providing employment for the poor. The patent system developed through the grant to 'projectors' of the sole right to manufacture such goods according to a particular method, and patents multiplied from the 1560s.

The coherence of all this activity should not be exaggerated. In part it was carefully planned. In part it involved reactions to short-term contingencies, or the initiatives of particular interest groups. The proposals of government were often challenged, modified, elaborated or subjected to exemption clauses in the course of their passage through parliament. Again, the impact of the regulative penal laws was diminished by their sheer number – there were so many by 1577 that Thomas Pulton published a handy abstract for magistrates – and by the limitations of the local government institutions charged with their enforcement. Nevertheless, the laws were enforced at least intermittently, sometimes through self-interested actions brought by informers, sometimes when local circumstances prompted magistrates to act. And if the legislation and policy of the two decades following the mid-century crisis emerged in a somewhat halting manner, it nonetheless reflected a common cast of mind and a certain consistency of purpose.

The sheer ambition of what was undertaken is striking. In its attempts to formulate solutions to pressing problems and to put them into execution, it represented a significant development in the conception of the economic and social role of the English state, and the bringing of important sectors of economic activity and social provision under national rather than municipal or manorial regulation. The measures introduced recognised shifts in economic realities and attitudes, while at the same time attempting to set the parameters of future development. They proposed ways of living with the imperatives of a more commercialised economy without giving free rein to the dynamics of the market and the elevation of self-interest in economic and social relationships. They permitted and indeed encouraged capitalist enterprise, but also endeavoured to define the scope of its activities. In addressing what one member of parliament described in 1571 as 'any matter for the commoditie of the Prince and of the common welth', they attempted to find the public good, according to their lights, and to arbitrate potentially conflicting interests. In short, they sought to reconcile the competing claims of commodity and commonwealth which wracked their society. Whether or not that objective was ultimately attainable, they provided a framework of law which retained some of the fundamental values of traditional social morality, and by doing so helped to shape the environment of change as the shock of the new gradually gave way to the acceptance of the unacceptable.

CHAPTER SEVEN

Economic expansion, c.1580–c.1650

In the half-century between the 1520s and the 1570s, the complex response to the challenges of demographic growth and price inflation had placed considerable strain upon established economic and social relationships throughout Britain – albeit to different degrees in different contexts. To many it brought new economic opportunities and enhanced material prosperity. To a growing minority, however, it brought greater insecurity and a gradual erosion of the viability of their domestic economies. In this situation, rapid and sustained economic expansion was needed if a larger population was to be supported and if the young in particular were to be enabled to 'make shift in the world', find employment and enjoy living standards at least comparable to those of their parents.

In the succeeding generations both the continuing need for economic expansion and the social, cultural and political tensions which it could breed were to be abundantly demonstrated. Throughout Britain population continued to increase. In Scotland a population of around 700,000 in 1560 had reached perhaps one million by the second quarter of the seventeenth century: a rise of some 30 per cent. In Wales, numbers grew by around 60 per cent from an estimated population of 250,000 in the mid-sixteenth century to one of 400,000 by 1650. In England, parish-register analysis suggests that crude rates of population increase remained high in the later sixteenth century, though slowing thereafter. As a result, the population of 2.98 million in 1561 had grown to over four million by 1601 and reached 5.23 million in 1651: an overall increase of 75 per cent.

The limited capacity of the economy to absorb population growth on this scale was evident in the continued rise in the prices of basic commodities. Average wheat prices in England almost doubled between the 1570s and the 1630s. Those of cheaper grains rose faster still. And, as before, the prices of livestock, dairy produce and manufactured goods lagged behind. The price of labour rose least of all, with the effect that by the 1630s the real wages of building craftsmen in southern England had been reduced to 68 per cent of their 1570s value. In Scotland, where the pressure of population growth was exacerbated by continued minor debasements of the coinage, the inflation of the later sixteenth century was even more severe.

None of this would seem to give grounds for optimism. Yet it also appears that population growth in England (and probably Wales) was faster and continued longer than was the case in Scotland and indeed in most of the European countries with which comparisons can be made. The implication is that, whatever population growth in England and Wales had in common with most of Europe in terms of its origins, it was being sustained by factors which were more peculiar to the English and Welsh situations. England in particular appears to have had a greater capacity to cope with increased numbers than was the case elsewhere. Moreover, estimates by J. R. Wordie suggest that in England prices actually rose *less* than might have been anticipated, given the enhancement of demand. Both considerations point to the likelihood of economic expansion and increased production on a scale that was rare elsewhere in Europe in this period outside the Netherlands. There is a good deal of further evidence that this was indeed so and that the cumulative experience of such expansion had profound implications for the structures of economic life in much of Britain.

i. *Expanding production*

Agriculture was the dominant sphere of economic activity and levels of agricultural production governed the growth opportunities of the economy as a whole. That agricultural output increased in this period is beyond doubt. Without such expansion, enlarged populations could not have been sustained. Measurement of the precise dimensions of growth is impossible, given the available evidence. Nevertheless, the direction of change is clear and there is much evidence of the manner in which it was achieved.

One major contributing factor was what is usually termed 'the extension of the cultivated area'. There was, in fact, relatively little land which was not put to some use in the mid-sixteenth century. But there were substantial areas which were exploited only intermittently, or at a low level of intensity. In the course of the later sixteenth and early seventeenth centuries much of this land was brought into permanent and more intensive cultivation. In Scotland, inroads were made on uncultivated 'commonty'. 'Outfields' were expanded into the waste. Settled areas were infilled by the sub-division of farming townships. The number of settlements doubled in Glenelg between the mid-sixteenth and mid-seventeenth centuries, while on Islay fifteen new farming townships had been created by 1614. In Wales there was much encroachment by both landowners and tenants upon upland pastures and wastes, including the turning of summer *hafotai* (shielings) into permanent farms. In England, woods were cleared in the Chiltern Hills and the west midlands. Shallow meres were drained at Myddle in Shropshire. On the Dengie coast of Essex salt marshes were 'inned' by the construction of dykes, drained and converted into permanent pasture land. Elsewhere, areas of former waste and pasture 'where the plough never entered' were brought into arable cultivation, as was some land which had formerly reverted to pasture, but was now considered to have 'gotten heart, strength and fruitfulnesse'. Most of this involved piecemeal local initiatives on the part of landlords and farmers anxious to increase the productive potential of their land. But there were also larger schemes, conducted with government backing and involving considerable capital expenditure and technical expertise, like the disafforestation of the royal forests of the west country between 1626 and 1632 and the systematic drainage and bringing into arable cultivation of vast tracts of fenland in Lincolnshire, Cambridgeshire and south Yorkshire in the decades after 1626.

Expansion of the acreage under regular cultivation was accompanied by a general intensification of cultivation. In part this was a matter of increasing output in order to meet local consumption needs and it could be achieved by simple intensification of effort in the form of more careful utilisation of manure resources, more assiduous weeding, or pest control by more frequent ploughing. Scotland provides some of the best examples. In the Lothians a report of 1627 spoke of the 'extraordinary labouring' of the land, while in the Highlands and Islands arable production for subsistence needs reached an almost horticultural intensity. Livestock manure, peat, turf, shell sand and seaweed were all employed to create areas of better and more workable soil which could bear a crop if sufficient labour was applied. In more favoured areas, however, intensification involved a greater degree of specialisation, a reorientation of the balance between arable and pastoral husbandry in accordance with what was deemed to be the most advantageous use of the land in particular farming countries. In Norfolk, for example, the eastern districts of the county became more oriented towards wheat production and the west towards barley, while pastoral specialisation increased on the heavier soils of the central area of the county. In the Forest of Arden in

Warwickshire, cattle rearing gave way to expanded arable production, notably of barley, and dairying. The east Durham lowlands, in contrast, saw the conversion of some land considered 'waisted and worne with continuall plowing' to pasture producing dairy produce, meat and horses for the coal-field population of the Tyne and Wear valleys. Proximity to London encouraged specialisation in wheat production in north-eastern Kent and in cattle-fattening, hops, fruit growing and market gardening elsewhere in the county.

Such specialisation for the supply of particular markets further encouraged the intensification of cultivation. In part this involved the spread of techniques of husbandry which were not in themselves new, but which were now more widely adopted. There is much evidence of increased manuring to raise the fertility of the land by spreading and ploughing in muck, lime or marl. Liming, for example, was widely adopted in the most fertile areas of Lowland Scotland, especially those like the Lothians and Berwickshire which were adjacent to urban markets. The period also witnessed the gradual spread across lowland England of the more productive pattern of mixed farming known as 'up and down' or 'convertible' husbandry. Previously a substantial part of the land, perhaps a third, had been allowed to rest fallow in any given year as part of a three-year rotation of grain, peas and beans, and fallow. Under convertible husbandry a greater proportion was laid down to grass for longer periods of years. Keeping a larger acreage under pasture at any one time increased livestock densities and provided more manure. The land regained heart better and its fertility was much enhanced, with the result that arable yields were greatly improved when it was periodically brought back into tillage. Ideally, this system would maintain or improve grain production, while at the same time increasing livestock production, for, as one contemporary put it, 'one acre beareth the fruit of three; the two acres are preserved to graze'.

Innovation of either kind could be facilitated by enclosure. As we have seen, the decades between the 1520s and the 1570s had witnessed a hiatus in the spread of enclosure. The last decade of the sixteenth century and the first half of the seventeenth century, however, brought a renewal of the trend towards enclosure in England. Between 1600 and 1650, for example, 40 per cent of the manors of Leicestershire and 18 per cent of the land area of Co. Durham were enclosed, while the period 1575 to 1674 saw the enclosure of some 17 per cent of the land in the south-midland counties, the heartland of open-field farming. In Wales too it is estimated that 90 per cent of the lowlands were farmed in severalty by 1640, while a good deal of upland pasture was also enclosed and absorbed into private ownership.

This second wave of enclosure differed from the late-medieval enclosure movement in two vital respects. In the first place, it was far less likely to involve the controversial conversion of formerly arable land to permanent pasture. Much of it was undertaken with a view to ensuring the continued practice of arable husbandry, the introduction of convertible husbandry regimes, or the control of access to upland commons. Secondly, it was usually accomplished not by the unilateral fiat of the landlord – though this did sometimes occur – but by agreement between landlords and tenants. This might involve a survey followed by the wholesale redistribution and consolidation of land-holdings, with each qualified participant receiving a proportional share of the former common. At Highley in Shropshire, for example, the enclosure of the common fields by agreement was accompanied by the division and apportionment of the common and woodland in 1618. Alternatively, enclosure might proceed piecemeal by agreement to allow previously con-solidated lands to be permanently enclosed. At Laxton in Notting-hamshire, which was never wholly enclosed, the demesne was enclosed by the landlord in 1635 and let as a single farm, while other enclosed farms emerged on the edge of the open fields by a gradual process of consolidation and exchange.

Whichever was the case, the central purpose was the creation of con-solidated, individually managed farms. Ambitious farmers favoured it, since it gave them the freedom to practise husbandry as they saw best, unrestricted by the views and practices of their neighbours. Intensive or innovative farming was certainly not impossible in the open fields, but it was deemed easier and more convenient when conducted in severalty. Landlords favoured it because enclosed farms commanded higher rents. Many of those affected did not welcome the change, as we shall see. But, among those whose decisions carried most weight, the trend was towards enclosure and in consequence the hold of communal and customary practices on agricultural organisation was weakened, and not infre-quently extinguished.

By 1619, it could be plausibly claimed that both 'the quantitie and qualitie of errable land and corne lands' in England had increased, and the innovations of the period do indeed appear to have raised both overall output and land productivity as measured by yields per acre. A survey of evidence from five counties in eastern and southern England suggests that cereal yields rose by around 12 per cent in the second half of the sixteenth century and by a further 4 per cent in the early seventeenth century. But it is unlikely that labour productivity rose. In the absence of major technological change, farmers and those whom they employed raised output above all by intensified effort. It may well be that from the perspective of agricultural economics they obtained diminishing returns for the additional labour expended. But that was not a calculation they were likely to make. Labour was abundant and cheap. To the subsistence peasant, the use value of the food produced was sufficient reward for effort. To the commercial farmer, increased output, however hard won, more than compensated him for higher labour costs while agricultural prices remained buoyant. English farmers, it was said, had 'growne to be more painfull, skilfull and carefull through recompense of gaine'.

The intensification of agricultural production and the development of a greater degree of specialisation imply the existence of larger and more integrated markets for agricultural produce. These were to be found, above all, in the supply of the growing towns and those rural areas with substantial non-agricultural populations. By the mid-sixteenth century the demographic contraction which had afflicted many late-medieval towns was over and was succeeded by a period of significant urban growth throughout Britain. In many towns this growth was roughly proportionate to the rise in national population. The population of Canterbury, for example, grew from around 4,000 to around 7,000 between 1570 and 1640. Some towns, however, were growing at a pace which far exceeded national population trends, above all the capital cities. Edinburgh more than doubled in size between 1560 and 1640 to reach a population of around 25,000. London, together with the adjoining parishes in Middlesex and Surrey, had already constituted a metropolis of around 70,000 in 1550. By 1600 the metropolitan population exceeded 200,000 and by 1640 it was close to 400,000 and still growing. All in all, it was a period of significant demographic urbanisation. The estimated proportion of the population of England and Wales living in cities of more than 10,000 inhabitants rose from 3.5 to 8.8 per cent between 1550 and 1650, while that of Scotland rose from 1.4 to 3.5 per cent.

As urban populations grew, vacant space within the medieval walls of the cities was gradually taken up for building. Existing housing was subdivided. Suburban developments spread outside city gates. In London, where these developments were most remarked upon, there were complaints of 'multitudes of people brought to inhabite in small rooms and . . . heaped up together and in a sort smothered'. And meanwhile the 'out parishes' to the east of the Tower of London grew in size from around 7,000 inhabitants in the 1570s to over 50,000 by the 1630s. The towns were increasingly crowded and insanitary. Even in normal years, levels of 'background' mortality were considerably higher than in the countryside. In years of crisis when epidemic disease – usually bubonic plague – swept through the cities, the results were disastrous. Yet despite this constant erosion, punctuated by periodic catastrophe, the towns grew. That they were able to do so was the result of continuous rural–urban migration. London, it has been estimated, needed an average of 6,000 migrants a year to replace its losses and continue to grow. And they came. Some came as what have been termed 'betterment' migrants with expectations of advancement, apprentices for example, or others with a known place to fill. Others came as 'subsistence' migrants, seeking any means of getting a living. The cities did not necessarily fulfil their hopes. More than a few sank into a life of marginality. But the fact that they came at all implies that there were opportunities of some kind to attract them.

Those opportunities lay for the most part in the reviving and expanding urban economies of the period. From the later sixteenth century, in Charles Phythian-Adams' words, the towns were 'recovering their basic *raison d'être* in both marketing and industry'. In Coventry the decades after 1570 witnessed a notable revival in marketing activity and the development of a more diverse manufacturing base. In Colchester and Norwich textile production expanded – in both cases with the aid of Protestant refugees from the Netherlands who introduced new products – while Norwich also saw marked growth in the numbers of apprentices entering the distributive trades.

In general urban economies were responding to a quickening of internal trade and the growth of rural demand for their products. Richard Carew captured the reciprocal nature of the process when he observed of Cornish farmers in 1602 that 'with the ready money gotten by his weekly selling of corn he setteth the artificer on work'. This was the fundamental relationship that reinvigorated the economies of country towns and provincial cities throughout the kingdom. And in the larger towns, where engagement in the supply of distant markets was superimposed upon the serving of local and regional hinterlands, the consequences were even more evident. The migrants who crowded into London's swelling eastern suburbs were employed there in the manufacture of textiles, metal wares, sugar, starch, soap and glass; in ship-building and its ancillary trades of rope-winding, sail-making, coopering and pulley-making; in the brewing and victualling trades which provisioned both the city and shipping; and on the wharves and the river. They engaged in all the multifarious activities spawned by London's role as England's leading centre of manufactures, premier trading city, largest consumer market, and the hub of internal commerce. The economy of London was, of course, exceptional in both its scale and its diversity, but the expansion so spectacularly evident there was also shared, albeit more modestly, by the revitalised urban economies of provincial England and Wales and Lowland Scotland.

The reciprocal relationship between agricultural development and urban growth extended also to the rural industrial districts of England and Wales, which witnessed comparable processes of expansion and diversification in the years between the accession of Elizabeth I and the Civil Wars. In 1551, as we have seen, the long expansion of England's premier industry, the manufacture of unfinished woollen broadcloth, had come to a shuddering halt. After a period of instability in the 1560s and early 1570s, broadcloth exports stabilised at a level close to that of the 1540s, though significantly below their 1550 peak. In the early years of the seventeenth century they rose modestly. By then, however, the dynamic sector of the textiles industry lay elsewhere, in the so-called 'New Draperies'. These were lighter textiles, more akin to modern suiting materials than the heavy broadcloth of the 'old draperies'. They were also fully finished cloths, varied and colourful in both nature and name: 'bays', 'says', 'mockadoes', 'perpetuanas', 'calimancoes'. They were cheaper than broadcloth, less durable and more adaptable to changing fashion, and found a readier sale in both domestic and overseas markets. In addition they offered other advantages. As finished cloths, they provided more employment in the finishing trades and increased demand for dyestuffs like woad, which established new cash crops and generated employment in agriculture. Moreover, as new products they lay outside the framework of statutes and regulations imposed from the 1550s to stabilise the manufacture of traditional woollens. The trade could be entered without formal apprenticeship and the nature and quality of its products was less rigidly defined. The employment of rural labour and the relatively unregulated nature of the industry helped English manufacturers to undercut the prices of their urban-based, guild-regulated Dutch and Italian competitors.

Initially the manufacture of New Draperies was centred in East Anglia and the south-east, where its establishment was greatly facilitated by the settlement of Protestant refugees from the religious strife of the Netherlands. (Norwich had almost 1,500 resident 'aliens' by 1568 and Colchester almost 1,300 in 1586.) They represented a significant influx of skills and expertise and they contributed much to the renewal of the textile industry in the region. In the cloth towns of the Stour Valley, for example, the broadcloth industry was in terminal decline by the early seventeenth century. The New Draperies, however, spread out gradually from Colchester via small towns like Braintree and Coggeshall and had established their dominance by the 1620s. In 1637, one Colchester cloth-ier, Thomas Reynolds, claimed to employ 400 households in spinning, fifty-two in weaving and thirty-three in finishing such cloths – and he was but one of many. Moreover, by that date their influence was being felt much further afield.

The New Draperies provide the most striking example of development in England's leading industry, but they were far from being the whole story of change. In Lancashire the manufacture of 'fustians' (a coarse linen–woollen mixture) expanded from the 1590s, centred on Manchester, but gradually spreading out into the parishes of south-east Lancashire. In the west country diversification into the production of heavy serges and 'Spanish reds' – dyed cloths using high-quality imported wool – provided partial compensation for the decline of broadcloth. The knitting of high-quality worsted stockings was established in London and in Norfolk and by the 1630s was spreading to involve rural parishes in Nottinghamshire, Leicestershire and Derbyshire.

The expanding range of woollen textiles, however, was only part of a larger process of innovation and diversification in English manufactur-ing, which was particularly evident in the establishment of 'import substitution' industries. Traditionally, a considerable number of the mis-cellany of non-essential manufactured goods consumed in Britain had been imported, primarily from the cities of the Netherlands. Under Eliz-abeth I, as we have seen, the privy council proved highly responsive to schemes promoting their manufacture in England, and numerous patents were granted to facilitate the introduction of the processes involved. Once established, many prospered and, as the original patents expired, some of the new processes were gradually diffused across the kingdom. Silk-weaving was established in Canterbury and in London by French Huguenot refugees. Glass-making was introduced to Kent and Sussex (again with the aid of immigrant expertise) and later spread to Shrop-shire, Staffordshire and Tyneside. By the 1590s it had captured the home market for window glass, by the 1620s for bottles and by the 1630s for drinking glasses and 'looking glasses'. The manufacture of starch, soap and paper, all previously imported, was widespread by 1640. Pins were still imported from the Netherlands to the tune of £40,000 a year in the 1590s, but by 1608 a native industry had been set up in the London suburbs, where it was said to employ between two and three thousand children, and by the 1630s pin-making was flourishing in the Glouces-tershire countryside. By the same decade lace-making had also become a widespread by-employment for countrywomen in Devon, Bedfordshire, Buckinghamshire and Northamptonshire, though the best-quality lace still came from the Netherlands.

For the most part these new industries were traditional in organisation, involving either small workshops, or decentralised production on
the domestic or putting-out systems. Few needed substantial investment
in fixed-capital equipment (glass production was an exception) and their
capital requirement usually took the form of the circulating capital necessary to finance the purchasing of raw materials, to pay workers and to
market the finished products. A number of other developing industries
of the late sixteenth century, however, were bringing a different face to
industrial enterprise in Britain: one of heavy capitalisation, centralised
production and concentrated plant.

Iron production was one such industry. Blast furnaces, utilising water-
driven bellows, had been introduced to England from Germany in the
mid-sixteenth century, encouraged by a government anxious to expand
munitions production. These were expensive undertakings to construct
and maintain, but the capital required was found, partly from London
investors and partly from major landowners anxious to develop their
estates. In 1574 there were fifty-one furnaces, and associated ironworks
operating in the Sussex Weald, three near Sheffield and a three more in
south Wales, and by the 1580s production of pig iron had tripled to
around 15,000 tons a year. By the early seventeenth century, eighty-five
furnaces are known to have been in operation, but their geographical distribution had altered. The relative position of the Weald was declining,
largely as a result of rising fuel costs, diminishing ore deposits and transportation difficulties. That of south Wales had grown as a result of the
region's attractive combination of ore and limestone deposits, plentiful
woodlands for the supply of charcoal, fast streams to drive water-
powered bellows and slitting mills, and coastal transportation. There was
further development in the west midlands too. By 1650 overall production was in the order of 24,000 tons a year.

Impressive as it was by the standards of the day, this five-fold increase
in iron production over a century was scarcely sufficient to keep pace
with the needs of the expanding production of metal wares, especially
in the west midlands. In contrast to the processes of iron production, the
metal trades remained traditional in structure, organised by the ironmongers of Birmingham, Wolverhampton, Walsall and Stourbridge on
the domestic or putting-out systems. But they demonstrated the
impressive capacity of those systems to respond to the rising demand for
edge-tools, nails, cooking utensils and other metal goods required in agriculture, building and shipping and for domestic use. Involvement in the
industry intensified in the small towns which specialised in particular products – locks in Wilenhall, saddlery wares in Walsall – and
spread more widely in the rural parishes of the area to which the iron-

mongers distributed rod- and bar-iron to be worked into nails or edge-tools. The production of metal goods expanded in quantity and – though it remained for some a winter by-employment – in continuity. By 1640 the expansion was such that imported iron, notably from Sweden, was required to supply the raw-material needs of the industry.

A similar juxtaposition of novel and traditional methods was to be found in the lead industry, which was also expanding to meet both domestic and overseas demand for the lead required for building, pewtering and military use. The more widespread adoption of the 'ore hearth smelting mill', which used water-driven bellows, freed the industry from the seasonality of smelting in 'boles' which depended on the wind, and permitted the smelting of lower-grade ores. The use of the 'water sieve' made possible more efficient separation of ore from mining waste. In consequence the somewhat decayed lead-mining industry of Derbyshire revived and grew markedly between the 1570s and the 1630s, and overall English lead production rose from under 600 tons a year in the 1560s to over 12,000 tons a year by the 1630s. On the one hand this growth represented increased activity on the part of the 'free miners', many of them also small farmers, who enjoyed ancient rights to prospect for lead in the Peak Country and who worked small mines in partnership, often on a seasonal basis. On the other hand it involved substantial investment by local landowners like the earls of Shrewsbury and Devonshire in smelting plant and in deeper, more highly capitalised mines employing large numbers of proletarianised 'cavers and hirelings'.

Both faces of production were also to be seen in perhaps the most spectacularly expanding industry of the period: coal mining. Britain is, of course, liberally endowed with coal deposits, and the exploitation of the most accessible outcropping seams for the supply of local fuel needs had long been known. As fuel requirements grew in the later sixteenth century, exacerbated in some instances by localised wood shortages, there was a general expansion of mining activity on the estates of both large and small landowners. Mines in Warwickshire, Staffordshire and Shropshire, for example, provided fuel for the forges of the west midlands. Those of south Yorkshire supplied the Sheffield area. A good deal of production, however, remained small in scale and traditional in nature. Mines were shallow, their depth being inhibited by drainage difficulties. Workforces were small and activity seasonal. Markets were highly localised, contained by the problems and expense of transporting such a bulky commodity by land.

In marked contrast were the mines now developing in those areas where river and coastal transportation created the possibility of expanding production to supply fuel to more distant markets – primarily those of the expanding urban centres, and above all that of London. Colliery development around the Forth constituted Scotland's principal sphere of industrial expansion in the period. (Scotland had no manufacturing sector of note outside the towns, a small lead industry producing 300–400 tons a year in the mid-seventeenth century, and only one operating blast furnace.) The substantial collieries of the region were shipping some 25,000 tons of coal a year in the 1620s, as well as supplying local fuel needs, which included those of salt pans in which salt was produced by evaporating seawater. Similarly large-scale undertakings in coastal south Wales shipped some 20,000 tons a year a decade later. Foremost among such areas, however, was the north-east of England: Tyneside and, from the early seventeenth century, Wearside. In the mid-sixteenth century Newcastle shipped an estimated 14,000–16,000 tons of coal per annum to London. From the 1570s, as London's growth entered its most spectacular phase, this trade, in John Hatcher's words, 'accelerated ferociously'. Annual shipments from the north-east to London alone reached 50,000 tons in the 1580s, 150,000 tons in the early 1600s and 300,000 tons in 1640, by which time a further 200,000 tons was also being shipped to provincial ports on the east and south coasts. Yarmouth, which had landed around 3,000 tons of coal in 1566–7, took almost 30,000 tons in 1637–8. King's Lynn, from where coal was carried up the Ouse and its tributaries as far as Cambridge and Bedford, took even more.

Production on this scale entailed a transformation of the mining industry in the north. The risks of investment in mining were great, but the potential profits were immense, and vast sums of capital were invested by consortia of Newcastle merchants and local landowners in the development of 'sea-sale' collieries. These became huge complexes, with numerous shafts (some several hundred feet deep), linked underground by complex networks of 'headways', and drained by elaborate hydraulic systems. While the coal trade remained seasonal, production became continuous. Large specialist workforces with an elaborate division of labour were employed in sinking, timbering and draining pits, the hewing, dragging, winding, and sorting of coal, and its transportation to riverside staithes, where it was stored ready for shipment downriver in keelboats to meet the collier fleets at the mouths of the Tyne and Wear. Ancillary industries were established to take advantage of the abundance of 'small coal' considered unsuitable for the sea-sale trade, but more than adequate to provide heat for glass-making, the manufacture of alum and copperas and salt production. (There were 153 salt pans at North Shields in 1605, employing 430 salters.)

As compared with the coal industries of most other areas, all this was utterly exceptional. Yet it existed. And the overall growth of the industry meant that by 1650 coal was Britain's principal source of fuel, not only for domestic heating, but also for the smithies, forges, lime kilns, salt pans, breweries, soapworks, sugar refineries, dyeing vats, brick kilns and numerous other industrial processes which consumed perhaps a third of total output. The impact of this abundance of cheap fuel was immense. If, as E. A. Wrigley has calculated, the energy value of a ton of coal is roughly equal to that of the firewood produced by an acre of coppiced woodland, then the northern coal field alone had increased England's fuel-energy resources by the equivalent of more than half a million acres between 1580 and 1640. Little wonder that one local patriot advised the English to correct their maps: 'Newcastle is Peru.'

ii. *Intensified commerce*

The expansion and diversification of production in both agriculture and industry built upon existing foundations. It did not involve technological innovation of a fundamental kind. Throughout Britain, however, it did involve intensified effort in the utilisation of existing techniques. And in the case of England and Wales, it also involved the widespread diffusion and adoption of the best contemporary practice within particular spheres of production, greater specialisation and increased involvement in non-agricultural employments. Moreover, the cumulative effect of these changes was to initiate a recasting of the regional geography of economic activity in England and Wales within a more integrated whole.

As we have seen, the period witnessed the emergence of a greater degree of specialisation in the agriculture of particular farming countries. Even more apparent were the distinctive local economies created by the growth of manufacturing and extractive industries. Both forms of differentiation were enhanced by the redistribution of population as people, above all the young, moved to those places which had the greatest capacity to provide them with a living. The migration to the towns which swelled urban populations was only part of this phenomenon. In the countryside, servants and labourers were attracted to those areas which most required their labour, where it was easier to acquire a small land-holding, or at least a cottage, or where common rights remained extensive. Cambridgeshire's population stabilised in the arable parishes of the south of the county, despite a continuing surplus of baptisms, and rose in the fenland parishes where extensive commons offered numerous means of supplementing the livings of cottager households. Much the same was true of Lincolnshire. In Leicestershire the early seventeenth century saw rising population densities in open, as compared to enclosed, parishes.

Such shifts of population were even more evident in the industrial areas. By the mid-seventeenth century the metalworking districts of the west midlands seemed to Richard Baxter 'like a continued village'. From the 1580s onwards waves of immigrants covered the commons of parishes like Sedgley and Smethwick with nail-makers' cottages, and in the century after 1563 the south-Staffordshire plateau saw a three-fold increase in population – well in advance of national population growth. There were similar surges of population in the lead field of Derbyshire, the coal fields of Durham and Northumberland, the weaving townships of East Anglia and in the Sussex Weald. 'As for worke for the poore,' reported the magistrates of the latter area in 1630, 'our parte of the countrey affordeth great plenty . . . by reason of our vicinity to the clothiers of Kent, who sette on worke the weemen and children and by reason of our iron workes, which yeelds employment for the stronger bodies.'

E. A. Wrigley estimates that the proportion of the English population living in cities of more than 5,000 inhabitants rose from 5.5 per cent in 1520 to 8 per cent by 1600, and 13.5 per cent by 1670. The rural population wholly engaged in agriculture fell from 76 per cent in 1520 to 70 per cent in 1600, and 60.5 per cent in 1670. The 'rural non-agricultural population', a category which includes the inhabitants of small towns as well as those of industrial villages, rose from 18.5 per cent in 1520 to 22 per cent in 1600, and 26 per cent by 1670. The figures are bold estimates, vulnerable to many qualifications. But the general trend which they describe seems well supported by independent evidence of the reconfiguration of economic activity in England in the later sixteenth and early seventeenth centuries, and the shifts in population distribution which that process entailed. The economic map of the country was gradually being redrawn and that this could occur also implies that its constituent local and regional economies were becoming more closely related. Had it not been so, the developments in agriculture and in industry which we have traced could scarcely have occurred, for they both depended upon and furthered the emergence of a more complex web of commercial interconnection.

Given the extent of population growth, an increase in marketing activity would of course be expected. The clustering of population in the towns and in market-dependent rural areas, however, probably meant that internal trade grew even faster than did overall population. Established arteries of internal trade grew in significance as the traffic along them increased. Shipments of grain to London from the Essex ports of Colchester and Maldon rose from roughly 1,000 quarters in 1565 to almost 13,000 in 1624, while those from the specialist grain-producing districts of north-east Kent grew from 12,000 quarters in 1587–8 to over 57,000 in 1638. The cattle-rearing districts of Wales and the north-west were drawn more deeply into an expanding droving trade. The coastal trade quickened on both the east and south coasts and in the Bristol Channel. The shipping of King's Lynn grew on the grain–coal axis established between East Anglia and the north-east, that of Swansea and other Glamorgan ports on intensified trade with Bristol and the ports of south-west England.

In addition, the networks of internal commerce elaborated and tightened. The river trade of the Severn valley extended its catchment area, to include not only the industrial districts of Shropshire and Worcestershire, but also Leicester, Lichfield and Warwickshire, and came to involve a more diverse range of commodities. The small port of Blakeney in Norfolk was dealing by the turn of the seventeenth century in coal and fish from the north-east, timber from Sussex and groceries from London, as well as exporting malt, rye, peas, butter and saffron. On the roads, carrier routes of a regular nature were being established in the most commercially dynamic areas of the kingdom. By the early seventeenth century many Kentish towns had scheduled services to London, the clothing and iron-producing districts of Gloucestershire had professional carriers linking them to Cirencester, Bristol and the capital, and the roads of Essex were beset by 'drugges and foure wheeled carts', some of them pulled by eight horses and carrying loads of thirty hundredweight or more. The strategic significance of the principal market towns was enhanced in a double sense. On the one hand they grew in importance as collecting places articulating medium-distance flows of goods within their hinterlands and connecting them to more distant markets. Leicestershire farmers equipped with wagons, for example, were now prepared to carry their corn over longer distances to find the best price, by-passing more localised markets. On the other hand, they served as the bases of tradesmen whose dealings penetrated deeply into the surrounding countryside, increasing the availability of a novel range of goods. Some did so directly, like Thomas West of Wallingford, Berkshire, who dealt in cloth, coal, fish, salt, nails, paper and other goods to customers in forty-five smaller communities. Some did so at one remove by supplying goods to the increasingly numerous pedlars or 'petty chapmen' who tramped their beats through the countryside carrying an assortment of goods either on pack-horses or on their own backs to be displayed in village streets or at farmhouse doors.

This intensification of internal commerce also involved the development of commercial practices which, if not entirely new, were now much more widely adopted. Of these the most salient, because it worried local authorities and led periodically to prosecutions, was the growth of private bulk dealing in foodstuffs which evaded the regulative framework of the traditional open marketplace. 'Engrossing', the swooping on markets by dealers who bought up supplies to the detriment of local consumers, had long been known and proscribed by law. Increasingly, however, the markets were 'forestalled' by deals which avoided the marketplace altogether. In 1612, for example, the yeoman William Fowler sold his crop direct to 'loaders' supplying the London food market at the Lion Inn and Cross Keys in Hertford. The farmers of Norfolk dealt similarly with the corn merchants of King's Lynn, and those of Sussex with the 'mealmen' of Rye. In 1617, one Essex dealer went a step further when he offered to buy twenty acres of wheat still growing at Wimbish. By the early seventeenth century such practices were commonplace – so much so in the Romford area that the market of this major collecting place no longer dealt in grain to any significant extent – and they were winked at by local authorities in most years. The professional middlemen who made it all possible were unpopular and frequently suspected of malpractice, not least because their activities created a freer market in foodstuffs in which the prevailing prices were bid prices determined solely by the interaction of supply and demand. But they were also increasingly recognised as indispensable if longer-distance markets were to be supplied. In both ways they furthered the development of more tightly integrated regional markets for agricultural produce, centred upon the major towns, in which the traditions of the regulated public marketplace were giving way gradually to what Professor Everitt terms 'a system of enterprise operating within a network of personal connections'.

More geographically extensive transactions in both agricultural and industrial commodities also encouraged the development of instruments of credit for the transfer of payments over long distances. They led to the introduction of the 'inland bill of exchange' – a written promise to pay which could be drawn upon elsewhere, or assigned to a third party. These were employed, for example, by William Herrick, a London goldsmith and agent for his brother Robert, a Leicester hosier, who wrote to William that 'many come to me . . . to leave money with me to have it in London'. In addition, dealings which extended beyond the circle of well-known and trusted individuals came increasingly to involve the use of 'conditional bonds' – formal contracts for the performance of a given transaction, which carried penalties enforceable at law.

The records of the law, indeed, provide one of our best indicators of the sheer scale of the growth in commercial activity in England during this period. A high proportion of civil litigation concerned failure to pay debts or to honour commercial agreements. And there was a massive rise in such litigation. In the central Westminster courts of King's Bench and Common Pleas, around 5,000 such cases were initiated each year in the 1560s – itself a doubling in the volume of litigation prevailing at the turn of the sixteenth century. By the 1580s around 13,000 cases were being initiated annually. In 1606 the figure was 23,147, and in 1640 it was 28,734. Comparable increases are also observable in the records of the other central courts and in those of the numerous local courts which handled commercial disputes in England's provincial towns. Moreover, such litigation was only the tip of the iceberg of commercial transactions being conducted by the early seventeenth century. It represented only the deals that went wrong – in all likelihood a very small proportion of the many that were satisfactorily concluded.

The evidence of the law courts confirms the validity of Tawney's view that 'it is through the widening of the influence of commerce and commercial transactions that the economic developments most typical of [this] period take place'. Whereas in 1500 much marketing remained highly localised and longer-distance commerce involved flows of goods across local societies which retained a considerable degree of economic autonomy, the dominant impression of much of England and Wales in the early seventeenth century is that of a society which was interconnected by commercial transactions as never before. This is most evident in the development of longer-distance markets for agricultural and industrial products which meant that by the mid-seventeenth century many rural households were linked as producers, or as consumers, or as both, to England's major cities – including London itself – by only one or two intermediaries. But it is also revealed in small things. In the Lutterworth area of Leicestershire, there was a marked reduction in the number of households which possessed the equipment to spin wool or flax. They no longer took their home-produced yarn to village weavers. They acquired their cloth from Lutterworth drapers. Prominent among the corn dealers of the same town were bakers who by the mid-seventeenth century consumed forty quarters of grain a week – enough to provide bread for twice the town's population. The additional loaves were sold from horse-panniers to the villagers of the surrounding countryside. The manorial oven had given place to the baker's delivery. This was a gradually commercialising society, in which both the livelihoods and the quotidian dealings of a far larger proportion of the population were increasingly shaped by markets.

The intensification of internal traffic of all kinds is perhaps our best indication of the growing commercial integration of the regional economies of England and Wales. The extent to which similar developments took place in Scotland, however, is questionable. Certainly, there are some signs of enhanced commercial integration. The food markets of Edinburgh and of other major towns in the south-east served to focus agricultural production in the region and by the 1630s there existed an east-coast market for grain which extended as far north as the Moray Firth. Again, at the turn of the seventeenth century the distinctive 'chiefly economy' of the western Highlands and Islands, which had traditionally been based on production to satisfy wholly local needs – the subsistence of the peasantry and the feasting and feuding of the clan chiefs – was beginning to be penetrated by greater involvement with Lowland markets through the export of cattle. As early as the 1580s cattle were being brought down from the shielings of Skye in August to be swum to the mainland and driven to the September fairs at Falkirk and Stenhousemuir, and by 1641 the Earl of Seaforth was contracting to deliver 300 beasts a year to an Edinburgh dealer.

Scottish economic development in this period remains underresearched. But it seems unlikely that the Scottish economy witnessed a galvanising of commercial activity comparable to that which took place south of the border. Scotland remained not only an overwhelmingly rural society, but also one in which the vast majority of the rural population lived in most respects outside a market economy. Most Lowland lairds still collected their rents in kind and marketed the produce themselves, while the Highland cattle trade was also developed by clan chiefs seeking to expand their cash income. The marketing in which their tenants engaged was for the most part what R. A. Dodgshon terms 'a trade in use rather than exchange values', engaged in to supply those needs not met by home production rather than in pursuit of profit. In addition, Scotland lacked England's widespread participation in rural manufacturing geared to the supply of distant markets, and its urban population was small. Save in the most favoured regions, essentially the major towns and their hinterlands, it seems unlikely that it possessed the broad foundation of consumer demand necessary for the development of closer commercial integration.

Nor was Scotland greatly involved in the other major source of the commercial dynamic of the late sixteenth and early seventeenth centuries: overseas trade. The development of coal and salt production provided Scotland with new export commodities to add to its traditional staples of hides, fish and coarse textiles. The trade of the east-coast ports expanded in volume and to some extent in geographical range. Sweden grew in importance as a trading partner, supplying timber, iron and flax. So did England, though not to a degree that would imply significant integration of the economies of the two British kingdoms. The economic union envisaged by James VI and I after 1603 was attractive to neither party. In the main, however, Scottish trade continued its traditional patterns of exchange with Scandinavia, France and the Netherlands. As Dr Whyte puts it, 'At a time when the horizons of European traders were widening to include the New World, Africa and the East Indies, those of Scottish merchants were firmly fixed on the North Sea.'

In contrast, the pattern of English overseas trade which had been established in the fifteenth century, and reached its apogee in the early 1550s, began to give way to a more diversified pattern of trade which linked the domestic economy more closely and more directly to a larger world economy. The established nexus of the cloth trade between London and north-western Europe continued, though the turmoil created by the revolt of the Netherlands against the Spanish crown led the Merchant Adventurers' company to shift their base of operations from Antwerp to Middleburg and then Hamburg. English merchants, however, were also venturing further afield – to the Baltic, Iberia, the Mediterranean, the East Indies and the New World.

The geographical expansion of English overseas trade has often been interpreted as the outcome of a search for new markets for English cloth in response to the commercial crisis of the 1550s. It was partly so. But it also involved the desire to establish direct access to a variety of high-profit import goods previously obtained via the Antwerp entrepot. In addition, it demonstrates a more generalised will to explore new commercial opportunities, stimulated perhaps by the growth of commercial information in the English trading community.

Such commercial exploration was presaged in the 1550s by voyages to Morocco, Muscovy and the Guinea coast – all of them concerned ultimately with the opening of routes to the east. From the 1560s, however, willingness to face the risks involved in the pioneering of new trades was enhanced by the restrictive policies adopted by the Merchant Adventurers in their management of the traditional cloth trade. The Merchant Adventurers – a body of fewer than 200 traders in most decades of the period – were anything but adventurous. They had an aversion to risk. Their response to market contraction was two-fold. On the one hand, they sought successfully to maximise their share of a reduced trade by using their political influence to exclude foreign merchants, by raising entry fees to the company and by policing the activities of 'interlopers' in the trade. On the other hand, they strictly 'stinted' the export quotas of members in order to stabilise profits. With opportunities in England's premier trade so limited, merchants of a more enterprising disposition had reason to look elsewhere.

Expansion came in two phases. The first began in the 1570s and focused upon the Baltic, Iberia and the Levant. In 1579 the Eastland Company was founded to establish direct links with the Baltic lands (a trade previously conducted either by merchants of the Hanseatic League based in London or via the Netherlands). This involved the export of finished cloths, and brought particular benefits to the emergent New Draperies and to northern cloth districts exporting through York and Hull. Of at least equal importance, however, was the securing of direct access to the sources of such import goods as grain, timber, pitch, hemp, flax and iron.

Trade with the Iberian peninsula and the Mediterranean was advanced by the establishment in 1573–4 of the Spanish Company, and in 1581 and 1583 of the Turkey and Venice companies, which merged in 1592 to become the Levant Company. These trades were all pioneered by 'new men' – London and Bristol merchants who stood outside the charmed circle of the Merchant Adventurers – and they were not primarily motivated by the search for export markets. Southern European markets for English cloth were limited. The New Draperies and other finished cloths exported to them were certainly able to undercut the prices of cloth produced in north Italy, and contributed to the decline of the Italian industry. But they were sometimes sold at or below cost by their exporters in order to finance the purchase of the import goods on which the profitability of the southern trades really depended: wine, dried fruit, fine wool, iron, silks and spices. By the early seventeenth century, the southern trade was well established. Imports of raw silk rose from 12,000 pounds weight in 1560 to 125,000 in 1621, and 213,000 in 1640, and those of currants from 9,000–10,000 hundredweight a year in the 1590s to 40,000–50,000 hundredweight a year in the 1630s. Meanwhile, the Levant merchants also became involved in the internal carrying trade of the Mediterranean, operating from their principal base at Leghorn (Livorno). Their success encouraged further expansion, and the foundation in 1600 of the East India Company to initiate direct trade with the sources of oriental spices – in particular pepper – a venture in which members of the Levant Company were heavily engaged.

Each of these Elizabethan trading initiatives involved the establishment of a chartered trading company to which the crown granted monopoly rights for the prosecution of a particular trade. Most of these were 'regulated companies' in which the directors of the company exercised a general oversight of the trade – which might include the maintenance of overseas factors and negotiation with foreign powers – and laid down regulations for its conduct. Ordinary membership was confined to 'mere merchants', who were licensed to participate on payment of an entry fee and traded as individuals, within the framework of the company's rules. Some, like the East India Company, were 'joint-stock companies'. These were associations of capital, open to any investor. Trade was conducted by the directors on behalf of the company, and the proceeds were shared among investors. Initially, the capital advanced was periodically repaid, but success encouraged resubscription and gradually share-ownership became permanent and a market developed in company stock.

As the trades concerned became well established, the monopolistic privileges of these companies tended to become increasingly resented by those whom they restricted or excluded – the parliament of 1604, for example, witnessed a vigorous attack upon the regulated companies. Their positive role, however, can scarcely be doubted. Individually they played a vital part in the pioneering of new trading systems, not least by reducing the risks involved to those with the enterprise to engage in them. Collectively, they brought about a diversification of English trade which was of the utmost importance. Their establishment of export markets for the New Draperies helped plug the gap created by the decline of the broadcloth trade. They created a larger, more diverse and highly profitable import trade in both luxury commodities and raw materials. And finally, by their success, they paved the way for the second phase of commercial expansion.

That came in the early seventeenth century and it encompassed the Atlantic. English involvement in the New World, of course, dated back to the Cabot voyages of the 1490s, and by 1600 already included voyages of exploration, illicit trade with the Spanish colonies of the Caribbean area, fishing, piracy and unsuccessful attempts at colonisation. Of these, the most economically significant legacy at the turn of the seventeenth century was the Newfoundland cod fishery. The number of vessels engaged in fishing the Grand Banks had risen from around forty in 1578 to around 150 in 1604, and was to reach between two and three hundred in the 1620s, not least because of the demand for dried cod in southern European markets now accessible to English merchants. The early seventeenth century, however, brought the establishment of permanent English settlements on the North American mainland and in the Caribbean, and with them the transformation of the potential for transatlantic trade.

The North American colonies were founded for a variety of reasons. Those established in New England after 1620 owed their origins to religious idealism. But even Puritans could not live by the Word alone and the economic viability of the northern colonies soon came to depend not only on family farming, but also on commercial dealing in fish, furs and timber. The Chesapeake and Caribbean settlements, in contrast, were founded primarily for their economic potential, and it rapidly became clear that their long-term future depended upon the establishment of colonial production of staple exports for British and continental European markets. The great merchants of the established companies had no stomach for that. They could secure a quicker and surer return on their capital elsewhere. And in consequence the development of the American trade fell to a further generation of 'new men', acting in partnership with planters who rapidly fell under their domination. They included younger sons of the minor gentry and yeomanry who lacked the means to enter the great trading companies, as well as shipmasters, mariners, retailers and tradesmen, most of them based in London and Bristol. Some had themselves been emigrants to the colonies. Some had begun by provisioning the colonists. They were often young, ambitious and willing to take full advantage of a commercial environment which was virtually unregulated and fiercely competitive as colonial production became established and expanded rapidly in the 1620s and 1630s.

Tobacco, a crop which required little capital or labour, kept well and fetched a good price in Europe, was the backbone of the new trade. Between 1622 and 1638 the quantity of tobacco imported to England rose from around 60,000 to some two million pounds weight a year. Prices fell dramatically and what had been a luxury commodity became an item of mass consumption for which the market was potentially enormous. The North Atlantic trade had been born, and by the 1640s, as Dutch entrepreneurs introduced sugar production to the Caribbean islands, it was rapidly maturing.

By 1640, then, English overseas trade had become more geographically extensive, more diverse in its nature and more complex in its structure. It would be mistaken, however, to exaggerate the extent of the transformation that had been achieved by that date. English trade remained heavily Eurocentric: the Indian and Atlantic trades held much promise but were still in their youth. The export trade continued to rely upon the sale of high-quality cloth, a relatively expensive commodity for which there was only a limited market, and, though it had diversified, it had not grown significantly in volume. The import trades had grown – the annual value of London's imports trebled between 1600 and 1640 – and the merchants who established them had demonstrated impressive enterprise. But they still played second fiddle to their Dutch competitors in most of the markets they had entered.

Nor should the significance of the changing patterns of overseas trade for the expansion of the domestic economy be exaggerated. The diversification of the cloth trade was of course of considerable importance to the stability of the clothing districts. Yet, insofar as trade expanded, it was import led. It fed domestic demand for a larger range of essentially luxury products. If the dynamic of the age was commercial, that dynamic was for the most part domestically generated, and the intensification of commerce which was such a marked feature of the period took place primarily in the inland trades. Estimates of the volume of English merchant shipping suggest that it may have tripled between the 1570s and the mid-seventeenth century. Yet whereas between 1582 and 1660 the tonnage committed to foreign trade rose by under one-third, that involved in the coastal trades rose more than five-fold. In 1660 overseas trade employed a significantly lower *proportion* of an expanded merchant marine than had been the case in the 1580s.

This points to the conclusion that, while overseas trade has an important place in the panorama of economic expansion which has been described in this chapter, that expansion was led by a growing domestic market for goods and services. Its sheer scale lends plausibility to the 'pessimistic', 'controlled conjectures' of Professor O'Brien and Dr Hunt that the national income of England and Wales more than doubled in real terms between 1566 and 1641. If this was indeed so, then it helps to account for the fact that population growth was sustained for so long, and for the evidence of growing material prosperity in the period. Yet, at the same time, prices continued to rise, real wages fell, and the period echoed to complaints of poverty and distress. Explaining that paradox requires a shift of emphasis from the means by which growing national wealth was created to the manner in which that wealth was distributed.

CHAPTER EIGHT

'Tumbling up and down in the world'

The ideal of the Tudor commonwealthsmen had been one of distributive justice, by which the members of each constituent group in society should be vouchsafed adequate maintenance for themselves and their households in accordance with their place and contribution to the common weal. The reality of the late sixteenth and early seventeenth centuries was that the distribution of the wealth generated by economic expansion was determined by marked variations in the capacity of different social and occupational groups to hold their own in an increasingly commercialised and competitive society.

i. Landlords

Landlords were in a position to do well. One of the striking features of the ethos of the nobility and gentry of the period was the extent to which, in Joyce Appleby's words, they 'identified themselves with the innovating forces of their times', and became 'deeply involved in the commercial restructuring of their country's economy'. In part this meant direct exploitation of the productive capacity of their estates. Some set examples of the benefits to be derived from more intensive use of the land, like Sir Thomas Pelham of Holland, Sussex, who introduced convertible husbandry on his home farm and enhanced its fertility by ploughing in turf ash and lime. Some invested in exploring the industrial potential of their estates, like Lord William Howard, who acquired boring-rods to prospect for coal on his Cumberland estates and in 1628 sent down northern experts to assist his son-in-law to do the same in Gloucestershire. Some engaged in trade, either as investors in joint-stock trading companies, or on occasion directly, like the Norfolk gentlemen who participated in the coastal grain trade. As members of a small and closely knit social elite, landowners were aware of one another's initiatives of this sort, and success bred imitation. Where they most influenced one another, however, was in their policies as rentiers.

In England and Wales this was the first great age of the estate surveyor. Landlords commissioned surveys of their manors which were of an essentially new kind. Unlike the surveys known since medieval times – which were simply listings of tenants and their obligations and which employed customary categories of holding size such as the 'oxgang' or 'virgate' – the new surveys involved exact measurement in statute acres and precise mapping. The resultant maps, and the accompanying survey books to which they were cross-referenced, presented a meticulous account of the manors concerned, their resources and the distribution of those resources both geographically and by tenancy. But, despite their impressive detail, they were also significant for what they omitted. These were maps neither of townships nor of parishes, but of ownership. The adjacent or intermingled properties of others were usually left blank. They were representations of the landscape from a single perspective, that of landed property, and they were undertaken primarily for the purpose of facilitating the efficient exploitation of its potential rental value.

Not every landlord undertook such surveys, of course. They were of greatest value when management was conducted from a distance. James Bankes of Winstanley in Lancashire – the resident owner of a single manor, which he knew intimately – contented himself with listing his tenants in his memorandum book, together with notes of their rents, the future rental potential of their holdings and desirable reallocations of particular parcels of land when their tenancies fell in. But those who did so best represent the changing tenor of estate-management policy.

Three prominent themes in such policy can be identified. The first was the further extension of leasehold tenure. Throughout England and Wales landlords grew more vigorous in their endeavour to whittle away the encumbrances imposed by inflexible customary tenures and to replace them with shorter, more frequently renegotiable leaseholds which were more adaptable to market trends. Where they were inhibited by well-defended claims to copyhold of inheritance, some adopted the expedient of selling the freehold to the tenants concerned – a temporary victory for the tenants, but one which could be reversed by subsequent reacquisition of the enfranchised land when opportunity arose. On the extensive Verney estates in the south midlands, for example, a consistent policy was pursued of buying up all freehold and copyhold tenements when they became available and converting them to leaseholds. Copyhold was by no means extinguished by such policies, but it was in retreat. Of fifty Yorkshire manors surveyed in the years 1620–60, only fourteen retained any copyhold tenants, and those who remained were of marginal significance in terms of the proportion of the land which they held.

The extension of leasehold was not infrequently accompanied by a second policy: the reorganisation of the land into larger, more compact farms. Two-thirds of the 'decayed' farmhouses listed in the 1607 investigation of enclosure in the midlands had been abandoned not because of enclosure and conversion of their land to pasture, but because the farms concerned had been 'engrossed' into larger units. The same trend is observable elsewhere – in Lincolnshire, Hampshire, Durham, Essex and south Wales, for example – and often enough such gradual consolidation was the prelude to enclosure by agreement between the landlord and the principal tenants.

Third, and of greatest significance for our present purpose, was the acceleration after 1580 of the upward trend in rents which had begun in the mid-sixteenth century. In the final decades of the sixteenth century many of the long leases granted up to a century earlier were falling in and being renewed for much shorter terms – usually of seven to twenty-one years – with higher fines and rents. By the mid-seventeenth century the extension of leasehold tenure and the cumulative process of renewal and enhancement had substantially raised the rental incomes of many estates. The extent to which comparable trends obtained in Scotland is very uncertain. To be sure, there were few legal inhibitions on Scottish landlords, and there were complaints of sharp rent increases in some areas where money rents had become established. Most landlords, however, continued to take rents in kind and derived their cash income from marketing the produce rendered. They stood to profit by doing so, especially if, as was the case among some Highland chiefs, they altered the balance of their demands in favour of the most marketable products of their estates. As yet, the dimensions of change in Scottish rural society remain frustratingly obscure. In many parts of England and Wales, however, a doubling or trebling of rental income was unexceptional, while some landlords did better still: the Myddeltons of Chirk, for example, achieved an astonishing ten-fold increase between 1595 and 1631. Between 1580 and 1640 rents for agricultural land were increasing faster than the prices of agricultural produce. This constituted, as Dr Bowden observes, 'a massive redistribution of income in favour of the landed class'.

That income was spent, in accordance with the values of the landed elite, on the nurturing of what contemporaries termed their 'house', 'charge' and 'port'. Some went on the expansion and consolidation of the estates on which the position of any gentle family ultimately depended. The land market remained relatively brisk until the 1620s, stimulated by sales of crown land necessitated by Elizabeth's long war with Spain (1585–1604) and James I's notorious extravagance. Some was productively invested in those estates. A great deal was spent on the advancement of children: on the education of sons at grammar schools, the universities and inns of court, or on the fees necessary to apprentice them to the more prestigious trading companies; on the instruction of daughters in ladylike accomplishments and the provision of their dowries. By 1625–49 the dowries of young gentlewomen were six or seven times higher on average than had been the case at the turn of the sixteenth century. They had risen faster than general inflation as gentle families competed to secure appropriate matches for their daughters among a relatively small pool of eligibles.

Considerable sums were also invested in the conspicuous consumption that was required either to reflect or to enhance the standing of elite families. This was a great age of building among the gentry and aristocracy. At one end of the scale, modest manor houses were remodelled, extended and improved. At the other, vast 'prodigy' houses were erected by members of the peerage. Between the two, the wealthier county gentry erected new 'seats' – country houses of more than ordinary scale and style. The number of such seats in Northamptonshire and Hertfordshire alone rose from around twenty to eighty between the mid-sixteenth and the mid-seventeenth centuries, most of the new houses being built from the late sixteenth century onwards. Furnishings and interior decorations grew more opulent. Dress became costlier – Sir John Oglander's wife Frances preferred a plain dress to oversee her household, but she needed silken gowns 'for her credit when she went abroad in company'. And leading gentry families went 'abroad' more often and for longer. This period saw the emergence of the London winter season, a growth in absentee landlordship, and the habit of spending landed revenues on the more sophisticated lifestyles afforded by the town. In 1632 Charles I fined some 250 noblemen and gentlemen for remaining in London after a royal proclamation had required them to return to their rural seats for the better government of the localities. That was a substantial minority of England's 2,000 or so noblemen and 'great' gentry. The political economists of the eighteenth century were not mistaken in viewing this period as one of rising consumption among landowners. Individuals might fail through ill-luck or ill-judgement, but as a class they prospered, and the manner in which their wealth was disposed provides a vital link between agrarian change, metropolitan growth and the developing import trade in luxury goods.

ii. *Tenants*

The experience of their tenants was far less consistent. Freeholders were, of course, insulated from rent rises and able to enjoy the full benefits of their husbandry. So were Scottish feuars, whose fixed 'feu duties' diminished rapidly with inflation, and copyholders of inheritance, who were in effect freeholders. But even among those who lacked such advantages, and who were obliged to cope with changing tenurial and rental conditions, there were those who were able to swim well enough with the tide. Those with large farms producing substantial marketable surpluses remained well placed to benefit disproportionately from the continued rise in agricultural prices and decline in labour costs. If they were also able to achieve higher yields by more painstaking or innovative husbandry, then their *net* yields and profits per acre would be proportionately even higher.

Many such farmers were commercially acute. The yeoman Robert Loder, who farmed 150 acres in Berkshire, had nothing to learn about economic rationality and adaptability. He calculated the profits made for him by his horses and his workmen – deciding in the latter case that it was more cost-effective to employ day-labourers than to keep servants in his household – and even worked out the benefit accruing from the dung deposited in his pigeon-loft. He attributed his successes to divine providence. In 1614, when his wheat crop produced 'a most marvellous yeld' of thirteen to one, he closed his accounts with 'The Lorde my God be praysed and magnified and glorified therefore. Amen, amen.' But he knew that the Lord helps those who help themselves, and the next year he increased his wheat acreage, since 'the profitte is greater'.

Loder was literate – an increasingly common accomplishment among English yeomen – and an unusually methodical record-keeper. But there is no reason to suppose that his cast of mind was exceptional, and indeed the evidence of agricultural change strongly suggests that it was not. As Tawney observed, 'it was the development of the large capitalist farmer which supplied the link binding agriculture to the market and causing changes in prices to be reflected in changes in the use to which land was put'. Such men could take rent rises in their stride. Indeed, by the early seventeenth century they must have anticipated them, and in their willingness to expand the scale of their operations they often contributed to them. John Norden's *Surveyor's Dialogue* (1607) describes farmers bidding up rents competitively in their anxiety to secure additional land, 'in a kind of madness . . . but in the best sense it is a kind of ambitious or rather avaricious emulation'. By their own initiatives on manorial land markets they advanced the process of engrossing and consolidating farms, which was favoured by landlords. They were often ready enough to cement that process by co-operating with their lords in enclosure by agreement. They had strong incentives to attempt to improve their yields, and where opportunity existed they also engaged willingly in a host of commercial and industrial activities supplementary to their farming.

Rent rises notwithstanding, the yeomanry, like the gentry, were carving themselves a larger slice of a bigger economic cake. It seems probable that this was also the case among the substantial single tenants of the more commercialised areas of the Scottish Lowlands, most of whom certainly produced for urban markets and some of whom leased grain rents from landlords and marketed the produce. Too little is as yet known of this emergent group in Scottish rural society. Among the yeomen of England and Wales, however, the evidence of prosperity in this period is abundant. The improvements in housing already observable in the third quarter of the sixteenth century both continued and spread in geographical incidence. So did the elaboration of domestic furnishing. The items of joined furniture, pewter tableware and bedding which had led the way grew in number and by the mid-seventeenth century were complemented by a proliferation of soft furnishings and domestic utensils. The distinctive textiles of the New Draperies, for example, can be identified in yeoman inventories in the form of cushions, hangings and coverlets, and they appear also in larger quantities of personal apparel. Yeoman households sent their sons to school to acquire the basic literacy and numeracy that was increasingly necessary if they were to hold their own in a more complex economic world. They were able to generate the cash portions used to establish some of them in trade and the professions. They provided larger dowries for their daughters. In all these ways, their experience can be said to have echoed, at a more modest level, that of the gentry. For many of the yeomanry a new household culture was emerging. It was most visible in material things. But it can also be said to have involved a heightened sensitivity to economic opportunity and responsiveness to material ambition.

Smaller tenants, in comparison, were less likely to be concerned with market opportunity than with gathering threats to the security of their existing position. Most of the cultivable area of Scotland was in the hands of such tenants. Given the limited nature of their exposure to commercial pressures, and in the absence – so far as we know – of significant changes in their tenurial position, the principal threat to their well-being was that of demographic pressure upon available resources. In an increasingly congested countryside, their principal response appears to have been that of intensified efforts to wring an adequate subsistence from an unpropitious environment. The difficulties of the husbandmen of England and of manorialised Wales were of a different nature. Whereas in the mid-sixteenth century many had shared with the yeomanry the initial benefits to be derived from rising agricultural prices, by the early seventeenth century the fortunes and interests of the two groups among the manorial tenantry were diverging.

Husbandmen were still numerous. At Laxton in Nottinghamshire in 1635 the forty-nine tenants of between five and forty acres were still the largest single group in the tenant population. Similarly, a sample of Essex manors in the period shows that 54 per cent of tenants held five to fifty acres, as compared with the 9 per cent who held more than fifty acres and the 37 per cent who held less than five. But, however numerous, they held a diminishing proportion of the land. The large middle range of the Essex tenantry held little more than a third of the land on the manors concerned, while the tiny minority of substantial tenants held more than three-fifths.

To be sure, such husbandmen were far better placed than the numerous tenants of tiny cottage holdings, let alone the wholly landless population. Dr Bowden estimates that in the early seventeenth century, a farm of 30 acres of 'moderately fertile' arable land, tilled with 'average efficiency' by family labour, would normally yield a net farming profit – after payment of rent and tithes – of perhaps £14–15 a year. Dr Howell calculates that in Kibworth Harcourt, Leicestershire, in the years 1606–14, the annual farming profit of a twelve-acre holding would amount to £3 12s. Such profits could sustain a family and provide a small surplus: 'a tolerable, though by no means easy existence', in Dr Bowden's words.

The crucial issue for such households, however, was that of whether they could sustain the viability of the small-farm economy under changing tenurial and market conditions. Some found difficulty in meeting the higher rents being demanded. At Kibworth Harcourt, for instance, the rent of a twelve-acre holding rose by ten shillings a year between the 1570s and the early 1600s. By the standards of the day, it was a 'reasonable' increase, but it cut deep into the precarious surplus of the small husbandman. Again, such peasant farmers were in a relatively poor competitive position. Their small crops and tiny flocks and herds gave them little entry into the market. They could not seriously contemplate expensive or risky innovations. Their lands were inadequately manured and at risk of exhaustion. They were vulnerable to harvest failures which could wipe out their modest surpluses, force them into rent arrears and plunge them into debt, while bigger men throve on scarcity prices. They lived under the threat of the engrossing yeoman whenever tenancies came up for renewal. George Owen wrote of the 'poor tenant' of Pembrokeshire standing 'in bodily fear of his greedy neighbour' at such times. And, as the process of engrossing advanced, they suffered also from the gradual erosion of the subsistence-oriented benefits of the common-field system. For, even without enclosure, the changing internal structure of the tenant community sounded the death knell of communal agricultural management. Increasingly, small tenants appeared marginal and archaic: one midlands observer wrote with contempt of 'the weak and unstocked husbandman', and another of the 'mouldy old leavened husbandmen who themselves and their forefathers have been accustomed to such a course of husbandry as they will practice, and no other', still sunk in an essentially subsistence-oriented mentality.

Despite all these difficulties, many husbandmen survived. Some had the good fortune to be tenants of complaisant landlords who did not trouble themselves to maximise the rental income from small tenants whose holdings seemed too insignificant to matter. Some continued to enjoy the supplements to their livings provided by large, unenclosed commons. Many diversified their domestic economies by engaging in industrial by-employments, like John Briercliffe of Whitehead, one of the numerous small copyholders of Lancashire's Forest of Pendle who had wool cards, spinning wheels and looms in their inventories. He had two sons and two daughters living at home to help sustain the family's dual economy. Best placed of all were those who lived close to urban food markets and who could specialise profitably in market gardening, fruit growing or small-scale dairying. Advantages such as these could help small tenants to survive and even prosper, sharing to a lesser degree the rising real incomes and increased consumption of the yeomanry.

They were worst hit where they were fully exposed to market forces without such compensating factors – above all in the arable lowlands. Studies of the changing distribution of land at Chippenham and Orwell in Cambridgeshire, Shelfanger in Norfolk, Crawley in Hampshire, and in the midland counties have demonstrated graphically how the middle range of holdings was gradually whittled away in this period by competitive failure and engrossment. In part that meant that individual husbandmen were unable to meet their obligations, fell into debt and were eventually forced to relinquish their holdings. In part it meant that would-be husbandmen were unable to compete for the tenancies which became available on the manorial land market against ambitious neighbours with longer purses. As small farm tenancies gradually diminished in number and accessibility, it became harder for the sons of husbandman families to establish themselves on the land. And if, as sometimes happened, the parental generation divided their holdings among their heirs to assist them to do so, this further reduced the number of middle-range farms while increasing that of vulnerable cottage holdings inadequate for the independent maintenance of a family.

The course of change varied locally and regionally, but by the mid-seventeenth century many rural communities were becoming increasingly polarised between, on the one hand, small groups of large-scale commercial farmers who held the vast majority of the land and enjoyed the greater part of the income derived from it, and, on the other, the many cottagers who scraped by on a few acres and whatever supplementary employment they could get. For the young, service in husbandry was becoming less a life-cycle phase for future husbandmen than a system of labour for the larger farms, which drew on the children of the smallholding population and prepared them for a future not as independent small farmers but as cottagers and labourers. The institution persisted, but its social meaning was changing.

Individual fortunes, of course, varied. But for husbandmen in general the economic climate of the early seventeenth century was fraught with risk. As a group they had become an embattled sector of the rural population: weakened by competitive failure on the one hand and less replenished by the young on the other. They clung to the land tenaciously if they could, but, where they survived, it was frequently less as independent peasant farmers than as semi-independent cottager-labourers or as smallholding industrial artisans.

iii. *Merchants, professionals and urban tradesmen*

It is far more difficult to generalise with confidence about the fortunes of the different groups engaged in commerce and industry. We know more about trends in overseas trade in this period than about the traders who shaped them – with the exception of particularly prominent individuals – and surprisingly little about the collective experience of the numerous self-employed producers and distributors who supplied domestic markets. Clearly, most towns were expanding in this period and there are good grounds to suppose that business opportunities were increasing in most sectors of the urban economy. Commercial development diversified the outlets for investment in both inland and overseas trade. Urban manufacturers enjoyed growing markets for their products among both the rural population and that of other towns. Urban growth created larger markets for those engaged in the processing and retailing of food and drink and generated more employment in the building trades. There was greater demand for the professional services of lawyers, scriveners, physicians and apothecaries, and for both skilled and unskilled labour. New wealth was generated in all these spheres of activity. Yet this did not necessarily entail the creation of a broad-based prosperity among those who were engaged in them.

All forms of business in this period were peculiarly hazardous. Many of those who undertook apprenticeships – the usual means of entry – did not succeed in establishing themselves independently, and among those who did subsequent business failure was common. Many businesses were under-capitalised. Rates of accumulation were painfully slow. Most transactions were conducted on 'trust', creating complex chains of debt and credit which rendered those involved in them vulnerable if they did not maintain a viable balance between the two, or were caught up in the knock-on effects of the failure of others to do so. Even the apparently successful could be brought down by unanticipated fluctuations in demand, or wiped out overnight by fraud, fire or other calamities. It was, of course, largely to counter such risks and to secure stable profits that the guilds and trading companies maintained their restrictions on entry, and sought to regulate standards, prices and trading practices. But they could not erect more than a partial barrier against misfortune. There were plenty of 'decayed' guildsmen, and no trading monopoly could secure a merchant against shipwreck, piracy or untimely death. They could, however, do a good deal to maximise the benefits of commerce for limited circles of participants.

For those merchants who were able to gain entry to the great trading companies, there were fortunes to be made in England's diversifying overseas trade. Of a sample of 140 Jacobean London aldermen, fifty-five (39.3 per cent) died worth more than £20,000 – excluding land-holdings – and seventy-eight (55.7 per cent) worth between £10,000 and £20,000. This was prodigious wealth by the standards of the day and probably brought them annual incomes of between one and two thousand pounds, placing them on a par with major landowners.

Entry to the great companies, however, was heavily restricted. The Merchant Adventurers were typical in their view that 'to ad more persons to bee marchants adventurers is to put more sheep into one and the same pasture which is to serve them all'. Apprenticeship premiums were high. Setting up independently required capital of at least several hundred pounds. Nor were the benefits equally distributed even among those permitted to graze a particular pasture. The Levant Company was

dominated by 'a highly ramified network of interconnecting family relationships, the members of which controlled a major share of the trade'.
In 1627–35, its twenty-four leading merchants (12 per cent of the
membership) enjoyed 54 per cent of the Levant trade, and also wielded
substantial influence in the East India Company. As one critic put it, they
were 'Born rich and adding wealth to wealth by trading in a beaten road
to wealth'.

Pioneering a new trade could also be a road to substantial wealth. As
we have seen, the southern European trades were initially established by
'new men', and in the early seventeenth century the emerging Atlantic
trades provided similar opportunities for those with the enterprise to
take the risks involved, and the luck – and ruthlessness – to survive. The
career of Maurice Thompson provides an outstanding example. Born to
a minor Hertfordshire gentry family, he emigrated to Virginia in his teens
and rose to become a ship's captain, a planter and a merchant. By his
thirties he was one of the dominant figures in what Professor Brenner
describes as an emergent 'colonial entrepreneurial leadership', linked by
'a veritable maze of business and family connections', controlling a
disproportionate share of the Atlantic trades and involved in every
significant colonial initiative.

Most overseas traders, however, especially those of the provincial
ports, were neither tycoons of the trading establishment nor audacious
opportunists. The five great merchants of the Eastland trade in the early
seventeenth century were flanked by forty-eight regular exporters and
seventy-five minor participants, and many of the Atlantic traders of
London and Bristol were small men who doubled as ships' captains and
shopkeepers. The net estates at death of such men were unlikely to exceed
one or two thousand pounds, and were frequently much smaller, and
their annual incomes were closer to those of the lesser gentry and substantial yeomen.

Similar distinctions can be observed among those engaged in the professions and in domestic commerce. Barristers could command an annual
income from fees ranging from several hundred to over a thousand
pounds. But they were few in number, and aspirants to the bar might well
need to spend a thousand pounds on legal education at the inns of court
and other costs before becoming established in practice. Opportunities
in the lower branch of the legal profession were growing rapidly, not least
as a result of the growing demand for legal services generated by commercial expansion. There was one attorney for every 20,000 people in
England in 1560; one for every 2,500 in a much increased population by
1640. But entry still involved apprenticeship to an established practitioner
and substantial start-up costs before a country attorney could establish

a practice yielding around fifty to a hundred pounds a year in fees. Again, some of the most lucrative inland trades were closely controlled by privileged groups like the Shrewsbury Drapers or the Newcastle Hostmen. The latter group, who held a monopoly of the booming coal trade from the Tyne, was dominated by around twenty 'Lords of Coal', who diversified into land ownership and mine ownership. Only twenty-six new Hostmen were admitted in the years 1600–59, and they required both substantial capital and family connections. Most branches of domestic trade and urban manufacturing were more open – at least to those whose families could provide an apprenticeship premium and who could muster starting capital of perhaps twenty pounds or more. The numerous factors, dealers, chapmen, shopkeepers and small masters of London and the provincial towns might end their careers with net assets of perhaps a few hundred pounds and enjoy annual incomes of perhaps fifty pounds: a comfortable living by the standards of the day, though often an insecure one.

Such openness, however, was never more than relative. In many crafts and trades the premiums demanded for apprenticeship, and even more importantly the capital required to set up an independent business, were growing. In most towns studied, the number of apprentices enrolled seems to have risen in a manner roughly proportional to urban population growth. Yet there were also greater numbers of lifelong journeymen in most urban crafts. Full citizenship was becoming a more socially circumscribed status in towns like Coventry or Worcester, and in London (where the proportion of adult males who were freemen of the city fell from around three-quarters in the 1550s to around half by 1640). The guilds of London have been described as becoming more 'hierarchically articulated' over time, with a widening economic and social distance between relatively small groups of leading masters and the journeyman 'yeomanry', while in Bristol similar developments gradually produced 'a somewhat more rigidly hierarchical social order'. Moreover, the spread of suburban manufacturing industries, which for the most part lay outside both the controls and the protection of the guild system, entailed a further increase in the numbers of unenfranchised wage-earners in the urban economy.

In such a situation, the principal benefits of expanding urban manufacturing flowed to those with the capital to establish independent businesses and positions of command within the structures of industrial organisation. For employees, real wages remained stuck at conventional levels for decades, while the cost of living continued to rise. Professor Woodward estimates that the annual costs of simply feeding a family of man, wife and three children at an adequate level in Hull and Lincoln rose from around six or seven pounds in the 1560s to over nine pounds in the early 1600s and more than fifteen pounds in the 1630s. Wage rates rose somewhat in the early seventeenth century, but failed to keep pace. In consequence, skilled tradesmen were obliged to work longer hours – if the work was available – in order to sustain their living standards. Among the building craftsmen of Hull, the best paid would have needed to work for 153 days to feed a family of five in the 1560s, and the worst paid for 192 days. By the 1630s, they would have had to find 229 and 306 days' work respectively, in a maximum working year of 313 days. Labourers in the same trades were even worse placed. They would have needed to find 256 days' work to feed such a family adequately in the 1560s, but 459 days' work in the 1630s – clearly an impossible task.

In short, if urban economies were expanding, they were also becoming more capitalistically structured. While small masters might achieve a modest prosperity, a larger proportion of urban craftsmen belonged to a skilled or semi-skilled journeyman proletariat struggling to cope with declining real wages and with the uncertainties of demand for their labour in what was frequently an overstocked labour market.

iv. *'Such as live of small wages'*

The same was true – and is often more graphically documented – in England's rural industrial districts. Some of these areas remained characterised by patterns of dual employment – as in the Leeds area, where a survey of 1628 describes a local economy based on numerous small farms, extensive commons and 'great Clothinge'. But, in many, industrial growth had produced concentrations of population almost wholly dependent upon wage-earning. In Sheffield township by 1616 even the 'best sorte' of householders were described as 'poor artificers': 'not one which can keepe a teame on his own land, and not above tenn who have grounds of their own that will keepe a cow'. The remaining inhabitants, 'the greatest part', were 'such as live of small wages, and are constrained to worke sore to provide them necessaries'. In 1622 the sheriff of Somerset described the 'multytude of poore cottages builte uppon the high waies and odd corners in every countrie parishe', 'stufte with poore people . . . that did gett most of their lyvinge by spinnying, carding and such imploymentes aboute wooll and cloath'. When trade was dead they were 'without worke and knowe not how to live'. In Wiltshire a year later, the oversupply of clothworkers was such that the clothiers had 'abated their wages what they please', so that many were 'not able to live by their diligent labours'. Similarly in Essex in 1629, it was complained, 'there were more alreadie of the weavers trade than could live one by another, for when trading is anything dead, as often in the yeare it is, there is not worke to be had for a number of them and . . . they imediatly fall into a miserable estate'.

In the 1620s, when these conditions were described, the situation in some textile districts was desperate as a result of repeated dislocations of the cloth trade. But even in better times the success of English manufacturing was to a large extent built upon the exploitation of the abundant cheap labour attracted to the industrial districts. The clothiers of the Stour Valley were said to 'care not how many workmen there be . . . for by that means they can have their worke done better cheape'. Some of them responded defensively that it was necessary to keep wages down in order to compete effectively with both other textile districts and overseas industries. But what that meant in practice was Suffolk weavers paid between four pence and eight pence a day in 1603 and Essex weavers earning two, three or four shillings a week in 1636. At those rates a man who worked six days a week for fifty-two weeks a year – a singularly unlikely situation – cannot have earned more than five to ten pounds a year: 'smale wages to mainteyne a familie, paie house rent and buy fire wood', as the Essex magistrates observed. While it was not unusual for Colchester clothiers to have net assets of a thousand pounds at death, it was reported of their workmen in 1629 that their 'wants are so great that they cannot be without worke one weeke' and that many had 'not soe much as a poore flock bedd to lye upon, but are forced to lye only upon strawe and can hardly gett that'. In 1636–7, a quarter of the population of Colchester were reportedly 'reduced to exceedinge greate povertie by the smalnes of wages'.

The fact that both the towns and the manufacturing districts continued to attract poor migrants is some indication of the bareness of the alternative living to be earned on the land. Dr Bowden estimates that at the usual daily wage rates of around eight pence a day in the south of England the annual earnings of an agricultural labourer cannot have exceeded £10.4 even if a man found work on every working day of the year, and he considers it unlikely that 'even the fullest employed agricultural labourer' actually earned more than £9.

A rare opportunity to test such estimates against evidence of the actual earnings of agricultural labourers is provided by the weekly farm accounts of Thomas Cawton of Great Bentley, Essex, for the year 1631–2. Much of the essential labour on Cawton's farm was provided by four living-in farm servants. In addition, however, he employed a substantial number of day-labourers at daily rates which varied from six pence to a shilling for different tasks, and at piece rates for threshing.

These farmworkers fell into three categories. First there were two regular employees, both with specialist skills. Thomas Bouling was a shepherd who was paid a basic retainer of £7 10s a year, and in addition earned further day-wages, mostly between April and September, for tasks ranging from carting, hedging and threshing to harvesting. His total earnings came to £10 5s 2d for the year, while his wife also earned a total of 19s 6d for seasonal weeding, haymaking and harvest work, giving a total family income of £11 4s 8d. John George was primarily a hedger and ditcher, who was also paid frequently as a thresher and for 'sundry work'. He was employed by Cawton for between one and six days a week during thirty-seven weeks of the year, with a long gap from early July to mid-September during which he got only one day's work building a haystack. In his best week of employment he earned £1 3s 9d; in his worst, only a shilling. His total earnings for the year came to £12 6s 5d.

Next, there were two men employed often, but for part of the year only. John Munford regularly worked several days a week between October and February – usually, it appears, as an assistant to John George. He earned £3 15s 7d, but thereafter disappears from the accounts. James Canterdell was fairly fully engaged in sowing and ploughing, often for six days a week, from October to January. He then disappears for six months, reappears fully employed in haymaking and during rye harvest for seven weeks, vanishes from the accounts again for a month, and finally reappears in the last week of September, paid for six days' sowing. He never earned more than sixpence a day or three shillings a week and in total was paid £2 1s 9d by Cawton during the nineteen weeks of the year for which he worked for him. Men such as Munford and Canterdell presumably worked for other farmers as well, but even if they did so it seems improbable that they would have much more than doubled the income they earned from Cawton. Finally, Cawton employed a substantial number of additional men and women – including Thomas Bouling's wife – as casual labour during the peak seasons for weeding (June), haymaking (July) and harvesting (August–September). They must have gained the greater part of their livings elsewhere.

Cawton's exceptionally detailed accounts make it clear that some fully employed, specialist farmworkers could earn a living comparable to that of a small husbandman – at least while they were in their prime. The annual earnings of most, however, probably fell well below Dr Bowden's optimistic estimate of nine pounds. Hence the importance for such people of the possession of an acre or two of land, a cottage garden, access to common rights or the chance to buy provisions at below market rates from their employers. For the increasing number of landless people who enjoyed few or none of these benefits, even the low wages paid in rural industry or to urban labourers must have seemed attractive.

In town and country alike, the final quarter of the sixteenth century and the early decades of the seventeenth century witnessed the emergence of a larger and more wholly wage-dependent labouring population, which probably constituted at least half the English population by the mid-seventeenth century. Agricultural intensification, urban growth and industrial expansion meant that there was work for more such people, but as we have seen it was often seasonal or highly insecure, while the constant pressure of greater numbers on the labour market meant that wages were low and underemployment a general reality.

The result was a growing problem of 'structural poverty' – poverty which derived not so much from individual misfortune or default as from the fact that for a growing proportion of the population periodic hardship was virtually inevitable, for the demand and rates of payment for their labour were such as to mean a diminishing capacity to meet their households' needs. This produced a distinctive life-cycle for labouring people. As servants they were cushioned by being housed and tabled in their masters' households, and could save their wages with a view to eventual marriage. As young adult cottagers or craftsmen they might manage well enough until they had perhaps two children, and even enjoy a modest surplus income. But too many mouths to feed meant straitened circumstances. Sickness, injury, premature death or simple unemployment could plunge their families into destitution. One such was the unemployed clothworker Richard Hammond, who petitioned in 1637 that 'my Charg is soe great that I can make shift noe longer for I have 5 Cheldren to keep and I had much adoue to keep them when I had work enough and I have made all the shift that I can'. Hammond sought work, not poor relief. He declared with evident pride, 'I never chardged the towne for a penny, not soe I desire now but Crave work . . . to mayntaine my Charg'. For such people, advancing age further diminished their employment chances and earning capacities. Old age – if they reached it – meant almost inevitable dependence on charity.

Many of these people, it has been said, were virtually 'economically superfluous'. To be sure, their lives were often enough economically marginal: cottaging where they could, scouring the resources of the commons, gleaning the fields, cadging assistance from kinsfolk and neighbours, moving from place to place if there seemed a better chance of scraping a living. They took what work they could get. Margaret Knowsley of Nantwich, Cheshire, was a labourer's wife who in 1626 had three young children and a baby, and was pregnant. She worked as a domestic servant to the parish minister, cleaning, laundering, gardening and fetching fuel and water, took seasonal agricultural work, knitted and provided medical services. Henry Savery of Stow Bardolph, Norfolk, left service in 1629, went to London, tried his luck as a seaman, returned home to work as a labourer, then left again with seven shillings in his pocket, and travelled to Suffolk, then London, then Yorkshire, and back to London – working his way 'up and down the country' – until he was taken as a vagrant in Highgate and returned again to Norfolk. It was easy enough for such people to slip into the ranks of the 'begging poor', or into vagrancy, but while they worked they were far from economically superfluous. The cheapness of their labour was not the least factor in the success of those who bought it, and collectively they generated a large part of the demand for food and other basic necessities on which economic expansion was based.

v. A polarising society?

If the national income of England and Wales doubled between the 1560s and the 1640s, the distribution of that income was markedly and increasingly uneven. This was an expanding economy, but one with a growing problem of structural poverty. It was a commercialising society in which involvement in markets was a more familiar dimension of everyday life and a source of new opportunities. Yet those whose competitive position was weak struggled for their livings in an environment of greater insecurity.

To be sure, their insecurity was hardly to be compared with the scraping existence, amounting perhaps to a general immiseration, which appears to have been the lot of the peasantry and labouring people of Scotland. Though inadequate documentation means that the full effects of demographic growth and inflation upon the Scottish people remain in many respects uncertain, the marginality of the subsistence of a high proportion of the population of the northern kingdom was graphically demonstrated in years of harvest failure. Famine afflicted Scotland on a national scale in 1585–7, 1594–8, 1623 and 1649–51, while there were more localised crises in the Highlands in 1602 and 1634–5. In 1623, perhaps the worst of these years, the crisis precipitated by two successive harvest failures took an appalling toll. Dumfries lost over a tenth of its inhabitants, Dunfermline perhaps a quarter and Kelso a third, to hunger and the diseases spread by famine conditions as desperate country people crowded into the towns in search of relief. At Burntisland in Fife, the parish gravemaster paid for 329 burials between April and November 1623 of 'parechinaries and other pore outland people': possibly a third of the local population.

England and Wales were not vulnerable to famine on such a scale, thanks in the main to their more productive agriculture, the more wide-spread existence of alternative means of gaining a living, and the capacity of a more integrated marketing structure to supply dependent areas with food. Nevertheless they were not spared from hardship. In the later 1590s, there were four successive harvest failures. Food prices rocketed. Demand for non-essential manufactured goods fell. Small farmers slid into rent arrears and debt. There was widespread misery among the labouring poor. In the most vulnerable areas of the upland north and west – where agricultural land was most marginal, numerous small-holders subsisted without adequate reserves to fall back upon, rural industry was depressed, local populations depended upon imported grain, and the transportation of relief supplies was difficult – there were famine conditions in the winters of 1596–8.

The worst-affected region was Cumbria, which had much in common with Lowland Scotland. Elsewhere, however, the dependence of a growing proportion of local populations upon production for long-distance markets was creating a different kind of economic vulnerability. In 1614–16, for example, the 'Cockayne Project', a misguided attempt to capture the broadcloth-finishing industry which involved prohibiting the export of unfinished cloth, precipitated an acute crisis in the industry. Netherlands merchants refused to buy the finished cloth. Exports plummeted. Dutch competitors seized the opportunity to expand their market share. The rapid disinvestment of clothiers who ceased to put out work produced widespread unemployment in the broadcloth-producing districts. Abandonment of the scheme in 1616 led to partial recovery, but the broadcloth industry remained beset by strengthening competition from the Dutch in a declining European market. By 1640 undressed cloth exports had fallen to less than half the level which had obtained prior to 1614. Again, in the 1620s, overseas markets for English cloth were dislocated first by warfare and currency manipulations in central and eastern Europe and then by hostilities between England, France and Spain. These circumstances precipitated successive slumps in first the northern European and then the southern trades, with particularly catastrophic results for the producers of the New Draperies. There was massive distress in the textile districts of the west country and East Anglia, and in many towns, and recovery in the 1630s was slow and uncertain.

Such periods of acute crisis might be dismissed as exceptional. But their lingering effects coloured the economic experience of the second, third and fourth decades of the seventeenth century, and they were exacerbated by further harvest crises in 1622–3 (which once again brought heavy mortality from malnutrition and its associated diseases in the upland north) and in 1630–1. Moreover, they highlighted the weaknesses of an economy and society which was gradually undergoing structural transformation. The capacity of agriculture to feed a growing population remained uncertain. The small-farming economy was increasingly threatened. Overseas trade and a cloth industry heavily reliant upon overseas markets were vulnerable to external dislocation, shifts in demand and foreign competition. The internal market was sufficiently integrated to create regions dependent for their food supply upon external sources but insufficiently developed to ensure the adequacy of that supply in conditions of scarcity.

Above all, these bouts of crisis threw into stark relief the gross disparities which existed in the distribution of an expanding national income – the extent to which, as Tawney observed, the seductive brilliance of the Elizabethan and early Stuart age 'gleams against a background of social squalor and misery'. There was, of course, nothing new about poverty or inequality. But the marked divergence in living standards and life chances between those who gained and those who lost in the decades around 1600, and the sheer growth in the numbers of the labouring poor have led many historians of England and Wales to view this period as one not only of economic expansion, but also of social polarisation.

So indeed it was. There were more opportunities both to acquire and to consolidate wealth. Yet a larger proportion of the national population was more deeply mired in a perennial struggle for economic survival. While the elite enjoyed in enhanced measure the habits of luxury which had always been their hallmark, the labouring poor struggled to feed and clothe themselves and shivered in cottages 'not fytte for any honest man to dwell in but onlie for beggars'. But it was something more too. For the period also saw the expansion and elaboration of what by 1640 social commentators were beginning to term 'the middle sort of people' – a composite body of people of intermediate wealth, comprising substantial commercial farmers, prosperous manufacturers, independent tradesmen and the increasing numbers who gained their livings in commerce, the law and the provision of other professional services.

The greater salience of such groups in the social order derived in part from the opportunities afforded by economic expansion for upward social mobility. For the most part, however, they were recruited not from below, but either from within or from above. The capital necessary to stock a large farm, launch a business or establish a professional practice meant that the majority of entrants to business and commercial agriculture were themselves the sons of yeomen of substance, tradesmen and professional men, or – in the case of the great companies and most prestigious professions – of the gentry. Whatever their individual origins, they were increasingly recognised as a distinctive grouping in society, distinguished from the landed gentry by their occupations and distanced from the 'meaner sort of people' by their prosperity and economic clout. Their growing presence was a matter of the first importance. The entrepreneurial initiative of such people – what Charles Wilson called 'a sense of market opportunity combined with the capacity needed to exploit it' – underlay the economic dynamism of the period. As the principal beneficiaries of change, they were able to place their own children in positions of advantage within a changing economic order. And collectively they constituted the core of the enlarged domestic market for an elaborating range of goods.

Whether we choose to emphasise the element of polarisation or to dwell instead upon the significance of a tripartite reconfiguration of the distribution of wealth and economic power is a matter of perspective and of purpose. Both were dimensions of a complex process of economic and social differentiation, of diverging life chances and living standards, which produced different outcomes in different local and regional contexts. Throughout the kingdom, however, the medieval conception of the society of estates was gradually losing its relevance. An alternative social order was emerging in England and Wales, composed along lines determined by new economic fields of force.

CHAPTER NINE

Redefining the commonwealth

The gradual decomposition of the Tudor conception of the common-wealth involved not only shifts in economic and social structures, but also adjustments of attitudes, values and social relations. By the turn of the seventeenth century, in Professor Clay's words, 'decades of population growth and inflation had wrought such a transformation that the economy and society to which mid-century conservatives had liked to hark back had, if it ever existed quite as they imagined, gone beyond any possible recall'. Forms of economic behaviour which had appeared novel and aberrant in the 1540s were becoming normalised virtually to the point of being taken for granted. Values and relationships characteristic of an earlier economic morality were gradually eroded in their con-straining force.

The term 'eroded' is used advisedly, for they had not vanished. Religious moralists could still denounce covetousness with a vigour Latimer would have applauded. Custom was still appealed to as a bulwark against detrimental change, and could indeed be reinvented to take account of new circumstances. Statutes and proclamations still employed the rhetoric of commonwealth to legitimise the purposes of public policy. Magistrates periodically – and sometimes vigorously – enforced the local and national regulations intended to contain the destabilising potential of economic change and restrain those 'cor-morants of the commonwealth' who sought only their own 'private lucre and gain'. But new words also were being coined in economic discourse to express new ideals, and old words were being redefined to take on novel connotations.

i. Discourse and practice

Perhaps the most significant of the new words was 'improvement', a term much used in the agricultural writings of the early seventeenth century. In that context, improvement initially meant the turning of land to more profitable use and the consequent enhancement of its rental value. To the proponents of improvement, the assumed purpose of agriculture was not subsistence, but profit and rent. They were hostile to the 'plodding and common course' of customary husbandry, drawn to the potential of employing reason and empirical investigation in agricultural practice, and infused with a powerful sense of the possibilities of change. Collectively, they shifted the focus of agrarian writing, and the term 'improvement' came to take on connotations of general betterment. The downtrodden husbandman defended by the Tudor commonwealthsmen was redefined as 'the rude, simple and ignorant clown, who only knoweth how to do his labour, but cannot give a reason why . . . more than the instruction of his parents or the custom of the country'. The new ideal was that of the industrious and innovative yeoman: the improving farmer.

That change of focus further involved a shift in definition of the interests of the commonwealth, from one centred upon a harmonious pattern of economic and social relations to one stressing the virtues of national productivity. For was not improvement of ultimate benefit not only to the individual but also to the commonwealth? To Richard Bernard, author of the popular *The Isle of Man* (1626), this was linguistic sleight of hand to be satirised in his portrayal of the arraignment of Covetousness, a villain who also went by the aliases of Good-husbandry and Thrift, and who was defended by his kinsman Sir Worldly Wise as a 'good Commonwealth's man'. Yet the discourse of improvement was a legitimising rhetoric of undeniably powerful appeal to the ambitious farmer or landlord. It profoundly influenced the developing genre of chorography, which represented rural England, in Andrew McRae's words, as 'a natural order of productivity' – a landscape eager to yield up its bounty – while discreetly neglecting to mention the productive relations by which its exploitation was achieved.

In the economic writings of the time there was also a new effort to understand, and thereby to legitimate, the mechanisms of a more complex economic order. Craig Muldrew has described how growing awareness of the sheer complexity of the networks of credit and interpersonal obligation underpinning a more commercialised economy led to an appreciation of the 'sociability of commerce'. 'There is nothing in the world so ordinarie and naturall unto men, as to contract, truck, merchandise, and traffique one with another,' declared John Wheeler in his *Treatise on Commerce* (1601). In such a context, market relationships could be perceived less in terms of the pursuit of private advantage and more as expressions of interdependence and trust. Society could be conceived of as an aggregate of such relationships bound together by contract. Again, Joyce Appleby has shown how the prolonged economic trauma of the 1620s 'brought many of the strands of economic development into a knot, tied together by a common crisis' and stimulated both official investigations and pamphlets which opened up the discussion to a broader public.

In a series of pamphlets written in the 1620s, Thomas Mun went beyond the cataloguing of the causes of the present crisis to the development of a model of the world of trade as a coherent, mutually supporting community in which 'by the course of trafficke . . . the particular members do accommodate each other, and all accomplish the whole body of the trade'. He argued that in such a system the health of trade was to be measured not by the balance obtaining between the 'treasure' gained by exports and expended on imports, but by the earnings, or residual credits, accruing from the whole process of commerce. Mun was developing a conceptual model of the market. In the same years Edward Misselden explored the nature of value, arguing that goods are not fixed in value, that exchange takes place only if it offers advantage to both parties, and that the market is the best means of determining both. He saw trade as subject to its own laws and regularities, defended the legitimacy of the profits made by merchants in the course of commercial exchange, and measured the well-being of the commonwealth in terms of the accumulated profits of its members. 'Is it not lawfull for merchants to seeke their *Privatum Commodum* in the exercise of their calling? Is not gaine the end of trade? Is not the publique involved in the private and the private in the publique? What else makes a commonwealth, but the private wealth . . . of the members thereof in the exercise of *Commerce?*'

None of these views was disinterested. Wheeler was secretary of the Merchant Adventurers' Company and a defender of its privileges. Mun was an East India merchant whose theories justified the export of bullion essential to that trade. Misselden was a merchant too, and one opposed to the official setting of exchange rates. But, while undoubtedly promoting particular interests, these men, and others like them, also demonstrated a growing willingness to come to terms with the complexities of commercial exchange, to explore its mechanisms and give frank recognition to its motivations. By doing so they introduced new elements into the discussion of economic policy. Nor are their writings the only examples of the extent to which contemporary opinion had diverged from the moral fundamentalism of earlier economic values.

The satirists of Jacobean and Caroline England lampooned the greed and acquisitiveness of their age, but in a mood which tempered scorn with resignation, and in full awareness that these vices permeated the whole of society. Others, however, celebrated merchants and clothiers as agents of national greatness, attributing to them classically aristocratic virtues of hospitality, magnanimity and patriotism. And still others vigorously appropriated a further range of traditional moral virtues and presented them as central elements in an avowedly commercial morality – notably diligence, sobriety, attention to business, trust, honest dealing and above all thrift. 'Thrift' expanded its meaning from being descriptive of a *condition* of material prosperity to encompass the *means* of acquiring such prosperity, means which were themselves undergoing redefinition. To the mid-sixteenth-century Bristol preacher Roger Edgeworth, 'He that feareth God will do good deedes, and will eschue the contraries, and his thrifte shall come accordinglye.' To Thomas Tusser, whose *Five Hundred Points of Good Husbandry* (1573) was the most popular poetical work of its day, the 'Ladder to thrift' was ascended by frugality and economical management. In Thomas Powell's *The art of thriving* (1635) – a work which took as its premises that 'all men are, or would be, rich', and that 'every man sits at the anvil or forge of his own fortune-making' – thrift and diligence were the way to riches. Those like Robert Loder who exemplified such virtues might still attribute their success also to the blessings bestowed by divine providence, but a subtle shift had taken place in their conception of meritoriousness. Such shifts of attitudes and values were of real consequence, for they both reflected and influenced changing economic practice. That this was so is particularly well illustrated by the transformation of attitudes towards two issues of peculiar symbolic significance – usury and enclosure.

Usury – the lending of money at interest by a contract involving no risk to the lender – was a practice proscribed by medieval canon law as contrary to the laws of God and of nature. It was forbidden in Old Testament texts and held to be an unnatural use of money (which, in the opinion of St Thomas Aquinas, was a mere token of value, and thereby incapable of reproducing itself). Not all forms of profitable money-lending were regarded as usurious. If a lender shared in the borrower's risk, then the loan became an investment meriting a share of the profits. Those who had initially lent freely were also thought to be entitled to 'interest' as compensation for a debtor's failure to repay the principal on time, and some canonists went further by permitting interest as compensation for the potential gain forfeited by the lender in freely advancing money to another. Such provisions could be written into the terms of contracts. Nevertheless, to contract intentionally for more than the principal of a loan without sharing the borrower's risk was deemed to be usurious, and usury was universally agreed to be oppressive, unchari- table, a manifestation of covetousness and the most potent symbol of all that the church found unacceptable in the commercial world.

At the turn of the sixteenth century, however, controversy had erupted in Europe over the proper definition of usury. The basic issue was that of intention. Traditionally the presumption had been that whenever money was lent at interest without risk, then the intention of the lender was sinful. Now, however, some canonists were prepared to concede that the sin of usury was not committed if the lender had no intention to commit an injustice, if the borrower entered willingly into the contract, and if the loan was mutually beneficial. These views, which reflected a greater willingness to recognise the legitimacy of commercial practice, provoked a sharp debate between those who insisted upon a strict definition of usury and those who, while continuing to abhor oppressive moneylending, questioned the strictness of the church's pro- hibition. This debate was inherited and developed by the theologians of the Reformation era. Luther took a relatively conservative position. Calvin, who was influenced by the liberal ideas of Charles du Moulin, was more permissive, as was Martin Bucer. But adherents of all confes- sions were divided on the issue. Their common ground was that secular rulers might choose to permit some lending at interest if it served the good of the community. Whether good Christians should participate was another matter.

In England the law vacillated. Statutes of 1487 and 1495 had prohibited usury, adopting a strict definition of the offence. In 1545 the charging of interest was permitted at rates of up to 10 per cent, with severe penalties for those who charged higher rates. Such latitude, however, shocked many contemporaries and the issue remained highly controversial. In 1552 the act of 1545 was repealed and usury, defined conservatively, was totally prohibited in a statute ringing with references to the authority of God's law. Even to a parliament which included many members of the mercan- tile community usury had no place in a Christian commonwealth. This conservative position remained dominant throughout the 1560s among those who preached or wrote about the subject, and was indeed little modified in principle by the Usury Act of 1571.

As we have seen, this act, which moderated the law of 1552, was pas- sionately debated in parliament and occasioned intense heart-searching by William Cecil, who worked through the arguments for and against a relaxation of the law at length in the privacy of his study. All parties were well versed in the theological debate over usury and all agreed that the central issue was that God's law and man's should be in concord. Where they disagreed was in their definitions of usury and in their views on what should be done about it – for, as all knew, it persisted, and frequently involved exceptionally high rates of interest. Some were prepared to permit lending at interest within clearly defined limits. If the offence could not be abolished it could at least be regulated for the good of the commonwealth. Others rejected such pragmatism, insisting on a strict interpretation of biblical precept and rehearsing the manifold evils to the commonwealth held to flow from usury. In the event usury was not legalised, save for the lending out of the capital of orphans and widows, a generally accepted charitable purpose. Loans at rates of up to 10 per cent, however, were tacitly permitted by the setting of mild penalties for such contracts (involving only the loss of interest). Such tolerance was intended to prevent the greater evil of 'heinous' usury, and for loans at higher rates severe penalties were imposed, far surpassing those of the 1545 act. As Norman Jones has argued, the act remained an act *against* usury: 'Rather than being . . . a victory of capitalism and protestantism over outdated medieval moral theology, the statute stands as a monument to the ways of thinking that created that moral theology'.

Within two generations, however, those ways of thinking were to be fundamentally transformed. Whatever the intentions of those who framed it, the Usury Act was widely perceived as legalising the charging of interest at rates of up to 10 per cent. Evidence from both probate inventories and the records of commercial litigation indicate that the amount of money lent by bonds carrying interest increased dramatically in the closing decades of the sixteenth century as economic expansion was fuelled by a developing commercial credit market. Nor did the law inhibit such a development. Cases brought to the courts by informers seeking to profit from the generous rewards offered for information on the practice of heinous usury served to mitigate the high interest rates often charged before 1571, but the lesser offence of petty usury was generally ignored. Indeed by the 1590s, 10 per cent was commonly accepted as the normal level of interest and printed tables were being published to facilitate the calculation of simple and compound interest at that rate. Regardless of its legal definition, 'usury' was being redefined in common parlance as the charging of an *excessive* rate of interest, and the word 'interest' itself was coming to signify a legitimate charge for lending, rather than the compensation due for the loss of a debt.

Despite these developments, conservative attitudes towards usury were far from eclipsed. They were passionately reasserted on a number of occasions, most notably in Roger Fenton's *Treatise on Usury* (1611). But Fenton and those who shared his views were struggling against a powerful new current of opinion. Other Protestant moralists were engaged in developing an alternative moral theology which placed its emphasis less upon positive law than on the primacy of the individual conscience guided by God, and on the virtue of voluntary adherence to high ethical standards in business affairs. Building upon the ideas of Bucer, Calvin and du Moulin, such writers argued that it was no sin to lend at interest if the loan was not inspired by covetous motives, if the interest was not 'biting', if it provided capital for productive investment on the part of the borrower, and if the lender was also willing to lend freely to the needy and to forgive the debts of the unfortunate. Within such parameters, usury was not deemed to be against charity in conscience, and in the most forthright formulations of such views the only usury prohibited was that which was uncharitable and hurtful to one's neighbour. To Sir Robert Filmer, who composed an answer to Fenton in the later 1620s, usury was 'no where in Scripture forbidden to Christians: but . . . is as lawfull as any other contract or bargain, unless the laws of the land do prohibit or moderate it as a point of state or policy'. In this matter, 'We are left to the lawes and customes of the Kingdome to guide us in our Contracts so long as they be not contrary to the rules of charity.'

By the 1620s, as Norman Jones has argued, law, theology and economic experience had 'combined unintentionally to relegate the ethics of economic relationships to the realm of conscience'. The aim of the theologians was to create individual Christians deeply sensitive to the demands of conscience in their worldly affairs. 'Less ardent souls', however, 'drew the moral from the theology that you could do what you felt was right.' Moreover, they did so in a context in which the practice of usury was now ubiquitous, and in which it was frankly recognised by practical men that 'as the world now goeth, and as men's manners now are, no common weale can stand without it'. Accordingly, the discussion shifted from the matter of the lawfulness of usury to that of points of 'state or policy'. Crown servants, notably Francis Bacon, considered whether loans could be registered and taxed. Members of parliament and economic pamphleteers debated whether the 'legal' rate of interest should be reduced. Did the relatively high price of money discourage investment in improvement? Did it lead merchants to abandon active trade in favour of moneylending? Did it adversely affect the price of land? Would the lowering of interest rates provoke a flight of capital abroad?

Such questions were central to the debates of the parliament of 1624 which eventually reduced the permissible rate of interest to 8 per cent, and they reveal how much had changed in fifty years. Whereas the heart of the matter in 1571 had been theological, now it was economic: the effects of the law upon the availability of business credit. The phrase 'All usury is forbidden by the law of God' was struck out of the bill in committee as a matter best left to the divines. The House of Commons dealt with usury as a purely secular issue, and the raising of religious objections in the Lords by the Archbishop of Canterbury resulted only in the adding of a proviso that nothing in the act should be construed 'to allow the practice of Usurie in point of Religion and Conscience'. Strictly speaking, all that had changed was that the permitted rate of interest had been lowered. The act of 1571 had been amended, not repealed. But the manner in which that modification was debated revealed a transformation in the members' conception of economic morality, and of the criteria by which they defined the good of the commonwealth.

The combination of economic and intellectual forces which transformed public attitudes towards usury can also be seen at work in the case of enclosure. As we have seen, enclosure had been stigmatised in the early sixteenth century as inimical to the well-being of the ploughman and to the strength of the nation, an innovation destructive of households, communities and commonwealth and a prime example of covetousness in action. During most of the century the pace of enclosure had slowed, in part because of the statutes prohibiting enclosures involving the conversion of tillage to pasture, in part because rising grain prices rendered such conversion less attractive to landowners. The continuing force of the powerfully negative image of enclosure, however, was amply demonstrated in the vigour with which enclosure in any form was resisted by tenants and commoners who felt their interests threatened by particular enclosure schemes, and by the sympathy with which their grievances were often heard by magistrates, judges and the privy council itself. The rhetoric of hostility to enclosure retained its resonance.

Yet the climate of opinion was also changing in response to the countervailing discourse of improvement. In 1593, in view of the 'great plenty and cheapness of grain', and 'the imperfection and obscurity of the law' regarding enclosures, parliament discontinued the statutes against the conversion of tillage. A flurry of enclosures followed in the midland counties. This relaxation of the laws, however, was ill timed, for it immediately preceded the prolonged dearth of the later 1590s. In 1597 the revival of the enclosure statutes was debated in the Commons, with revealing results. Sir Francis Bacon expressed the government's desire to see the statutes reimposed, with an entirely traditional attack on enclosure as the cause of depopulation, the decay of tillage, idleness and the impoverishment of the realm. Another member took the opportunity to attack covetousness, declaring, 'it is strange that men can be so unnaturall as to shake off the poore as if they were not part of the bodye', and conjuring up the old image of a land 'where sheep shall devoure men'. It was hard for those who opposed the bill to find an effective language of response: Henry Jackman, a London cloth merchant who represented a Wiltshire borough, could only question the allegations of impoverishment, though he wrote in his notebook that 'Men are not to be compelled by penalties but allured by profite to any good exercise.'

Yet while the statutes were revived they were subjected to so many exemptions as to render them virtually ineffective outside the midland counties, and further qualified by the permission granted to suppress tillage on one part of an estate if grassland was ploughed up elsewhere (in effect licensing the practice of convertible husbandry). Moreover, in 1601, when their repeal was again debated, a more coherent opposition case was voiced. Sir Walter Raleigh pointed out that other countries abounded in corn, which could be imported more cheaply than it could be produced at home, and that the Netherlands, which grew little corn, were well supplied by this means: 'And therefore I think the best course is to set it at liberty, and leave every man free, which is the desire of a true English man.' This attempt to appropriate the patriotic card was quashed for the government by Sir Robert Cecil's retort that 'I think that whosoever doth not maintain the Plough, destroys this Kingdom.' The statutes remained in force. But Raleigh was not abashed, urging, in a related debate, his desire to 'let every Man use his Ground to that which it is most fit for, and therein use his own Discretion'. The old rhetoric might still carry the day, but the debate reveals the extent to which, as W. R. D. Jones puts it, 'unity of belief concerning the type of society which it was the duty of the government to maintain had broken down'.

In the early decades of the seventeenth century, support for Raleigh's views was gathering strength. In 1607, in the aftermath of an alarming outbreak of enclosure rioting in the midlands, the government ordered a new enquiry into enclosure and there were subsequent prosecutions of offenders. But the ambivalence now surrounding the whole issue was amply demonstrated by a privy council memorandum of July 1607. This carefully rehearsed both the advantages and disadvantages of enclosure and recommended that, while action should be taken against depopulating enclosure, other forms of enclosure should remain arbitrable, to the end that 'the poor man shall be satisfied in his end, habitation, and the gentleman not hindered in his desire, improvement'. Such thinking underlay the establishment in 1618 of a commission of judges to license retrospective dispensations from the tillage statutes, freeing those who had made enclosures from molestation by informers provided that they had neither caused depopulation nor deprived others of their 'lawfull use of Common'. It also underlay the repeal in 1624 of the 1563 legislation against conversion of tillage, and a growing disinclination to enforce even the exemption-ridden measures of 1597.

The 1620s witnessed a rash of new enclosures throughout the kingdom, an acceleration of change in which the crown itself was by now deeply implicated in response to the energetic attempts of its surveyors to raise the revenues of the crown estates by the improvement of commons. Such projects were carefully justified. The drainage and enclosure of Sedgemoor, for example, was announced in 1618 as likely 'to tend to the good of our commonwealth, the relief and right of the . . . lawfull commoners . . . and the just increase of the revenue of the crown'. But there was not much doubt about the dominant motive. And where 'habitation' and 'improvement' were irreconcilable, improvement was increasingly likely to carry the day. The draining of the eastern fens, initiated with crown support, was represented as a project which would bring a barren and unprofitable wasteland into cultivation, provide work for idle hands, alleviate the poverty of the region, and add a new and fecund province to the commonwealth. The fact that the area was already occupied by thousands of fenlanders who derived a poor but independent living from its numerous resources was overlooked, and the formidable resistance to drainage which they sustained for three decades was gradually worn down while successive governments, if not wholly deaf to their appeals, demonstrated severely impaired hearing.

Much the same was true of the disafforestation and subsequent enclosure of the royal forests of the west country, and of numerous lesser enclosure disputes of the early seventeenth century. As Joan Thirsk observes, the changing attitude of the crown 'positively encouraged gentlemen everywhere to go and do likewise'. And not just gentlemen. Substantial farmers were also drawn to the benefits of severalty and willing to consent to enclosures. Where their interests and ideals diverged from those of their neighbours, local resistance to enclosure was less likely to involve the concerted action of manorial communities than that of the lesser tenantry and cottagers who had most to lose from the extinction of common rights.

The old attitudes were not dead. In the 1630s renewed anxieties about grain supplies led to the establishment of new commissions to discover unlawful enclosures and to exemplary prosecutions by the privy council in the course of which Archbishop Laud demonstrated his personal hostility to enclosers. They lived on also among the defenders of the commons and those who were prepared to champion them. When a new burst of enclosure threatened the common fields of south Leicestershire in the 1650s, the Rev. John Moore, whose father had shown sympathy to the rioters of 1607, remonstrated urgently in both sermon and print against a process which 'made Farmers, Cottagers; and Cottagers, Beggars', and an economic mentality encapsulated by 'those heathenish speaches . . . May I not make the best of mine own?' But the tide was running strongly against him. His neighbour the Rev. Joseph Lee responded with a fierce denunciation of the inconveniences and inefficiencies of common-field farming – 'God is the God of order, and order is the soul of things, the life of a Common-wealth: but common fields are the seat of disorder, the seed plot of contention, the nursery of beggary' – and with a barrage of rhetorical challenges asserting the rights of property and the legitimacy and beneficial consequences of economic individualism. 'May not every man lawfully put his commodity to the best advantage?' Was it not 'an undeniable maxim, That every one by the light of nature and reason will do that which makes for his greatest advantage'? 'By what Law of God or man is every man bound to plow his land . . . whether there be need of corne or no, although he can make more advantage to himself by pasture?' 'The advancement of private persons will be the advantage of the publick', and 'if men by good husbandry . . . do better their land, is not the Commonwealth enriched thereby?' Moore persisted in organising petitions to parliament and won the support of Cromwell's Major-General Whalley. But the bill for renewed restraint on enclosure presented in 1657 found no sympathy there. Assumptions had changed since 1597. As the Master of the Rolls observed, 'he never liked any Bill that touched on property'.

These changes in public attitudes towards usury and enclosure are indicative of a broader process of transition in the economic culture of the period, of gradual movement between one dominant set of values and another. Central to that process was a developing awareness of the claims of alternative interpretations of economic behaviour, and a growing willingness to accept the legitimacy of those claims. It involved less pure innovation than shifts in the definition and description of behaviour, and changes of emphasis and priority. But cumulatively it effected a significant moral repositioning.

Change of this kind bred ambiguities and tensions which were resolved in several ways. For the most part they were resolved by expediency in the day-to-day conduct of economic affairs. Given the existence of a spectrum of alternatives in opinion, people could choose, as Richard

Grassby argues, 'to accept and follow those interpretations of the normative order which best suited their purposes'. They adjusted their behaviour, now reluctantly, now with truculence, to the pressures of change, the demands of economic survival or the lure of gain. To be sure, economic transactions frequently remained embedded in immediate personal relationships and there were limits to the extent to which any individual could pursue personal advantage in defiance of the expectations of those with whom he dealt without fatally damaging his personal credit. Nevertheless, not all transactions were of an equally personal nature. Geographical and social distance could diminish such inhibitions. And adjustment to the norms of a more competitive economic environment could proceed by daily accretion through the myriad of decisions taken and transactions concluded in the course of simply earning a living.

Secondly, they were resolved by the exercise of power. Where different opinions existed on the subject of proper conduct in economic affairs, not all carried equal weight, and not all had equal capacity to prevail. Sometimes the issue was forced. That might mean outright coercion, as when Lady Grace Manners made 'threatening speeches' against free miners claiming the right to work lead on Smerrill Grange in Derbyshire, and then drove them from their mines with a private army recruited from her tenants. It might mean the exertion of social authority, as when Henry Hastings bulldozed an improvement scheme through the manor court of Puddletown, Dorset, in 1629, despite 'great debate' and 'questions moved' by his tenants. It might mean the assertion of economic dominance, as when leading guildsmen arbitrarily changed their journeymen's wages or conditions of work, corn-badgers engrossed the supplies of a country market, or enclosures 'by agreement' meant in effect the agreement of the principal land-holders. Those who proceeded with too high a hand might find themselves the objects of resentment, litigation or even riot. But not everyone had the temerity to dispute the purposes of the powerful, and those who did so could still suffer for it. When the copyholders of Earles Colne, Essex, led by two prominent tenants, took their lord to court over their wood rights in 1622, they gained an arbitrated settlement which was entered in the court rolls of the manor 'for everlasting memory'. They proved that he had been wrong to note on the corner of his account book, 'I can prescribe any custom.' He punished their presumption by doubling their rents.

Finally, tensions could be resolved by authoritative adjudication: by decisions of the courts, interventions by the privy council, or by parliamentary statute. The positions adopted by government carried most weight of all. They might tend one way, as when copyholders were granted the protection of the royal courts, or another, as when municipal magistrates endorsed the decisions of guild-masters. They could vacillate, as has already been illustrated by the changing attitudes of parliament to usury and enclosure. Alternatively, authority could simply stand aside. Growing areas of economic activity remained unregulated. Laws passed in one climate of opinion could be allowed to atrophy for want of enforcement in another. When this was so, as Richard Grassby notes, the absence of external sanctions could render social values more 'subjective and indeterminate', more exposed to the reconfiguring forces of expediency.

Shifts of this kind were taking place in the attitudes of English government during the last decades of the sixteenth and early decades of the seventeenth centuries. Early Elizabethan government, as we have seen, had combined a willingness to lend an ear to projects which offered to expand national resources and employ the poor with an essentially conservative vision of the magistrate's role. This stance underlay William Lambarde's 'charge' to the grand jury of Kent in 1583 that their duty was to seek 'the quiet of the good and the correction of the bad, the stay of the rich and relief of the poor, the advancement of public profit and the restraint of injurious and private gain'. And it was also expressed in a management of the crown estates, which involved, alongside the defence of the crown's interests, a distaste for agrarian change and what Professor Hoyle calls 'a commitment to an ideal of social organisation in which landlord and tenant lived in peace'. He adds, however, that subsequent generations gradually lost patience with such an ideal. In agrarian change, as Paul Slack puts it, the crown became 'a player rather than an arbitrator'. Under the early Stuarts improvement was endorsed. 'Projectors' and 'searchers' were empowered to ferret out opportunities to raise revenue by challenging crown tenants' rights to their lands and obliging them to 'compound' financially for their confirmation. Royal proclamations might still employ the rhetoric of commonwealth, but the crown's own practice owed rather more to the demands of expediency. Its regulative measures were tainted with fiscalism, a willingness to exploit the law for its own financial ends. All this was politically inept, a contribution to the deteriorating credibility of a Stuart monarchy which fell apart in 1640. But it also betrayed a growing moral confusion concerning the role of authority in the face of change. In that climate of uncertainty, government did not wholly abdicate its traditional responsibilities, but it came to define them less ambitiously. As Professor Clay puts it, 'the rear-guard action against change itself was gradually converted into a policy of simply trying to ensure that the distress of the poorest members of the community never reached the intensity which would produce a breakdown of the public peace'.

ii. Overseeing the poor

The most positive outcome of governmental concern was the development and implementation of a national poor-relief system. This was an extraordinary undertaking – one without parallel elsewhere in the Europe of the day, where welfare initiatives were for the most part confined to the towns and to private philanthropy. It has been described by Paul Slack as 'both an intellectual and above all a political achievement' – involving a developing understanding of the nature of poverty, a capacity to formulate practical relief policies and the will to secure compliance with their requirements – and its eventual institutionalisation in thousands of local communities was to exert a profound influence on social attitudes and social relations.

Both the formulation and the implementation of policy were gradual. The law of 1572 had empowered local magistrates to survey the poor and to impose compulsory taxation for their relief. It remained based, however, upon a dichotomous perception of poverty, inherited from the middle ages, which sharply distinguished the deserving 'impotent' poor from those whose poverty was deemed to be the consequence of their own moral default. It left the greater part of the poor, who were neither conspicuously 'impotent' nor 'masterless', vagrant and outside the household structure of settled society, in a distinctly ambiguous position. Nor was it widely enforced outside the larger towns.

In the succeeding generation, it was added to with the issue by the privy council, under William Cecil's guiding hand, of 'Books of Orders' detailing measures to be taken to combat crises occasioned by plague (1578) and dearth (1587). Both drew upon the experience of urban government. But, while the former remained for the most part applicable to the epidemic-prone cities, the latter – which included searches of corn stocks, and measures to provision local grain markets and control prices in time of scarcity – were extended to the countryside. After their initial issue in 1587, dearth orders were reissued, and energetically followed up with flurries of peremptory letters requiring their implementation, in each subsequent harvest crisis of national significance between 1594 and 1631. They became so normalised as the appropriate response to food scarcity that where magistrates were slow to impose them angry crowds not infrequently acted unilaterally to 'stay' shipments of grain in their localities and to force their sale to the poor – a form of 'petitioning in strength and in deed' which was usually successful in stimulating more urgent action from local authorities.

Surveys of need resulting from the law of 1572, and above all from the local implementation of dearth orders, had the gradual effect of modifying perceptions of the problem of poverty. A more intimate knowledge of its circumstances led to fuller recognition of the problems of 'labouring persons not able to live off their labour', a recognition reinforced by investigations of the industrial depressions of the early seventeenth century. Moreover, they enhanced awareness of the need for greater regularity in the provision of relief at the level of the parish. In the wake of the crisis years of the 1590s, the laws were overhauled in a manner intended to clarify responsibilities and to simplify procedures in the interests of their more effective implementation. The poor laws of 1598 and 1601 fixed responsibility for the assessing and raising of rates, the relief of the impotent, the apprenticing of poor children and the setting to work of the able-bodied squarely upon the shoulders of parish churchwardens and 'overseers of the poor'. Parish officers were also empowered to whip vagrants and to return them to their places of origin. Henceforward the system was to be emphatically the responsibility of the parish, with county justices exercising a supervisory role, hearing appeals and when necessary ordering the incarceration of 'incorrigible rogues' in 'houses of correction' (originally envisaged in 1576, but required to be established in every county from 1610).

The next half-century saw the gradual implementation of the parochial relief system. In 1600 poor rates were already established in most towns, and thereafter they became increasingly common in rural parishes, their adoption being hastened by the responses of both local and central authorities to the emergency years of the 1620s, 1630s and late 1640s. Inevitably, the process was gradual and uneven. Not infrequently it involved a degree of foot-dragging by parishioners reluctant to accept the burden of regular local taxation. Yet by 1640, after the energetic monitoring of enforcement by Charles I's privy council in the wake of the crisis of 1630–1, the poor rate was an accustomed fact of life in many parishes. By the 1650s the system was operational in perhaps a third of England's 10,000 parishes and well on the way to the near-universal implementation which was accomplished in the third quarter of the century.

Long before then, however, the surviving account books of parish overseers reveal what were to become the characteristic features of the system. Those deemed able to contribute to the rate were listed and assessed. The impotent poor were identified and paid weekly pensions. Orphan children were placed in households and subsequently apprenticed. Occasional 'extraordinary' relief payments were made to those of the able-bodied poor suffering from temporary crises which rendered them unable to sustain their households. In addition, parish officers were frequently made responsible for the administration of private charitable donations to the local poor – involving, for example, the regular distribution of bread or the periodic provision of clothing. And some made determined efforts of their own to combat the impoverishing consequences of scarcity. At Cawston, Norfolk, during the dearth of 1596, for example, households were categorised in accordance with their degree of need and provided with access to stocks of rye and peas in a particular order and at variable prices.

The poor-relief system as a whole, then, was designed to meet both the potentially destabilising levels of general impoverishment precipitated by short-term economic crises and the more permanent problem of poverty occasioned by long-term economic and social change. Its formulation and implementation demonstrated the exceptional capacity of English government when it chose to act decisively. That the system could be afforded at all also demonstrates England's relative wealth: a tax base of 'substantiall inhabitants' existed to fund the system on a regular basis. In Scotland, in contrast, laws passed in imitation of the English example in the 1570s did not include provision for a compulsory rate and there is little evidence of their enforcement in rural parishes for over seventy years. Yet that the system was needed at all reveals the chronically unequal nature of the distribution of England's wealth, and the perennial fragility of the household economies of the labouring poor. It was characteristic of the situation that at Cawston in 1601 (not a crisis year) a parish officer listed the householders of the parish as being either 'persons of ability' or 'others'. Sixty-eight householders (41 per cent) were 'persons of ability' able to contribute to the rate. The 'others' unable to contribute included the members of twenty households (12 per cent) possessing a house and cow, fifty-seven households (34 per cent) lacking a house and cow, and finally twenty-two households (13 per cent) actually in receipt of relief. The labouring population of the parish was clearly not undifferentiated, and only a small proportion were actually dependent on the parish at that moment, but most of the rest might reasonably have been termed 'at risk'.

The poor laws were intended to meet the needs of such a situation, and within limits they were capable of doing so. Their implementation, however, both reflected and furthered the shifts in attitudes and social relations which accompanied the changing structures of local economies. On the one hand, 'persons of ability' largely accepted their responsibility to provide for the poor – an acceptance encouraged, as the Sussex justices put it, 'partly by the perswasions of us and of their ministers' and partly 'of their owne charytable disposition'. Without this nothing could have been achieved. On the other hand, there were limits to that sense of obligation.

The whole system was highly discretionary. Though nationally uniform in its basic structures, it was also parochial in the extent to which local discretion was permitted in its operation. It was crucial to the acceptance of the system by those who financed and administered it that they were permitted to determine local levels of need and to set their rates accordingly. Perhaps predictably, they were rarely generous. The sums paid in weekly pensions were not usually such as to provide full maintenance for the recipients. In late-Elizabethan London, Dr Archer estimates that they amounted to perhaps a third to one-half of the necessary costs of maintaining a pauper household. They were intended to supplement the incomes of people who were expected to provide what they could for themselves, like Joane Dan of Pluckley, Kent, who was described at her burial in 1603 as 'a poore old maid that lyved partlye by the parish . . . but she wrought mutch for her lyving as longe as she was able, spinning and carding wouls diligently'.

Discretion extended also to the determination of who was deserving of parish relief, and in this regard the system was – and was intended to be – manifestly discriminatory. The impotent poor who were regularly relieved were, in Paul Slack's words, 'few and conspicuous': the aged, the orphaned, the chronically sick. Preference was shown for women and children. In Pluckley they made up more than four-fifths of those relieved, while men received help only occasionally and briefly. At Aldenham in Hertfordshire, 'poor labouring men' were prominent among those relieved only in the dearth crisis of 1631, and even then few received relief for more than a month or two. Yet the marginality of their livings at the best of times is suggested by the fact that a quarter of those relieved are known to have become dependent paupers at later stages of their lives. Parish pensions were granted only to those who otherwise would have faced chronic indigence. They were not intended to cut very deeply into the penumbra of marginality which extended beyond that core of deep poverty. This was made explicit in a 1603 survey of St Martin's in the Fields, London, which reveals that, while 8 per cent of the households in the parish were in actual receipt of weekly alms, a further 19 per cent could be described as those 'that want [that is, need] relief and are likely to come to have relief'. But not yet.

Among those who received relief, moreover, assistance was conditional upon conformity to the behavioural expectations of the overseers. To this extent, it was an instrument of discipline. London overseers, who were 'determined to mould the morals of those in their care', were far from unique. Privately established charities, which extended occasional relief to a larger range of labouring people, were particularly given to explicit definition of the the criteria of deservingness. Gilbert Spence's charity at Tynemouth was to be 'carefully and warylie distributed' by the overseers, 'alwaies regarding that no part therof be given to needles lewde and idel persons, nor to drunkards, swearers or infamous persons'. The dependence of the poor upon the good opinion of 'the parish' was also firmly demonstrated in Wiltshire during the dearth of the 1640s, when entitlement to purchase subsidised grain was restricted to the impotent poor and to such others as could secure a certificate from the ministers and four or five 'chief inhabitants' of their parishes declaring that 'they are laborious and painfull and by reason of their hard charge of children they are not able to maintayne their familie by their hard labour'.

If the discretionary nature of relief was evident in the selection of those assisted, it was even more apparent in the determination of parish officers to exclude those deemed not to be the responsibility of their parish. Those who lacked the 'settlement' conferred by birth or long residence were routinely rejected, and the poor laws provided a powerful incentive to exert control over immigration to the parish. The laws regulating the erection of cottages or the 'harbouring' of 'inmates' (lodgers and sub-tenants) were among the most vigorously enforced of the penal laws, as in Earles Colne, Essex, where cottaging required the permission of the lord of the manor and six chief inhabitants, or in Pluckley, Kent, where in 1635 action was taken against twenty-seven cottagers, described as 'so poore that many of them descend, the rest are likely to descend to receive alms of the parish'.

In this, the chief inhabitants, who were commonly also the principal local employers of labour, needed to balance the benefits of a ready supply of day-labourers against the potential charge such people might engender for the poor rate. It is scarcely surprising that action against cottagers or inmates was often taken retrospectively, when they ceased to be useful and became instead what one contemporary called a 'sore discommodity'. But some parish officers also learned from experience to become proactive. One common solution was to demand that those who encouraged cottagers or inmates should give surety that those received would not 'fall upon the parish'. Another was to attempt to prevent the marriage and settlement of potential paupers. One labourer of Terling, Essex, found when the banns were called for him and his proposed bride in 1617 that 'the parishe would not suffer them to marry'. A year later Anthony Addames of Stockton, Worcestershire, married 'an honest young woman', but found the parishioners 'not willing he should bring her into the parish, saying they would breed up a charge among them'. He had to find a cottage elsewhere, though they still let him work in Stockton.

The paradox of the parochial relief system was that it was at one and the same time an expression of social responsibility and inclusion and an instrument of coercion and exclusion. Relief, in John Walter's words, 'presupposed membership of a community' – a community with a surplus and regular structures for the transfer of part of that surplus to the needy. Yet it also demonstrated the highly stratified nature of that community, the ambiguous position of the poor within it, and the fact that its boundaries and rules were determined by tight oligarchies of leading employers and ratepayers. The ambivalences which it engendered are well illustrated in the speech made by Alexander Strange, vicar of Layston, Hertfordshire, to the parish vestrymen in 1636. Layston had permitted twenty families of cottagers to settle in recent years, many of whom had already required relief. To Strange, the cause of the problem was 'the roote of all evil, covetousness' – the covetousness of those who profited by providing cottages 'to the visible hurt and prejudice of that little commonwealth wherof yourselves are the principall members'. His solution was that such persons should be fined, that cottages should be bought up and pulled down, that charitable relief should be confined to 'auntient poor . . . such as have been a good tyme dwellers', and that no incomers should be accepted save 'honest men, good labourers, and such as with God's blessing will be able to support and maintayne themselves and famlys without being a charge to the parish'. Strange used some old words, but his gloss on them was new. His commonwealth was both socially and geographically bounded and his hostility to covetousness was excited not by the dispossession of the poor, but by its consequences for the poor rate.

To many of the officers who implemented the English poor laws their parishes were little commonwealths in Strange's sense. As 'principall members' they attended to the needs of the settled poor at not inconsiderable cost in time and money. Yet at the same time the experience of doing so enhanced their sense of social and moral distance from the poor, excited their prejudices, bureaucratised the extension of neighbourly charity and taught them how to estimate the relative utility of the poor as an economic resource. As for the poor themselves, the system extended to them certain entitlements. It cushioned the blows of lifecycle crises. It endeavoured to ensure that they did not starve. Yet such rights as were accorded them were conditional and gained at a cost. As John Walter has argued, if the labouring poor had been largely delivered by 1650 from the threat of crises of subsistence, they had also become only too familiar with the realities of what was for many a 'crisis of dependency'.

iii. *Life chances*

Economic expansion between the 1570s and the 1640s thus involved not only increased production and commercial intensification, but also a significant recasting of the occupational structures of England and Wales, shifts in the distribution of wealth and subtle changes in economic attitudes and social relations. Economic development made it possible for the population of England in particular to grow faster and for longer than was the case elsewhere. Yet the benefits of change were poorly distributed. Its costs were evident in the growing economic insecurity of thousands of households. And despite the ameliorative measures of the relief system, those facts gradually began to bite. From the 1590s, the rate of population growth was slowing, by the 1620s it was slowing markedly, and by 1650 it had stopped. The demographic expansion which had more than doubled the population between the 1520s and the 1640s was over.

Traditionally, the cessation of demographic growth in early-seventeenth-century Europe has been largely attributed to the effects of rising rates of mortality, and in particular to the growing susceptibility of populations pressing hard on available economic resources to periodic 'crises of subsistence'. Within Britain, the experience of Scotland perhaps comes closest to that model. As we have seen, the available evidence suggests that by the early seventeenth century the pressure of growing numbers upon Scotland's severely limited economic resources had become acute. The widespread susceptibility to famine of what may have been an increasingly immiserated rural population is one measure of this. Another, more indicative perhaps of the bare prospects facing the young in what was still primarily a subsistence economy, is the extraordinary level of Scottish overseas migration in the period. In the early seventeenth century, and especially after 1610, an estimated 90,000 people left Scotland. Some 20,000 to 30,000, most of them small tenants and cottars from the south-west, migrated to Ulster. Most of the rest went to Scandinavia and Poland, some as pedlars and merchants, but most as mercenary soldiers recruited for the armies of the Thirty Years' War. Licences to recruit 47,000 men were granted by the Scottish government between 1625 and 1642, some 14,000 in 1625–7 alone. Most of these migrants were, of course, young men, and it is possible that migration on this scale more than accounted for the natural increase of the Scottish male population in the second quarter of the seventeenth century. The arresting of population growth in Scotland, and indeed the possible reduction of the Scottish population by 1640, then, can be accounted for largely in terms of the growing incapacity of the Scottish economy to support its people. England and Wales were spared that fate. Migration to the English colonies before 1640 involved substantial numbers, but a much smaller proportion of a population over five times larger than that of Scotland. And while England and Wales certainly endured mortality crises between the 1580s and the 1640s, they were relatively free of those crises precipitated by food scarcity which so devastated Scotland in the same period. Even in the 1590s, famine was mostly confined to the most economically marginal areas of the north and west. In 1623 it has been documented only in some upland districts of the north. Thereafter such crises are conspicuous by their absence.

Crisis mortality occasioned by epidemic disease, above all by bubonic plague, was more common. But plague was principally a phenomenon of the towns, spilling over occasionally into those rural areas which were closely connected to them. The experience was ghastly, yet it is perfectly clear that the towns experienced no difficulty in replacing their epidemic losses while the rural areas remained demographically buoyant. Parish-register analysis further suggests that other forms of mortality exercised limited influence on the stabilisation of English population growth. Life expectation at birth remained relatively good in the late sixteenth and very early seventeenth century, averaging around thirty-eight years. From the second quarter of the seventeenth century it worsened. Infant and child mortality increased and average life expectation fell before stabilising at a significantly lower level in the later part of the century. It is unlikely, however, that this trend exerted a powerful influence on the braking of population growth which had already occurred by 1650. That phenomenon appears to have been largely attributable to declining fertility.

As we have seen, rates of fertility had been falling gently throughout the later sixteenth century. In the early seventeenth century they fell more sharply. Between the final quarter of the sixteenth century and the third quarter of the seventeenth century, crude birth rates fell from 33.2 to 28.6 live births per thousand population and the gross rate of reproduction fell from 2.3 to 1.9. The reasons for this trend are not wholly clear, but there is strong reason to believe that it was primarily the outcome of the connection between prevailing levels of living standards and marital opportunity.

In the first place the decline in fertility rates closely followed, with a time-lag of some ten to fifteen years, the deterioration of real wages in the period. This suggests a relationship between living standards and fertility, though it does not in itself explain the nature of the causal mechanisms involved. Marital opportunity provides the explanatory link. In a pre-contraceptive age, couples could exert little direct control over their fertility within marriage and actual rates of marital fertility do not appear to have changed significantly in the early seventeenth century. What people could do, however, was to decide when, and indeed whether, to marry, and the evidence suggests that it was changes in the age and incidence of marriage which were the principal influence on trends in the overall fertility of the population.

In many English parishes the average age of first marriage – and in particular that of brides – was rising in the early seventeenth century. This was not uniformly the case. At Terling in Essex, Colyton in Devon, and Banbury in Oxfordshire, for example, the age at first marriage for women rose little between the late sixteenth and the early seventeenth centuries. At Bottesford in Leicestershire, it actually fell slightly. But in Shepshed, Leicestershire, it rose by a year, in Hartland, Devon, by two years and in other parishes in Warwickshire, Hertfordshire and Lincolnshire by up to three years. What this suggests is that some local economies were witnessing a significant tightening of marital opportunities.

That this was so is further suggested by the fact that marriage rates were falling. The number of marriages per one thousand population aged 15–34, for example, fell from 9.69 to 7.11 between 1586 and 1646, with most of the change occurring after 1610. Most striking of all, however, is the evidence provided by estimates of the proportion of the female population never marrying. These suggest that, of those born around 1566 who might be expected to have married around 1590 and whose fertile lives would have extended until perhaps 1610, only 4.2 per cent failed to marry. Of those born around 1586, of marriageable age around 1610 and fertile until perhaps 1630, however, some 17.4 per cent failed to marry. For those born around 1606, the comparable figure was an astonishing 23.6 per cent. These extraordinary figures indicate a brutal deterioration in the opportunity to marry and form households in the early seventeenth century. But, however startling, they are fully compatible with the evidence of economic change and its consequences for different social groups.

At all social levels, marital opportunity was dependent upon the capacity of prospective couples to establish and sustain a viable household economy. Yet members of different social and occupational groups had differing notions of what that entailed in terms of the minimum living standards below which they were loath to descend when embarking on the risks of family formation. They were also subject to varying constraints upon their likelihood of achieving that standard. Given these realities, the young adults of the period can be crudely divided into three marrying populations. For those born to families of substantial property, expectations in terms of living standards were high, but their likelihood of achieving the economic threshold for marriage was also high. Young men could expect to be established upon the land or to be placed in the higher echelons of trade and the professions. Young women would be provided with substantial dowries. At the level of the individual, their personal fortunes would of course be influenced by a host of contingent factors, but as a group their marital prospects were excellent. The children of families of small property had lower expectations and could expect less in the nature of family 'advancement'. Their path to economic maturity might be more dependent on their own efforts and capacities and subject to greater insecurity. Nevertheless, if they had the advantages of apprenticeship, marriage portions appropriate to their status and the prospect of a modest inheritance, their chances of attaining the level of economic security necessary for marriage were good. Labouring people had the lowest expectations in terms of minimum living standards, but were also those least likely to have the benefit of familial assistance beyond goodwill and the passing on of a few household goods. They had to make shift for themselves. Their marital prospects were correspondingly uncertain, subject above all to local variations in the demand for their labour.

These differences of experience are concealed within demographic statistics relating to whole populations. Awareness of their existence, however, is essential to any satisfactory explanation of the impact of economic change upon marital opportunity in the early seventeenth century. It is unlikely, for example, that the children of the landed, mercantile and professional elites or of the 'principall inhabitants' of provincial communities were significantly affected. Parents might fret over the mounting costs they faced in establishing their sons or providing dowries for their daughters. The need to meet the inevitable 'charge' of children was an added incentive to improve their estate rentals and enhance their profits. But, while individual families sometimes encountered difficulties, we have no reason to believe that as a group there was any decline in their ability to meet such obligations. Daughters of the gentry and yeomanry and of substantial citizens, who frequently married in their late teens or early twenties, were the youngest marrying groups in rural and urban society respectively.

The economic uncertainties of the early seventeenth century were likely to bear down more heavily on people of small property, on those for whom marriage was linked to leasing and stocking a small farm or establishing themselves independently in a craft or trade in an increasingly competitive environment. It is perhaps significant that of the many patients suffering from forms of depression treated by the Buckinghamshire clergyman–physician Richard Napier – most of whom were neither rich nor poor – a third were in their twenties, and many expressed anxiety about their economic fortunes, uncertain capacity to get a living and marital ambitions. If the economic prospects of this segment of the population were overcast with insecurity, however, this was perhaps more likely to encourage prudence and delay in marriage than to blight hopes of marriage altogether.

Those whose marital prospects were most vulnerable to dislocation were of course the labouring poor. When and where their labour was in demand, such people were able to marry relatively young. Phillip Stubbes was sharply critical of such imprudent behaviour in his *Anatomy of Abuses* (1583). Yet in the early seventeenth century, and in particular from the 1610s, they faced not only declining real wages, but also diminishing access to common land, repeated dislocations of formerly prosperous industries and the tightening control over settlement and cottaging exerted by parish poor-law authorities.

An unexpected insight into the effects of increasing economic insecurity upon the marital opportunities of the poor is provided by the history of extra-marital fertility. The sexual anticipation of marriage during serious courtships was by no means unusual in this period. Pregnancy at marriage was common. Illegitimate births were often the outcome of breakdowns in intended marriages among the poor, and to this extent their incidence provides a partial indicator of the relative security of their marital expectations. This being the case, it seems highly significant that the proportion of births registered as illegitimate in English parishes rose markedly between the 1590s and the 1610s. This temporary peak in illegitimacy was almost certainly the outcome of the dislocating effects of the economic crisis of the 1590s, and of the continuing insecurity of the marital plans of labouring people thereafter. By the 1620s, however, the incidence of illegitimacy was declining, to reach a nadir in the mid- to late seventeenth century. Given what we know of the falling rates of nuptiality in the early decades of the seventeenth century, the decline in illegitimacy can hardly be attributed to a revival of secure marital opportunities among the poor. It suggests rather an adjustment of attitudes and behaviour, involving the exercise of greater caution in the conduct of courtships in the face of a deteriorating climate of marital opportunity – a shift also reflected in the fact that rates of bridal pregnancy were in decline as well.

The peak in illegitimate births at the turn of the seventeenth century, then, may represent a point of transition in the marital prospects of labouring people. Marriage for the poor was at the best of times a gamble on their prospective ability to support a family. The pessimism of their 'betters' on that score was evident enough in the pains taken by some parish authorities to discourage it. The evidence of both the rising ages of marriage and declining rates of nuptiality in the early seventeenth century suggests that such pessimism was increasingly shared by the poor themselves. For a very substantial minority of the population marriage was becoming a gamble which they were either unwilling or simply unable to contemplate.

The stabilisation of population in early-seventeenth-century England was therefore not simply a 'homeostatic' adjustment to a darkening economic climate, but more specifically a response which reflected England's changing economic and social structure, and in particular the deteriorating life chances of a much enlarged wage-labouring population. For, if a fifth of English women were not marrying, the great majority of those women were surely drawn from the labouring class, and they must have represented a significantly higher proportion of that class than they did of the population at large. A commonwealth based upon households had become one in which a substantial segment of the population was no longer able to sustain a household without periodic public assistance, and in which a further substantial minority could not establish an independent household at all. There can be no more graphic illustration of the social transition unleashed in the sixteenth century by demographic growth and inflation.

CHAPTER TEN

Specialisation and integration c.1650–c.1750

In the century between the Reformation and the Civil Wars, England and Wales had witnessed a long-term process of economic expansion. Resources were more fully utilised. Manufactures were diversified. Capital was accumulated and productively invested. New sources of both supply and demand were tapped. There was significant change in occupational structures, with a declining proportion of the population being engaged in agriculture. Commercial activity intensified. The social relations of production between landlords and tenants, masters and employees shifted in response to the demands of the market. The flows of resources within household economies became more dependent upon the involvement of their members in markets as both producers and consumers. There was a developing discourse of improvement and productivity, and an enhanced sense of the possibility of economic growth. By 1641 national income may have doubled since the 1560s, and possibly quadrupled since the 1530s.

With the benefit of hindsight, all this seems clear. Yet it is equally evident that the economic development that had taken place was socially and regionally uneven in its impact and that in important respects it remained insecure. The benefits of change in terms of rising real incomes and living standards were poorly distributed. The domestic basis of demand for goods and services beyond the essential requirements of subsistence remained socially narrow. Overseas trade and the livelihoods of the many who depended on foreign markets for their products remained highly vulnerable to both short-term dislocation and foreign competition. The early seventeenth century was punctuated by crisis. The 1640s brought the interruptions of commerce and industry, heavy taxation, plundering and destruction occasioned by four years of Civil War.

As Britain emerged from the Civil Wars it was by no means obvious to contemporaries that the economic future was bright. Advocates of agricultural improvement like Walter Blith or Joseph Lee wrote with a somewhat embattled air. Commentators on trade and manufactures still lived in the shadow of the bitter experiences of the 1620s, assuming a world of weak demand and limited markets to be struggled for in an intensely competitive environment. They looked enviously and apprehensively at their ingenious and industrious Dutch rivals, seeking to discern the secret of their prosperity and apparently inexhaustible entrepreneurial vitality.

Yet within fifty years England itself had become a paradigm of economic success. A country which had relied on supplementary imports of Baltic grain in years of scarcity had become a major exporter of agricultural produce. Industry was still more widespread, diverse and competitive. The tonnage of merchant shipping had risen substantially and was increasingly deployed in long-distance trade. The English state was able to raise hitherto scarcely conceivable levels of revenue through a sophisticated system of public credit and to expend it on wars which served the dual purpose of defending the revolutionary settlement of 1688–9 and combating French hegemony in Europe. By 1700 England had emerged as a great power. The English – whose self-esteem in matters economic had so recently been uncertain, to say the least – were celebrating a novel sense of identity as 'this trading nation', and the Scots were being drawn by the glamour of English wealth into a political union in which the hope of economic advantage seemed to Alexander Fletcher 'the bait that covers the hook'.

This apparent reversal of fortunes was so startling that to many contemporaries it appeared a providential deliverance. To some historians the contrast between the earlier and later seventeenth centuries is such that they have attributed the difference to the political changes of the Civil Wars and Interregnum – above all to the removal of constraints supposedly placed upon capitalist development by the policies of early Stuart government. This interpretative perspective is illusory. The events of the 1640s and 1650s certainly had their influence upon particular spheres of economic life, as we shall see. But they did not constitute a watershed in economic development. England's eventual economic success had deep roots. English capitalism had already come to a series of accommodations with government and had more still to make. There was no single turning point. Nor were the economic achievements of the later Stuart era the outcome of a sudden release of pent-up energy. They were hard won over three generations, and long remained in doubt. Their accomplishment, in a period which in many parts of Europe witnessed relative economic stagnation, was the result of creative and ultimately successful adaptation to the demands of a changing context in the world outside Westminster.

i. *A new context*

Central to that changing context was demographic stability. In 1651 England's population stood at approximately 5.23 million. During the remainder of the seventeenth century compound annual growth rates rarely rose higher than 0.2 per cent per annum, and between the 1660s and the 1680s they were actually negative. By 1701 the population had fallen slightly, to approximately 5.06 million. Growth rates picked up again in the early eighteenth century, but only modestly, and by the late 1740s the population had reached only 5.63 million. The Welsh population, meanwhile, remained stable at around 400,000 throughout the later seventeenth century, rising to perhaps 490,000 by 1750, while in Scotland the evidence suggests a stable population of not more than one million.

In the English case, the reasons for this relative stability seem clear. Fertility, as measured by the gross rate of reproduction, reached its early modern nadir in the third quarter of the seventeenth century. Thereafter, it recovered slightly, but remained relatively restrained and did not regain its late-sixteenth-century levels until the second half of the eighteenth century. Meanwhile, any potential which existed for renewed population growth appears to have been choked off by two factors.

First, mortality worsened. The late seventeenth and early eighteenth centuries saw a deterioration in both infant and child mortality and a fall in average life expectation at birth, which was as low as thirty-three years during much of the period. It seems paradoxical that mortality was so adverse in a period which witnessed the final disappearance of the bubonic plague from English demographic experience, the last major outbreak occurring in 1665–6. The diminution of crisis mortality of this kind, however, did not prevent the existence of relatively high levels of 'background' mortality. The research of Dr Dobson suggests that this was frequently associated with, on the one hand, low-lying districts of the country which suffered from stagnant water supplies, and, on the other hand, areas of urban and industrial development, or which lay on significant trade routes. This suggests that, while some areas were perennially unhealthy, deteriorating mortality may have been the outcome of the growth of denser concentrations of population, and the greater ease with which infectious diseases were communicated in a more closely interconnected society. The major threats to life lay not in spectacular epidemics, but in gastric infections associated with flies and contaminated food and water, in airborne infections which throve on close human contact, and in smallpox, which was by now endemic in the population. The second factor counteracting any tendency to renewed population growth was migration. Within England, continued migration from the countryside to insanitary urban centres did much to wipe out the birth surpluses of the healthier rural areas. Whereas in more buoyant demographic conditions the role of the towns as 'devourers of mankind' had done little to check upward population trends, in the late seventeenth and early eighteenth centuries urbanisation exerted a much stronger restraining influence. It has been estimated that the migrants needed to fuel London's growth alone accounted for half of the baptismal surplus of the rest of England in the late seventeenth century and dampened growth potential significantly in the early eighteenth century. Moreover, in the second half of the seventeenth century, some 240,000 people left England to settle overseas – primarily in the expanding North American colonies. Migration on that scale was sufficient to cancel out the remaining potential for population growth, and does much to explain the negative growth rates of the decades before 1690.

In demographic terms the century after 1650 represented a new era. The same was true of price trends. The prices of wheat and rye fell gradually from the 1650s to the 1680s and then – except during the bad harvest years of the 1690s – fluctuated at around 20 per cent below the price levels of the early seventeenth century, with particularly low prices being recorded in the early eighteenth century. The price of barley also fell, though holding up rather more in the early eighteenth century, probably as a result of greater demand for malting barley. In contrast, the prices of livestock remained fairly stable in the later seventeenth century and rose modestly thereafter, while industrial products also held their price in the late seventeenth century, but fell from the 1710s by some 10 per cent.

The impact of all this on the living standards of consumers was considerable. While wage *rates* grew only slowly in the course of the period, the *real incomes* of wage-earners rose substantially for the first time in more than a century. The purchasing power of the wages of agricultural labourers rose by almost a quarter between the 1650s and the 1680s, and improved again during the second quarter of the eighteenth century when especially good harvests in the 1730s and 1740s meant that food prices were particularly low. Urban consumers also benefited. Between the 1630s and the 1690s the number of days' work needed to feed a family of five in Hull fell from 229 to 125 days for the best-paid building craftsmen, from 306 to 143 days for the worst-paid craftsmen and from an impossible 459 to a more feasible 251 days for builders' labourers. For wage-earners, the struggle to provide for a family had been massively eased by the turn of the eighteenth century. Moreover, there was no demographic pressure to cancel out the benefit of rising real wages, and the changing age structure of the population meant that the dependency ratio of young children to adults was reduced. For those who could find regular work, a new level of purchasing power was released for goods over and above those required for basic subsistence. And if this was true of wage-earners, it was of course even more true of the many house-holders of the middle rank who enjoyed much more substantial incomes from the profits and fees earned in commerce, manufacturing and the professions.

The essential features of the new context, then, were demographic sta-bility, declining grain prices, stable or mildly rising livestock prices, stable or gently falling industrial prices, significantly improved real wages, and the enhancement of the potential purchasing power of a substantial pro-portion of households. Moreover, all these trends were occurring within the more commercialised environment which had emerged by the mid-seventeenth century: one in which the livelihoods of individual households had become increasingly dependent on the markets for their products, skills and labour within a substantially more integrated economy. In consequence, the implications of the changing economic context were worked out through the responses of households engaged in different spheres of economic activity in local economies all over the kingdom. And the result was a reinforcement of the processes of economic development set in motion in the very different conditions of the preceding century. It can be summed up baldly as enhanced regional specialisation and intensified commercial integration within an emergent national economy which was increasingly influenced by participation in a nascent world economy. Such a summary, however, does little justice to the complexity of the processes involved, and it is to these that we must now turn.

ii. *Regional specialisation: an overview*

A starting point is provided by the illuminating work of Ann Kussmaul on the changing patterns of regional economic specialisation in late-seventeenth-century England – a reconfiguration which she describes as 'a sharp early modern discontinuity in the English rural economy'. This discontinuity is revealed in her analysis of the changing patterns of the seasonality of marriage in a sample of 542 rural parishes. As Kussmaul demonstrates, different seasonal patterns of marriage were associated with particular local economic structures. Marriages tended to be concentrated in the slack periods of the working year. In areas of predominantly arable husbandry, couples tended to marry in the autumn, after the harvest. In pastoral regions spring or early summer marriages were more common. In predominantly industrial parishes, or in towns, however, there was no pronounced seasonal pattern.

The late seventeenth century saw significant shifts in the geographical distribution of these seasonal patterns. In East Anglia and the south-east, for example, the existing predominance of the arable pattern was strengthened as some previously pastoral parishes shifted towards autumn marriage. In the east midlands, in contrast, there was change from a largely arable to a predominantly pastoral pattern of spring marriages. In the west midlands and the south-west, some formerly arable parishes became non-seasonal, while in the north there was a similar increase of non-seasonality in previously pastoral parishes. Finally, an already existing predominance of non-seasonality was strengthened in the areas around London, and in the industrial districts of the north-west, the west country and the midlands.

Overall, Kussmaul is able to demonstrate the emergence of a much stronger pattern of regional differentiation in the seasonality of marriage, which she interprets as reflecting 'the spatial rearrangement of economic activity over the English countryside': that is, the enhancement of regional specialisation within the national economy, and 'the completion of the transition from bounded and localised to economically integrated regions'. Her remarkable bird's-eye view of change in the English countryside thus provides an initial perspective on the course and consequences of a set of intersecting developments in agriculture, industry and trade which completed the early modern restructuring of the economy of England and Wales, and which can be found reflected in the dynamics of marriage and household formation among thousands of ordinary people.

iii. Agriculture

In agriculture, the key to change is to be found in Kussmaul's comment that among the landlords and farmers of the late seventeenth century 'the lessons of commercialisation were not erased by the reversal of relative prices' between grain and livestock. Faced with the need to sustain their incomes in a changing market situation they adapted their husbandry in order to seek the most profitable use of their land. The commercial decisions to be made were far from easy, for the situation confronting them was complex. Prices for different agricultural products did not move in a synchronised manner. Within the general price trends already sketched, there were regional and local differentials, though these were narrowing over time. Farmers rarely kept detailed records, and they were initially far more likely to be aware of short-term price fluctuations than of the longer-term trends which could shape strategic thinking. Nevertheless, within the myriad of individual responses to changing times, some broad patterns can be discerned.

In tracing those responses it is important to remember that markets for agricultural products were not declining. Rather they were stabilising and reorienting. This being the case, commercial farmers seeking to sustain their profits and incomes were under pressure both to reduce their unit costs of production and to compete for a larger market share. And this in turn placed a greater emphasis upon the potential benefits of 'improvement'. In many arable areas of England and Wales the use of fertilisers appears to have intensified. Some farmers within easy reach of major urban centres or industrial districts diversified into the pro- duction of fruit, vegetables, hops or industrial crops for which there were good markets – the price of hops, for example, rose by almost a third between 1640–79 and 1710–49. Many made efforts to increase their live- stock production. The practice of convertible husbandry became more prevalent and more efficient from the mid-seventeenth century as a result of the more widespread sowing of fallow crops such as turnips, clover and other 'artificial grasses' and the development of a market in seed. Turnips were most commonly used on the lighter soils of, for example, Norfolk and Essex, while clover was adopted on heavier land. Clover and rye grass became commonplace in north Worcestershire and south Staffordshire between the 1650s and 1670s, for example, while in the Gower peninsula in Glamorgan there was said to be 'much clover grass and seed' by 1697. The immediate purpose of this practice was to increase fodder production, but by cleansing the soil of weeds and enhancing nitrogenisation, it had the further benefit of improving arable yields when the land reverted to tillage. The later seventeenth century also saw the more widespread 'floating' of water meadows – the artifi- cial flooding of meadow land in winter to protect it from frost, deposit silt and thereby encourage earlier and richer hay crops. This improve- ment was especially prevalent in the pastoral areas of the west.

None of this was in itself new. It did not constitute an 'agricultural revolution'. Nevertheless it did involve what Dr Emery, writing of Welsh agriculture, calls 'a sequence of interrelated changes in agriculture which (for particular periods of time and areas) produced a measure of improvement'. Professor Kerridge describes it as a more 'general introduction' of improvements in husbandry techniques which laid the foundation for a more 'complete adoption' of such techniques in the eighteenth century. Landlords, whose rentals were threatened by falling prices in many areas, were happy to encourage this. They, or their estate stewards, were in a better position to take a broader, more strategic view of the changing times, and some of them set examples. It was not unusual for a gentleman farmer to lead the way and for the yeomanry to follow. For the same reasons, they also undertook the further consolidation of their land into larger, more economically efficient farms. And they smiled upon, or promoted, those enclosures by agreement with their major tenants which arguably provided farmers with the opportunity to exercise greater flexibility in production choices and definitely increased the rental value of formerly open land.

All this contributed to the regional reorientation of land use described by Kussmaul. The mainly arable complexion of the eastern and south-eastern counties was consolidated. This was still a relatively high price region for cereals. Its farmers benefited from their proximity to the markets of London, the urbanised south-east and continental Europe – some 283,000 quarters of grain were being exported annually by the early 1700s, a trade encouraged by the payment of government bounties for corn exports when prices were low at home. The midlands, in contrast, became predominantly an area of livestock husbandry, while the pastoral orientation of the north and west intensified. This growing regional specialisation should not be exaggerated into a picture of regional homogeneity. The complex configurations of landscape and soil types meant that there was still a considerable degree of variation in husbandry at the sub-regional level. In Oxfordshire, for example, the fertile lowlands produced wheat and malting barley for London, while the upland north of the county supplied the metropolis with cattle, sheep and cheese. But the evidence suggests a definite trend towards greater regional specialisation among those larger farmers who were most responsive to the commercial climate, held a still growing proportion of the land, and thereby exerted the greatest influence in determining the complexion of their farming countries. This in turn made easier the gradual diffusion of innovations by example. John Aubrey, in describing agricultural change within his lifetime in Wiltshire and Herefordshire, was able to name improvers and to trace their influence. Clover, he tells us, was introduced to Wiltshire by Nicholas Hall of North Wraxall, around 1650: 'It turned to great profit to him, which hath made his neighbours to imitate him.'

Taken as a whole, the process of specialisation and improvement also expanded agricultural output. There was a general increase in livestock density. Cereal yields in the arable areas of the east and south rose by some 50 per cent in the century after 1650, with most of the improvement coming in the early eighteenth century. Professor Overton estimates that overall agricultural output rose by some 14 per cent between 1661 and 1741. And at the same time, estimates of the proportion of the population primarily employed in agriculture suggest that it fell from around 60.5 per cent in 1670 to 55 per cent in 1700 and 46 per cent in 1750. In short, the period witnessed increases in the productivity of both land and labour in response to the demands of a more competitive commercial climate.

iv. *Towns and trade*

Regional specialisation in agriculture was both encouraged by and served to further two additional developments which are signalled by Dr Kussmaul's findings: urbanisation and the growth of the non-agricultural rural population. The towns and the industrial districts provided the most concentrated markets for agricultural produce. Growing agricultural productivity in turn permitted the shift of labour into non-agricultural occupations and, as prices fell, created greater purchasing power among consumers.

One of the most striking features of the period is the fact that, despite the overall stabilisation of population, the population of the towns and of rural industrial districts continued to grow both absolutely and relatively. The regional redistribution of the population which had begun in the preceding century continued and indeed accelerated. Professor Wrigley's estimates suggest that while the rural agricultural population fell, as described above, the proportion of the population living in cities of more than 5,000 inhabitants rose from 13.5 per cent in 1670 to 17 per cent in 1700 and 21 per cent by 1750. The 'rural non-agricultural' population – which included the inhabitants of smaller towns – increased from 26 to 28 per cent and then 33 per cent between the same dates. As might be expected, a good deal of the growth in the urban population was occasioned by London. By 1700 London contained some 575,000 people and was already the largest city in Europe. By 1750 its population had reached 675,000. Yet, while London continued to grow in *absolute* terms, its *relative* share of the population of England stabilised after 1700 at around 11.5 per cent. By then the continued growth in the proportion of the population inhabiting major urban centres was becoming primarily a matter of growth in other towns. In 1600, England had twenty towns with populations in excess of 5,000. In 1670, it had twenty-six, which now included, significantly, the expanding industrial centres of Leeds, Birmingham and Manchester. By 1700 it had thirty-two such towns, the new additions including the developing ports of Sunderland and Liverpool and the dockyard town of Chatham. Whereas the larger provincial towns collectively constituted only 4 per cent of the national population in 1670, by 1700 that proportion had risen to 5.5 per cent and by 1750 to an impressive 9.5 per cent.

Such growth involved a further rearticulation of the urban hierarchy in England. London remained at the top of that hierarchy, unquestionably. But some of the older regional centres had either stabilised in population, or grew only slowly. York, for example, historically the greatest of northern cities, stabilised at around 12,000 inhabitants. The principal centres of growth were of two kinds. On the one hand there were the ports, especially those of the west. Between 1670 and 1750 Bristol's population grew from 20,000 to 50,000, and that of Liverpool from under 5,000 to 22,000. On the other hand, there were the industrial centres. Norwich grew rapidly from 20,000 to 30,000 inhabitants between 1670 and 1700, and then more slowly to reach 36,000 by 1750. Over the whole period 1670 to 1750, Newcastle grew from 12,000 to 29,000, Leeds from 6,000 to 16,000, and Birmingham from 6,000 to 24,000 inhabitants. This shift in relative significance was especially pronounced in the early eighteenth century. Between 1700 and 1750 the population of a sample of ten 'historic' centres grew by only 18 per cent, while that of eight ports rose by 58 per cent and that of four 'new' manufacturing towns (Birmingham, Manchester, Leeds and Sheffield) by a remarkable 159 per cent. The urban system was becoming, in Professor Corfield's phrase, 'more visibly polycentric', and the dynamic underlying its growth and rearticulation lay in trade and industry.

The later seventeenth century was once conventionally referred to as the age of the 'Commercial Revolution' – a conceptualisation of the changing scale and pattern of English overseas trade which laid particular emphasis upon the growth of long-distance trade, and above all upon extra-European trade with the Americas, Africa and the East. That term may seem exaggerated. There was much that did not change in English trade in the later seventeenth century. Most of the established trading relationships within the European arena retained their importance, and indeed grew. Yet they did so within a changing context for which the notion of a transformation of trade is entirely appropriate, for the overall pattern of English trade was undoubtedly shifting radically in the period as the initiatives of the early seventeenth century were consolidated and extended. The essential nature of that development can be grasped by considering four areas of change.

First, we can consider the export trade in domestically produced goods. In 1640 the English domestic export trade remained overwhelmingly dominated by the export of woollen cloth. In that year 92.3 per cent of London's domestic export trade was in woollens, divided between the Old and the New Draperies in roughly equal proportions. By 1700 the comparable figure was 72.8 per cent: the dominance of the cloth trade had been greatly reduced. This change was not the result of absolute decline in the woollen trade – though the New Draperies became proportionately much more significant. Rather, it was the outcome of growth in the relative significance of other domestic exports. Foodstuffs (mostly grain and fish) and raw materials (notably lead, tin, coal, hides and salt) collectively constituted only 5.1 per cent of London's export trade in 1640, but 12.3 per cent in 1700. Non-woollen manufactured goods, such as metal wares, leather goods or other textiles, similarly emerged into prominence, rising from 2.6 per cent of London's domestic exports in 1640 to 15.1 per cent in 1700. The domestic export trade was diversifying.

Secondly, there were significant developments in London's import trade. Imports from established European trading partners grew substantially. Between the 1630s and 1700 the value of silks and wines imported from the Mediterranean and Iberia almost doubled. Linen and canvas imported from the Netherlands and Germany rose more than three-fold in value and iron and steel from Scandinavia more than sevenfold. Yet, despite this growth, a declining *proportion* of the import trade was being conducted with north-western and southern Europe. The southern trades, for example, accounted for only 29.6 per cent of London's imports in 1700, as compared with 43.7 per cent in the 1630s. In contrast, a growing proportion of imports now originated in the East or the Americas. Imports of pepper doubled in value between the 1630s and 1700, those of tobacco more than doubled between the 1660s and 1700 alone. In addition there was massive growth in two essentially new trades. Imports of Indian 'calicoes' (cotton textiles) rose fourteen-fold, and sugar imports five-fold from the 1630s to 1700. Moreover, the latter trade involved a development of the first significance, since sugar, which had previously been obtained from the Levant or from Dutch suppliers based in Brazil, was now imported on a massive scale from plantations established in the 1640s in England's West Indian possessions. In consequence, between the 1630s and 1700, East India goods rose from 11.3 to

16.2 per cent, and American goods from 5.3 to 18.5 per cent of London's imports. The significance of the extra-European trades established in the earlier seventeenth century was growing markedly.

If the East Indian and American trades collectively constituted more than a third of London's import trade by 1700, they also laid the foundation of a third development: the re-export trade. For a very substantial proportion of the goods imported from these sources were first landed in England and then re-exported to European customers. Approximately one-third of the sugar, two-thirds of the tobacco and nine-tenths of the pepper landed in England are believed to have been re-exported. By the 1660s the re-export trade was already of equivalent value to 20 per cent of the import trade and 28 per cent of the domestic export trade. By 1700 the comparable figures were 34 and 45 per cent respectively. Moreover, these figures for the value of the trade, impressive as they are, somewhat mask the sheer scale of growth, since the flood of colonial products now being imported greatly reduced the prices of these goods. Sugar, tobacco, calico cloth and spices, sold in small quantities, were within the reach of ordinary consumers, and they were swiftly consumed. They created a mass market of European dimension. For England, which for two centuries had relied on the export of high-quality woollens, of considerable durability, for which there was limited demand, an entirely new trade had come into existence, supplying a potentially vast market.

Finally, the extra-European trades facilitated not only the establishment of the re-export trade with Europe, but also the development of more complex multilateral trading systems, usually designated the 'triangular trades'. These included, for example, the linkages between England, the Newfoundland cod fishery and southern Europe, or between England, India and other east Asian destinations. The most notable, and the most sombre, was the 'Atlantic Triangle', involving the export of manufactured goods to West Africa, the acquisition of slaves from coastal suppliers, their transportation and sale in the West Indies and the southern American colonies, and the return of colonial goods to England. The Atlantic slave trade, which from 1672 was in the hands of the Royal Africa Company, was a ghastly business, involving the export of over 1.4 million slaves between 1662 and 1749, almost a fifth of whom died in transit. English merchants did not invent it, but they came to dominate it and pursued it ruthlessly, and it is indicative of the commercial temper of the age that for a century it aroused little humanitarian comment. Slave labour was the key to the rapid exploitation of England's thinly peopled colonial possessions through the development of the plantation system, especially in the West Indies, where the slave population grew from around 1,500 in 1650 to some 115,000 by 1700. The slave trade was therefore fundamental to the Atlantic trading system, to the profits which it generated, and to a major element of England's growing commercial power. To those who never witnessed its conduct or its human consequences, that was enough.

The restructuring of English trade was clearly apparent by the 1680s and well established by 1700. Thereafter there was further consolidation and growth within the framework created in the later seventeenth century. In the early eighteenth century the domestic export trade with the Netherlands, the German states and France suffered from the effects of warfare, and of protectionist measures aimed at the development of self-sufficiency in those markets. But trade with the Baltic and the Mediterranean remained buoyant, the colonial import trades retained their dynamism, and Germany, Holland and France remained open to the re-export trades, which doubled in the thirty years after 1700. Moreover, in the early eighteenth century the Atlantic and East Indian trades came to involve the export of a larger quantity and greater range of British manufactured goods, including guns, cottons and metal wares attractive in African and Asian markets and to the growing population of the North American colonies. Altogether, between 1700 and the early 1750s, the estimated value of the English import trade grew by a further 40 per cent, that of the re-export trade by a further 76 per cent and that of the domestic export trade by 91 per cent. Trade had been transformed.

The expansion of overseas trade created both income and employment. The total annual value of English trade is estimated to have risen from around £8.5 million in the 1660s to £12.2 million around 1700 and £20.1 million in the early 1750s, an overall increase of £11.6 million per annum, which was equivalent to over £2 per head of population. The bulk of the net profits of trade would, of course, have gone to a few thousand overseas merchants. But the benefit of the vast sums expended in its prosecution must have been spread out much more broadly to the many more who were involved in shipping, the supply and distribution of goods and the developing commercial infrastructures of the ports. The total tonnage of English merchant shipping rose by almost two-thirds between 1660 and 1702 alone, and three-quarters of that increase, significantly, was in the tonnage employed in foreign trade. Nor can there be any doubt concerning the direct influence of England's burgeoning trading strength on urban growth.

The results, predictably, were most obvious in London. In 1700 London still handled close to three-quarters of all English overseas trade. It was the home port of half the merchant fleet, the dominant centre for ship-building and repairing and the many ancillary crafts involved in shipping supplies, the principal centre of sugar and tobacco processing and of many other manufacturing industries linked to overseas trade (for example, silks). But, increasingly, the benefits of expanding trade were to be seen also in the 'outports', for the degree of London's dominance was declining, especially in the Atlantic and re-export trades. By 1700 some 35 per cent of tobacco and 17 per cent of sugar imports (by value) were handled by the outports, which also dealt with around a third of the export trade in manufactured goods to the West Indies and a quarter of that to the North American mainland. Bristol grew on the Atlantic trade, as did Liverpool, which emerged from relative obscurity to eclipse nearby Chester as the principal port for the Irish trade, and then to challenge, and eventually usurp, the position of Bristol in the slave, sugar and tobacco trades. New docks were constructed there in the 1710s and 1730s, the navigation of the Mersey was improved to link the port more effectively to the industrial towns of south Lancashire, and the modest market town of Elizabethan times was transformed into what Defoe called 'a large, handsome, well built and increasingly a thriving town'.

v. *Manufacturing*

The robust health of trade was also of immense significance to the development of manufacturing industries. To quote Pat Hudson, 'it is impossible to understand the evolution of the domestic economy, and particularly of those sectors and regions which spearheaded industrial change, without considering the direct and indirect impact of external trade'. The fortunes of the woollen textile industries, of course, remained heavily dependent upon overseas markets. But the new trades also developed growing markets for both traditional and novel manufactured goods. Already in 1686 London exported 598 different commodities (in 329 ships) to Barbados, Jamaica, the Chesapeake colonies and New England, to a total value of £212,000. These included textiles, clothing, metal wares and a host of miscellaneous manufactures – 3,000 drinking glasses, for example, and 6,000 saddles. Bristol merchants invested in sugar-refining and in the production of ironware, glass, pottery, soap, brass and copper within the city's hinterland, and in the developing metallurgical industries of south Wales, all of which activities were intimately related to the Atlantic trade.

These developing overseas markets were thus of powerful significance. But most of the products of manufacturing industries were still consumed at home. As has already been shown, cheaper food substantially raised the real incomes of wage-earners, providing a margin above what was required for basic subsistence needs – at least during some stages of the family cycle – which could be employed for the purchase of simple manufactured goods such as linen, calicoes or domestic utensils. Moreover, additional income was being generated in trade and manufactures themselves, especially among the swelling ranks of the 'middle sort of people'. They not only shared the benefit of cheaper food, but also had larger surplus incomes for a variety of goods usually described as the 'decencies' of life, as distinct from both luxuries and necessities: more and better clothing, ceramics, clocks, mirrors and other domestic goods.

In a population which had stabilised at around five million, the domestic market was therefore large and growing. To take but one example, the pioneer statistician Gregory King calculated in the last decade of the seventeenth century that on average half a household's income was spent on food and about a quarter on clothing. The demand for that clothing meant the annual consumption, among other items, of over three million hats and ten million pairs of stockings, twelve million pairs of shoes, eight million pairs of gloves or mittens, and ten million shirts or smocks, most of which were now bought ready-made. Lipson suggested that by 1721 the total value of the home market for British products amounted to about forty-two million pounds – rather more than five times the value of the export and re-export markets combined – and more recent calculations suggest that even this high figure may be a significant underestimate.

Taken together, the growing domestic and overseas markets encouraged the bulk manufacture of standardised goods, and the development of a still larger, stronger and more flexible industrial base. In textiles, the west country saw growth and further diversification in the production of high-quality woollens primarily for overseas markets. The woollen industry of the West Riding of Yorkshire grew on the production of cheaper cloths aimed primarily at the domestic market, though the emergence in the last decades of the century of worsted production also ate deep into the overseas markets formerly dominated by East Anglian producers. Halifax doubled in population in the century after 1664, primarily as a result of the thriving worsted trade. Lancashire also witnessed important new departures. Woollen production continued in the Rochdale, Bury and Colne areas, where by the 1720s between half and two-thirds of the male occupations noted in the parish registers were those of textile workers. But in south Lancashire the linen industry relocated to the Warrington and Wigan area, producing not only linens for the home market, but also sailcloth and canvas for the shipping of Liverpool. And around Manchester the period witnessed the establishment of cotton manufacture, in imitation of the cheap and popular calicoes introduced to British consumers by the East Indies trade. By 1700 a million and by 1740 two million pounds' worth of raw cotton was being imported annually to supply this new industry, and by the 1750s the Manchester area was completely dominated by cotton production. There were 4,674 looms at work in Manchester and its immediate hinterland by 1751, and the cloth they produced sold readily both at home and to the West African and American markets.

These were notable precursors of things to come, but as yet many of the most important developments lay outside cloth production. Exploitation of the potential of the recently invented stocking-knitting frame led to the growth of the ready-made hosiery industry. There were around 400 knitting frames at work in London in the 1650s, but 2,500 by 1727, by which date the industry had spread to further locations in the midlands. Around 5,500 stocking-knitting frames were being operated by cottagers in Leicestershire, Nottinghamshire and Derbyshire in 1727, and 12,000 in 1750. The pottery industry was also taking off in Staffordshire. Production of coarse earthenware and of Delft-ware (which imitated Dutch products) increased substantially after 1660, the manufacture of stoneware developed from the 1680s, and overall employment in the potteries more than trebled between 1660 and 1750.

Meanwhile, the metalware industries were expanding dramatically. In 1672, when the total population of the large parish of Sheffield was around 4,200, there were already over 200 smithies at work in the town itself and a further 600 within a ten-mile radius. By 1736 the growth of the industry had been such that the population of the parish was 14,500, and its products had been diversified to include not only the knives, edge-tools and nails long associated with Sheffield, but also scissors, files, metal buttons, razors and forks (a novel product reflecting changing table manners among the genteel). Defoe commented on the blackened houses of Sheffield 'occasioned by the continuous smoke of the forges, which are always at work'.

In the west midlands there was growth and diversification on an even larger scale, especially from the 1690s. Nails, edge-tools and saddlers' ironware were produced in greater range and diversity and were joined by the expanding manufacture of pots and pans, kettles, buckles and buttons, steel 'toys' (such as jewellery and snuff boxes), 'japanned' and enamelled metal boxes (which copied popular Asian imports) and guns. All of these goods and more found markets both at home and in America, the West Indies, Africa and southern Europe. West Indian planters, for example, used their commercial credits with English customers to order vast quantities of cask nails, hoes, cane knives, oxchains and – a further reminder of the underside of colonial development – slave collars. The population of Birmingham quadrupled between the 1660s and 1750, while that of Wolverhampton almost trebled, and industrial activity penetrated even more deeply into the countryside of the whole region.

On a lesser scale, similar developments in local and regional industrial specialisation were also proceeding elsewhere: in the boot and shoe industry of Northampton, Devonshire lace-making, and the brewing industry of Burton-on-Trent, for example. But the point is sufficiently made. This was a period of very significant growth in manufacturing industries. And all of this activity, of course, required raw materials. Some of these were imported, as was the case with, for example, cotton, a good deal of iron and steel, and the finest-quality wool. But a great deal was domestically produced. The demands of the leather and woollen industries were primarily met by the graziers of the midlands, Wales, the west country and the north. Iron, steel and brass production was expanded in Wales, the west midlands, south Yorkshire and on Tyneside. From the 1670s tin- and, from the 1690s, copper-mining grew in scale in Cornwall and Devon. The established lead field of Derbyshire saw intensified production in the late seventeenth century, and there was expansion also in North Wales, Cardiganshire and the north Pennine dales.

The position of coal as the ubiquitous fuel not only for domestic hearths, but also for forges and most industrial processes requiring heat was emphatically consolidated long before Abraham Darby pioneered its use for smelting, and with formidable consequences. Production expanded on every British coal field. North-eastern England, where output grew from around half a million tons in 1650 to well over a million tons by 1700 and two million by 1750, remained dominant, but the early eighteenth century in particular also saw very substantial growth in coal production in south Wales, the west midlands, Yorkshire, Lancashire, Cumberland and Scotland. Larger and deeper collieries were developed. Drainage technology was elaborated, and in the early eighteenth century began to include the use of the earliest steam engines, following the example set in Cornish tin mines. The transportation of coal from pitheads to riverside staithes was revolutionised by the development in the north-east, and later adoption elsewhere, of wooden railways for horse-drawn wagons. From the 1660s, and especially after 1690, a network of such 'wagonways' spread out from the Tyne and Wear, creating access to rich seams previously considered uneconomic because of their distance from water transport. One proud coal owner considered his wagonway comparable to the Via Appia, and the comparison was not inappropriate. These were among the greatest civil engineering projects undertaken in Britain since the departure of the Romans. They were prodigiously expensive to build and to maintain, but they were the key to success in a highly competitive trade, and the very fact that they were undertaken at all speaks volumes about the spirit of the age.

It was not all a tale of growth. Part of the changing regional geography of economic activity in this period was the decline of industry in some areas, notably the rural south-east. The Wealden districts of Sussex and Kent were undergoing gradual deindustrialisation. Iron production contracted markedly, unable to compete effectively with the emergent industries of south Wales and the midlands. Only fourteen blast furnaces and thirteen forges remained in operation in 1717 as compared to the thirty-six furnaces and forty-five forges working in 1653. Cloth production never fully recovered from the slumps of the early seventeenth century, and entered a long decline, losing markets to the New Draperies of East Anglia. By the 1720s Defoe could write of the Cranbrook area that 'there was once a very considerable clothing trade carried on . . . but that trade is now quite decayed'. Nor was all well in the East Anglian industry itself, which was increasingly challenged by northern competitors. The Essex industry had seen its best days by the early eighteenth century, while that of Suffolk was close to extinction. Once-proud cloth towns like Lavenham were forced to depend upon the preparatory combing and spinning of wool for the looms of Norfolk.

Such cases serve as a reminder of the element of relocation involved in the increasing concentration of industrial activity in the north, the midlands, Wales and the west. But it was a minor element. For the roots of industry went deep in most of those regions. Their increasingly industrial character owed more to an accelerating process of 'agglomeration' – a greater density of involvement in industrial production. The west midlands provide a prime example of this process. There was a proliferation of small – and some large – units of production, and a growth in the size and density of the population involved in industry. The multiplication of products already noted was accompanied by a diversification of manufacturing processes – the application of water power to tinning; greater use of the metal stamp, the turning lathe and the drawbench for malleable metals – and encouraged ancillary and spin-off developments ranging from the production of coal, steel, copper and brass to that of pitch and tar. In the towns from which out-production was organised there was development in warehousing, in the provision of credit and exchange facilities, and in carrier services linking the area to London, Liverpool and the inland ports of the Severn.

Such agglomeration – which could be equally well exemplified by Tyneside, Hallamshire or the West Riding – created large and experienced workforces, facilitated the transmission of skills, enhanced flows of information regarding markets and innovations in organisation and technology, aided the formation of local partnerships to raise capital, and in general encouraged further complementary development. It resulted in the formation of highly specialised regional economies, and indeed distinctive industrial cultures. If their roots sometimes reached quite deeply into the past, the later seventeenth and early eighteenth centuries saw their full emergence as part of a new regional structure, a configuration of what Pat Hudson terms 'internally integrated but outward looking' socio-economic zones, locally distinctive, yet national and international in their roles and orientations.

vi. *Traffic*

In a period of demographic stability, the interconnected processes of agricultural specialisation, urbanisation, expanding trade, industrial agglomeration and regional differentiation described above would have been scarcely conceivable had not England and Wales already possessed a society and culture in which the dominant actors in the economy were highly attuned to commercial impulses. It could not have proceeded as it did had they not already possessed an economic structure sufficiently integrated to facilitate the working out of those impulses in local and regional economies all over the kingdom. To that extent, the economic achievements of the later seventeenth and early eighteenth centuries were built upon the developments of the preceding century. What made this period different in the sheer pace of change, however, was the exploitation of the potential of new sources of demand both at home and overseas, demand which was more broadly based socially, more extensive geographically, and which encompassed a proliferating variety of goods. This is turn was both reflected in and advanced by what David Rollison calls a second and still more powerful 'wave of intensification' in the internal commerce of England and Wales.

This was an age of improvement in communications and in commercial organisation as well as in agricultural technique and industrial expertise. Coastal traffic had long taught contemporaries to regard the sea, in T. S. Willan's striking phrase, as 'merely a river around England, a river with peculiar dangers, peculiar conditions and peculiar advantages'. Increasingly they also sought to exploit and to improve the further advantages of the country's extensive network of navigable rivers and to tackle the problems presented by the sluggishness and expense of overland transportation. Some forty acts for the improvement of river navigation were passed between 1660 and 1750, with significant effects. The Don navigation scheme of the 1720s, for example, made the river navigable to within three miles of Sheffield, whereas previously the nearest lading point at Bawtry had been accessible only after a twenty-mile journey over difficult roads. In addition 'turnpike trusts' were established by local initiative and provided with parliamentary authority to improve the quality of the roads with toll income. To take only one regional example, every major route serving the manufacturing districts of Gloucestershire was turnpiked between 1690 and 1740.

Moreover, it was an age of intensifying traffic through all these veins and arteries of commerce. Coastal trade grew and diversified around the entire seaboard of England and Wales. The tonnage of English merchant shipping engaged in coastal traffic grew by some 27 per cent between 1660 and 1702 alone, with the greater part of that increase now occurring outside the east-coast coal trade. There was growth in the numbers and size of the vessels plying the major rivers and in the quantity and diversity of the goods they carried. The port books of Gloucester, for example, reveal that an annual average of 443 boats passed through the city in the 1670s, but 736 in the 1720s, while the number of commodities traded in them rose from around 150 to over 400. In 1637, seventy-two tons of cheese had passed downriver through Gloucester and seventy-nine tons of miscellaneous groceries had passed upriver. The respective figures for the early 1720s were 289 and 1,539 tons. Even more impressive were the growing tonnages of industrial products passing downriver from the midlands. The four tons of ironware handled in 1637 had become 596 tons by the 1670s and 1,456 by the 1720s. No salt or earthenware was handled in 1637. In the 1670s, seventy-one tons of salt and 475 crates of earthenware were registered annually, and by the 1720s, 4,274 tons of salt and 2,519 crates of earthenware.

Improved roads linked producers to the inland ports which gave them streamlined access to major markets. Lechlade in Gloucestershire, for example, grew from the 1650s as the lading point for both the agricultural and industrial produce of an extensive hinterland: up to 200 wagons of cheese were said to have been delivered to its cheese fair in 1719, while the clothiers of the Stroud area brought their cloth there by land carriage 'and so carry it down to London'. They also made possible an increase in both the number and frequency of carrier services along the major routes. By 1700 eight towns on the London-to-Harwich road had weekly carrier services, three had twice-weekly services and one had a thrice-weekly service. By the 1740s the routes and stopping places of the increasingly numerous carriers were being regularly advertised in an emergent provincial press. Moreover, they performed financial as well as transportation services. For those unable to secure a convenient 'return' payment by inland bill of exchange, the well-defended trains of the carriers were a relatively secure means of transferring cash across country. The 'normalisation' of more complex and geographically extensive transactions was reflected in the fact that commercial litigation, which had witnessed explosive growth in the preceding century, underwent a marked decline in the later seventeenth and early eighteenth centuries. Commercial transactions of this kind were more familiar, procedures more established and their outcomes more secure.

By all these means interregional trade was facilitated, stimulated and intensified. The cumulative outcome was that by 1750, as the historian of agricultural marketing puts it, 'if a national market was not in existence . . . it was strongly emergent'. The same was perhaps even more true of other sectors of the economy. At the heart of the whole system, of course, stood London: the principal centre of trade, finance, manufacturing and specialist services, and the largest market for both agricultural and industrial products. London was the focal point of what Guy Miège breathlessly called 'this vast transport of provisions and commodities', the central 'concourse of carts and wagons by land, of ships and barges by water'. But, if London's role in the articulation of the national economy remained fundamental, it was perhaps less totally dominant than had been the case a century earlier. In both their internal structures and their external orientations, the developing provincial economies of the later seventeenth and early eighteenth centuries had not only a greater distinctiveness, but also a greater degree of independence within the whole. With their increasingly specialist functions and command of whole spheres of economic activity, they developed dynamics of their own in the furtherance of their particular roles within both national and international divisions of labour. And in the growing urban centres they possessed little Londons of their own.

From such central places, whether as mediators of metropolitan influence or as independent hubs of entrepreneurial initiative, both traffic and economic influence spread out, through the thriving thoroughfare towns like Cirencester or Guildford, Swansea or Wrexham, Newark or Doncaster, and down to smaller towns and villages. Reconstruction of the flows of goods and people through the market town and river port of St

Ives shows how its neighbouring villages in Cambridgeshire and Huntingdonshire came to constitute what Dr Carter calls a kind of 'dispersed
urban conglomerate'. In this sense they illustrate the manner in which
the process of urbanisation involved not only the growth of major urban
centres, but an intensifying relationship of exchange between rural and
urban society, and the transmission of commercial influences right down
to the level of the village.

One sign of this was the continued decline of the open market as the
locus of most retail purchases and the proliferation of shops kept by permanent retail traders in small towns and the larger villages. Between 1649
and 1675 more than 6,000 shopkeepers in some 1,500 locations are
known to have issued trade tokens of their own in lieu of the small
change needed for minor purchases by their customers. By 1759, the
excise commissioners reckoned that there were 141,700 retail outlets in
England, of which only 21,600 were in London. They were kept by men
like Abraham Dent of Kirkby Stephen, Westmorland, who stocked goods
ordered from no fewer than 190 suppliers in fifty-one different places.
Such local tradesmen showed how far the local economies of England
and Wales had moved from the era of relative local self-sufficiency represented by those other north-countrymen Richard Lowson and Odonell
Selbye. They symbolised the culmination of a process of commercial
transition. As John Brewer puts it, 'the shopkeeper linked the market
town and local community to a network of markets that stretched
beyond the nation's boundaries and across oceans and continents',
linking its participants into an increasingly integrated whole: an elaborating world economy, a commercial civilisation in which Britain played
a core role.

CHAPTER ELEVEN

The state and the Union

Change in both the domestic economy and its relationships with the larger world also implied a changing role for government. As we have seen, throughout the sixteenth and seventeenth centuries the assumption prevailed that public authority had both the right and the responsibility to regulate economic and social affairs for the common good. Essentially there were three well-established aims of public policy. First, it was directed towards the maintenance of good order and social stability by, for example, the regulation of the market, the redress of economic grievances, the alleviation of severe poverty and the protection of employment. Secondly, efforts were made to support and encourage those economic activities which were deemed to have particular bearing on the military potential of the nation, its security and its independence: tillage; shipping; the manufacture of munitions. Thirdly, there was a general concern with the protection and enhancement of national wealth – a project which by the seventeenth century was largely encapsulated in the notion of securing a favourable 'balance of trade' by encouraging exports, limiting imports, fostering import substitution industries, and augmenting, or at least conserving, those stocks of precious metals which were essential to maintain the circulating coinage.

These basic aims and the assumptions which underlay them held much of their force throughout the period. As we have seen, however, there were changes over time both in their relative significance as priorities of government and in the ways in which they were interpreted with regard to specific economic issues. The economic developments of the later seventeenth and early eighteenth centuries brought further shifts of this kind, consolidating and advancing those changes in economic culture which can already be discerned in the early seventeenth century. As Joyce Appleby puts it, 'opportunities for enterprise grew at a much more rapid rate than the capacity of government to oversee them', and economic practice increasingly violated earlier patterns of expectation. The republican state of the 1650s might call itself a 'Commonwealth', but the use of that term to express a broader social ideal was giving way to the concept of 'the public good'. This was a phrase, as Paul Slack points out, less freighted with 'problematic associations'. It gave fewer hostages to fortune in the discussion of public policy, and was friendlier to the increasingly powerful notion of 'improvement' and the growing approbation of the values of production, productivity and profitability which provided an alternative set of standards for discriminating between the claims to consideration made by different groups in society.

i. *'Policies of "Potency"'*

One result was a gradual sea-change in domestic economic policy. The governments of the day were no longer concerned even to make gestures in defence of the traditional agrarian order. Many of the statutes governing cloth manufacturing became effectively obsolete. The growth of trade outside the regulative framework of the open marketplace was regarded with complacency. The regulation of prices and wages gradually fell into disuse. After the passage of the Act of Settlement of 1662, which clarified the basis of entitlement to parochial relief, central direction of the poor-law system was relaxed. It was not a matter of Tudor and early Stuart paternalism being swept away in a tide of ideological hostility to authoritative intervention. It was characterised rather by simple neglect of some of the former preoccupations of central government. Dr Innes calls it a period of 'disengagement' in domestic policy. But it would be inappropriate to regard the period as one heralding *laissez-faire* in the sense of nineteenth-century free-market dogma. For there was still a substantial corpus of law and public policy directed at economic goals. Indeed, it was growing. The difference was that it was now animated by different priorities, less concerned to deflect threats to domestic social stability and increasingly preoccupied with the regulation of trade and industry as a means of promoting national power.

Adam Smith was later to characterise the results as the 'mercantile system', and subsequent historians of the economic writings and protective measures of the period elaborated his insights into the notion of the theory and practice of 'mercantilism', an economic system held to be characteristic of the later seventeenth and early eighteenth centuries. In fact there was no very coherent theory of 'mercantilism' as such. Rather, the economic policies of the time emerged piecemeal from a set of commonplace assumptions which had long influenced commercial policy and which had hardened in the light of the troubled experience of the earlier seventeenth century.

Central among those assumptions were a general pessimism about the potential for economic growth and the simple but powerful notion of the 'balance of trade'. It was assumed that there was a finite cake of commerce to be divided up among competing nations. Demand for goods was limited in a world in which most people commanded very limited purchasing power. Markets were inelastic. Technological change was slow and unlikely to bring productive breakthroughs giving one nation a marked competitive price advantage over others. It was therefore wise to guard existing export markets jealously, to develop and protect domestic production, to seize where possible the lion's share of any new market, and to supply any deficiencies in domestic resources by an international commerce in which exports should always exceed imports. The generally favourable balance of trade resulting would support employment and shipping, draw in 'treasure', and buttress the security and power of the nation.

Whether or not these assumptions remained wholly appropriate in the late seventeenth century, they had an undeniably powerful influence. The resulting enactments and regulative practices were described by Clapham as 'policies of "Potency"': 'economic policies which were only in a secondary sense economic'. They were justified by the perceived need to foster the strength of the kingdom and to secure its independence of other states in the economic sphere. That all this added up to a type of economic nationalism is beyond doubt. The specific policies justified by such objectives, however, did not necessarily imply a centrally directed plan for the creation of an aggressive commercial system. Rather, as John Brewer puts it, they constituted 'a loose and flexible structure, whose configuration changed over time' – in particular as specific interest groups strove to persuade the government of the day to lend them its backing by arguing that their interest was most closely identified with the national interest. And taken as a whole, the result was the piecemeal emergence of a framework of legislation within which market forces operated to the advantage of whatever groups had proved most persuasive. A highly competitive economic environment was assumed. Within that environment, however, there was no abstract notion of the universal virtue of free competition. The whole idea was to pursue economic advantage by laying out a playing field that was not level; to load the dice in one's own favour; to win.

The outcome of such attitudes was most obvious in commercial policy. As we have seen, the central dynamic of the time was commercial, and the experience of the time was that in an intensely competitive struggle for markets, as Jan de Vries observes, 'foreign trade seemed to be a species of warfare'. By the mid-seventeenth century, after a long struggle to expand and reorient overseas trade, English merchants had established a colonial trade of great potential. There was therefore every incentive to keep it in English hands, which meant above all to keep it out of the hands of the Dutch, the overwhelmingly dominant force in the international carrying trade. As the preamble to an act of 1664 stated, the whole purpose of planting colonies was that they should be 'beneficiall and advantagious' to England, in 'making this Kingdome a Staple not only of the Commodities of those Plantations, but also of the Commodities of other Countryes and Places, for the supplying of them . . . it being the usage of other Nations to keepe their . . . Trade to themselves'.

The result was the Navigation Acts, initiated by the act of 1651, passed at a time when there was great danger of the colonial trade falling into Dutch hands, and confirmed, revised and extended in 1660 and subsequently. The act of 1651 laid down that goods of Asian, African or American origin could be imported only in English or colonial shipping. European goods could be imported only in English ships, or ships of their country of origin. The masters and most of the crews of English ships should be of English nationality, and aliens were also prohibited from participating in the domestic coastal trade and fisheries. In 1660 these regulations were elaborated by the placing of higher import duties on European goods carried in foreign ships, the requirement that the colonies' own imports should be carried only in English or colonial shipping, the prohibition of alien factors (commercial agents) in the colonies, and the enumeration of categories of colonial goods which henceforward could be shipped to European markets only after first being landed in English ports. Most of this was clearly aimed at the Dutch. It was initially difficult to enforce, but in the ensuing twenty years it was backed up three times by naval war, and its effectiveness increased after the capture in 1664 of the Dutch colony of New Amsterdam (New York). Though based upon earlier precedents in the regulation of individual branches of trade, the Navigation Acts were of the greatest significance as a general declaration of future intent and of considerable practical benefit both to English shipping and to all those who stood to gain from establishing a firm grip on the profits of the colonial and re-export trades.

The Navigation Acts were therefore of considerable symbolic and practical importance. Equally significant, however, was the fact that, within the framework which they provided, government policy remained highly pragmatic in relation to particular commercial interest groups.

The great chartered trading companies, for example, were much concerned to restrain the activities of unlicensed 'interlopers' who poached upon their monopolies. The directors of the companies remained firm advocates of the virtues of a 'well-regulated' trade – not least in the interests of sustaining the profits of their principal members. Those assumptions, however, were somewhat shaken by the experience of growth in those areas of trade which remained unregulated (notably the American trades). Those who interloped in other trades were prone to argue that freedom from the monopolistic grip of the companies would lower prices, increase the volume of sales and thereby enhance profits in the long run.

All of these arguments were essentially self-interested, and the government adjudicated among them on a pragmatic basis. Where the regulative role of companies was no longer deemed to be of major significance for the security of a particular branch of commerce, company monopolies were gradually reduced – not usually by abolition, but by measures to open up membership through the reduction of entry fines. By such means the Eastland trade was effectively opened to all would-be participants by the later 1670s, as was the Merchant Adventurers' monopoly by 1688, and the Muscovy Company's after 1698 when fines were drastically reduced. Where a company's privileges were still deemed to be of real practical importance to the protection and prosecution of trade, however, they were confirmed and even extended. The Levant and East India companies were both rechartered in 1661. The former, which still sponsored and protected annual fleets to the Mediterranean, retained its effective monopoly until 1753. The latter – though much resented and subject to frequent attack – repeatedly proved capable of persuading governments to confirm its massive privileges, and gratefully reciprocated by providing them with loans. In 1698, after a decade of particularly vocal attacks, the enemies of the company succeeded in establishing a 'new' East India Company in return for a loan of two million pounds to the government. Four years of competition between the 'new' and 'old' companies, however, ended in accommodation in 1702 and a merger in 1708. The East India monopoly survived. Nonetheless, the period did witness a shift from the assumption on the part of government that trades should ideally be 'well regulated' to the assumption that such regulation was permissible where special justification existed.

This kind of pragmatism was assisted by what Dr Innes terms a 'reconfiguration at the centre' of decision-making from the later seventeenth century. Under the Restoration regimes, the privy council ceased to be the dominant forum of policy-making that it had been under Elizabeth and the early Stuarts. Central government became more 'polyarchic' with the emergence of a variety of influential departments (the Treasury, the Cabinet, the Board of Trade) which exerted influence and were co-ordinated by leading statesmen, and above all with the massive increase in the authority and influence of parliament, especially after 1688 when it was in session annually. This, it has been argued, created a context in which government tended to be involved less in the formulation of an overall economic strategy than as a centre of power which was 'reactive' to initiatives promoted by special-interest groups. The activities of such groups were by no means novel: their voices had always been heard both in parliament and in privy council petitions. But the changing institutional context gave them additional scope, and parliament in particular became increasingly available to them through developing techniques of co-ordinated lobbying, pamphleteering and petitioning.

Many piecemeal additions and adjustments to the corpus of economic and social regulation resulted from such activity – a new tariff here, a new regulation there – and a growing number of locally or sectionally sponsored initiatives were furthered by private acts of parliament, as in the case of turnpikes, navigation improvements, and increasingly enclosures. It was all indicative of a situation in which the entrepreneurs of the period were anxious to have freedom to conduct their businesses unhampered by regulation when it suited them, but only too happy to get the power of the state behind them when by doing so they could ensure their competitive advantage, their possession of particular markets or their protection from threatening competition (especially overseas competition), commonly arguing their cases on 'balance of trade' assumptions.

Professor Hey has shown how the Culter's Company of Sheffield 'fought many a battle to defend its members' interests, arguing for free trade or for restrictive practices with no regard for logic except that of pleading for their own advantage'. In 1660 they sought to free the importation of Spanish iron, against the hostility of local iron masters who sought protection. In 1718, they secured an act to prevent skilled workmen from being seduced to work abroad. Both initiatives were entirely characteristic of the age. So too were the battles resulting from the craze for imported oriental fabrics which peaked at the close of the seventeenth century. The East India Company did well from the trade. But it was opposed by an alliance of domestic woollen and silk producers, whose markets were threatened and who agitated for prohibition in the 1690s. The Levant Company, meanwhile, saw its interest in encouraging domestic silks and cottons for which it was the principal importer of raw materials. Members of parliament who were close to, or effectively lobbied by, different interest groups were long divided, but in 1701 an act was passed which prohibited the *wearing* of *finished* fabrics imported from Asia, but permitted the continued import of such fabrics for *re-export* purposes. This pragmatic resolution of the problem gave comfort to the silk lobby and encouraged the development of domestic cotton production, a nascent import-substitution industry which gained further protection when the import of printed calicoes was prohibited in 1721.

ii. Wars and taxes

Such instances are illustrative of the changing direction of public economic regulation in this period, and of the complex realities underlying the notion of the 'mercantilist' state. The period also, however, witnessed significant developments in the influence of the state in another sense: the growth of its role as an independent actor in the economy. For the generation following the Revolution of 1688 saw the emergence of what John Brewer terms the 'fiscal–military state' in Britain, the outcome of a revolution in public finance which was in turn a response to the escalating financial demands of war.

By the standards of the time, the kingdom of England was relatively rich. Despite the poverty in which many lived, it had a wealthy landowning class and a broadly based prosperity among the 'middle sort of people' who had benefited from economic change. The crown, however, had never succeeded in tapping that wealth effectively. Prior to the Civil Wars, the revenues of the crown depended upon its own estates, customs duties, a patchwork of residual feudal dues and occasional 'extraordinary' taxes granted by parliament, usually to meet the exigencies of warfare. Taxes were granted with great reluctance, not least because of parliament's distrust of the crown's purposes. They were also inefficiently assessed and collected, with the result that income from taxation rose little in real terms between 1540 and 1640, despite rising military costs. In addition there was considerable unwillingness to lend money to the crown, which had proved itself, especially under James I, to be an untrustworthy debtor. Yet the later seventeenth century saw the transformation of both the fiscal capacity of the state and its consequent capacity for effective action, above all in war.

This reversal was the outcome of developments which, in Dr Roseveare's words, 'transformed the willingness, rather than the ability, of the English people to pay high taxes, lend large sums and above all repose great trust in the financial institutions of their parliamentary government'. Resistance to Charles I had in part been provoked by his ministers' attempts to expand the crown's income by fiscal expedients of questionable legality. Yet the Civil War years demonstrated a surprising willingness, at least in areas of parliamentarian support, to accept the burden of higher direct taxes voted by parliament. Suffolk, which had reluctantly yielded £8,000 to Charles I in 'Ship Money' in 1639, was paying £7,500 a month as its contribution to parliament's 'monthly assessment' in 1644. Again, in 1644 parliament successfully introduced the 'excise', a system of indirect taxation modelled on Dutch precedents. If the regimes of the Interregnum were somewhat more fiscally successful than their predecessors, however, it was a success based ultimately on military power and one which lacked legitimacy in the eyes of many of their subjects.

Under the restored monarchy of Charles II, parliamentary control of taxation revenues was unambiguously established, and anxiety to avoid potential sources of conflict brought higher grants of regular taxation income to the crown in the form of the hearth tax, customs and excise. Steps were also taken, under the Treasury administration of Sir George Downing, to improve public credit. Loans raised to finance the second Dutch War were repaid by a system of 'Treasury Orders' which involved their repayment in strict chronological order from specified branches of the revenue. Despite these good intentions, however, the demands of war put massive strain upon what remained inadequate fiscal resources. The 'Stop of the Exchequer' of 1671 postponed repayment of the crown's creditors and brought disaster to some of the financiers who had lent to the government. Its credit severely damaged, the crown fell back on the old expedients of borrowing from coerced public bodies, such as the City of London or the East India Company, or from 'tax farmers' – the consortia of plutocrats who bought the right to collect taxes and who could be prevailed upon to advance loans in anticipation of their receipts. Expanding trade brought higher customs revenues, but the system of public finance remained deeply flawed. It was inadequate to meet the costs of emergency expenditure, and reform remained inhibited by distrust of the political purposes and religious complexion of the Restoration monarchy.

From 1688 the situation was transformed in less than a decade by a series of developments justly termed a 'Financial Revolution'. The catalyst was the pressure imposed by the need to finance the wars fought to defend the revolutionary settlement of 1688–9: a settlement approved of, albeit sometimes reluctantly, by the bulk of the political nation. Parliament was now fully in control of the public revenue. Annual estimates were made of need, supply was voted, and accounts were subject to public audit. Given these safeguards, parliament proved prepared to sanction a series of devices necessary to raise money for war. The Land Tax introduced in 1690 provided a reliable annual income from direct taxation which initially facilitated the raising of loans on the guaranteed security of parliamentary taxation. By 1692–3, however, the huge sums needed to maintain the military effort on both land and sea could no longer be raised simply by anticipating the yield of annual taxation. England's capacity to sustain the war was in question and further expedients were adopted in the parliamentary sessions of 1692–3 and 1693–4. Longer-term borrowing was undertaken through the sale of annuities, which were also secured by parliament. Lotteries were introduced, and proved highly popular. In 1694, the Bank of England was established, not as a central bank as such, but as a means of mobilising resources for the state. It initially involved subscription to a loan of £1.2 million, with interest of 8 per cent and eventual repayment guaranteed from taxation. The loan was advanced in the form of sealed bills which the government used to pay its creditors. They in turn were able to use the bills in their own dealings, with the option of returning them to the Bank for payment when necessary to satisfy their hard cash requirements. The circulating medium was enhanced by the issue of secure bank notes and in 1696 steps were taken to stabilise the coinage, which had deteriorated markedly in quality, with a boldly enacted recoinage. Meanwhile, a market rapidly developed in the new range of transferable state securities which formed the core of an emerging London stock exchange.

The measures of the 1690s have been described by D. W. Jones as 'haphazard and improvised', a piecemeal grafting of the new on to the old. But they succeeded – just – in enabling the war effort to continue through to the inconclusive peace of 1697. Once established, however, they inspired a degree of confidence in the fiscal probity of the state which transformed the situation when war with France was renewed in 1702. By 1714, at the end of the War of the Spanish Succession, the government debt amounted to £48 million, of which £40 million was 'funded' by parliamentary pledges to pay the interest and eventually the capital. In 1717, sinking funds were established for the orderly reduction of the debt. The fact that the success of the new financial structure was still not guaranteed was demonstrated in 1720 by the 'South Sea Bubble', an ill-advised attempt to privatise the national debt by converting it into South Sea Company stock, which led to wild speculation and a crisis of confidence that temporarily threatened disaster. But, with the restoration by Walpole of secure repayment of the state's creditors, confidence was restored and in the 1720s the complex of innovations settled into a stable, routinised system of public credit.

Fundamental to the whole edifice was of course the political will to create and sustain an effective system of taxation which made possible the servicing of a massively increased public debt. Prior to 1714 this was largely achieved from revenues raised by the land tax – essentially a tax on rental income from land, which was initially set at 20 per cent in some of the wealthier southern counties. The land tax, however, was never reassessed and the burden gradually shifted from the land towards the income yielded by indirect taxes: the customs, stamp duties and above all the excise charged on a host of common items of consumption. Basic necessities were exempted, but the system was undoubtedly and increasingly regressive. Nevertheless, it worked. Taxes were on the whole efficiently collected by a new body of public officers, and the public revenue rose massively. By the 1720s it stood at eight times the level of the income enjoyed by Charles I in the 1630s. But even earlier the impact of the system had been formidable. It is estimated that in 1700 some 9 per cent of national income was being taken in taxation, while 30 per cent of taxation revenue was required to fund the national debt. A regime had been created, as O'Brien and Hunt note, with 'the political support, the administrative capacity, and the fiscal base required to accumulate and service a perpetual debt'.

This transformation of the fiscal strength of government also transformed its capacity for effective action, and Professor Brewer's term, the 'fiscal–military state', derives its aptness from the fact that so much revenue was spent on the prosecution of war. Military expenditure as a proportion of estimated national income was around 2 per cent in 1685. In 1710, after over two decades of almost uninterrupted warfare, it peaked at 14.5 per cent. After 1714 it stabilised at around 5 per cent even in peacetime, largely because of the costs of maintaining the navy.

The effects of all this were potentially destabilising. Contemporaries complained that high taxes penalised both landowners and consumers only to enrich a limited number of financiers and state creditors ('the monied interest'); that they pushed up prices, raised production costs and damaged competitiveness; that warfare endangered trade, and raised the costs of marine insurance and coastal transportation. Nor were such fears groundless, especially in the 1690s. Small landowners were almost certainly hard hit by the rising burden of taxation. More generally there was a serious risk of a decline in domestic spending and of falls in output and employment. Some branches of trade were seriously dislocated. Around 4,000 merchant ships were lost to enemy action in the years 1688–97. Bristol alone lost 200 vessels in 1688–93. There was a real risk that King William's war might destroy the English trade surplus which ultimately made possible the remittance of funds to sustain the war in Flanders. The country limped home to the peace of 1697.

In the War of the Spanish Succession, however, a series of fortunate circumstances combined to ensure that the war was fought against a background of expanding home exports. The discovery of gold in Brazil led to a boom in the Portuguese trade. The dislocation of Baltic grain production and of the textile industries of Saxony and Silesia by the Great Northern War of 1700–21 made possible the expansion of English grain and textiles exports to Russia, the Low Countries and Germany. In addition, the Atlantic trade held up well and the balance of trade with India improved markedly. Competition between the 'old' and 'new' East India Companies in the years of peace 1698–1701 had resulted in massive investment in the East which meant that during the war years it was less necessary than formerly to export the bullion required to drive the trade. That England not only survived economically but also prospered despite the massive costs of Marlborough's war was to a considerable extent due to this unlooked-for combination of circumstances. As D. W. Jones observes, 'Albion was extremely lucky as well as perfidious.'

Yet in the longer term there were also positive consequences of the emergence of the government as by far the largest actor in the economy as a borrower, spender and employer, and the benefits extended well beyond the confines of the 'monied interest'. It is estimated that throughout the early eighteenth century military expenditure actually exceeded private investment in the English economy. And a great deal of that expenditure had the effect of stimulating production and expanding employment. In 1711 the royal dockyards on the Thames and Medway employed over 3,500 men, and close to another 3,000 were employed in Portsmouth and Plymouth. The dockyards were the largest enterprises of their day, and the ships they built and repaired among the most expensive items of capital equipment. A third-rate naval vessel cost around £15,000, and a first-rate vessel £30,000 to build at a time when even large private businesses rarely had capital goods worth over £10,000. Constructing them created demand for timber, canvas, rope, leather, brass and copper, not to mention the numerous varieties of nails, latches, chains, anchors and ordnance produced for the navy by iron masters like Sir Ambrose Crowley. Again, clothing and equipping armies and fleets which totalled 116,000 men in the 1690s and 112,000 in the 1740s generated demand equivalent to the populations of several large cities. In addition, many people of the middle rank found employment in the administration of the system, notably in the excise service. Many were able to enjoy secure incomes from their investment in government stocks.

Higher taxation is thought to have encouraged efforts to reduce costs in both agriculture and industry. In trade there were benefits accruing from the military defeat of trading rivals, their exclusion from markets, and the seizure of their colonial territories. Such advantages underlay the popularity of the 'blue-water' strategy of conducting naval and colonial war directly, while subsidising continental allies to bear the brunt of land campaigns in Europe. All in all, the balance between the advantages and disadvantages of the changing economic role of the state seems likely to have been a positive one. For England and Wales, military expenditure and the taxation necessary to support it does not appear to have caused stagnation or regression of the kind experienced by the Dutch economy in the same period. Initially that outcome may have owed as much to good luck as to good judgement, but in the long term, as with the Dutch a century earlier, the pursuit of profit and the pursuit of power seem to have gone hand in hand.

iii. *The bait and the hook*

That the emergence and subsequent development of the fiscal–military state was of considerable significance to British economic development can scarcely be doubted, though the precise nature of its significance remains to be fully explored. From 1707, of course, it was no longer an English, but a British state, and the Union of the kingdoms of England and Scotland in that year raises a further set of problems regarding the impact of political developments upon the course of economic change.

The early seventeenth century had not been kind to Scotland. Population growth had ground to a halt with a series of devastating mortalities, which demonstrated the marginal capacity of the agricultural economy to feed the population, and helps to explain the extraordinarily high rate of emigration among young men. And if the wars which followed the National Covenant of 1638 removed the need to emigrate among those whose best option in life seemed to lie in military service, the armies of the Covenant and of Montrose made their own contribution to the kingdom's distressed condition by spreading and prolonging the epidemic diseases which culled the population in 1646–9, and by the devastation wrought in the course of a bitterly fought internal war. To Oliver Cromwell, who had campaigned there, Scotland appeared 'a very ruined nation'.

He exaggerated. By English standards, Scotland was certainly poor, and unfavourable comparisons between the two were a commonplace of contemporary travellers' accounts. But Scotland's economy was not devoid of vitality. On the contrary, it was one, in Professor Devine's words, 'in which the commercial enclave was becoming stronger'. In the course of the later seventeenth century, the population of Edinburgh grew by almost a third and that of Glasgow by a fifth, to reach levels of 35,000 and 18,000 respectively. Glasgow emerged as Scotland's second city. In rural society, landlords were granting more secure written 'tacks' to their tenants, for longer terms of ten or more years. Single tenancies of farms were becoming more common than joint tenancies in counties like Midlothian and Berwick, and the fact that agricultural prices were declining, and with them the value of rents rendered in kind, led some to take their rents wholly or partly in cash. The latter development brought some tenants into more direct contact with the market and its imperatives. There was significant growth in the numbers of small non-burghal markets in the countryside, over 300 being authorised between 1660 and 1708. Moreover, the study of relative market prices suggests the emergence in the Lowlands of more integrated sub-national grain markets centred upon Edinburgh and Glasgow and gradually coalescing into a single Lowland price zone by the early years of the eighteenth century. The potential for agricultural improvement was recognised by permissive acts of the Scottish parliament authorising enclosure (1661), the exchange and consolidation of holdings (1669) and the division of commonty and runrig lands (1695). Grain production was encouraged by the prohibition of grain imports in 1671 and the granting of bounties for exports in 1695. And if these measures were for the moment more representative of aspiration than actual change, there was real development to be noted in the livestock trade. Some 18,600 cattle were driven across the border to English markets via Carlisle in 1662, and by the 1680s the annual trade was in the region of 30,000 beasts. The growing cattle trade led to the creation of enclosed cattle parks in Galloway for the supply of English markets, and the further incorporation into a market economy of the Western Highlands, where clan chiefs engaged increasingly in the marketing of cattle via the great fairs at Falkirk and Crieff. By the turn of the century, sheep were also being driven to England in large numbers from the Central and Eastern Borders.

In industry and trade there were more signs of change. The Scottish parliament was sensitive to the country's relatively backward and dependent status in these spheres and passed a variety of measures intended to encourage enterprise by banning luxury imports, naturalising skilled foreigners, removing duties on raw materials and facilitating the formation of joint-stock companies. The Bank of Scotland was chartered in 1695, based in Edinburgh and with branches in other leading cities. In 1661 parliament also confirmed earlier measures designed to counteract labour shortages in the coal and salt industries by tying colliers and salters to their masters for life through the bondage system – a form of effective serfdom that remained in force for more than a century and long aroused no more comment than did colonial slavery. On the most pessimistic estimate, total coal production was in the order of 225,000 tons by the 1690s, close to a ten-fold increase on the output levels of the 1620s. Linen production involving the employment of cottar families in the putting-out system also expanded markedly, both in the east, in Forfarshire, Fife and Lowland Perthshire, and in the west, in the Lanarkshire and Renfrewshire hinterland of Glasgow. By 1700 at least 1.2 million ells of linen (c.1.23 million yards) were being exported to England, of which over two-fifths was destined for London. From the 1650s the trade of Edinburgh and the east-coast ports revived from its Civil War dislocation and expanded modestly, while in the west Newport Glasgow was established for ships of burthen in 1668 and efforts were made to penetrate the growing Atlantic trade through illicit commerce with English colonies.

In the later seventeenth century, then, the Scottish economy was neither supine nor stagnant. The problem, rather, was that its areas of growth were distinctly patchy, that they involved development from a relatively low point of departure, and that the most successful initiatives rendered Scots increasingly dependent upon the markets supplied by their wealthier southern neighbours.

Edinburgh and Glasgow were growing, but outside those cities the population of some other significant towns was stable or declining. Aberdeen's population fell by 30 per cent and Perth's by even more in the later seventeenth century, while growth among the smaller burghs appears to have been confined to those in the environs of Edinburgh and Glasgow and to those on border trade routes. Grain markets were more integrated, but oatmeal prices fell drastically until the 1680s, possibly because there was less of an urban market to sustain them than was the case in England. The agricultural depression was far worse for commercial farmers than in the English case. Indeed, in Professor Devine's view, the commercial sector of the Scottish rural economy, though growing, remained a 'relatively small enclave' and 'it would be an exaggeration to conclude that the rural Lowlands in general were on the move by 1700'.

If part of the rural economy of Scotland was geared to the expanding livestock trade and to the supply of the leading towns, most of the Scottish countryside remained, in Dr Dodgshon's words, 'geared to subsistence and hemmed in by its constraints'. This was emphatically true of the Highlands, but it was also true of the Lowlands. Small farms predominated in most areas. While 36 per cent of the farms of Midlothian, which served Edinburgh, were larger than a hundred acres in size by the 1690s, this was true of only 5 per cent of farms in Renfrewshire and 2 per cent in Aberdeenshire. Half the farms of Renfrewshire were smaller than thirty acres, and 45 per cent of those of Aberdeenshire below twenty acres in extent. Multiple tenancy of farms remained commonplace. There was little enclosure outside the Lothians, the Berwickshire Merse, the Glasgow area and Galloway. Outside the regions of specialist livestock production, rents were still usually taken in kind, as was the case with three-quarters of the rents of the Strathmore estate in Perthshire and Forfarshire in 1695 and two-thirds of the rents of the Melville estate in Fife in 1715. This was still a predominantly subsistence economy, and the subsistence it provided remained fragile. Yields of oats, Scotland's staple crop, were low at the best of times – usually in the range of three- to five-fold, which was half the yield expected in England – and in the disastrous harvests of the later 1690s Scotland's continued vulnerability to nation-wide famine was tragically demonstrated. In the capital a refugee camp was established in Greyfriars churchyard and the city council minuted that the poor of Leith were 'starving and dying upon the streets'. Aberdeenshire lost a fifth of its population to famine (perhaps a third in the Highland parishes of the county) and losses in Scotland as a whole probably totalled 13 per cent.

Nor should developments in other sectors of economic activity be exaggerated. The Scottish Parliament might seek to encourage domestic manufactures, but the actual results outside the Glasgow and Edinburgh areas were limited, not least because of the severely limited nature of the domestic market. The Scottish peasantry exerted little demand for manufactured goods, while if the real wages of urban wage-earners recovered somewhat in the later seventeenth century they did not rise significantly. The Bank of Scotland was poorly capitalised, proved very cautious in its policies and did little to expand credit – its branches outside Edinburgh proved unprofitable and closed after a year. Moreover, protective measures intended to encourage Scottish industries brought damaging reciprocal action from stronger trading partners. In the closing years of the century new tariff barriers and war with France badly affected the export of salt, fish and coal to France, coal to the Netherlands and grain to the Scandinavian kingdoms, while the manufacture of cheap woollen plaids in Aberdeenshire, Banff and Kincardine declined with the loss of French, Swedish and Dutch markets. As was the case in agriculture, the most hopeful developments in Scottish industry – coal and linen – were heavily and increasingly dependent upon access to English markets.

By the 1690s, much the same could be said of trade. Glasgow merchants were endeavouring to break into the Atlantic trade, and they proved enterprising smugglers, but serious participation was greatly hindered by the English navigation laws. Only seven ships a year were trading to the Americas from Glasgow in the 1680s. That Scots were not lacking in overseas enterprise is demonstrated by the foundation in 1695 of the Company for Trading to Africa and the Indies, and the raising within Scotland of the prodigious capital of £400,000 sterling – believed by contemporaries to represent half the capital in Scotland. But the fate of the company also demonstrated the relative weaknesses of Scotland's position.

Initially the company was an Anglo-Scottish venture, aimed at outflanking the Royal Africa and East India Companies from a Scottish base. Opposition from those powerful interests, however, achieved the rapid withdrawal of potential London investors. The Scots proceeded alone, and on the initiative of William Paterson (one of the founders of the Bank of England) conceived the visionary, or harebrained, scheme of colonising the Isthmus of Darien, establishing an overland passage between the Atlantic and the Pacific, and opening a new route to the East. The resulting Darien expeditions of 1698 and 1699 ended in complete disaster. English trading interests were hostile. Spain was affronted. William III stood aloof, anxious to avoid the dislocation of his diplomatic manoeuvres regarding the imminent problem of the Spanish succession, and forbade the English colonies to give aid. Two thousand lives were lost to tropical disease and Spanish attacks, and with them most of the capital invested in the scheme. The Darien scheme seemed to prove, as Professor Whyte puts it, that 'The Scots desperately needed international trade, but international trade did not need the Scots.' It brought to a miserable end what Bruce Lenman calls 'a decade of indescribable anguish, both physical and psychological'.

All this provided the essential context for the debates which led to the Union of 1707. Both political and economic union had been considered at various times since the Union of Crowns of 1603. It had been briefly achieved in the 1650s after the Cromwellian conquest of Scotland, but had otherwise foundered upon the reluctance of both partners to the match. This left the Scots in a galling position: technically independent, yet in a subordinate position within what one pamphleteer of 1701 called 'a state wherein we are not considered as subjects, nor allies, nor Friends, nor Enemies, but all of them only when, where, how and how long our Task Masters please'. From an economic perspective, the commercial sector of Scottish agriculture and Scotland's most dynamic industries were increasingly dependent on the English market – perhaps half

Scotland's foreign trade was with England in 1700. Yet England had no such dependence on Scotland – only 1.2 per cent of London's imports came from Scottish sources in 1699–1701. And the Scots were excluded from participating in the English economic system in other respects. Most Scots were acutely conscious of their national identity and anxious to preserve their national integrity. They resented political domination and feared the possible consequences of inclusion within the developing English tax system. Yet the experiences of the 1690s had also made many equally conscious of Scotland's relative economic weakness, and among their rulers there was a powerful minority described by Professor Lenman as 'avid for the economic growth which alone could increase their disposable incomes'.

By 1701, English interest in union had become urgent for essentially political reasons. Following the Act of Succession, it was imperative that Scotland recognise the Hanoverian succession on the death of the childless Queen Anne. The security of the revolutionary settlement depended upon it. Yet the Scots, irked by the disadvantages of the dual crown, seemed reluctant to do so. This being the case, the English government, which would initially have settled for simple recognition of the joint succession, became increasingly conscious of the security benefits of full political union, and it was perfectly prepared to use its economic leverage. The Aliens Act of 1704 threatened the exclusion of the Scots from English markets if they failed either to enter into negotiations for union or to recognise the house of Hanover's claims by Christmas 1705. Negotiations began.

In Scotland the issue was fiercely debated, with economic issues well to the fore. Perhaps surprisingly, access to the English colonial system was not a major issue. The opponents of union included many merchants, and some were optimistic about the potential of developing other trades in a fully independent Scotland. The crux of the matter, however, was the question of the English market for linen, coal and cattle – the only areas of commerce in which Scotland enjoyed an undoubtedly positive trading balance, and matters very close to the hearts of many Scottish landowners. In the event such considerations carried the day, both among the Scottish commissioners appointed by Queen Anne to negotiate the Treaty of Union and in the Scottish parliament, which, despite substantial opposition, eventually endorsed it. Indeed, while the continued autonomy of both the Church of Scotland and the Scottish legal system were prominent among the articles of the treaty, the majority of the remaining articles were concerned with economic issues. The Scots were accorded full freedom of trade with England and Scottish ships became ships of Great Britain for the purposes of the navigation laws. The customs and excise services were unified, but Scotland was granted temporary exemption from certain potentially damaging duties. Provision was made for the standardisation of the coinage and of weights and measures on the English model. The burden of direct taxation was apportioned equitably in a ratio of 1 : 42, which was taken to represent the relative wealth of the two kingdoms. Scotland accepted a share of responsibility for the National Debt, but was compensated with 'equivalent' payments, one of which was earmarked to recompense those who had suffered losses in the Darien scheme. It was a reluctant union, driven by political contingency and made acceptable by economic sticks and carrots. But on 1 May 1707 it came into effect.

Was it a union by absorption, characterised more by domination of the weaker partner by the stronger, or one of fusion, characterised more by co-operation within the new framework? In economic terms, many Scots feared that it would be the former. In the long term it gradually became the latter. But initially it was neither. As Professor Devine observes, 'the settlement merely offered a context, with both opportunities and risks'. The risks of Scotland's reduction to a dependent satellite status comparable to that of Ireland were not realised. England was not seriously interested in outright domination of Scotland beyond the issue of military security. Despite the commercial links which had developed in the later seventeenth century, the Scottish economy was not so closely linked to that of England that it could speedily be subjugated to English economic interests even if that object had been desired. To that extent, the relative autonomy of much of the Scottish economy protected it. Scotland was mostly left to the Scots. On the other hand, the Union provided a new framework for Scottish enterprise. Scotland was now included in the largest and richest common market area in Europe. Its merchants had open access to the colonial trade. Its entrepreneurs were more closely connected to flows of commercial information, technological innovation and capital. Yet initially the consequences were very limited, and, if the fears of 1707 were not realised, neither were the more extravagant hopes aroused by the Union debate.

Ultimately the economic future was shaped by the Scots' own responses to the new conditions obtaining after Union, and that took time. In agriculture the earliest effects were seen in the continued growth of the droving trade. The lairds did well, but the evictions of tenants in Galloway to make way for enclosed grazing parks provoked one of Scotland's few outbreaks of peasant unrest in the anti-enclosure Levellers' Revolt of 1723–5. More broadly, there was gradual continuation of the institutional changes which had begun to emerge in the later seventeenth century. Written tacks became more general. Leases lengthened again, often to nineteen years. The shift towards money rents was accentuated, first by increases in the money element, and then, especially from the 1740s, by full conversion. Single tenancies continued to advance in numbers and with them larger farms were created. An entrepreneurial farming class was expanding. But there seems little doubt that in most of Scotland really significant development in the rural economy came after 1750.

In industry and trade the anticipated benefits of Union were also slow to materialise. Markets for coal and for linen were relatively stagnant in the early decades of the eighteenth century. By the second quarter of the century, however, there was marked improvement as Scotland's business class began to realise the potential of their access to the English and increasingly the colonial markets. Coal production had probably trebled by 1750. Glasgow, which had imported 200,000 pounds of tobacco annually in the 1680s, landed two million pounds a year in 1715 and nine million pounds in 1743 – figures which may well be significant underestimates of the real volume of the trade, given the widespread prevalence of customs evasion. By the 1730s the city was already Britain's premier tobacco port. In 1743–4 the portbooks show that ninety-nine ships entered from the Americas and eighty-eight cleared for American destinations – as compared to the seven ships engaged in the American trade in the 1680s – while a very extensive trade was pursued with Ireland, Scandinavia, France and Holland, a good deal of it involving the re-export of tobacco. The linen trade also expanded rapidly from the 1720s. Over two million yards were produced in Scotland in 1727–8 and over seven million yards by 1747–8, half of which was produced in Lanarkshire, Renfrewshire and the west and much of which was exported to colonial markets.

By 1750 to most Scots the economic consequences of the Union had confirmed neither their hopes nor their fears. In specific sectors of the Scottish economy, however, it had brought real benefits. They derived not so much from the direct influence upon Scotland of England's economic dynamism – for Scotland remained to a very large extent a separate economic sphere – as from the energy with which some Scots were seizing and exploiting the opportunities provided by a new economic context. If as yet they had succeeded in galvanising only limited sectors of the Scottish economy, their achievements were very much the shape of things to come in the century after 1750.

In the second quarter of the eighteenth century it can hardly be said that there yet existed a British economy. What did exist, however, was a British economic system, centred on England and Wales, but with an infra-

structural reach extending across much of the known world, a system
into which Scotland's slow, and as yet partial, integration was part cause
and part consequence of the creation of what Swift called the 'crazy
double-bottomed realm' of Great Britain. That system was scarcely
the outcome of conscious planning. It was the result of a myriad of
responses to changing circumstances extending back for two centuries
and more. But it had been assisted into being in the late seventeenth and
early eighteenth centuries by a state dominated by a landed aristocracy,
yet responsive also to commercial interests, which had created and sustained political and legal conditions which, on balance, were conducive
to economic development.

In its basic structures, it remained what E. A. Wrigley terms an
'organic economy' – still dependent for the most part on human and
animal muscle-power, assisted by wind and water, and not yet the
'mineral-based energy economy' which it was to become with the
harnessing of coal, iron and steam to unleash a kind of mechanised
productive power scarcely dreamed of in 1750. The coal industry, already
a formidable presence, perhaps pointed the way, but as yet few if any
were looking in that direction. Indeed, in many respects the productive
techniques of the 1740s were closer to those of the 1540s than to those
of the 1840s. But there was, of course, a difference. If Britain remained
an organic economy, much of it had also become, as Wrigley insists, an
advanced organic economy, characterised by a highly productive
agriculture, large commercial and industrial sectors, sophisticated
commercial organisation and a growing capacity both to accumulate
capital and to deploy it productively. If the economic advances of the era
of industrialisation were scarcely anticipated, the people of much of
early-eighteenth-century Britain were 'doing with exceptional success
what other pre-industrial economies had normally done less well'. For
the most part they still conducted their economic lives in household
units, but in households operating in a context which had changed dramatically over two centuries. To appreciate fully the nature of those
changes, and their outcome in individual lives, we must return to the
more intimate economic dynamics of the household.

PART THREE

Living with the market, c.1660–c.1750

In 1695, Gregory King, Lancaster Herald of Arms and a notable exponent of the emergent science of 'political arithmetic', composed an account of English society. Like Edmund Dudley almost two centuries before, he had a particular purpose in doing so, though a somewhat different one. Dudley's purpose, as we have seen, was essentially moral. He sought to prescribe the conditions for the flourishing of the commonwealth in England – an objective in which 'worldly prosperitie' had an important place, but one subordinate to a larger vision of justice and tranquillity which would contribute to the ultimate achievement of the 'honour of god'. To that end, Dudley had constructed his elaborate allegory of the commonwealth, stressing those roles and relationships which, if properly conducted, would bring harmony and well-being to the whole. Gregory King's purpose was rather more specific. He was engaged in an attempt to estimate 'the state of the kingdom and the value thereof' in order to justify his view that England's wealth was declining as a result of the wars and taxation precipitated by the Revolution of 1688. To that end, he constructed a statistical table – 'A Scheme of the Income and Expense of the several Families of England Calculated for the Year 1688'.

In King's 'Scheme', as in Dudley's commonwealth, the household remained the basic unit of society. He reckoned that England's population of 5.5 million was made up of 1,360,586 families, estimated the average family size and income of different social groups, calculated their average income and 'expense' per head, and drew conclusions as to whether or not their domestic budgets were in surplus or in deficit. If King conceived of England as an aggregate of households, however, his table and its supporting calculations implied that they inhabited a very different social and economic world from that envisaged in Dudley's work.

Dudley conceived of society as being composed of three great orders or estates, differentiated by social function. King distributed his house-holders into no fewer than twenty-six different 'Ranks, Degrees, Titles and Qualifications' – or, as he called them elsewhere, 'classes' – differentiated by levels of income and expenditure. Like Dudley, he assumed the social leadership of a landed aristocracy: the titular nobility and four ranks of gentility clustered at the top of his table. But neither of the other two orders of medieval social theory was recognisable in its traditional form. The clerical estate had become one among several professions, with its members divided into three categories distinguished by levels of income. The 'commynalite' had been similarly disaggregated into eight-een component groups, labelled not by the old status terminology of yeoman, husbandman, citizen or burgess, but by occupation or source of income, and ranked for the most part according to wealth. Moreover, the most fundamental distinction in King's scheme did not lie between the roles of the three estates, but was of a radically different nature. In his summarising 'General Account' he grouped together all those house-holds whose incomes exceeded their necessary expenditure as those 'increasing the wealth of the kingdom'. All those whose necessary expense, however modest, exceeded their incomes, were deemed to be those 'decreasing the wealth of the kingdom'.

In King's estimate those 'increasing the wealth of the kingdom' com-prised approximately 38 per cent of all families and, by virtue of their larger households, which included servants and apprentices, some 49 per cent of the English population. Among them were numbered the nobility and gentry (1.2 per cent of all families); those who farmed the land as freeholders or tenant farmers (24.3 per cent); members of the various civil professions and military officers (4 per cent); those engaged in commerce as merchants, shopkeepers and tradesmen (3.7 per cent); and finally independent artisans (4.4 per cent). All of these groups were taken to have average family incomes of at least forty pounds a year, while most professional families had in excess of one hundred pounds and merchants and gentlemen more than two hundred pounds a year. Those 'decreasing the wealth of the kingdom' comprised some 62 per cent of all families and 51 per cent of the total population. They included the households of common seamen and soldiers; 'labouring people and outservants'; 'cottagers and paupers'; and finally some 30,000 vagrants who did not live in family units. Their estimated average family incomes ranged between six and twenty pounds a year.

The reliability of King's figures was questioned at the time and has been disputed since. For our purposes, however, what is more important is his perception of England's economic and social structure. King conceived of England not as an amalgam of functionally interdependent orders, but, in Joyce Appleby's words, as 'an aggregation of private wealth'. The well-being of the whole was determined not by the performance of the God-appointed duties of each estate, but by the extent to which the surplus income of those 'increasing the wealth of the kingdom' exceeded the deficit of those 'decreasing the wealth of the kingdom' – which in King's view it had done in 1688 in a ratio of approximately 3 : 1. Within his overall 'Scheme', the relative economic fortunes of the members of each component class depended not upon their appointed 'degree', but upon what Max Weber would have called their 'market capacity': their ability to generate income and to command resources within a competitive market economy. Many such economic classes were distinguished by King. But, as he explained in his responses to his critic Robert Harley, he also believed that they could be resolved, on the basis of their per-capita domestic consumption, into three broad groups: 'the better sort', 'the middle sort' and 'the poorest sort'. To judge by the details of his 'Scheme', that tripartite distinction depended among those 'increasing the wealth of the kingdom' upon their possession of landed property, financial capital or specialist professional knowledge, and among those 'decreasing the wealth of the kingdom' upon their possession of little more than their power to labour.

The economic world implied by King's calculations was therefore radically different from that which had been assumed by Edmund Dudley two centuries earlier. Both were based upon the household. But Dudley's householders were for the most part small producers enjoying a considerable degree of self-sufficiency, whose engagement in commercial relationships was relatively limited and localised, and whose activities were contained by what E. P. Thompson called 'the organic compulsions of the manor and guild'. King's householders engaged, according to their different capacities, with the demands of an economic environment in which the market was the central mechanism and the power of capital was far more salient. It was a far richer society, in which the 'better' and 'middle' sorts of family enjoyed a purchasing power well in excess of their necessary expenses. Yet it was also a more highly differentiated society in which the livings of more than half the population were dependent upon the uncertainties of the market for their labour.

To this extent King's laconic 'Scheme' encapsulated the outcome of two centuries of economic and social change. What it did not explore, however, was the manner in which its component households had adapted to, and indeed continued to shape, their changing economic environment. It tells us little or nothing about the strategies which they adopted in different market sectors and situations, the conventions governing their daily economic practices, the options and constraints which they encountered, their shifting roles and identities, or the many ambiguities of attitude and behaviour which derived from the persisting significance, within a fundamentally transformed economic structure, of older values and relationships. In short, it describes some of the parameters of their economic life, but remains silent on the subject of their economic cultures. If we are to appreciate fully the outcome of the process of commercialisation which had so radically accelerated in sixteenth- and seventeenth-century Britain, and which was in some respects still far from complete at the turn of the eighteenth century, we must ask how people had learned to live with the market: as the landowners and farmers of capitalist agriculture; as those who deployed capital in commerce and industry; as those who sold their labour; as those who reflected on the economic transition of the age and tried to understand it.

CHAPTER TWELVE

'A nobleman, a gentleman, a yeoman': the landed interest

In 1500 Britain's component societies had been overwhelmingly rural and its constituent economies predominantly agricultural. It was a world in which most people gained their subsistence directly from small family farms, in which their access to the land was shaped by the structures of lordship and customary tenurial systems, and in which their agricultural practices were constrained by the expectations and compulsions of the manor and the barony. At the turn of the eighteenth century that world remained partially in being. Despite urban growth, most of the population still lived in the countryside, and, despite the spread of rural industries, most of those who did so still derived their livings primarily from agriculture. Nor was peasant farming a thing of the past. In much of Wales and in most of Scotland, the small farm, worked largely or wholly by family labour, still remained the norm – four-fifths of the householders of Highland Aberdeenshire were small-farm tenants in 1694. And in England too small farms remained numerous, especially in areas which retained extensive commons and in the open-field parishes of the midlands. Half the tenants of the Belvoir estate in Leicestershire in 1692 held less than twenty acres, and a further third held between twenty and eighty acres. In Scotland most rents still came to the laird in kind, and in England and Wales many surveys and rentals still recorded the rights accorded by copyhold tenancies and manorial custom and archaic rents which represented recognition of lordship more than a capitalist levy upon the produce of the land.

There was much that spoke in the accents of the past. Yet, at the same time, in much of England and Wales both the institutional structures of rural society and the basic imperatives of the rural economy had been transformed by two centuries of cumulative change, in a manner which was also increasingly evident in Scotland. The spread of leasehold tenures and the process of enclosure entailed a hardening of property rights over the land. The ambiguities of custom were gradually washed out by the powerful certainties of ownership and contract. Probably not more than a third of English tenancies were still customary in 1700, and an estimated 71 per cent of the cultivable area was already enclosed. The manor was a unit of management rather than a tenant community, and its court a registry of land transactions rather than an institution of communal regulation. The composition of rural society had been recast by the process of engrossing. If 50 per cent of the Belvoir tenants of 1692 were smallholders, it was also the case that they collectively held only 2 per cent of the land, while more than half was in the hands of the 18 per cent of the tenantry who farmed holdings of more than a hundred acres. And if farm tenancy was still the norm in much of Scotland, it was also the case that in the Lothians and the Merse only 15 per cent of householders in 1694 were tenants. Such institutional and structural changes reflected change in the dynamics of the rural economy and in attitudes towards the nature of agricultural production. What had been the subsistence activity of most was now increasingly a matter of specialist production by large-scale farmers engaged in supplying consumers in distant markets. With that shift came a change in the place of agriculture within the emergent national economy. It was becoming a particular form of business rather than the commonly assumed way of life. And as this became the case, those who engaged in it as landowners and commercial farmers became subject to redefinition as a distinctive element within the larger structure of economic life: the 'landed interest'.

i. *Securing the estate*

At the head of the 'landed interest' stood the great possessors of property in land: the nobility and the landed gentry, and in particular the owners of substantial estates. Much of the institutional transformation of the rural economy had been accomplished at their behest, or with their compliance, and its character reflected their priorities and their values. Tawney wrote of the 'calm, proud faces' of their portraits, which hang still on the walls of the country houses from which they ruled Britain, staring down on us with 'the unshakeable assurance of men who are untroubled by regrets or perplexities, men who have deserved well of their order and their descendants'. They were not all so untroubled in life, to be sure. Their conventional portrayal was part and parcel of what E. P. Thompson termed the 'theatre' of the great, a representation of the innate superiority of a traditional ruling order which was intended to convince the onlooker and to instil deference to its social and political hegemony. And if they deserved well of their descendants, it was not least because of their capacity to adapt to changing times. For the landed class was nothing if not culturally amphibious. Its roots were in the land, yet many of its members spent much of the year in town and all were familiar, to one degree or another, with the worlds of commerce and finance. They stood for tradition and hierarchy, but they were thoroughly imbued with the values of the market. They revered lineage and ancestry. Yet they measured one another first and foremost in terms of the round figures of estimated annual income. They stood upon their honour, and were capable of a haughty condescension towards those engaged in trade. Yet they appreciated to the full the benefits of capitalist enterprise. They were patricians, but they were also rentiers, responsive to economic pressures and fully aware that their port, social ascendancy and political clout depended ultimately upon the efficient exploitation of their property.

For any landed family, the first priority was continuity: the preservation of its established place in society, which in turn involved the maintenance of the integrity and economic viability of the estate. In the central decades of the seventeenth century that objective had been threatened for many landowners by the trauma of the Civil Wars and Interregnum. Heavy war taxation, military plundering, inability to collect rents and the unavoidable neglect of properties had weakened the position of many gentry households. Roughly a quarter of the landed class of England and Wales suffered 'sequestration' of their estates, involving the seizure of the bulk of the income by parliamentary commissioners as punishment for 'delinquency' (active support of the king) or for their Catholicism. Some royalist estates were ultimately confiscated and sold, as were the lands of the crown, the episcopate and cathedral deans and chapters. The eventual outcome in terms of the potential redistribution of landed property, however, was surprisingly slight. Parliament remained dominated by landowners, most of whom shared Oliver Cromwell's view that the established social order of 'a nobleman, a gentleman, a yeoman' was 'a good interest of the nation'. They had no desire to destroy their royalist kinsmen and neighbours. From 1646 the latter were permitted to 'compound' for their delinquency and to recover their estates on payment of fines, and by 1650 most of them had done so. Many confiscated estates were bought back by their former owners acting through agents, and others were recovered at the Restoration of the monarchy in 1660, as were the estates of the crown and the church. The Civil Wars and Interregnum brought no lasting reconstitution of landed society, though they were a period of massive strain for many landed families and left behind a legacy of indebtedness and straitened circumstances.

Weathering the lingering aftermath of that storm was assisted by two mid-seventeenth-century legal developments which very much reflected the priorities of the landed class: the 'strict settlement' and the 'equity of redemption'. The strict settlement was essentially a device for effecting the orderly transmission of landed property between the generations in a manner which would both preserve the integrity of the estate and provide for the future of all those whose well-being depended upon it. It was an agreement, executed at the time of the marriage of the heir to an estate, whereby the present owner and the heir were granted only life interests in the estate. As life tenants, they were prevented from selling any part of the settled patrimony, which was to be transmitted intact to the as-yet-unborn eldest son of the marriage. At the same time, provision was made for the jointure which would maintain the heir's bride in the event of widowhood, and for the portions of the heir's brothers and sisters. In this way the strict settlement attempted, in Professor Trumbach's words, 'to balance the claims of family continuity and greatness, embodied in the position of the eldest son, against a satisfactory provision for younger children and for wives; to mediate between the conflicting claims of kindred and patrilineage'. As such it rapidly recommended itself to the owners of great estates and was widely adopted by them during the 1660s and 1670s, while subsequently becoming common also among the lesser gentry.

The equity of redemption was a legal doctrine, developed in chancery case-law, which extended greater security to those who sought to raise capital by the mortgaging of property. Prior to the 1650s mortgaging was an extremely risky expedient. The mortgagee frequently took possession of the property concerned and even the slightest infringement of the terms of the loan could result in its forfeiture. Under the equity of redemption, which may have developed in part as a means of assisting heavily indebted former royalists to regain their lands, the mortgagor retained possession of the land, and was secured from foreclosure so long as the principal was eventually repaid, with interest. Mortgages could also be extended, provided interest was paid. These developments, together with the greater availability of mortgage funds provided by metropolitan bankers or brokered by country attorneys, enabled landowners to raise capital more safely and easily to meet their necessary occasions – the payment of dowries and portions, perhaps, or the financing of building or improvement – without resorting to the sale of parts of their estates. All that was required was the capacity to generate sufficient rental income to maintain interest payments and eventually to repay the principal.

The equity of redemption thus complemented the strict settlement as a means of conserving the patrimonies of the landed class. But, while both devices offered greater security, neither could guarantee a family's retention of its place in landed society. Not all estates were settled, and, of those which were, the strict settlement was incapable of permanently preventing the alienation of land. The contingencies of demographic misfortune meant that many fathers died before the marriages of their heirs, thereby frustrating the renewal of settlements in unbroken succession generation after generation. Settlements could also be broken by private act of parliament if their provisions proved impossibly restrictive to the present life tenants of estates, especially those in economic difficulty. In practice, landed families needed to be able to enjoy periodically the flexibility to rethink their strategies, and if necessary to dispose of land. The real significance of their continued employment of the strict settlement lay less in its effectiveness in binding the hands of landowners than in the manner in which it enshrined a particular set of aspirations – aspirations of permanence which could not always be realised. Nor did the greater availability and security of mortgages necessarily rescue landowners in difficulty. Edward Lloyd of Llanforda adopted many expedients in his struggle to repair the Civil War losses sustained by his father, including the mortgaging of part of his small estate, but he failed to sustain the burden and was forced eventually to sell. So too was Richard Willoughby of West Knoyle, Wiltshire, who was crushed by the fact that two-thirds of his income was committed to the provision of his widowed mother's jointure and the payment of interest on a mortgage raised to provide marriage portions for his five sisters. In the final analysis the maintenance of the integrity of the estate, and of the continuity to which landed families aspired, depended not so much upon legal instruments as upon the success of the broader strategies of estate management within which they were employed.

ii. Managing the estate

Successful estate management meant in practice exploiting the estate's income-generating capacity while also controlling expenditure beyond that necessary to sustain a family's standing. On smaller estates such management was the direct responsibility of their owners – men like Sir Edward Dering of Pluckley in Kent, who, concerned at his sagging rent

roll in the early 1670s, adopted a course of 'generall frugalitie' and considered twenty-two projects 'as may be beneficiall by way of improvement'. There was no formal training for such duties. Landowners learned
their business as if by osmosis, absorbing the lessons to be garnered from
the example of their parents and their neighbours. And that process was
not confined to the male heirs to the patrimony. Many young gentlewomen acquired business sense as well as genteel accomplishments – an
awareness of the essentials of estate management which they were
expected to deploy at different stages of the life course. Sarah Fell kept
the accounts of her father's estate at Swarthmore, Lancashire. Alice
Thornton's mother not only improved her husband's estate by bringing
a dowry of £2,000, but also by 'her wise and prudential government of
his family and by her care was a meanes to give opportunity of increasing his patrimony'. Lady Elizabeth Bowes, like many widows, nurtured
the family's lands and coal-mining interests in Co. Durham during the
long minority of her eldest son, before stepping back into the role of
dowager when he came of age in 1718.

On that occasion Lady Elizabeth encountered her son's marked reluctance to return from London to take up his responsibilities. In that, he
was not alone. Absentee landownership had always been an inevitable
feature of the lives of great magnates whose estates were widely scattered. But in the later seventeenth and early eighteenth centuries it also
became increasingly part of the way of life of most landowners of substance. In part this was because of the political involvement of leading
gentlemen in parliament. In part it arose from the uniting of estates
through the marriages of heiresses to husbands who were socially appropriate, but geographically distant – a not uncommon phenomenon in a
period in which adverse demographic conditions meant that a substantial minority of landed families failed to produce male heirs. Many Welsh
estates passed into the hands of English landowners in this manner. In
part it was simply a matter of preferring the amenity and sophistication
of urban and in particular metropolitan society. 'Surely you don't think
me such a fool', protested William Bowes, 'as to prefer the Charms of a
stupid, dull, country life to the pleasures of the Town.' Some resided permanently in their town houses, like Sir John Lowther of Whitehaven, who
lived in London and visited his Cumbrian estates only eleven times in the
years 1666–98. Many others chose to reside in town during part or all of
the winter social season, and to visit their principal country seats during
the summer, perhaps following a spring jaunt to such developing spa
towns as Bath or Scarborough. Edinburgh was described as 'the ren-
dezvous of taste, and winter quarters to all our nobility who cannot
afford to live in London'. But, whatever the case, absenteeism had two

very obvious implications. First, it involved additional household expenditure – the Welsh landowner Sir Thomas Hamer spent £636 on a six-week visit to London in the winter of 1700–1, and it cost the Gloucestershire MP Sir Thomas Chester £755 to maintain his family in London between January and May 1735. Secondly, it required the elaboration of the system of estate management at a distance.

Both needs were met by the members of the emergent profession of estate stewardship. In the absence of their employers, estate stewards (or in Scotland 'factors') took responsibility for the management of the home farm, the maintenance of the country house and park, the tenanting of the estate, the exploitation of woodlands and mineral resources, the receipt of income, the keeping of accounts and the transfer of funds to meet the landowner's immediate expenditure. On smaller estates, or those where the owner's absence was only seasonal, the steward might be a local lawyer, surveyor or substantial farmer engaged part-time in the overseeing of a client's affairs. On larger estates they were commonly full-time managers, not infrequently gentlemen by birth and sometimes kinsmen of the owner. In the case of the greatest estates they could be part of a complex management structure. The Duke of Newcastle, for example, had a 'man of substance' running each of his scattered properties and a Chief Steward in London charged with the co-ordination of the whole. The circumstances varied, but the essentials of the steward's role remained the same. He undertook all that the landowner would have done had he or she been present, and in return was rewarded with a salary or fees, a variety of perquisites and the exercise of considerable local power. Save in the case of the most complacent or irresponsible of landowners, however, he acted with the knowledge and consent of his employer. For, if landowners were increasingly absent from their estates, they were not ignorant of their affairs. The duties of the steward involved incessant correspondence, such as that which kept the Duke of Hamilton minutely informed of day-to-day affairs on his Scottish estates – the completion of sowing; the quality of the harvest; the state of the grain market; problems with tenants; the progress of his coal and salt interests, and scraps of personal news. In this way stewards informed and proposed; landlords disposed. There was little that was too trivial to bring to their attention, and the resulting files of letters provide ample testimony to the assiduity with which the economic potential of many estates was exploited.

Many stewards were exceedingly active managers with a sharp eye for any means of improving the profitability of their masters' lands. Where appropriate, this might include investment in industrial undertakings, in more efficient managing of woodlands, in transportation, or in urban development. The Earls of Southampton, Salisbury and above all Bedford benefited hugely from London property development. The Lowthers of Whitehaven invested in coal mining and salt-production and established a new town and port facilities which gave them a further interest in the tobacco trade. The Liddells of Ravensworth and the Boweses of Gibside were major players in the Tyneside coal industry and they had many counterparts in the developing coal fields of the midlands, in Scotland and in Wales. Some fortunate and enterprising families were able to derive a major part of their income from such undertakings. In Cornwall, for example, the Eyns drew 44 per cent of their income from their copper-mining operations in the years 1727–31. But for most landed families such opportunities were a welcome supplement. The truly vital part of their incomes was that derived from the management of their agricultural estates.

Maintaining and if possible improving income from agricultural land presented a different set of difficulties in the late seventeenth and early eighteenth centuries from those which had obtained a century earlier. Then the principal problem had been that of revising forms of tenure and customary levels of fines and rents in order to tap the farming profits being made in a period of rising agricultural prices. Now most tenures were leaseholds, granted for periods of between seven and twenty-one years. Landlords drew most of their income from annual rents rather than periodic fines, and 'rack rents' adjustable with the state of the market were increasingly common. Yet grain prices had fallen significantly and livestock prices had stabilised. The rewards for the commercial farmer were neither so large nor so easily won as they had been in Elizabethan and early Stuart times, and the rental incomes of landlords were threatened as a result. In 1680 the author of *Britannia Languens* lamented that 'our late wealthy yeomanry are forced to sink their rents on the gentry continually [that is, fall into arrears] or else to fling them up their farms'. A decade later Richard Baxter described vividly the situation of small husbandmen, now fully immersed in a market economy and struggling desperately to meet their obligations in an adverse commercial climate. 'If their sow pig or their hens breed chickens,' he wrote, 'they cannot afford to eat them, but must sell them to make their rent. They cannot afford to eat the eggs that their hens lay, nor the apples or pears that grow on their trees (save some that are not vendible) but must make money of all.'

Baxter carefully exempted from his account of the husbandman's plight 'freeholders that pay no rent', and those who benefited from the exceptional market opportunities provided by London, or other great cities, or whose domestic economies were supplemented by a trade. But his discrimination in doing so lends all the more power to his depiction of the struggling small-farm economy, and there is a good deal of independent evidence which not only supports his testimony, but also shows that the difficulties of the times extended to more substantial tenants as well. A survey of the probate accounts of Lincolnshire farmers from the 1660s to the 1680s reveals that while the median value of the inventoried goods of yeomen was £149 – a substantial sum – the median net value after payment of debts was only £26, and 20 per cent of those surveyed died insolvent. They included men like Richard Holmes of Markby, whose goods were valued in 1683 at an impressive £562, but who owed £270 to his landlord for several years' rent arrears, as well as other debts. Husbandmen in the same county had a median inventoried wealth of £62, but a median net estate of only £13, which made them little better off than farm labourers. Moreover, almost 30 per cent died insolvent, like William Presgrave of Steddington, half of whose estate was required to pay off rent arrears to two landlords.

The estate accounts of the later seventeenth century are liberally dusted with references to such tenants – 'dead insolvent'; 'went off in debt'; 'carried away his goods by night and went off insolvent'; 'nothing to be had: the man is dead and his wife and children are maintained by the parish' – and the implications for landlords were deeply threatening. Arrears built up. Rent levels were often forced down in the arable south and east, though they held up better in the livestock-oriented north and west. From the 1680s the situation was somewhat more stable until the abundant harvests and depressed prices of the 1730s and 1740s brought further distress to the farmers of predominantly arable regions. But profit margins in agriculture remained relatively slim. Dr Bowden estimates that in the conditions of the early eighteenth century a specialist livestock farmer with a hundred acres in the west country would be likely to make a net profit of less than £53 a year with which to maintain his household, while an eastern arable specialist with the same acreage would have a net profit of just over £35, and a midland sheep grazier could expect a net loss. And by that time the burdens of the landed interest had been added to by the land tax, which was paid directly by freeholders, copyholders and those farmers with leases for lives, but borne by the landlord in the case of land tenanted at rack rents. It is unlikely that the gross annual return on landed property exceeded 5 per cent of its value, and the net return was significantly lower than that which could be achieved by other forms of investment. 'How much better money yields than land,' mused Lord Hervey in 1707, 'which after taxes and repairs allowed never answers above three per cent,' while in 1724 Lord Chandos repented 'that I have laid out so much money in land and wish I have kept my money in the funds'.

Yet landownership meant so much more than an annual return. It conferred social distinction and political influence. Landowners of substance were under an inherited obligation to maintain and if possible advance both. And they continued to lay out money in land, drawn on still by the ideal of the consolidated estate, focused upon a principal seat, which entrenched their families in the soil, society and power structures of particular countries – however rarely they chose to visit them. The Lowthers eagerly snapped up small estates intermingled with their west-Cumbrian properties, the Mansells of Margam bought consistently to fill out their Glamorganshire holdings, and vigilant stewards regularly advised other ambitious magnates of opportunities to do likewise. Nevertheless if land brought returns not measurable by a financial statement, landownership was also a business. Financial returns must be maintained and if possible improved, and in the conditions of the time that meant tenanting the land with those farmers most likely to achieve levels of profit that would ensure the regular payment of rent.

iii. *Strategies of 'improvement'*

Three strategies were widely adopted to further that end. The most fundamental of these was the consolidation of the structures of large-scale capitalist agriculture by reducing the numbers of small tenancies and augmenting large farms. 'A steward as much as in him lieth', wrote Edward Lawrence in his *The Duty of a Steward to his Lord* (1727), '. . . should endeavour to lay all the small farms, let to poor indigent tenants, to the great ones.' By the time Lawrence wrote, this was conventional wisdom. Larger farmers were better able to stock and equip a farm, to carry more livestock, to afford better seed and the dressing of the land. They achieved higher profits for reinvestment, and above all they paid higher rents more reliably. Accordingly, there was a gradual attrition of small tenancies in many parts of England and Wales, most notably in the midlands. It was a process which aroused surprisingly little comment, and no literature of agrarian complaint comparable to that of the sixteenth century, for it no longer involved the challenging of entrenched customary rights, was conducted in a normative climate conducive to 'improvement', and above all proceeded slowly. 'To alter farms and to turn several little ones into great ones', opined Lawrence, 'is a work of Difficulty and Time.' It should be accomplished 'without oppression', for 'it would raise too great an *Odium* to turn poor Families into the wide World, by uniting Farms all at once, in order to make an Advance on Rents'. He advised stewards to take the 'more reasonable and popular' course of waiting until such farms fell in at a tenant's death, and then to resume possession rather than 'continuing the farms to the poor remains who may as well betake themselves to other employments'.

In addition, the steward was advised 'to be zealous, for his lord's sake, in purchasing all the freeholders out as soon as possible'. Small freeholds, or copyholds of inheritance which remained outside the commercial rental market, could be converted into leaseholds, or amalgamated with larger holdings, and their acquisition could also further schemes of rationalisation and improvement. Thus the Hon. Beaumont Hotham's steward at Wilton, Yorkshire, wrote to his master in 1743 urging the acquisition of a farm which would complete a long-standing process of consolidation of ownership: 'By purchasing the farm you may have it in your power to inclose and make land worth 15 s[hillings] an acre that is now in tillage and only let at 5 s[hillings].' Comparable processes of rationalisation motivated the systematic purchase of small freeholds and secure copyholds on the Dashwoods' estate at Kirklington, Oxfordshire, between 1684 and 1750, at Chippenham and Orwell in Cambridgeshire, at Highley in Shropshire, Terling in Essex, and in many other places.

As a result of such policies, a small farming population which was still substantial in numbers, if not in the acreage under its control, was gradually eroded. A survey of south-midland estates, for example, reveals that the total acreage held in farms of thirty to sixty and sixty to one hundred acres fell markedly in the course of the later seventeenth and early eighteenth centuries, while that given over to farms of more than a hundred acres rose proportionately. On the Leveson-Gower estates, more than half the land was still held in farms of under a hundred acres in the 1710s, but less than a third by the 1760s. Village communities in which small farmers had remained numerically, if not economically, preponderant were completing the transition into societies of large-scale capitalist farmers, semi-independent cottagers and landless labourers. And if that process was much less advanced in some other parts of Britain, it was nonetheless making itself felt. On the Powis estate in Montgomeryshire, the financially embarrassed owner lost patience with his small tenants in the 1720s and issued instructions that all arrears of rent should be collected 'or els drive the people out of the country, for my lord had as good be without tenants as to have such as pay no rents'. In Lowland Scotland the rapid transition to money rents – which on the Melville and Leven estates in Fife meant that by the 1710s close to half the lairds' incomes came in money, as compared to only a tenth in the 1670s – placed greater emphasis on the desirability of reducing the numbers of multiple tenancies to create larger holdings for the commercial farmers who could securely pay them. Whereas as late as the 1730s more than half the tenancies on the Douglas estate in Lanarkshire were still multiple tenancies, that figure had been reduced to less than a fifth by the 1750s. By that date, in Professor Devine's view, 'multiple tenancy was not only in retreat, but was fast being eliminated', while single tenancies meant bigger farms and the creation of a smaller, but more commercially viable, 'independent farming class'. In the Highlands too the structure of the clans was being eroded by the desire of chieftains to realise larger disposable incomes from their land, often on the advice of professional consultants employed to further that end. On the Argyll estates a more direct proprietor–tenant relationship redefined the nature of obligation in the Clan Campbell. Tacksmen were removed, or transformed into large tenants or factors. Land was let to the highest bidder irrespective of clan loyalties. By 1715, Professor Whyte concludes, 'the clan had been virtually destroyed by commercialisation'. MacLeod of Dunvegan and MacDonald of Sleat went further by devising a scheme to export peasant families to the colonies as indentured labour. They failed, but their proposal foreshadowed the shape of things to come.

All this was with a view to the creation of larger, more commercially attuned and more profitable farm tenancies. Once created, however, they needed to be filled, and to be kept filled, with the right kind of farmer. That was not necessarily easy. It might seem paradoxical in a rural society in which many young people aspired to hold a tenancy of their own, and in which landlords were engaged in reducing the numbers of their tenantry, that their stewards should complain of a shortage of tenants. Yet the essence of the matter lay in what a tract of 1673 called 'the want of tenants with good stocks to manage the farms they take': that is, with adequate working capital. Under the older agrarian dispensation the initial stocking of a small family farm had been largely a matter of inheritance. Ongoing needs were met by reserving part of the crop as seed, by breeding or by purchases from retained earnings, and labour costs were low. To a considerable extent the system was self-sustaining. Under the new commercial order, the initial capital required to stock a large farm was much greater. Inputs in the form of superior seed, better livestock, land dressings and maintenance costs were more substantial. Labour costs were higher, and so were rents. Farmers with the wherewithal to undertake all this were fewer in number, in high demand and apt to be choosier about the tenancies they undertook.

This being the case, a second prominent strategy of estate-management was the nurturing of relations with the most desirable sort of farmer – those who combined a reputation for industry, competence and honesty with 'good stocks to manage the farms they take'. At bottom, such relations were played out according to essentially commercial ground rules. The obligations of tenants were laid down in their leases, and they in turn could bargain hard over their terms. In 1680, the steward reported from the Fitzwilliam estate in Norfolk that two good tenants were threatening to give up their tenancies and move elsewhere 'unless your Lordship be kind to them', while a third was demanding that the rent owing on his present farm be cancelled and that he be granted a reduced rent for two years on a new taking. Some tenants preferred short leases and rack-rents for the flexibility they gave them to renegotiate their leases annually, and the mobility of tenants could be considerable. Both parties to the lease were also well aware of the potential conflict of their interests. Viscount Cholmondeley, who had employed tenant bailiffs on his Cheshire estate, found that they 'beat down' the rents – it 'being against their interest' to do otherwise – and therefore appointed a minor gentleman as his steward, and expected him to 'effect the gentleman's interest' and to scorn that of 'the clowns'. Tenants in return were often, in Dr Hainsworth's words, 'formidably stubborn, alert to their own interests and capable of defending them against what they perceived as assaults from either landlord or steward'. They might defer to their landlords' social position, hat in hand, but such deference could also be decidedly conditional. 'If my lord be so very haisty to call of me for moneys faster than I can possably gett it,' wrote one Yorkshire farmer to Lord Irwin's steward in 1690, 'I must be forced to give his Lordshipp his land into his own hand.' And the same truculent independence was exhibited by farmers on the Earl of Dorset's estate in Staffordshire and Derbyshire. 'I assure you, my lord,' reported his scandalised steward, 'several tenants in these parts keep landlords in a kind of awe for fear they should throw up their land,' concluding ruefully, 'so the world is thrown upside down.'

In such a context, relations with tenants were conducted with discretion, for it was in the economic interests of landlords to do so. In contrast to the situation obtaining in the sixteenth century, landlords' financial self-interest now reinforced rather than undermined the traditions of paternalism. Rent arrears were tolerated in bad years, and slow payment was often the case even in better times – half the rents due on Lady Day (25 March) 1685 on one Somerset estate had still not come in by August that year. Ruthless maximisation of the rental was relatively rare, as was the eviction of otherwise good tenants who encountered difficulties. Most landlords were well aware of the fact that, as one Welsh steward instructed his master in 1730, 'if a landlord has the character of being severe to his tenants . . . he will never have no body live under him but poor slaves as cannot leave him', whereas if his reputation was good, 'foreigners will come and will be ready to give the value for anything as is to be let'. They could be assiduous in playing the role of the good landlord: generously engaged (from a distance) in the dispensation of patronage; finely aware (from their stewards' letters) of details of individual circumstance; minutely attentive (when present) to the bestowal of that appearance of concern which could transmute disparities of rank and interest into a bond of personal identification. Lady Bowes knew that such things mattered when she urged her reluctant son to come north and meet his tenants. So did John Rouse, who wrote from darkest Suffolk two days after Christmas 1704, 'I've just come from Ipswich to drink ale with the tenants; and as soon as that ceremony's over, shall return from whence I came.' His ennui was palpable, but the obligation was kept.

If the rituals of paternalism were intended to maintain the semblance of common interest, the mutual concerns of landlords and tenants found more concrete expression in a third strand of estate-management strategy: the fostering of a culture of agricultural best practice. As we have seen, the market trends of the late seventeenth and early eighteenth centuries encouraged both increased regional specialisation and the more widespread introduction of improved methods aimed at lowering unit costs of production in a more competitive environment. The extent of such investment in improvement should not be exaggerated. In most of Scotland there was very little change at all before the later eighteenth century, though the shift towards larger farms undoubtedly prepared the way for more rapid development thereafter. Much of upland Wales was scarcely amenable to improvement by the techniques available at the time, and in the better favoured areas of the country innovation was modest and gradual, usually involving a shift towards a greater emphasis upon livestock production and the introduction of clover. In England too, innovation diffused slowly and patchily, in a manner which Dr Thirsk has described as seeming almost 'random and unpredictable'. But of course it was neither. Those who undertook it were aware of the possibility of improvement. They were conscious of the fact that, given their location and potential markets, it might turn to their profit; and they were in a position to finance it.

In all this the estate system had a role to play. Landlords, and more particularly their stewards, were well aware of the literature and practice of improvement and took an interest in both. Watkin Owen, steward of the Gwydir estate, owned a copy of Worlidge's *Systema Agriculturae* (1669) in the 1680s, and fifty years later Edward Wynne, steward of Bodewryd, borrowed and copied passages from Bradley's *Compleat Book of Husbandry* (1727) as well as Lawrence's *Duties of a Steward*. The Duke of Somerset took notes on his tenants' farming practices in the 1720s. The Earl of Strathmore joined the Society for Improving the Knowledge of Agriculture, tried out clover on his home farm, and instructed his factor on 'the method of Farming in England'. It can hardly be said that landlords generally took the lead in promoting innovation. Most of the revenues of their estates were devoted to current rather than to capital expenditure. What they did do, however, through their stewards, was to encourage best practice. Their leases were for the most part unambitious in the specification of improvements to be undertaken. Nevertheless, they usually required 'proper' or 'husbandlike' adherence to the expected standards of the day, and often prescribed the maintenance of fences and drainage ditches, woodland planting, and the dressing of the soil with lime, marl or manure. Beyond that, some of them set examples. Prominent among the innovators of the period were minor gentlemen and estate stewards with home farms to manage, and both they and those who followed their lead learned principally from example. Edward Wynne held office in the diocese of Hereford and modelled the home farm he managed on one he had observed at Ross-on-Wye. He bought his clover seed there in 1717. The spread of sainfoin, coleseed and convertible husbandry in parts of Lincolnshire was almost certainly attributable to the successful example of the Massingberds of South Ormsby. Of the eight earliest farm inventories revealing the use of clover in mid-Gwent, four came from adjoining parishes. Two of them belonged to gentlemen who were kinsmen and two to yeoman farmers who were father and son.

In addition, the estate system could welcome and facilitate the following of such examples by substantial farmers with the will and the capital to undertake improvement. Leases of seven to twenty-one years could encourage medium-term initiatives. Stewards and tenants could strike deals over the costs of improvements, and landlords could be persuaded to finance long-term improvements like drainage schemes or the erection of new buildings which could be expected, eventually, to lead to improved rentals. In these various ways, it has been suggested that the system had the capacity to call forth more investment than either party would have been likely to have undertaken alone.

Such processes were slow, and their geography uneven, and in consequence the late seventeenth and early eighteenth centuries are not conventionally thought of as a period of significant change in rural Britain. The period lacks the high drama of both the institutional changes of the sixteenth century and the technological advances of the later eighteenth and early nineteenth centuries. It was, nonetheless, a vital period of consolidation in much of England and Wales, while in Scotland it witnessed significant departures from tradition. Central to both was the elaboration and extension of an estate system through which the continued social and political ascendancy of a traditional landowning elite was underpinned by the rents yielded by a capitalistically structured agriculture. By the second quarter of the eighteenth century, agriculture in Britain was already well advanced towards the achievement of its distinctive combination of intensive cultivation and large-scale enterprise. The estate system played a vital role in the creation of the institutional and cultural context necessary for that development. Behind its deceptively archaic trappings, it ensured that agriculture was primarily a business for both landlords and their tenants. And though it exploited the idiom of tradition, it normalised the expectation of change and adaptation in the pursuit of commercial opportunity. With the consolidation of the estate system the early modern transition in agrarian social relations was completed, and its associated economic culture further ensured that, if technological revolution in agriculture was yet to come, the cast of mind that made it possible had already crystallised.

CHAPTER THIRTEEN

Capital and 'credit': the 'middle sort of people'

The estate system was central to one aspect of Britain's increasingly distinctive economic identity: a highly productive and improvement-oriented capitalist agriculture. At the turn of the eighteenth century, however, the attention of those most conscious of Britain's growing economic strength was focused elsewhere – upon the world of commerce and manufactures, and upon the activities of those members of the trading, manufacturing and professional classes whose efforts were most visibly increasing the wealth of the kingdom. They were those described by Daniel Defoe in 1709 as 'the middle sort who live well', and a proportion of 'the Rich who live very plentifully'. As Roy Porter puts it, they were 'the swelling, prosperous middle ranks': Britain's 'stout midriff'.

That phrase perfectly captures their essential position in the social and economic structure, but it disguises their heterogeneity. In occupational terms, they included people as various as merchants, lawyers, medical practitioners, clothiers, ironmongers, mining engineers, shipmasters and what Porter calls 'an anthill of petty traders, horse dealers, builders, inn-keepers, and manufacturers who excelled in turning a penny for themselves'. In all, Gregory King's table suggests that they comprised some 12 per cent of English households in 1688, while in 1759–60, after a further two generations of commercial development, Joseph Massie's comparable calculations suggest a total of 22 per cent of households. In terms of income, King and Massie agreed that the lower threshold of this broad social grouping was set by a household income of at least forty pounds a year. Yet they also made it clear that many professional men, merchants and manufacturers could expect annual incomes of between three and ten times that level, while a few plutocrats had incomes of such stratospheric magnitude as to render their inclusion among the 'middle ranks' something of a misnomer. In terms of social status, some – notably great merchants and leading professionals – enjoyed effective gentility. Others were recognised as the 'principal inhabitants' or 'better sort' of their provincial communities. Still others were simply termed 'householders': a usage implying a degree of economic and social soundness which distinguished them from the poor.

Heterogeneous as its membership might be, the notion of a 'middle sort of people' placed between the landed gentry and the labouring classes has a general validity – as contemporaries recognised by their frequent employment of the term. And if it was a distinctly elastic category, those encompassed by it had certain broad characteristics in common. Of these, the two most frequently singled out by historians are their independence and their prospects. Unlike the gentry, they had to work for a living, but unlike labouring people they did so independently. They frequently employed others, but were rarely themselves employees. In addition, most of them were able to generate a significant income by the standards of the day (at least forty pounds a year). This placed them in a position, in Peter Earle's words, 'to accumulate on a regular basis and so improve themselves'. Both their independence and their hopes of advancement in the world, however, depended upon a third characteristic: their possession of capital.

i. *Three kinds of capital*

The capital which underpinned their position was in the first instance economic – a stock of money or goods which could be turned over to generate profit and an income: capital in the conventional sense of the word. But they also possessed capital in two further senses: first, the 'cultural capital' of acquired skills, knowledge and demeanour, and secondly, the 'social capital' of connection to networks of association, obligation and support. Both had the potential to be transformed into economic capital. And all three forms of capital were derived in the first instance from an individual's family of origin.

This fact is most clearly revealed in the processes of entering and becoming established in the worlds of trade, industry and the professions. Entry required training, and that did not come cheap. For the most part it was still acquired by forms of apprenticeship. That might mean by formal indenture, in the traditional manner, but increasingly it involved serving a less formal clerkship or assistantship in a master's business. (The number of formally enrolled apprentices was declining in most major cities in the early eighteenth century.) Such a training was necessarily preceded by schooling at a grammar school, or one of the 'dissenting academies' founded for religious nonconformists, or at a commercially oriented 'writing school'. In Scotland from the 1690s burgh schools often taught book-keeping and the basics of navigation, while some Scottish youths were sent to the mercantile schools of the Netherlands. The quality and relevance of this preliminary schooling varied, but it would include at least a good level of literacy and the basics of numeracy. Thereafter the apprentice would acquire in a master's place of business, or perhaps in an overseas station, the necessary knowledge of production processes, commercial letter-writing, the weights and measures peculiar to particular trades, financial management, forms of action or of treatment, or whatever else was appropriate, in addition to such less tangible skills as sensitivity to the market, risk avoidance, commercial judgement and the arts of nurturing contacts and clients.

All this required initial investment on the part of a family. At the turn of the eighteenth century apprenticeship to one of the great merchants of Bristol or Liverpool cost a premium of £150 or more, while in London it was likely to fall in the range of £200 to £500. Even apprenticeship to a master craftsman cost between ten and fifty pounds in the capital. It is therefore unsurprising that throughout Britain urban apprentices were usually of gentry, yeoman or commercial and professional backgrounds – the last of these categories being particularly prominent. Nor was entry much more open in small towns and in areas of rural industry. The iron-mongers of the west midlands, for example, were for the most part either the sons of established ironmongers or else from local commercial and farming backgrounds. Moreover, the establishment of a child involved not only the financial costs of schooling and a premium, but also the deployment of a family's social capital. As Michael Mascuch expresses it, 'the network of social association provided by the family was itself a form of personal property' which could be invested in the young. Family networks were crucial to the determination of a youth's occupational options, and in a world in which personal recommendation was vital, the mediation of kin and 'friends' could be crucial in the placing of a youth with a good master. Adam Montgomery, a Glasgow factor based in Stockholm, was not alone in his practice of selecting his apprentices from among the children of his kinfolk and friends.

Such circumstances were equally evident at the point of establishing an independent business. In those trades in which guild or company membership remained important, it was increasingly acquired either by patrimony, or by redemption (that is, purchase). Starting up a business usually required an initial capital of at least a hundred pounds, while in

the most prestigious trades it could be much more, and it was singularly
unlikely that any aspiring youth could save such a sum from a journeyman's wages. On the contrary, it was usually raised from parents or
kin in the forms of inheritance, gift or loan, or from the charitable
loan funds maintained by some companies (which required both membership and recommendation), or in the form of credit extended by
an established network of connections. William Stout of Lancaster,
for example, was a yeoman's son who was able to set up his shop with
£141 acquired by inheritance and small loans from his siblings, goods to
a similar value advanced on credit by London suppliers to whom he
was personally recommended, and the goodwill of his former master. A
good marriage could also help, for, as Professor Hunt observes, marriage
among the middle sort 'cannot be understood without some reference
to the capital needs of business'. But a good match itself depended
upon both connections and prospects. The portion of the bride was
expected to be equalled by the fortune of the groom, and to this
extent it usually consolidated rather than established a new household's
capital. Many young businessmen thought it prudent to delay marriage
until they were reasonably well established, like Thomas Gent of York,
who confessed, 'it was my fortune to dread wedlock, fearing so great an
expense as that state of life requires'. In sum, as Dr Earle has demonstrated in his analysis of London business careers, there was a clear relationship between the size of the premium required to enter a particular
commercial occupation, the start-up costs required to establish an independent business, and the average fortunes accumulated by those involved
at the time of their deaths. As he notes, 'in most cases, those who ended
up rich started off rich, or at least pretty well-off'. Well-off, one might
add, in all three senses, for in the absence of any one of the three essential forms of capital, the potential of the others could not easily be
realised.

Nurturing all three forms of capital remained essential in the development of business and professional careers. The great advantage of
commercial capital, as compared with landed property, was its liquidity
and flexibility. Merchants, dealers and manufacturers could inject capital
into the economy, create markets, finance industrial undertakings, float
new ventures and provide employment. Their enterprise was essential to
both the extension and the intensification of productive activity, and they
could anticipate relatively good returns on their investment – usually
between 6 and 12 per cent in overseas trade (though sometimes more),
and around 15 per cent in the domestic trades. Commercial capital,
however, lacked the security and permanence of land. It was deployed in
an increasingly competitive environment. If business activity in the early

eighteenth century was less inhibited by the corporatism and frater-
nalism of companies and guilds than had formerly been the case, it was
also correspondingly riskier. Accumulation of capital could be painfully
slow in the early stages of a business career, especially when household
expenses could swallow up a very substantial proportion of the income
generated, and reserves were usually limited.

In addition, ready money was perennially in short supply and most
business inevitably involved the extension of medium- to long-term
credit. Manufacturers obtained their raw materials on credit, often paid
their workers in arrears, and extended credit to their customers, settling
their own obligations as and when payments came in. In long-distance
trade, transfers and payments could be spread over years. Shopkeepers
and tradesmen became involved in complex webs of debt and credit
which ramified throughout and beyond local economies. James Green, a
Braintree grocer, was heavily in debt to a London wholesaler in 1728, and
was himself owed money from 327 customers in the Braintree area,
ranging from servants to local notables. Payments were irregular because
most people's incomes were irregular and this could leave a tradesman
dangerously exposed if obligations were not met at periodic 'reckonings'.
The Lancashire mercer Roger Lowe, for example, had a total inventory
valued at only sixty pounds at the time of his early death, including only
twenty-nine pounds' worth of shop goods. Yet he was turning over some
£200 worth a year of goods obtained on credit from suppliers in Warrington, Wigan and Liverpool. Hence the practice, when money was
short, of going round 'dunning' debtors for payment, or if necessary
bringing to bear the threat of litigation in local courts to accelerate
payment. But neither expedient was necessarily effective. William Stout
of Lancaster was forced to write off 'desperate' debts totalling £220 from
248 customers in the years 1688–97 – the equivalent of two years' profits in a decade of trading. And when payment was not forthcoming,
tradesmen might have to borrow in order to sustain their own credit. In
1746 a principal role of London pawnbrokers was said to be that of supplying 'the middling sort of tradesmen' with money to pay wages, household expenses and suppliers, 'by reason of the great credit they are
obliged to give their customers'. At a higher level of the trading world
the gold and silver plate proudly displayed by merchants of substance
was also a form of reserve, which needed periodically to be turned into
cash.

In such a situation, as Peter Earle explains, 'the central problem of the
businessman's life was to keep this complex of payments and receipts in
some sort of balance and to ensure that over time more money came in
than went out, so that he and his family had enough to live on and there

were regular additions to his capital'. That was far from easy, given the complexities of their dealings, the relatively primitive nature of account keeping, and the many contingencies affecting their ability to meet their obligations. As a result, the relative affluence of the middle sort was tinged with insecurity. Business fortunes were, in Dr Grassby's phrase, 'congenitally fragile'. The letters, diaries and autobiographies of tradesmen are seasoned with cautionary tales of business failure among their neighbours and associates and the risk was never far from their minds. 'Troubled in my thoughts by reason of the debts I did owe and for fear I should miscarry,' confessed Roger Lowe to his diary. And the burden of anxiety was the worse because the lack of a legal distinction between business and personal liability meant that failure shattered individuals and families rather than institutions. In 1707 Defoe distinguished the 'poverty of inheritance' suffered by 'people born to labour' from 'the poverty of disaster', which he regarded as falling 'chiefly on the middling sorts of people who have been tradingmen, but by misfortune, or mismanagement, or both, fall from flourishing into debt, bankruptcy, jails, distress and all sorts of misery'.

Given this context, the valued independence of the middle sort could be more apparent than real. It rested, somewhat precariously, upon a variety of what Dr D'Cruze terms 'hidden dependencies' within their spheres of association. And if some of these relationships placed them at risk, others could be drawn upon for support. For one of the most vital of assets in the making and sustaining of a business career was a network of contacts whose assistance could be drawn upon with some confidence – in the raising of capital, in the secure transfer of payments, as intermediaries in the brokering of deals, or as providers of commercial intelligence and advice, 'motioning' one another towards opportunities. For many businessmen, the most trusted of such individuals were kinsmen, among whom the bonds of family obligation and solidarity could be brought to bear to reinforce commercial relationships. Accordingly, the business world was to a high degree meshed together by ties of blood or marriage. As Professor Devine observes of Scottish merchants, 'nepotism had a basic commercial rationale', and some trades were virtually dominated by extended family networks. In the iron industry, for example, the Fells of Hallamshire were linked to the Fells of Cumbria and intermarried with the Milners who operated in the west midlands, Wales and Cumbria, while the Lloyds of Montgomeryshire and Flint also had marital links with the ironmasters of the west midlands. They were all Quakers. At a humbler level, the boatmen of Bridgnorth, Shropshire, included so many masters from the same families, sometimes with identical names, that they needed to be distinguished by nickname. Thus the Head family included Richard 'Silver' Head and Richard 'Arseward' Head, as well as Edward 'Lemon' Head and John 'Wackey' Head.

As the example of the Quaker ironmasters already indicates, shared religious affiliation could be another bond of trust and obligation, especially among the members of religious minorities. Both Quaker and Jewish merchants dealt extensively with co-religionists in the Atlantic trades and in other spheres of enterprise. Long-standing partnerships could be similarly binding, as with the Sitwells of Sheffield, who formed partnerships with members of the Parkin family over two generations. And more broadly it was in the economic as well as the social interest of any tradesman to maintain good relationships with his peers within the local community, nurturing them in the vigorous associational world of guild drinkings and dinners, clubs, friendly societies and masonic lodges, or service in parish and municipal office. Most of the capital invested in the West Riding woollen industry came from loans raised locally among people well known to one another. Most transactions were sealed with the personal commensality of 'clubbing' together to buy a drink.

The texture of this business milieu can be appreciated in the chequered career of the apothecary Simon Mason. The son of a Huntingdonshire lawyer, he was sent at the age of ten to live with his uncle, a Hertfordshire physician. After a few years, his uncle asked him whether he would 'go to the University of Cambridge and be bred a Physician, or go to London and be bred an Apothecary'. He chose the latter and was apprenticed to a London apothecary known to his uncle. On completion of his training, his mistress attempted to match him to the daughter and heiress of a neighbouring haberdasher, but his affections became engaged elsewhere when he met another young woman through a family connection. He married and set up shop with the assistance of his former master, who recommended potential clients, but the business failed when his father-in-law was forced to renege on the payment of his daughter's expected portion. At this point Simon's father saved him by arranging for him to become a journeyman to a Cambridge apothecary. He subsequently returned to London to establish a public house in partnership with his brother-in-law, while lodging with his sister. But he was unhappy with this situation, and in 1734 secured a position as an apothecary hired to care for the poor of two London parishes. This brought him to the attention of a leading parishioner who directed him to an apothecary in need of a journeyman. From that position he advanced to become a partner, and eventually inherited the business, while continuing his parish work, which served as a further source of connections and business within the urban community.

ii. *Right living and domestic consumption*

Simon Mason's early career was both shaped and sustained in adversity by a variety of overlapping social networks, and such networks were vital to the coherence of a competitive commercial society locally, regionally, nationally and internationally. At the heart of each of these, however, was an individual household, and in an environment fraught with risk the most immediate strategy of security was the maintenance of a well-ordered household, one exhibiting 'good rule', 'family order' or 'right living'. That, in effect, meant the proper performance of their roles by all members of the household in order to sustain it as an economic unit. But the obligation to do so fell most heavily upon the master and mistress.

For both sexes the ideal, as propounded in the popular advice litera-ture directed at householders of the middle rank, involved conformity to an exceedingly demanding conception of domestic virtue. Men, as the principal providers, were enjoined to be diligent, regular in their habits, conscious of the need to 'redeem the time', sober, thrifty, prudent and responsible. Such counsels of perfection can hardly be expected to have been fully realised in practice. Nor were they, especially with regard to sobriety – Roger Lowe was not the only tradesman who 'could not trade if att some time I did not spend 2d.' in ale. Yet there is a good deal of evidence in the diaries and autobiographies of men of the middle sort that they had a strongly internalised sense of their responsibility for pur-suing a long-term strategy of family sustenance. 'A man is bound to provide for his family, and lay upp for them,' wrote Ralph Josselin, 'this scripture alloweth, commandeth, requireth.' And he did his best to do so, making vigorous efforts to expand his income while his family grew, devoting a third of his entire life's earnings to the maintenance, educa-tion and eventual setting up of his children, and exhibiting considerable satisfaction when he had settled one of them in life. Edmund Bohun recalled that at the most critical stage of the family cycle 'there went so much money to my children, that I became very melancholy, and feared I should be ruined by it'. He insisted that his primary motivation in seeking advancement was the 'necessity to support my family'. Failure to do so entailed a powerful sense of personal inadequacy, and was also likely to be regarded by others as evidence of moral and prudential shortcomings.

The role of the mistress of the household both complemented and overlapped with that of her husband, and her ideal virtues were those attributed by the Sussex shopkeeper Thomas Turner to his wife Peggy: 'Conduct, Prudence and good Oeconomy'. Most tradesmen's wives were expected to be familiar with and to assist in the conduct of their husbands' business – like Peggy Turner, described by Thomas as 'very busy today in putting up the goods for the Audit' – and to be capable of continuing it, if necessary, in widowhood. Some ran independent businesses of their own, especially in the provisioning and clothing trades, to diversify the family's sources of income. Edinburgh's trades-people included numerous female shopkeepers and lodging-house keepers, as well as 'rouping women' (dealers in second-hand furniture) and 'pudding wives'. In London, Simon Mason's wife took in needle-work. Mrs Sharrett of Ludlow baked 'bisketts, sugar cakes, Naples and makcroones . . . for sale'. Alice Beilby of Selby and her daughter Rebecca were 'assistant one to the other in managing the trade of pipe-making'. Around 1700, some 6 per cent of the members of Edinburgh's Merchant Guild were widows, and, whether as widows or in their own right, women were actively running 10 per cent of the London businesses insured by the Sun Fire Office in the 1720s. Ann Morrell of Oxford com-bined both roles, continuing her first husband's ironmongery business after his death, diversifying into the vintner's trade, taking her second husband into that business and acquiring the Crown Inn with him, and then continuing to manage it alone after his death. In addition, all women, whether active in the generating of family income or not, were expected to take a primary role in the thrifty management of the house-hold's resources. The *Athenian Mercury* described the ideal wife as 'One whose Prudence can secure you from an Inspection into her Family Accounts and divert the Curse of trifling into Poverty'. Thomas Turner knew it well. 'How do I severely know the want of her', he wrote after Peggy's death, 'in the careful and regular management of my family affairs.'

The avoidance of 'trifling into Poverty' by 'careful and regular man-agement' meant above all the control of consumption. As Gregory King's 'Scheme' makes clear, it was one of the defining features of households of the middle rank that they had a margin of income comfortably above that required to supply the basic necessities of life. They were capable of a higher level of per-capita consumption, and contemporaries expected them to possess a certain standard of material comfort. They enjoyed superior housing: in the Hearth Tax assessments of the 1660s and 1670s they usually inhabited houses with three or more hearths. They could afford fuel and candles to warm and light their homes. They ate better, dressed better and slept more comfortably. They could meet the initial expenditure required to equip their households adequately, and they were in a position, if they so chose, to add subsequently to their stock of domestic goods.

The evidence is that in the late seventeenth and early eighteenth centuries they did so choose, increasingly often. Studies of domestic inventories show that by the third quarter of the seventeenth century the households of the middle sort were already well equipped with basic domestic furnishings: tables and chairs, beds and bedding, pewter, cooking equipment and so forth. In the succeeding fifty years, however, their world of goods underwent considerable elaboration. Traditional items of furnishing were possessed in larger quantities and in more varied forms. Goods which had previously appeared in the inventories of only a small number of high-status households – like looking glasses, earthenware, books, pictures, window curtains and table linen – became more common. And certain new goods began to appear with increasing frequency, notably clocks, china, more elaborate kitchen equipment, utensils for the preparation and consumption of hot drinks like coffee and tea, and table settings of knives and forks.

Such trends are of no small importance to our understanding of economic change in the period. They confirm the existence of a growing market for a wide variety of manufactured goods, some of them imported, but most domestically produced. Moreover, they reveal something of the sociology and geography of participation in that developing market. Sociologically it was very much a phenomenon of the gentry and of the trading and professional classes. Yeomen farmers lagged behind in the acquisition of new types of domestic goods, and husbandmen and labouring families were scarcely involved at all. Geographically, London led the way in evidencing the new consumption trends, as might be expected, though it was closely followed by other urban centres and by some of the more commercialised rural areas – Kent, for example, and those parts of north-eastern England closely linked to the metropolis by the coal trade. Hot drink utensils were appearing in Kentish inventories by 1685, but are not traceable in Staffordshire until 1725. China, which was still entirely imported, was possessed by some Durham households in the 1680s, but appears in rural Cambridgeshire inventories only in the 1720s. Comparison with Scotland is difficult, given the relative paucity of surviving inventories. Such evidence as exists suggests a comparable expansion of domestic comfort and amenity among the gentry and high-status urban households, though most Scottish families continued to live much more simply than their English counterparts.

That gentry households were quick to take advantage of opportunities to enhance their already generous living standards by the acquisition of newly available goods is scarcely surprising. The consumption of luxury goods had always been one of the means by which they expressed their social superiority. The implications of the evidence of changing patterns of consumption for the behaviour and aspirations of the middle ranks, however, appear more problematic. It was not simply a matter of their enjoying greater access to a wider variety of desirable domestic goods. A propensity to indulge in greater consumer spending cannot simply be assumed, especially among people whose values placed such emphasis upon prudence and thrift in the management of the domestic economy. Indeed, some who could certainly have afforded to participate in the new world of goods emerging at the turn of the eighteenth century appear to have been relatively resistant to its attractions – notably yeoman farmers. For this reason, a good deal of attention has been devoted to explaining the underlying motivation of changing patterns of consumption among the middle sort.

Central to any such explanation is the notion that goods have both practical and expressive functions. Their possession makes possible the enjoyment of a particular degree of material comfort or convenience. At the same time, however, it also involves the cultivation of a certain sense of selfhood. To this extent, consumption is a form of self-fashioning, a way of assuring oneself that one possesses certain attributes and tastes. But it is not simply self-directed, for the adoption of a particular pattern of material life also inevitably imparts messages to a larger social audience. Such points were not lost on observers of changing patterns of material culture in early-eighteenth-century Britain, and in explaining that phenomenon they usually relied upon the notion of imitation inspired by social emulation. 'We all look above ourselves,' observed Bernard Mandeville, 'and fast as we can, strive to imitate those that some way or other are superior to us.' 'The poor will be like the rich and the rich like the great,' agreed Defoe, '. . . and so the world runs onto a kind of distraction at this time.' The new consumption habits of the middle sort, in short, involved the 'aping' of the gentry, the staking of claims for status in a more complex and fluid social environment.

There was undoubtedly some truth in that. Early newspaper advertisements placed by provincial shopkeepers alluded none too subtly to the social cachet attaching to the goods they had for sale. But the matter was also much more complex. In the first place, studies of inventories of goods make it clear that, in terms of the pace of adoption of new consumption habits, people of the middle sort were not simply following a lead set by the gentry. On the contrary, members of the professions and of the wealthier dealing trades appear to have equalled or even preceded the gentry in their possession of many of the new items of consumption, while less wealthy tradesmen and craftsmen were not far behind. To a very large extent the commercial and professional classes were among the pacemakers of change. Secondly, it would be a considerable exaggeration to maintain that these people were attempting to emulate the expansive lifestyles of fashionable society. Even the wealthiest of them usually aspired, in Dr Grassby's words, to unaffected lifestyles of 'quiet civility rather than aristocratic splendour', while those of lesser means, like the ironmongers of the west midlands described by Dr Rowlands, were engaged in the creation of 'homes of dignity though not pretension'. The diffusion of new consumption habits certainly spread by example and imitation, but such imitation did not necessarily imply the mimicking of social superiors. Rather, it involved the spread of influence through the networks of association of the middle sort themselves, as when Elizabeth Brockbank, the wife of a Lancashire parson, eagerly sought advice from her Newcastle cousin, Ann Turnley, concerning 'the best way of making coffee'.

In short, the middle sort were themselves innovators; they helped to initiate new standards of domestic consumption. Their engagement in new consumption habits was conducted with a restraint which was as much voluntary as imposed by the limitations of their means. And inasmuch as their behaviour was imitative, it was usually imitative of people like themselves. All this implies that the changing material culture of so many middle-rank households at the turn of the eighteenth century was part of a process of middle-rank self-definition. That process involved the cultivation of both a self-identity and a public identity as persons of solid worth, prosperity, refinement, restraint, responsibility and respectability. The former enhanced their self-esteem. The latter brought public recognition. It distanced them from their social inferiors and secured inclusion within the social milieu of a disparate group of people who found common ground not only in commercial interaction, but also in a particular style of domestic life and the sociability which accompanied it. If the control of domestic consumption was vital to the accumulation of economic capital among the middle sort, it was also the case that their changing patterns of expenditure had a part to play in the accumulation of the social capital of group membership and the cultural capital of public reputation.

iii. *Credit and reputation*

Reputation mattered a great deal. For despite the emergence of a more competitive business environment and widespread acceptance of the legitimacy of the pursuit of personal gain, the commercial culture of the time did not endorse an ethic of ruthless competitive individualism. On the contrary, what Thomas Turner contemptuously referred to in his diary as the 'cankerworm of self interest', or 'sordid self interest', was generally condemned. Those who were held to exhibit it in its most naked form – the scrabbling 'stockjobbers' of the emergent London stock market – aroused deep hostility and repeated attempts at legislative restriction. 'A generous person', Samuel Richardson advised the young tradesman, 'must needs be better pleased, the more capable he is of advancing himself without hurting others.' To an extent the guilds still fostered such attitudes, as was the case in the Edinburgh incorporations, though Professor Houston detects a growing tension between those members who wished to adhere to traditional restrictive practices and those who found them irksome. But, even where commercial society was increasingly a conglomerate of competing households, it was also, as Dr Muldrew writes, one of 'competing but interdependent households which had to trust one another.' The market was an arena fraught with risk, but its functioning depended upon the extension of credit and, with that, exchanges of trust. And for this reason, considerable cultural emphasis was placed upon the virtues and values essential for the maintenance of a creditworthy society.

Accordingly, the business ideal of the time was not that of the buccaneering entrepreneur, but that of the person of 'credit' and 'reputation'. It was an amalgam of private and public virtues which coalesced in a model of both personal and commercial integrity. It involved all those qualities already alluded to as characteristic of the householder of merit: diligence, discipline, regularity, weight – the whole cultural complex symbolised in the clocks that increasingly graced the halls and parlours of the middle sort. And it involved also social responsibility, adherence to corporate norms of behaviour, reliability in the honouring of obligations, financial probity and honest dealing.

All this was of immediate practical consequence. For the establishment and maintenance of 'credit', in the sense of reputation, was essential to the establishment and maintenance of financial credit. Failure to do either had harsh material consequences. 'He that breaks through his honesty', warned Defoe, 'violates his credit.' Loss of reputation entailed loss of the trust which was fundamental to the capacity to do business effectively. And it was usually swiftly communicated, among local networks of businessmen, in the gossip of the Exchange, and along the chains of connection linking together a commercial world in which mercantile correspondence was spiced with personal observations and served as a vehicle for the exchange of informal character references.

The ubiquitous insistence upon the importance of personal credit and reputation reflected the demands of a changing economic environment;

one in which the complexities of individual dealings had outgrown the capacity of traditional institutions of commercial regulation to control them, and in which the risk of malpractice was insufficiently provided for by the safeguards of commercial law. To this extent the elaboration of the model of individual commercial probity was a further dimension of the process of bourgeois self-definition. To be sure, there was little about its constituent elements that was truly new. The ideal of the upright businessman drew upon values long expressed in the ordinances of the guilds – fair dealing, good fame and recognition of collective responsibility. It owed at least something to the notion of gentlemanly honour. It endorsed behavioural traits – the avoidance of idleness, conscionable behaviour and sobriety – which were familiar enough prescriptions of traditional religious morality. And for many it was underpinned by religious sanctions. Misfortune could be interpreted as God's correction for personal failings and success as a providential blessing. Joan Dent, the widow of a Quaker weaver who remained in trade and built up a formidable fortune, described herself to her executors in 1715 as 'one that has taken pains to live, and have through the blessing of God, with honesty and industrious care, improved my little in the world to a pretty good degree'. 'It is the Lord that creates true industry in his people,' she added, 'and that blesseth their endeavours.'

Joan Dent construed her career as no less contributing to the honour of God than a medieval guildsman or merchant would have done, though she was perhaps readier than they might have been to emphasise her own deservingness, and more comfortable about the legitimacy of her accumulative efforts. To this extent, her testament might be held to illustrate the 'puritan' or 'protestant' ethic which allegedly legitimated material gain as the evidence of divine approval. But in truth her attitudes were Protestant in idiom rather than in essence. If the moral earnestness of the godly life could certainly contribute to business success, and if the anxieties and insecurities of a commercial career might render people more receptive to a religious doctrine of self-discipline and spiritual watchfulness, the connection between the two was conjunctural and contingent rather than causal. Both the commercial world of the late seventeenth and early eighteenth centuries and the providential theology which enabled some of its members to understand their personal experience of its challenges and opportunities were of independent origin. The godly were never more than a prominent minority among those engaged in industry and commerce. And the commercial ethics of the time were not peculiar to Dissenters, or to Protestants, or for that matter to Christians. They were the broadly shared outcome of a larger process of cultural adaptation whereby elements of varied origin were appropriated, modified and fused under the pressure of the demands of a changing economic environment. By 1700 that process of selection, adaptation and mutation had provided the members of commercial society with a set of values which they could claim, with some justice, as being peculiarly their own. It enabled them to function more effectively and securely in a complex and competitive economic milieu. More, it helped to define, and to confirm the integrity of, their place in the world.

iv. *Gentlemen–tradesmen*

They were increasingly confident of that place. If all went well, the more successful members of the middle ranks were able to accumulate capital in the course of a life and to diversify their economic activities and investments – acquiring leases of urban property, lending to other businessmen within their networks of connection, financing mortgages, investing in industrial projects, in shipping or in the public funds. They might invest in land too, following the old path from the acquisition of trading wealth to the purchase of a country estate and entry, or re-entry, into the landed gentry.

Some certainly did so, like Sir Stephen Fox, a London merchant who laid out £100,000 establishing an estate in Wiltshire between 1672 and 1686. But by the early eighteenth century only a minority of even the greatest plutocrats took that course. This was partly because the costs of entry into the true landed elite were unacceptably high. Landed estates were conventionally valued at twenty to twenty-five times their annual rental, which meant, for example, that £4,000 would need to be paid for an estate that would yield even a modest gentry income of £200 a year. Few had that kind of capital sum at their disposal, and, of those who did, the return on land was insufficiently attractive to justify its withdrawal from business. A landed estate, of course, brought social and political advantages, and these remained sufficiently attractive to some – notably, it appears, to leading lawyers and state servants, who were prominent among the purchasers of estates in Northamptonshire, Hertfordshire and Northumberland in the early eighteenth century. But most businessmen who chose to invest in landed property preferred at most to acquire a small country house and park within easy reach of their urban bases and to remain fully engaged in trade and industry. In 1683 John Evelyn found the Epping area of Essex full of 'over grown and suddenly monied men' (among them Sir Josiah Child) and the same was true of those parts of Kent, Surrey and Hertfordshire adjacent to the metropolis, and of the countryside around Birmingham, Leeds, Glasgow,

Edinburgh and other major cities. The most successful trading and professional families certainly intermarried with the landed gentry, but they
had a limited desire to join them. The leaders of trade and finance – the
'monied interest' – now constituted an influential segment of Britain's
increasingly composite ruling class, and they appear to have preferred to
retain their own distinctive place within it.

If they were little attracted to the prospect of becoming landowners
on a significant scale, however, they were more attracted to at least some
elements of gentility as a cultural ideal. And that attraction extended to
many more among the middle sort. A householder with an income from
profits and fees of even one or two hundred pounds could never have
aspired to ownership of a small estate, but such people could afford, as
we have seen, to live in comfort and some style. As the builders, or
tenants, of elegant, brick-built, classical houses, laid out in uniform
streets and squares, they were prominent in the remodelling of urban
landscapes in the late seventeenth and early eighteenth centuries. They
were also promoters of such civic improvements as the erection of new
public buildings (including exchanges), paving, lighting and the laying
out of promenades and gardens. They subscribed to philanthropic projects like the founding of infirmaries. They were active participants in the
development of a commercialised polite culture, ranging from the sociability of the coffee house (which was also, of course, an important place
of business) to the assemblies, public performances and race meetings of
the urban season. As the founders and readers of newspapers and as
patrons of bookshops, lending or subscription libraries and public lectures, they had a central role in the development of a 'public sphere' of
critical discussion and a culture of sensibility and self-improvement.
Within the privacy of their homes, they cultivated also a more refined
domesticity. Among professional people, merchants and the wealthier
tradesmen and manufacturers, the home and the place of business were
increasingly likely to be physically separated. Their wives were less likely
to be actively engaged in the family business, and more preoccupied with
a role in household management which was expanding to embrace
status-confirming forms of consumption and genteel entertainment – not
least more elaborate cooking and the taking of tea – a shift of role in
which many, if not most, were willing participants.

Much of this involved, for the more substantial members of the middle
ranks, the enjoyment of a material culture which they shared with
members of the gentry and frequent interaction with members of landed
society not only in a business capacity but also through participation in
spheres of sociability open to all those who could afford them. But if some
of the middle sort aspired to a genteel style of life, it was one which

expressed a very distinctive conception of gentility. Those who espoused it have been described as the 'pseudo gentry', a term which has its utility, but which is also much too disparaging both in its attribution of pretence and in its implication of uncritical social emulation. A better term is that coined by Defoe, who detected a hybrid social category in the 'Gentleman–tradesman' – an 'amphibious creature', in Moll Flanders' opinion; a 'land–water thing'. Many business people and professionals desired to be regarded as gentlemen, and increasingly they were so regarded, for as Guy Miège observed, while 'Gentlemen . . . are those properly who, being descended of a good family, bear a coat of arms', 'the title of Gentleman is commonly given in England to all that distinguish themselves from the common sort of people by a genteel dress and carriage, good education, learning, or an independent station'. Many of the middle sort had some or all of those qualities. And as Dr French points out, 'in appropriating the concept of gentility to themselves, these people were turning both it and themselves into something different'. The material culture of polite society was at least as much their creation as that of the gentlemen they supplied. So was the culture of what Peter Borsay calls the 'Urban Renaissance' of the late seventeenth and early eighteenth centuries. And so indeed was a concept of gentility which had become detached from the possession of broad acres. Gentlemen–tradesmen and their wives moulded the concept of gentility to suit their own needs and produced in the process a notion of its attributes which was appropriate to people of business. Their ideal of gentility was civic, respectable and virtuous, incorporating work, thrift, prudence and temperance and exhibited not so much in heraldry as in good character. If they usually deferred to the social and political authority of the landed gentry, they were also advancing a claim to parity in exhibiting the attributes of a redefined gentility, the outcome of what Dr Grassby terms 'a bilateral process of acculturation within propertied society'.

For most of the middle ranks, however, their place in the world was not that of the 'Gentleman–tradesman' but that of the independent householder. These were people like Robinson Crusoe's fictional father, to whom Defoe attributed in 1719 the view that the 'Middle State' was 'the best state in the world', or the very real Essex woolcomber Joseph Bufton of Coggeshall. Bufton kept notes on the blank pages of his almanacs of the sermons he had heard and the books he had read. In 1699 he copied out these lines:

> Thrice Happy's he who in a Middle State,
> Feels neither want nor studys to be great,

He eats and drinks and lives at home at ease,
Whilst warlike monarchs cross the raging seas.

Bufton must have known full well that many people of his sort periodically crossed raging seas of their own, and felt the threat and sometimes
the actuality of want. But, perhaps for that very reason, he endorsed an
ideal of security. The middle-rank culture and identity which he
embraced was moulded by the imperative of regularly achieving the
modest surpluses which could secure a family in the present and provide
for its members' futures. Most people of the middle sort lived their lives
within what Michael Mascuch terms such 'attenuated horizons of expectation'. They were linked to a larger commercial world, but embedded
in their own local communities. They were 'principal inhabitants' and
'sufficient householders' rather than members of polite society. They
were less heroic entrepreneurs than people who cautiously turned over
their limited capital and strove to sustain their credit. They were
concerned less with social advancement than with maintaining their
position and that of their children within the broad middling ranks into
which they had usually been born. If they succeeded in that, they could
avoid exposure to what Crusoe's father called 'the Miseries and Hard-
ships, the Labour and Sufferings of the Mechanick part of Mankind'.
That was reason enough to accumulate what they could, and by their
efforts to do so they also increased the wealth of the kingdom.

CHAPTER FOURTEEN

Dependence and independence: labouring people

'The Mechanick part of Mankind' were those described by Guy Miège as 'such as get their livelihood either in a mechanick or servile way'. They were conventionally identified as 'the Hands and Feet of the Body Politick'. But if their labour was essential, and recognised as such, it brought no honour. Nor was it well rewarded. Among the most striking features of Gregory King's 'Scheme' was the yawning gap between the estimated annual family income of the least well-off of the middle sort – forty pounds – and that of the best paid of his four categories of labouring people: twenty pounds. He assumed that most labouring families earned even less, and, despite their significantly lower levels of expenditure on 'food, housing, clothes and all other necessaries', he found most such families to be marginally insolvent. The average family of 'labouring people and outservants', for example, earned seven shillings a year less than was required to maintain its members at the level of consumption considered appropriate to people of their station. Hence the paradox that the three-fifths of English families whose productive labour sustained the national economy were considered to be 'decreasing the wealth of the kingdom'.

Defoe was more optimistic and more conscious of the differentials that existed among the wage-earning population. He distinguished four groups: 'the Working Trades, who labour hard but feel no want'; 'Country People . . . who fare indifferently'; 'The Poor that fare hard'; and finally 'The Miserable, that really pinch and suffer want'. In fact such distinctions could be still more elaborated. For the blunt terms in which contemporaries tended to homogenise the 'meaner sort' or 'poorer sort' of people concealed a considerable variety of market situations and life chances. The uneven development of a capitalist agriculture and the variegated nature of capitalistically structured industries had produced not a simplification but rather a diversification of economic classes. And what has been termed the 'plebeian culture' of the late seventeenth and early eighteenth centuries was far from monolithic. It encompassed the diversity engendered by the many different ways in which particular groups of people experienced and responded to the processes of economic development. Central to that diversity were differences in the relative dependence or independence of labouring people in two vital senses. First, their different capacities to maintain themselves without reliance upon public relief. Secondly, their ability to enjoy some measure of self-direction in the pursuit of their livelihoods. Both were vital to the experience and to the identities of those who lived by their labour.

i. *Lives of labour*

The capacity of labouring families to subsist independently depended upon the work available in particular local and regional labour markets, the level and purchasing-power of their wages, and the degree to which their domestic economies relied upon such earnings – all matters which could vary considerably with occupation, locality, age, sex and the peculiarities of individual family circumstances.

Most labour markets remained highly localised. Structures of employment varied locally according to agricultural specialisation, the presence or absence of rural industry and the particular combinations of commercial and manufacturing activity which distinguished the major towns. Within such local and regional economies, employment opportunities were contained by the relatively short distances over which the personal contacts central to most hirings could be established and maintained. Servants in husbandry engaged at the hiring fair at Spalding in Lincolnshire, for example, travelled on average only six to eight miles between masters. Workers in the putting-out industries were recruited locally by the capitalist masters who organised production. Urban labour markets might draw upon more extensive rural hinterlands, but even these were relatively contained. A survey of migration to the towns of six English regions reveals that the median distance travelled was only fifteen miles, and that those employed in relatively low-status occupations were least likely to have moved far. And within the larger cities recruitment was further localised by the 'houses of call' associated with specific trades: the taverns and alehouses which served as labour exchanges for the craftsmen, seamen, building workers and so on of particular districts. Geographically, then, we must think in terms not of a single labour market but of a series of overlapping regional, sub-regional and local labour markets. But, even at the most localised level, labour markets were far from unified. On the contrary, they were heavily segmented, the employment opportunities and expectations of those who sought work being markedly differentiated by their levels of skill, by gender and by age.

Defoe distinguished three levels of skill among wage-earning men. The highest level was that of 'mechanics or craftsmen' who were 'guides or masters in such works or employments': those artisans who had served either an indentured apprenticeship in a particular trade, or at least a comparable period of training. Some were semi-independent small masters who worked principally for capitalist entrepreneurs, like the cutlers of Sheffield or the smiths of Birmingham. Most were skilled employees, like the journeymen tailors or hatters of London. But, whichever was the case, they possessed the 'property of skill': the specialist knowledge and manual dexterity which differentiated them from the unskilled and secured them the dignity of a craftsman's identity. Below them were what he termed 'workmen or handicrafts' who laboured hard but 'have yet some art mingled with their industry': those semi-skilled workers in town or country who lacked formally recognised training, but had acquired sufficient expertise in one or more of the processes of agriculture or manufacturing to secure them fairly regular employment. Below them again were 'all the drudges and labourers in the several productions of nature or of art': those willing to perform any task requiring their muscle power and a modicum of experience, but who could claim neither the mastery of a specialised trade nor any occupational identity more precise than that of 'working men or labourers'. These were the 'unskilled' in the sense that the skills which they possessed were so widespread that they commanded no particular premium.

If the labour market for men was segmented by differentials of skill, the market for female labour was set apart by entrenched assumptions regarding the forms of work deemed appropriate for women. Women were excluded from most of the skilled trades – the exceptions being such distinctively female trades as millinery or 'mantua-making' – and were therefore almost by definition confined to the spheres of semi-skilled or unskilled work. Even there, employment opportunities were largely restricted to what were conventionally regarded as female roles. Most single women were employed either as domestic servants or as servants in husbandry engaged in dairying rather than in heavy field work. Most married women, in contrast, were primarily dependent on their husbands' earnings, supplementing their family incomes by wage work which was for the most part casual, intermittent and badly paid: seasonal agricultural tasks; sewing, cleaning, washing and nursing; hawking goods in the streets. Widows made shift to live as best they could in much the same ways. In the industrial districts both might find more regular employment, though there too their role was usually restricted to 'female' tasks: carding wool or spinning yarn, knitting, plaiting straw, lace-making or the like. The female nail-makers of the west midlands were unusual in their engagement in a task which was not gender-specific, though it was the least skilled of the metal trades.

Differentials of skill and gender were further compounded by those of age and life-cycle stage. Labour markets continued to be entered young – albeit gradually – by both sexes. William Hutton, son of a Derby wool-comber, recalled how in 1729, when he was six, his parents held 'consultations . . . about fixing me in some employment for the benefit of the family'. They considered 'winding quills for the weaver' and 'stripping tobacco for the grocer' for fourpence a week, but 'it was at last concluded that I was too young for any employment'. He started work a year later at a silk manufactory. Most children of labouring families were engaged in some kind of work from about the age of seven, and at this stage their range of employment was influenced more by their capacity than by gender. Thomas Tryon, son of an Oxfordshire tiler and plasterer, began carding and spinning wool at around seven, and recalled that 'at Eight Years of Age I could spin Four Pound a day which came to Two Shillings a Week'. Others found casual agricultural work, often alongside their mothers. Full engagement in the labour market and the crystallisation of gender differentials came in the early to mid-teens when many children left home to enter agricultural or domestic service, to be apprenticed to local tradespeople, or otherwise set foot on the ladder which led by stages to full adult employment. Anthony Wood began work, 'by leave of his father', as a boy 'jagger', leading horses for a Derbyshire lead-smelting works. At fourteen he was working underground as an ore carrier and by nineteen he was cutting ore himself for a man's wages.

By the time he reached his fifties, however, Anthony Wood was working as a weaver. Whereas the major discontinuity in women's working lives was that occasioned by marriage, that for labouring men came with advancing age and declining health and strength. Seventy per cent of seamen were aged between fifteen and twenty-nine, and almost 90 per cent were under forty. By that age, unless they possessed particular skills, or had been promoted mate, they were usually obliged to seek work onshore. Coal miners suffered a similar declension in employment status as they passed their prime – the lists of 'old decayed work people' drawn up for the parish of Whickham, Co. Durham, in the mid-eighteenth century included more than a few men who can be identified as well-paid coal-face workers in the local pits a decade or two earlier. Advancing age did not bring retirement, save among those completely incapacitated and reduced to dependence on parish relief. But it brought a marked deterioration in employment opportunities. Faced with that situation, people did what work they could. Robert Couper, an Edinburgh journeyman cordiner (shoemaker) was licensed in 1745 'to mend and vend old shoes', since 'by reason of old age and other infirmity . . . he was rendered incapable to work new work'. Robert Walker of Eccleshall, Staffordshire, was a former skinner and 'an honest poor man' who in old age used his literacy to make a living by reading for hire and teaching children. Phyllis Denham was still sorting coal at a Tyneside pithead at the age of eighty.

A further enduring characteristic of labour markets was that the demand for labour was highly seasonal and irregular. This was most obviously the case in agriculture, with its slack season from November to February, and its periods of peak activity associated with lambing, haymaking, harvesting and so forth. But many other occupations were also affected by the weather. Fishing and coastal shipping had seasonal peaks and troughs. Building activity slackened in the winter – the journeymen masons, plasterers and housepainters of London were said in 1747 to be idle for four or five months of the year, and so, by implication, were those who supplied their raw materials. Excessive rainfall brought drainage problems which could interrupt mining activity for weeks on end. And then there were other forms of irregularity. London tailors were busiest during the fashionable season and hard put to stay in work outside it. The ironworkers of the famous Crowley firm depended heavily upon naval orders, which meant a pattern of periodic boom and slump. In short, most forms of production involved marked fluctuations in the demand for labour, and, given the small productive units which were characteristic of the period, employers were prone to keep on valued key workers during slack times but to lay off the rest.

Taken together, the structural features of local labour markets carried significant implications for both the earning capacity of wage-workers and the experience of labour in the period. Given the localised and segmented nature of labour markets, both the forms and levels of payment varied considerably. People might be paid by the year, by the day, by the job or by the piece. Payment might be in cash or in kind, or a mixture of both. Malcolm McGibbon, for example, was rewarded for a ditching job with the promise of half a cow when it came to slaughter, half a crown in English money, the cancellation of a debt for twenty-one shillings Scots, and a deal board 'that he got for his son's coffine'.

Given such complexities, comparison can be difficult, but generally speaking daily rates of pay were higher in the south than in the north or west, higher in the towns than in the countryside, and highest of all in London. At the turn of the eighteenth century, agricultural labourers' wages ranged from eight to twelve pence a day in England and from six to ten pence a day in Wales, and were customarily lower in the winter than in the summer. Craftsmen and industrial workers were also paid locally customary rates. That meant that in most northern towns building craftsmen were paid eighteen pence a day or less around 1700, as compared to eighteen to twenty pence a day in southern towns. There were exceptions. Craftsmen in York, Hull and Beverley equalled or surpassed the southern rates, for reasons peculiar to the labour markets of those cities. Building labourers in northern towns, however, were unlikely to earn more than ten or twelve pence a day as compared to twelve to fourteen pence in the south.

Within particular local economies, as might be expected, wages varied according to age, skill and gender. Servants in husbandry worked for their board and lodging and a small annual money wage which rose with age and levels of responsibility, female servants being paid less than men. More generally, skilled workers were generally paid 30 to 50 per cent more than the unskilled for a day's work, and women received half to two-thirds the wages paid to men. The results of such differentials can be illustrated by the peculiarly variegated and well-documented local economy of the coal-field parish of Whickham, Co. Durham. There, in the mid-eighteenth century, general agricultural labourers earned eight to ten pence a day; carpenters twelve to fourteen pence; masons sixteen to eighteen pence; and wagonwrights fourteen to twenty pence. At the colliery, horse-drivers (some of whom were boys) earned eight to twelve pence a day, and 'putters', who dragged coal underground to the pit shafts, earned twenty-two pence. The hewers who cut the coal were paid according to their output, which was usually high, making them the best paid of all. At the other end of the scale were the women who 'wailed', or sorted, the coal, or shovelled it into heaps at the pithead. They were paid four and six pence a day respectively.

Such figures tell us a great deal about the differentials which existed in the earning capacity of wage-earners, both between and within particular local economies. Yet translating them into estimates of the actual annual earnings of labouring people is exceedingly difficult, given what we know of the irregularity of employment, and the simple fact that we very rarely have precise information on the numbers of days, weeks or

months actually worked by individuals in this period. Levels of participation in the labour market appear to have been high, yet there was also
extensive underemployment. Servants engaged on annual contracts were
fully employed, and servants in husbandry may have supplied an estimated one-third to one-half of the labour needs of agriculture. Among
the adult population as a whole, however, continuity in employment was
not to be expected save among a minority of exceptionally skilled and
valued employees. Most workers were engaged for the duration of a particular job, or in the case of seamen for a 'run' or voyage, while general
labour was usually hired on a daily basis. The bulk of the labouring
population, both male and female, therefore constituted a large pool of
partially employed labour, which was drawn upon selectively as need
arose. Collectively, such people formed a penumbra of casual labour
which was likely to be at least as large as the maximum variation in seasonal demand for labour, and was in some circumstances even larger.
Work was always possible, but it could not always be obtained. For some,
periods of fairly regular employment were punctuated by lengthy bouts
of idleness. For others, days of work were scattered intermittently across
the year. As Dr Schwarz puts it, 'there were islands of steady employment, inhabited by colonies of skilled workmen . . . but, by and large,
the world was in a state of flux'.

In addition, most people lacked a stable occupational identity. This
was very much the case among adult women, as has frequently been
observed. But it was also the case for most men. Multiple occupations,
or engagement in a series of occupations successively, was a commonplace experience, indeed a necessary expedient. The listing of the householders of Eccleshall, Staffordshire, prepared in the mid-1690s and
annotated by Bishop Lloyd of Lichfield, provides many examples. 'Curly'
Wollam was a general labourer, thresher, thatcher and weaver: 'a very
honest man, laborious and Religious'. Thomas Lightwood was a cottager
and cobbler, and a 'good worker', but want of work led him to take up
chimney-sweeping, an occupation which earned him a sooty appearance
and the nickname 'The Devil'. Mark Assleby was a labourer, a broom-
gatherer and a basket-maker. He also sold cabbages, onions and pickles.
Similarly in Whickham, the general labourers of the parish flit intermittently through the records of employment – now employed in agricultural work, now working on a wagonway maintenance gang, now
shovelling coal at the riverside staithes, now helping to erect a colliery
horse-gin. As Sir James Steuart wrote of the labouring people of early-
eighteenth-century Scotland, 'had you asked them . . . how they lived,
they would have told you "By the Providence of God". The answer
was good and proper. Their industry was then so miscellaneous; the

employment they found was so precarious and uncertain, that they could not give it a name.' These were wage workers for whom the very notions of consistent employment or a reasonably predictable cash income were alien to their experience.

If this was the lot of most labouring people of the time, it becomes easy to understand the importance to them of access to a variety of supplementary resources. Some industrial districts remained characterised by dual economies in which employment in manufacturing or mining was combined with running a smallholding. Often enough the industrial 'by-employment' had gradually become the tail that wagged the dog. But the continued existence of such multiplex domestic economies provided a vital safeguard for many people. If they were in gradual decline in the worsted districts of west Yorkshire, the woollen districts of Lancashire and Somerset and the metalworking parishes of Staffordshire, they remained very much alive among Hallamshire cutlers, the wagonmen of the northern coal fields, the lead miners of Derbyshire and the yeoman clothiers of the Yorkshire woollen districts.

Similarly, agricultural labourers and village craftsmen might hold small plots of land which, if insignificant in estate surveys of tenanted land, were a very significant supplement to their livings. This was very much the case in Scotland, where most agricultural labour was provided by cottars like those of Plowlands, Fife, who in 1714 received a house, kailyard and small plot as part of their conditions of hire, or those who were paid wages by Lady Baillie at Polwarth, Berwickshire, in the 1690s, and in their turn sold her poultry, eggs, butter and wool produced on their own holdings. But it was also the case, if less systematically so, in many parts of England. In unenclosed areas, possession of a tiny holding would further provide access to common rights, which were also attached to some cottage tenancies, or in some manors permitted to all inhabitants. In the estimate of Dr Shaw-Taylor, a cow's grazing, the right to gather fuel, the means to fatten a pig, a half-acre garden and the right to glean for ears of grain in the open fields after harvest could collectively provide resources equal to the annual cash wages of a labourer. And if few possessed all these advantages, many possessed some of them. Gleaning rights alone could enable labourers' wives to gather grain of value equivalent to two months' wages.

Such advantages meant that rural labouring families might still engage in a good deal of self-provisioning, and in the production of goods for sale. It was doubtless on the commons of Eccleshall that Mark Assleby gathered his broom and his basket-making materials, and in his own garden that he grew his cabbages and onions. And there were equivalents also in the working worlds of those wholly divorced from the land.

Miners were commonly provided with housing and house-coal as part of their remuneration. Seamen might enjoy the 'privilege' of a little cargo space to carry goods which they traded on their own account. Shipbuilders could take home 'chips' of wood. Tailors kept scraps of unused materials, or 'cabbage'. Dockers could find rich pickings in the form of 'breakages'. Edinburgh journeymen were allowed 'bounty' products, supposedly for their own consumption, but usually sold. Employers might occasionally fulminate against such customary perquisites of the trade, but by and large they were tolerated, and in the urban world, as in the rural, forms of what Dr Schwarz terms 'non-monetary appropriation' were part of the package of resources which supplemented the money wage.

Then there was credit. Labouring people are underrepresented in the inventory record of debt and credit and in the small-debt litigation of municipal courts; but they are present nonetheless, sometimes lending to one another, sometimes being sued for small sales credits unpaid. And this can be only the tip of the iceberg, for credit must have been fundamental to people whose incomes were even more irregular and uncertain than those of the middle sort, but whose obligations to one another were less likely to be recorded, and whose debts to tradesmen were unlikely to provoke litigation. In some highly seasonal occupations it was certainly systematic. 'What must become of the poor keelmen?' protested the coalowner George Liddell in 1729, when it was proposed to delay the start of the Newcastle shipping season by a month:

They give over work the beginning of November and many of them had not then a shilling before hand. They live upon Credit and a little labouring work till they get their binding money at Christmas. That money goes to their Creditors and they borrow of their fitters to buy provisions . . . and so they put off until trade begins. Now if they are not to begin until about Ladyday, half of them will be starved, for as their time of working will be so much shorter trades people will not trust them.

To be deemed creditworthy must have kept many a labouring family off the parish at times of hardship, and indeed it has been suggested that the periodic forgiveness of small debts owed by the poor probably constituted a hidden supplement to the formal poor-law system. If so, however, it was one which was provided not only by sympathetic tradespeople, but also by labouring people themselves. Credit was probably the most tangible form of the complex of bonds of mutuality within the trade, the neighbourhood and the extended family which, though largely invisible to the historian, certainly constituted another of the resources which supplemented the uncertain prop of the money wage.

The economic world of labouring people in the late seventeenth and early eighteenth centuries was thus one of great heterogeneity, varying in its specifics from area to area, and within any local economy between different segments of the wage-earning population. Moreover, its structural characteristics were not in themselves new; they can be identified throughout and beyond the early modern period. What had changed in the course of the sixteenth and seventeenth centuries was the proportion of the population whose domestic economies were structured by such realities. Demographic growth and the expansion and consolidation of a capitalist agriculture had created a greatly enlarged population of landless or near-landless labourers in the countryside. Commercial and industrial development had markedly increased the proportion of the population inhabiting the larger towns and the rural industrial districts. Among urban craftsmen the proportion of lifelong journeymen had grown. In rural industry the dual economy was in gradual retreat. In all these ways, the wage-dependent population had expanded and diversified. If the process of 'proletarianisation', in the sense of the elimination of sources of family subsistence other than wages, was very far from complete in much of England and most of Scotland and Wales, it was nonetheless an increasingly prevalent reality.

In the late seventeenth and early eighteenth centuries, as we have seen, some of these trends continued. At the same time, however, they were accompanied by more positive developments in both the demand for labour and the levels and purchasing power of wages. Population had stabilised, but commercial and industrial expansion accelerated, and the result was an enhancement of the demand for labour in a variety of urban and rural economies. The supply of labour was not deficient in absolute terms. As we have seen, unskilled labour remained abundantly available in most areas. But employers were not always able to secure an adequate supply of skilled and semi-skilled labour when and where it was most required. In agriculture, increased specialisation and the intensification of husbandry regimes created localised labour shortages and competition among employers edged up agricultural wages – by 25 to 50 per cent in parts of southern and eastern England in the century after 1650. In areas of industrial expansion the demand for semi-skilled workers drew in more members of labouring households who were familiar with, or could quickly learn, simple manufacturing processes, with knock-on effects in other sectors of local labour markets. Fully skilled labour was in particularly short supply. In Halifax the opportunity to earn high wages as specialist woolcombers and drawloom weavers in the rapidly growing worsted industry led some small clothiers to abandon their previous independence. The growth of trade placed a premium on the services of seamen, with especially significant wage increases during the periods of prolonged warfare after 1688 when merchant shipping competed with the Royal Navy for experienced men. Urban expansion created demand for both skilled building craftsmen and labourers, with the result that wages rates rose by 20 to 25 per cent in London between 1650 and 1720 and even more in other towns in both the south and the north. These matters remain insufficiently explored in detail for many regional economies, but the available evidence points consistently to a growth in the demand for labour and rising levels of remuneration. And meanwhile, as we have seen, falling food prices increased the real incomes of even those workers whose money wages remained relatively stable, such as the labourers of Scottish towns.

Taken as a whole, then, the late seventeenth and early eighteenth centuries were relatively good times for labouring people in Britain, though the extent of the improvement in their living standards should not be exaggerated. Certainly they could eat better, even if their diet was somewhat monotonous. (In Scotland the staple was some thirty-seven ounces of oatmeal a day.) They were also better clothed in all likelihood. It took only two days' earnings for a Hull labourer to buy three yards of fustian in the 1690s, and the same length of linen would have cost him only a day's pay. Patterns of consumption also changed to include such items as sugar, treacle, coal, tobacco, tea, petty items of personal adornment like ribbon, lace and buttons, and a range of modest domestic goods. The inventory of the Crowley manufactory's Tyneside warehouse in 1727 provides an indication of the goods on which the relatively well-paid Crowley ironworkers might spend their surplus income. It included cloth in great quantities and variety and the thread to sew it; ready-made breeches, stockings and shoes; fire irons, pots and pans, candles, bread and tobacco. And alcohol was abundantly available everywhere.

These matters were not insignificant. But labouring people are unlikely to have participated in the more elaborate consumption trends of the period, and indeed attempts to estimate their probable incomes and domestic budgets tend to underline their severely limited capacity to do so. In the agricultural parish of Terling, Essex, in the late seventeenth century, a labourer who found work for 220 days of the year (four days in most weeks and five in some) would have earned a total of £11. A tailor working the same number of days would have earned £12 and a carpenter £16 10s. Yet payments made by the poor-law authorities of the parish suggest that keeping a family of five at the level deemed appropriate for the poor would have cost £13 14s a year. In Whickham, Co. Durham, detailed information on wages paid in the mid-eighteenth century indicates that agricultural and general labourers earned around £8–£12 for a working year of 220 days or more. Coal miners and master craftsmen earned £15–£20 for a comparable year's work, and a tiny number of elite workers could earn around £25 or more. The necessary expenditure to keep a family of five in this area is estimated at £14 16s 4d. In short, even with a working year of 220 days – a generous estimate in the conditions of the time – and in the improved conditions of the period, only a minority of skilled workers could have maintained their families adequately on their own earnings. In Scotland they faced an even harder struggle: around 1750 a Stirlingshire labourer would have earned only a third of what was required to maintain his family at levels of physical efficiency.

Obviously, the subsistence of most such families demanded the additional earnings of wives and children. Andrew Morgan of Eccleshall worked in the 1690s as a towdresser, a linen weaver and a gardener. His wife was a seamstress. His two daughters, aged fifteen and thirteen, span. Any surplus income enjoyed by such people would most likely have been concentrated in particular phases of their life-cycles: in early adult life, before the birth of their children or at that point when some children were old enough to contribute significantly to the family's income. In 1752, for example, John Brabbon earned almost nineteen pounds as a hewer at Northbanks Colliery in Whickham, and his son, aged ten, brought in close to eight pounds more as a horse-driver in the same pit. These were the Brabbons' high times. But between those two phases most labouring families probably faced a struggle to get by, and later, when advancing age reduced parental earning power, assistance from their families would have been even more necessary if relative economic independence was to be sustained.

Such realities did not release significant purchasing power for goods other than the basic necessities of food, clothing, fuel and shelter. And they certainly did not render any kind of accumulation likely. Mathew Burtoft of Burningham in the Lincolnshire fens was very well off for a rural labourer, with an inventory valued at £29. He had a couple of acres of land, and common rights, seven cows and calves, two pigs, poultry, and a good range of agricultural tools. There was a spinning wheel too, probably used by his deceased wife, or his daughters. But his two-room cottage was only meagrely furnished with essentials for eating, sleeping and storage. John Croft of Eccleshall was a day-labourer regularly employed by a local yeoman. His goods comprised two bedsteads, a bolster, four blankets, two pairs of coarse sheets, a chest, a box, two old cupboards, his tools (a shovel, a mattock and an axe) and his clothes: the total value was £2 15s. These men were not paupers. Burtoft had done well. His debts came to only half the value of his inventory and there was money to apprentice his son to a trade for £3 and to give his daughters 13s 4d each towards their marriages. And even Croft was among the upper echelon of the rural labouring population. Most labouring people's goods were not inventoried for the simple reason that they did not possess goods worth over £2 to leave. In the industrial parish of Old Swinford, Shropshire, 72 per cent of the adult men and unmarried women who died in the years 1689–90 were excused probate for this reason. Among such people there could be no significant transfer of accumulated wealth or goods across the generations.

What the evidence suggests cumulatively is that there was a high level of what Paul Slack terms 'shallow poverty' among the wage-earning population, much as Gregory King observed. The English Hearth Tax assessments of the 1660s and 1670s certainly confirm this, with rates of exemption from the tax for reasons of 'poverty or smallness of estate' ranging from around a fifth of all households in parts of rural Cambridgeshire and Cheshire, through around a third of households in most rural areas, to half to two-thirds of households in most industrial districts. In cities, around two-fifths of households tended to be exempt, the households concerned being concentrated in the poorer parishes. Yet, at the same time, close local studies show that relatively few of those exempted were actually in receipt of parish poor relief at the time. They were managing to keep their heads above water in all the ways detailed above. But they were subject also to a myriad of uncertainties and insecurities which could temporarily or permanently undermine the precarious viability of their household economies. The industrious family of Andrew Morgan, described above, was eventually reduced to dependence on the parish by his sickness and his nine-year-old son was taken into the Eccleshall workhouse. William Hine of Aldenham, Hertfordshire, needed relief for a year and a half when his wife died, leaving him with four children aged between eleven years and fourteen months. He came off the parish when he remarried. Nathan Hadnell of the same parish became 'very weake and unable to work' in 1680. After his death, and burial at parish expense, his widow Mary and their three children were relieved until she remarried, and by doing so re-established a viable household economy. Abraham Thurston of Nayland, Suffolk, was a skilled weaver who managed to make a living in most years, despite the decline of the Suffolk cloth industry, and took on pauper apprentices for the parish. But he needed relief for three months in the slump of 1719, and periodically thereafter. In 1742 his daughter, a spinner, was taken into the Nayland workhouse and Abraham followed her there himself in 1746, when he was sixty-one.

Insecurities like these were a perennial feature of life for labouring people, the contingencies of individual misfortune being periodically exacerbated by the more general traumas of industrial slumps or bad harvests. And they were endured generation after generation. The poor laws were necessary because of the inability of so many wage-earning households to maintain consistently an independent domestic economy. Yet most people did so, most of the time. That they were able to do so might be held to provide evidence of the relative prosperity which flowed from a nascent capitalist market order. In fact it provides rather better evidence of the courage and resourcefulness with which they coped with its demands.

ii. *Labour disciplines*

Resourcefulness and a good deal of courage could be shown in other ways too, not least in the manner in which labouring people contrived to exercise some influence over their place within the economic order and the terms and conditions of their labour. From the perspective of their employers and social betters, that place was clear. It was expressed in the notion of the 'utility of poverty'. The poor, as John Bellers put it in 1714, were 'the Kingdom's greatest Treasure and Strength, for without Labourers there can be no Lords; and if the poor Labourers did not raise much more Food and Manufactures than what did subsist themselves, every Gentleman must be a Labourer'. Moreover, the poverty of the many was essential not only to sustain the privileges of the few, but in the interests of national greatness. A large labouring population meant cheap labour. Cheap labour made possible the maintenance of competitiveness, the expansion of markets, the buoyancy of profits and the accumulation and investment of capital.

The fundamental assumption underlying all this was not in itself new: it was not far removed from Edmund Dudley's view that the duty of most was 'to lyve in labor and pain, and the most part of their tyme with the swete of ther face'. But it was now presented in a more secular guise and with a more elaborate economic justification. Nor did such views command universal assent: Defoe and Child both advanced the argument that high wages might be beneficial to the economy. But the utility of poverty was generally accepted as conventional wisdom, not least because it was consonant not only with the economic interests of employers, but also with established notions of authority. For this was a moral and political as well as an economic doctrine: a new spin on the age-old need to justify, and thereby strengthen, an existing structure of inequality and subordination, rendering it natural, commonsensical, something to be accepted with resignation.

At the same time, however, it coexisted uneasily with another old idea: that labourers, as Dudley had observed, were apt to 'grudge' or 'murmur' against their condition, and that they were given to the sin of idleness. Contemporary economic discourse echoed with allegations that labouring people were not only 'rude' and 'boorish', 'rough and savage' in their demeanour, but also full of 'insolence, disobedience, disregard and contempt . . . towards their masters', even infected with 'leveling Principles', and with 'this maxim: that *Adam Left No Will*; they are his sons, and ought to have a share of their father's possessions'. Above all, they were held to be unwilling to work when wages were good, the assumption being that they adhered to customary expectations regarding consumption and would work only so long as was necessary to achieve them, spending the rest of their time in idle pursuits. 'The Poor, if Two Dayes work will maintain them, will not work Three,' opined Francis Gardiner in 1699: in hard times manufactures were 'never so well Wrought'; in times of plenty they 'spend the more in Drinking'.

Such allegations concerning the 'leisure preference' of labour were probably greatly exaggerated. They cannot simply be dismissed, and probably had some foundation in specific contexts, notably that of skilled workers during periods of brisk demand, who may have been willing to work hard enough when work was available, but not to the maximum capacity expected by their employers. There may also have been a life-cycle element in such behaviour, with youthful workers, lacking family commitments, preferring to enjoy days of ease rather than to maximise their earnings with sustained labour. But it seems improbable that voluntary idleness was widespread among the unskilled. Cottagers with plots of ground or common rights may have found it more in their interests to tend their own land or animals on some days rather than taking paid employment, but that was a matter of a preference for alternative work, rather than leisure. Poor nutrition may have rendered some physically incapable of sustaining an intensive work routine. But for most of the rural poor work was not sufficiently available and income neither so predictable nor so adequate as to justify behaviour of the kind complained of by employers. Joseph Massie's investigations led him to the conclusion that while 'Choice, Idleness, or Drunkenness' occasioned some of the poverty of labouring people, 'the general cause is Necessity' – above all the fact that they lacked either land or other means of independent subsistence and were at the mercy of the fluctuations of trade in a commercial economy.

Exaggerated or not, such views were widespread among both employers frustrated by the difficulties encountered in sustaining or expanding production and economic savants preoccupied with the productive potential of the nation. And predictably their recommended solution to the perceived problems of the labour market lay in the dual disciplines of low wages and moral improvement. The poor should be forced to work hard by sheer necessity, and taught to work hard by being more thoroughly imbued from childhood with the habit and duty of labouring in their station for as little as possible. As we have seen, however, wage levels did not always answer to the task. However vehemently low wages were recommended as an economic nostrum, both money wages and real wages gradually improved in the course of the later seventeenth and early eighteenth centuries. In practice, therefore, the emphasis shifted to the task of rendering labouring people more industrious and compliant.

The conventional strategy for achieving that end was through the exercise of what we might call authoritarian paternalism. Exasperated as they were by the supposed collective failings of labouring people, employers frequently remained sensible of their own traditional social obligations. They were even more attached to the claims to authority that went with them. They commonly preferred to think of themselves as 'masters' and of their workers as 'servants', a choice of terms which implied the existence of constraining bonds of reciprocal obligation, but within parameters defined from above, and on terms which smothered the independence of the subordinate in expectations of deference and obedience.

Such a model of labour relations could work well enough within the household. Servants were hired on annual contracts. They worked under their master's or mistress's eye and at their immediate command, an intensive form of labour discipline. It was in order to obtain such a supply of permanently available labour that many farmers and gentlemen reverted to the keeping of greater numbers of servants in the late seventeenth century. In Scotland cottars were similarly under the eye of the tenant and could be turned out if they failed to satisfy, a vulnerability shared by those regular farmworkers in England who inhabited tied cottages. It could also work well enough within the small workshop, especially if journeymen lived in, and among the tiny crews of coastal vessels. But relationships of this kind were less easy to sustain in larger manufactories, or in shipyards, in collieries or on the bigger vessels engaged in long-distance trade. Where concentrated production, co-ordinated labour and the need to keep expensive fixed-capital equipment fully employed placed a particular premium on good time-keeping and regular working practices, some employers attempted to establish them in novel forms. At his Tyneside ironworks, Sir Ambrose Crowley created a generous welfare system for what he termed 'my people', while at the same time imposing a rigorous code of labour discipline to ensure that his employees showed 'a due regard in doing their duty by labouring to do their utmost in the lawful promoting my interest and answer the end of their being paid'.

Comparable forms of industrial paternalism were also emerging in the coal industry. But such innovations were hardly practicable in most of the manufacturing industries of the time. In the rural putting-out industries most work was done in household units scattered over large areas, while major urban manufacturers also employed outworkers like the journeymen tailors of London and Edinburgh, who received materials and patterns from their employers but did the cutting and making-up on their own premises. All such workers had in common the fact that they retained control of the labour process, and it is no accident that the bitterest complaints of idleness were commonly directed against them. As for the vast majority of casual unskilled labourers, the establishment of a lasting bond of mutual obligation with a particular employer was scarcely relevant at all. Insofar as these groups encountered the mores of authoritarian paternalism, it was likely to be not in the context of novel regimes of labour management but in the routine administration of the poor laws.

Parish poor-law authorities dominated by leading ratepayers who were also commonly the leading local employers continued to accept the duty of relieving the poor, while simultaneously asserting the right to discipline their behaviour. Widow Dickenson of Aldenham learned as much when the vestry ordered in 1701 that if she did not 'forthwith put her daughter to service . . . she shall be stricken out of the collection and be wholly excluded from any further relief'. The child was thirteen. And such developments as took place in the system tended towards the same end.

In Scotland, parish poor relief became more widely established in the later seventeenth century, especially in the towns, with funds raised from voluntary contributions, fines, pew rents and other means being administered by the Presbyterian kirk sessions. If the Scottish system differed from that of England in that the imposition of compulsory rates was strongly resisted, however, it shared the expectation that those relieved should be demonstrably 'deserving'. Pensions were awarded in Edinburgh on the approval of an elder and two deacons, and failure to attend church meant their withdrawal. In England and Wales the Settlement Laws made more efficient the regulation of local labour markets, tolerating incomers when their labour was needed, and facilitating their ejection in hard times. The badging of those relieved by the parish, required by law in 1697, added a new element of humiliation to those like the Norfolk labourer described in 1700 as 'taking the patch upon himself and family'. Obliging cottagers to sign over their property as a condition of relief was a means of reducing the numbers of cottages with common rights.

The Corporations of the Poor set up in many cities in the period 1698–1712 to centralise relief and establish municipal workhouses were profoundly influenced by the Reformation of Manners movement and took a particular interest in the inculcation of industry, sobriety and piety among the poor. So did the charity schools established by the Society for the Promotion of Christian Knowledge, which were deemed 'Nurseries of Industry', and the many workhouses created in large parishes and market towns following Knatchbull's Act in 1723 with the dual purpose of reducing the costs of relief and moulding the demeanour of those relieved. At Ashwell, Hertfordshire, for example, relief was denied to any who refused to enter the workhouse, while those who did were obliged to sign over their goods, to work and to attend religious services, while being forbidden to leave without the vestry's permission, or to go into the streets to idle and gossip, all to ensure that the workhouse would 'not fail to answer the end for which it was established, to be a house of good manners, piety, charity and industry'. The chaplain of Edinburgh's workhouse was disciplined in 1748 for being too sympathetic to the inmates. It was alleged against him that he had prayed 'that the managers might be enabled to render the people's lives as sweet, easy, and comfortable as possible', but had neglected to offer prayers 'that the people might be made as submissive, contented and grateful as their condition required'.

All this undoubtedly had its effects. It was perhaps no accident that it was in Swallowfield, Berkshire, a parish tightly controlled for a century, that John Evelyn met in 1685 an exemplary poor woman of 'humility and contentednesse' who earned four pence a day by spinning, maintained her aged parents and spent her time 'continually working, or praying, or reading'. Yet it would be difficult to argue that the poor laws significantly advanced the larger purpose of transforming the poor into a docile and compliant workforce. For just as employers generally failed to peg, let alone reduce, wage rates, so also local poor-law authorities usually failed to transform the nature of the relief system. Workhouse schemes were frequently abandoned after a few years because they were not financially viable. And in most English parishes poor-law expenditure gradually rose as increased numbers were relieved and weekly pensions grew more generous.

The problem was, as Paul Slack expresses it, that 'in practice the poor law made the recognition of poverty easier than its denial and the granting of relief easier than its refusal'. Whatever the rhetoric of the vestry meeting, parish overseers confronted real need among their poorer neighbours and were forced to acknowledge its claims. And where they hardened their hearts, local magistrates were liable to respond to appeals. 'The poor' was an expanding category. A system initially established to secure social stability in conditions of demographic increase had slowly transmuted into a system for coping with the life-cycle crises and inherited poverty of a greatly enlarged labouring population in conditions of demographic stability. And while it remained an instrument of regulation, reflecting the mores of local elites, its growing familiarity rendered it subject also to the development of assumptions about entitlement. No one wanted to 'take the patch', but the expectation that they could do so if circumstances demanded was becoming a new element in customary expectations. In all these ways the poor laws exemplified the ambiguous nature of the relationships of masters and their employees, the 'better sort' of people and the labouring poor.

iii. *'Standing on their terms with their masters'*

The labouring people who were the object of so much attention looked upon the same economic and social landscape with different eyes. From their perspective the central problems arising from their betters' attachment to the notion of the utility of poverty were those of maintaining the economic viability of their households, of securing favourable terms and conditions for their labour, and of keeping a measure of independence in the limited sense, as Robert Malcolmson puts it, of retaining 'a certain social and psychological space of one's own'.

In part this involved an attachment to tradition, the retention where possible of those spaces for self-activity which remained to them in the interstices of the prevailing economic and social order. Cottagers clung tenaciously to the common rights which ensured the survival of quasi-independent smallholder economies alongside the dominant structures of capitalist agriculture. Artisans cherished the guild traditions whereby company officers were expected to take cognisance of the interests and grievances of journeymen and masters were obliged to respect the rules regarding apprenticeship, pay and conditions. Those without benefit of either form of custom knew at least how to exploit the ambiguities of paternalism, to maintain the show of deference that could establish claims to consideration or secure a favourable response to appeals for help.

Yet such traditions were fragile. In the countryside the continued consolidation of property ownership restricted access to common rights. Enclosure extinguished them – and 70 per cent of England's cultivable area was enclosed by 1700. In the towns the authority of the guilds was waning. The companies of London had abandoned most of their controlling functions long before 1750, and elsewhere guild membership among masters was in decline. Employers uninhibited by guild sanctions and disposed to show, as Clapham observed, 'no more observance of national regulations than was convenient' could set what terms they chose for their employees. And more generally the reciprocities of paternalism were markedly asymmetrical. Masters might like to think of their employees as 'servants' when requiring their compliance, but in a cold economic wind their own sense of personal obligation was prone to wither. They were content to shift responsibility for the maintenance of employment to the market, and by the final quarter of the seventeenth century magisterial attempts to assess appropriate wage levels had been abandoned in most counties. Increasingly, therefore, labouring people were obliged to find additional means of protecting their interests, to develop alternative forms of identity and organisation which might draw extensively upon inherited notions of the proper relationship between masters and men, but which were also creative adaptations to the economic conditions and opportunities of the times.

Some were relatively poorly placed to do this. Agricultural workers inhabited village worlds in which they were, to use Michael Mann's phrase, 'organisationally outflanked': geographically dispersed; dependent on the goodwill of a particular employer if they were regularly hired; in daily competition with their fellows for a day's work if they were not; embedded in local power structures controlled by others; and vulnerable to the petty vindictiveness which was the other face of village paternalism. In such a milieu it would be a brave man or woman who tried to bargain too determinedly with an employer. Yet rural labourers were not incapable of doing so, as is sometimes implied. At Ashwell, Hertfordshire, some allegedly 'agreed not to work ... in harvest but upon excessive wages'. Those brought in to help construct Hull citadel in the 1680s, 'knowing our want of men', refused to work unless they were paid the going rate for urban building labourers. It was harvest time and they knew they could find work elsewhere. Such people understood their local labour markets very well, and it is not unlikely that other rural labourers were similarly well informed by their networks of informal association. We know all too little of how hirings of day-labour were conducted in this period. But if rural wage rates rose, as they did, it must have been because labourers bargained when they could, knowing that their fellows did likewise. A man could hold his hat in his hand and still find ways to remind a farmer of what his neighbour paid.

The dynamics of the rural labour market remain in many ways obscure. Elsewhere, however, and in particular among the skilled and semi-skilled workers of the towns, the industrial districts and indeed the oceans, there is evidence enough of the capacity of working people to organise themselves and to act collectively to defend, and where possible to advance, both their economic interests and their self-respect. In London, journeymen and small masters disillusioned with the insouciance of their company officers sometimes attempted in the later seventeenth century to achieve incorporation in their own right. When that was denied, they formed their own clandestine associations. They had a long tradition of association to draw upon, frequently inhabited the same districts and used the same 'houses of call'. Moreover they were also able to conceal their actions behind the public face of a novel form of voluntary association, the friendly society or benefit club. Such societies, which were usually trade-based, required regular contributions to a 'box', provided sickness and old-age insurance for their members, and involved periodic meetings governed by rules of orderly conduct. According to Defoe they were widespread in the metropolis and in other towns by 1697. They existed throughout Britain by the second quarter of the eighteenth century.

Among urban artisans such societies clearly grew out of the guild tradition of mutuality. But they were also something more, by virtue of their restricted membership and clandestine functions. In 1727 Edinburgh journeymen tailors used their box to maintain 'refractory persons . . . till their masters should be compelled to yield to their demands'. And in the manufacturing districts to which they spread in the early eighteenth century they represented a distinctly novel development in the formal association of rural industrial craftsmen. By the 1710s they were well established in the west-country woollen districts and a sufficiently threatening presence to be banned by act of parliament in 1726, a ban which was extended to the silk, iron, linen and leather industries in 1749. But they continued underground. And, literally underground, miners were another category of industrial workers with a marked propensity for collective organisation, facilitated by their geographical concentration, the co-ordinated nature of their work, and their ability to meet undetected in their pits. Scottish colliers were forbidden by law to leave the service of their masters without permission and a testimonial. But they were not slaves. They were paid wages, were well aware of the variations of pay and conditions within their industry, and were much given to 'brothering': the articles of a 'brothering' association at Cowden Colliery, Midlothian, were concealed in the men's Friendly Society box. Similar associations also existed throughout the English mining industries.

Such evidence reveals the crystallisation, by the turn of the eighteenth century, if not before, of a set of industrial cultures and associated collective identities which might be distinctive in their specifics, but which also shared certain characteristics. Particular patterns of work and organisation gave rise to traditions of behaviour which became the customs of the trade. In some instances these had roots which went back for centuries. In others, however, they were invented traditions, the product of novel circumstances. The mine or the ship, for example, might be regarded in one sense as what Marcus Rediker calls a place of 'cultural dispossession' for those who entered that unfamiliar world. But, as he also stresses, both became the setting for the development of distinctive work cultures which involved not only acquired skills, but also associated attitudes, values and expectations. Each trade had its own customs, its own rituals of entry and of belonging, its own songs, costume, and even gait, its own languages of speech and gesture – like the habit of Tyneside keelmen and pitmen of 'spitting on a stone' to express a sense of grievance, or to pledge solidarity with the aggrieved. Each conferred its own sense of identity. Each had its own kinds of public or sequestered association – and by the early eighteenth century many of these forms of association were continuous.

All this could provide a platform for standing 'on their terms with their Masters'. For their masters were also expected to operate within frameworks of industrial custom which were collective creations. To do so was to be 'good honest gentlemen' as west-country weavers put it; to do otherwise was 'unmasterlike'. Open assaults upon customs held to be bastions against detrimental change could be met with fierce and well-organised resistance. In 1718 the weavers and woolcombers of Devon struck to prevent their masters from taking excessive numbers of apprentices and to defend the prices of their work, sustained by friendly societies which 'fed them with Money till they could again get employment, in order to oblige their masters to employ them for want of other hands'. In 1731 the pitmen of the Durham coal field resisted unilateral increases in the size of the 'corves' or baskets by which their output was measured: 'laying in' working pits, burning the new corves, electing colliery representatives, holding mass meetings, confronting the leading coalowners 'in a Body', and, when negotiations failed, embarking on a concerted campaign to destroy pithead machinery and 'fire the corves' which was averted only by the arrival of troops.

Industrial action on this scale was rare. For the most part it was not needed. But it happened. In some industries it could be recurrent – the notorious keelmen of the Tyne struck successfully six times between 1701 and 1750, and the weavers of Gloucestershire and their masters were said to live 'in a perpetual war with one another'. And it was remembered. Like the food riots which also disturbed the industrial districts in years of bad harvest, it demonstrated the contingent nature of hierarchy and authority. To this extent it formed the backdrop to the numerous minor frictions which were more characteristic of industrial relations in the period: the sallies and concessions which attended the maintenance or modification of customs, the settlement of grievances, and above all the determination of wages. London journeymen enforced closed shops by refusing to work with 'irregular' labour. Edinburgh cordiners attempted to 'make new laws at their own hand' and backed their wage demands with withdrawal of labour. West-midlands nailers insisted on being paid 'such rates as are given in the country' and recompensed employers who failed to comply with deliberately bad workmanship. Seamen and colliers haggled over the details of the 'articles' they subscribed when signing on for a season's work or a voyage. They engaged in frequent minor stoppages to demand the modification of those terms if the conditions of work changed, and both also knew when to desert.

There were limits to what could be achieved by such means. As Adam Smith later observed, 'In the long term the workman may be as necessary to his master as his master is to him, but the necessity is not so immediate.' In the event of major industrial crises, employers were usually in a position to hold out longest. And when necessary they could call upon public authority. Edinburgh's town council gave moral, judicial and financial support to masters in dispute with their journeymen. Parliament was willing to provide private legislation to prohibit combinations in particular industries – as the west-country weavers' societies learned – and the Durham miners were not the only rumbustious workforce to be quelled by troops. Workers were most successful in asserting their demands in the favourable circumstances of periods of brisk trade, when stoppages were most damaging to masters and their workpeople therefore had more clout. They knew it and adjusted their tactics accordingly.

Nevertheless, the fact that such circumstances were not uncommon in the late seventeenth and early eighteenth centuries, and that they were repeatedly acted upon, is a major reason for the emergence into historical visibility of what Rediker calls 'a robust world of working class self-activity'. Organised workforces with common sets of expectations, strong senses of collective identity and a truculent self-confidence certainly existed, and they could place real constraint on managerial authority. They could also respect a good master who treated them with the consideration which they took to be their due. They could express solidarity with their masters in the common defence of the interests of the trade – especially against foreign competition. Nor were they opposed to the structures of a capitalist market economy as such. They were the product of its development. They understood its ways very well. What they sought was to have a voice in determining the limits within which market forces were permitted to operate. By doing so, they exerted some influence on the manner in which they lived with the market.

Conclusion

This book has attempted to describe and to explain a long and complex transition in economic life. That transition can be defined, readily enough, as a process of commercialisation. A patchwork of loosely articulated, primarily agrarian, regional economies, which contained commercialised sectors, was transformed into an integrated economic system in which market relationships were the mainspring of economic life, a capitalist market economy, albeit one which retained more traditional elements. To give something a name, however, is not the same thing as explaining it. The explanation of the processes that give the early modern period its distinctiveness in the economic history of Britain does not lie in such labelling. It lies, rather, in the details: in the interconnectedness in time of changes in forms and levels of production, in patterns of economic organisation and in structures of economic power; in the actions of those whose initiatives and responses shaped those processes; in the shifting nature of the social relationships within which economic activity was embedded, and of the cultural values which gave it meaning and purpose.

The processes of change which recast economic life in Britain between the sixteenth and the eighteenth centuries were set in motion blindly. They were animated by a growth in the demand for goods which was partly external in origin and partly generated by the demographic resurgence and inflation of the sixteenth century. They were kept in motion by the changing dynamics of those webs of relationships which bound people together in particular spheres of economic life and by the priorities and strategies which shaped their responses to change. Some of these were already in being – the search for security and stability in the maintenance of household economies; the structures of lordship and tenancy; the networks of interdependence and exchange at local, regional and

national levels. They were adapted to pursue existing objectives in changing circumstances. Others were established, or emerged into greater
prominence, in response to the pressures and opportunities confronted
by succeeding generations. Lordship was transmuted into landlordship.
Property rights hardened and grew exclusive. Tenant communities
polarised, and as they did so loosened their grip on permissible agricultural practice. The relationships of masters and journeymen in the guilds
which had been the social embodiment of handicraft production became
more distanced and conflictual. The putting-out system spread. Wage
dependency became more salient and more permanent as a mode of economic existence, gradually introducing new dimensions into the social
relations of production. Commercial networks elaborated and intensified, precipitating shifts in the roles and identities of farmers, craftsmen,
merchants and labourers. Changing relationships between government
and the myriad of different groups with claims on its support or its
protection were expressed in fluctuating policies of encouragement or
restraint, intervention or disengagement. The state itself grew in significance as an independent actor in the economy, asserting new claims
of its own upon society. The outcome of all this was shaped by the differing capacities of individuals and groups to hold their own in a changing context; by the corrosive force of expediency; by changes in their
aspirations and in their sense of the priorities of economic life. And often
enough it was determined by the conflict which hammered out new patterns of relationships, established the dominance of new expectations,
and gradually created an economic culture more attentive to the requirements of the market and posing fewer objections to the logic of its
demands.

For the most part these developments were slow, hesitant, uncertain
and uneven – spread over eight generations; variable in the force of their
impact; longer, less urgent and often less perceptible in the living than
they are in their historians' telling. If it is possible to discern, as E. P.
Thompson saw it, a 'great arch' of capitalist development stretching from
the central middle ages to the eighteenth century, it is by no means so
apparent that those who constructed their part of that span had any clear
sense of intention. Some may have laboured purposefully. Most muddled
through. Innovation was often enough, as Professor Sacks puts it, 'the
consequence of makeshift efforts to cope with immediate social and economic problems'. The pace of change varied as comparable processes
worked themselves out in different economic, social and institutional
contexts. Particular regions and social groups within them had their own
chronologies of development. For much of the period the dynamics of
change were far more apparent in England, or parts of England, and in

those areas of Wales most connected to the centres of the English commercial system, than in Scotland. Scotland was not spared the initial
shocks of demographic growth and inflation; but, insofar as we are able
to tell, economic life in Scotland was not galvanised by those forces to
anything like the same extent. Most households in the rural Lowlands
remained outside the commercial system until the later seventeenth
century, and the Highlands were only slowly incorporated thereafter: a
separateness of experience which was the outcome of a separateness of
institutions and a more constraining range of economic options.

Nevertheless, if the geography and sociology of change were uneven,
it remained the case that, even where greater continuity with the past was
preserved, it could be more apparent than real, for it was maintained
within changing contexts which almost inevitably affected its meaning.
The poverty and backwardness of the Scottish Highlands, for example,
were only truly apparent when Highland chieftains learned to view their
lands as a source of rental income to be generated by commercial
activity, rather than as sources of men and tribute. Moreover, while the
impact of change varied, it was nonetheless sufficiently widespread to
make possible the identification of significant turning points chronologically, periods when departure from tradition was more perceptible, or
when the velocity of change accelerated. If the mid-sixteenth century
witnessed the fiercest denunciation of economic innovation, the protest
of that age was in a sense pre-emptive, the rhetoric of men who remained
confident of their power to resist detrimental change. It was in the later
decades of the sixteenth and the opening decades of the seventeenth centuries that the conception of a society of estates defended by the commonwealthsmen truly decomposed in England, crumbling in a tide of
economic expansion and commercial intensification. Again, the later seventeenth and early eighteenth centuries brought a further acceleration of
the process of change – this time in a context which meant that it rested
on a broader base socially and geographically, and was less vulnerable to
the forms of negative feedback which had halted population growth and
slowed the momentum of economic expansion in the second quarter of
the seventeenth century. This was a period also in which the social and
cultural restraints on change were weaker: a better context for working
out the fuller implications of the transformations of economy and
society which had been accomplished in England by the 1620s, and were
now being extended to Scotland.

There were turning points also in people's awareness of the nature and
direction of the economic dynamics of the early modern period. If
change had been set in motion blindly, it became more purposeful over
time, as those with a clearer apprehension of the opportunities of the

times and a greater propensity to identify themselves with the forces of change made more deliberative and more powerful interventions in the process. Some were also coming to terms with it intellectually. In the mid-sixteenth century the response of the commonwealthsmen to commercial development had been one of passionate rejection. For them the trump card in the determination of economic claims remained the unchanging will of God. But already there were many for whom the imperatives of the times, and the right of each man to do what he would with his own, provided sufficient justification for swimming with the economic tide, and thinkers like Thomas Smith who accepted the expediency of working with the grain of human self-interest and adjusting policy to the prevailing habits of mankind.

In the succeeding century and a half, and especially from the 1620s, ideas concerning the structures and dynamics of economic life emerged piecemeal. They were often formulated in response to immediate problems and not infrequently involved the legitimation of particular interests in debates over policy. But they also involved a search for order and meaning in economic affairs. And from the debating of specific issues general maxims were developed, maxims embodying an emergent sense of the interconnectedness of economic relationships and processes and alternative criteria for the evaluation of economic behaviour. People had long known that the market was a system of power, animated by the pursuit of economic advantage. Only gradually, however, as society became more thoroughly permeated by commercial relationships and assumptions, and more willing to concede their claims to priority, did the system acquire recognition and legitimacy as a system of order, subject to its own laws and constraints, as distinct from a maelstrom of rampant acquisitiveness.

'Ideas that move people need a context,' as Michael Young writes. By the late seventeenth century the context for the consolidation of economic knowledge existed. The political arithmeticians were anxiously engaged in the effort to assess and analyse the sources of the wealth of the kingdom and to estimate the direction and magnitude of economic forces with a view to developing the productive potential of the nation, and with it national power. Other contributors to the economic discourse of the times were developing and refining the concepts which would eventually be systematised by the political economists of the eighteenth century into the notion of what Joyce Appleby terms 'a natural order of economic relations': one which purported not only to describe and to explain an existing pattern of economic relationships, but also to justify and to extend it. In 1750 that still lay in the future, but the materials for the construction of that intellectual edifice already lay to hand, and with

Hume they were finding expression in an attempt to render the historical development of a commercial order in England intelligible and, in doing so, to endorse its values.

As yet, most people knew little of all that. They were not engaged in imagining the economic system as a whole, though they were aware enough of the manner in which its dynamics impinged upon their own lives. They were preoccupied not so much with the search for meaning in economic affairs as with the more immediate problem of getting a living. And they pursued that quotidian objective within an economic order which presented a somewhat messier set of realities than those envisaged by the founders of economic science. For if it bore the face of a commercial civilisation, it remained still a mixture of forms, structurally, geographically, culturally and in its congeries of social identities, shot through with ambiguities and inconsistencies. By the eighteenth century, Roy Porter argues, English society was 'capitalist, materialist, market-oriented; worldly, pragmatic [and] responsive to economic pressure': but it was also 'unashamedly hierarchical, hereditary and privileged' in its stuctures of power and authority. Britain was a 'trading nation', the world's dominant commercial and industrial power, and Europe's most rapidly urbanising society: yet most of its people still inhabited the countryside, some of them in a manner which would have been familiar to their distant ancestors. Britain had become one of the world's richest societies and one in which wealth was broadly distributed in the middle ranks: but also one which contained a vast reservoir of poverty. Its rulers cherished liberty while retaining a firm grip upon the slave trade, and valued independence and freedom of association while criminalising such plebeian expressions of those ideals as were deemed inconvenient. It was a society increasingly permeated by market values. Yet it was also one in which much economic activity was still embedded in personal relationships and influenced by their demands; in which new beliefs and assumptions could be absorbed while older ones were retained, familiar but strangely out of place; in which awareness of economic self-interest was still qualified by notions of family duty and social obligation; in which antagonisms of interest could still be smothered by traditional patterns of authority; in which assertions of economic power could be tempered by benevolence – but in which benevolence was qualified by a readiness, where necessary, to resort to brutal coercion. It cherished tradition, ancestry and custom. Yet it was sustained by an economic order which was experienced by many as restless, demanding and unstable, one which entailed a 'decoupling from permanence' in Robert Colls' striking phrase.

This was not quite what the savants imagined. It was not quite what anyone had wished. But it was the world the British peoples had made for themselves over three centuries, and the one they had to cope with, bearing up as best they could.

> And this is all the good tidings amount to:
> This principle of bearing, bearing up
> And bearing out, just having to
>
> Balance the intolerable in others
> Against our own, having to abide
> Whatever we settled for and settled into
>
> Against our better judgement.
>
> Seamus Heaney, *Weighing In* (1994)

Further reading

This bibliographical guide identifies many of the works which I have found most valuable in preparing this book. It is not a comprehensive bibliography. However, it provides a starting point for further reading, and many of the works listed contain specialist bibliographies which can be utilised by readers anxious to explore specific issues more deeply. The guide is organised by chapter. In each section I have listed the works bearing most directly on the contents and arguments of a particular chapter. An additional section lists some of the many local and regional studies which have done much to illuminate the details of economic and social change in the period. I have drawn upon them repeatedly for illustration throughout this book, and they are especially to be recommended to readers with an interest in particular areas. To facilitate their use, they are categorised here by type of study (manors and parishes; towns and cities; counties and regions) and within those categories alphabetically by author. Only book-length studies are included. A final section lists a number of unpublished dissertations from which I have quoted evidence. I am grateful to their authors for permission to quote from their work. Throughout this guide, the place of publication of books is London unless otherwise stated. Works included more than once in the chapter sections are referred to by abbreviated titles on the second and subsequent occasions.

Abbreviations:
 AgHEW, IV: *The Agrarian History of England and Wales*, vol. IV: *1500–1640*, ed. J. Thirsk (Cambridge, 1967)
 AgHEW, V: *The Agrarian History of England and Wales*, vol. V: *1640–1750*, ed. J. Thirsk, 2 parts (Cambridge, 1984)
 EcHR: *Economic History Review*
 P&P: *Past and Present*
 TRHS: *Transactions of the Royal Historical Society*

INTRODUCTION: EARLY MODERN BRITAIN: APPROACHES
AND INTERPRETATIONS

The works of the principal contemporary commentators on economic and social change in the sixteenth and early seventeenth centuries are available in modern editions, notably *Utopia* in *The Complete Works of Sir Thomas More*, ed. E. Surtz and J. H. Hexter, vol. 4 (New Haven, 1965); *A Discourse of the Commonweal of this Realm of England: Attributed to Sir Thomas Smith*, ed. M. Dewar (Charlottesville, 1969); *Harrison's Description of England*, ed. F. J. Furnivall, *New Shakspere Society*, 6th Series, vols 1 and 5 (1877–8); *The State of England Anno Dom. 1600 By Thomas Wilson*, ed. F. J. Fisher, Camden Miscellany XVI, *Camden Society*, 3rd Series, 52 (1936); *The History of the Reign of King Henry VII and Selected Works of Francis Bacon*, ed. B. Vickers (Cambridge, 1998), and *Oceana* in *The Political Works of James Harrington*, ed. J. G. A. Pocock (Cambridge, 1977). Additional contemporary comment can be found in *Tudor Economic Documents*, ed. R. H. Tawney and E. Power, 3 vols (1924) and *Seventeenth-Century Economic Documents*, ed. J. Thirsk and J. P. Cooper (Oxford, 1972). For the writers of the Scottish Enlightenment, see D. Hume, *The History of England from the Invasion of Julius Caesar to the Revolution in 1688*, 6 vols (Indianapolis, 1983), esp. vols 3–6; D. Hume, *Essays: Moral, Political and Literary*, ed. E. F. Miller (Indianapolis, 1987); Sir James Steuart, *An Enquiry into the Principles of Political Economy*, ed. A. S. Skinner, 2 vols (Edinburgh, 1966); Adam Smith, *An Inquiry into the Nature and Causes of The Wealth of Nations*, ed. E. Cannan (Chicago, 1976); J. Millar, *An Historical View of the English Government from the settlement of the Saxons in Britain to the Revolution in 1688*, 4 vols (1812), esp. vols 2–4. T. B. Macaulay's *History of England from the accession of James II* (1848) has been frequently reprinted. Karl Marx's account of early modern Britain is to be found in *Capital*, vol. 1 (1954), Part VIII.

D. C. Coleman, *History and the Economic Past: An Account of the Rise and Decline of Economic History in Britain* (Oxford, 1987) provides a lively and controversial account of the development of economic history as an academic discipline. N. B. Harte (ed.), *The Study of Economic History: Collected Inaugural Lectures, 1893–1970* (1971) has a valuable introduction and also reprints the inaugurals of many major figures, including Ashley, Unwin, Clapham, Tawney, Eileen Power and F. J. Fisher. They convey a strong sense of the changing aspirations and preoccupations of leading practitioners of the subject. G. M. Koot gives a cogent account of the emergence of the discipline in *English Historical Economics, 1870–1926: The Rise of Economic History and Neomercantilism* (Cambridge, 1987), which is continued in his 'Historians and Economists: The Study of Economic History in Britain, c.1920–1950', *History of Political Economy*, 25 (1993). Also useful is A. Kadish, *Historians, Economists and Economic History* (1989).

The works of the English Historical Economists remain essential reading. Those quoted here are J. E. Thorold Rogers, *Six Centuries of Work and Wages:*

The History of English Labour (1884), 11th edn (1912); W. Cunningham, *The Growth of English Industry and Commerce*, 2 vols (1882), 6th edn (1925), and W. J. Ashley, *An Introduction to English Economic History and Theory*, part II: *The End of the Middle Ages* (1893). The works of their early-twentieth-century successors quoted or alluded to include: G. Unwin, *Industrial Organisation in the Sixteenth and Seventeenth Centuries* (Oxford, 1904); W. R. Scott, *The Constitution and Finance of English, Scottish and Irish Joint Stock Companies to 1720*, 3 vols (Cambridge, 1910–12); R. H. Tawney, *The Agrarian Problem in the Sixteenth Century* (1912), Harper Torchbooks edn (New York, Evanston and London, 1967); R. B. Westerfield, *Middlemen in English Business, 1660–1760* (New Haven, 1915); N. S. B. Gras, *The Evolution of the English Corn Market from the Twelfth to the Eighteenth Century* (Cambridge, Mass., 1915); and A. Clark, *The Working Life of Women in the Seventeenth Century* (1919).

Ephraim Lipson's formidable textbook *The Economic History of England* went through many editions, culminating in the 12th edition of vol. 1 (1959) and the 6th edition of vols 2–3 (1956). It remains in many ways illuminating. The tone of post-Second World War writing on the period, however, was set by J. H. Clapham, *A Concise Economic History of Britain from the Earliest Times to 1750* (Cambridge, 1949). The numerous textbooks which attempted from the 1960s to synthesise the research achievements of the post-war decades (and in doing so created a new consensual interpretation of the period) include: P. Ramsey, *Tudor Economic Problems* (1963); C. Wilson, *England's Apprenticeship, 1603–1763* (1965); L. A. Clarkson, *The Pre-Industrial Economy in England, 1500–1750* (1971); B. A. Holderness, *Pre-Industrial England: Economy and Society, 1500–1750* (1976); D. C. Coleman, *The Economy of England, 1450–1750* (Oxford, 1977); D. M. Palliser, *The Age of Elizabeth: England under the Later Tudors, 1547–1603* (1983); and C. G. A. Clay, *Economic Expansion and Social Change: England, 1500–1700*, 2 vols (Cambridge, 1984). Christopher Hill's avowedly Marxist *Reformation to Industrial Revolution* (1967) kept alive an alternative perspective, as, in his own way, did W. G. Hoskins' *The Age of Plunder: King Henry's England, 1500–47* (1976). All are valuable and Clay provides an extensive bibliography. For overviews of the 'new social history' which emerged in the 1970s, see K. Wrightson, *English Society, 1580–1680* (1982); R. Porter, *English Society in the Eighteenth Century* (1982); J. Youings, *Sixteenth-Century England* (1984) and J. A. Sharpe, *Early Modern England: A Social History, 1550–1760*, 2nd edn (1997).

Scotland and Wales have, until recently, been less well served with general accounts of the early modern period. I. F. Grant's *The Social and Economic Development of Scotland before 1603* (Edinburgh, 1930) long remained the standard work, supplemented by S. G. E. Lythe, *The Economy of Scotland in its European Setting, 1550–1625* (Edinburgh and London, 1960). T. C. Smout's *A History of the Scottish People, 1560–1830* (Glasgow, 1969) did much to stimulate a new wave of interest in the economic and social history of early modern Scotland, the results of which are now summarised in I. D. Whyte, *Scotland before the Industrial Revolution: An Economic and Social History, c.1050–c.1750* (1995). Bruce Lenman's *An Economic History of Modern Scotland, 1660–1976* (1977) provides a vibrant account of the latter part of the period. There is no single volume devoted to the the economic and social history of early modern Wales, but valuable survey chapters can be found in G. H. Jenkins, *The Foundations of Modern Wales, 1642–1780* (Oxford, 1987); T. Herbert and G. Elwyn Jones, *Tudor Wales* (Cardiff, 1988); P. Jenkins, *A History of Modern Wales, 1536–1990* (1992); G. Williams, *Renewal and Reformation: Wales, c.1415–1642* (Oxford, 1993).

PART ONE: HOUSEHOLDS IN A LANDSCAPE, C.1470–C.1550

The best edition of Dudley's work is *The Tree of Commonwealth by Edmund Dudley*, ed. D. M. Brodie (Cambridge, 1948). An interesting recent discussion of its significance can be found in N. Wood, *Foundations of Political Economy: Some Early Tudor Views on State and Society* (Berkeley, Los Angeles and London, 1994). For commercial development in medieval England, see R. H. Britnell, *The Commercialisation of English Society, 1000–1500* (Cambridge, 1993).

Chapter 1: Household economies: structures and roles

Life in the great households of the period is vividly illustrated in F. Heal, *Hospitality in Early Modern England* (Oxford, 1990). For household structure more generally, see P. Laslett and R. Wall (eds), *Household and Family in Past Time* (Cambridge, 1972), and T. Arkell and A. Whiteman, 'Mean Household Size in Mid-Tudor England: Clackclose Hundred, Norfolk', *Local Population Studies*, 60 (1998). Concepts of the family are discussed in N. Tadmor, 'The Concept of the Household-Family in Eighteenth-Century England', *P&P*, 151 (1996), which makes points equally relevant to the early sixteenth century. The standard work on service is A. Kussmaul, *Servants in Husbandry in Early Modern England* (Cambridge, 1981). Apprenticeship is examined in many urban studies, one of the best discussions being S. Rappaport, *Worlds within Worlds: Structures of Life in Sixteenth-Century London* (Cambridge, 1987).

Status and occupational distinctions are more fully introduced in Wrightson, *English Society*, and Smout, *Scottish People*. Urban occupational structures are particularly well explored in C. Phythian-Adams, 'The Economy and Social Structure', in *The Fabric of the Traditional Community*, Open University Course A322: English Urban History 1500–1780 (Milton Keynes, 1977). See also Hoskins, *Age of Plunder*, and J. Patten, *English Towns, 1500–1700* (Folkestone, Kent, and Hamden, Conn., 1978). Unwin's *Industrial Organisation* still provides the best introduction to the structures of manufacturing, and S. L. Thrupp, *The Merchant Class of Medieval London, 1300–1500* (Chicago, 1948) remains of great value. The best recent study of rural industry is M. Zell, *Industry in the Countryside: Wealden Society in the Sixteenth Century* (Cambridge, 1994). E. A. Wrigley's important estimates of the changing proportions of the urban, rural agricultural and rural non-agricultural populations are to be found in his article 'Urban Growth and Agricultural Change: England and the Continent in the Early Modern Period', *Journal of Interdisciplinary History*, XV (1985).

R. E. Pahl's *Divisions of Labour* (Oxford, 1984) provides a stimulating historical introduction to the problem of changing roles in the household economy. C. L. Powell, *English Domestic Relations, 1487–1653: A Study of Matrimony and Family Life in Theory and Practice as Revealed by the Literature, Law and History of the Period* (New York, 1917 and 1972) is an excellent introduction to the prescriptive 'domestic conduct books' of the period. Women's property rights are examined in A. L. Erickson, *Women and Property in Early Modern England* (1993); T. Stretton, *Women Waging Law in Elizabethan England* (Cambridge, 1998); and R. Houston, 'Women in the Economy and Society of Scotland, 1500–1800', in R. A. Houston and I. D. Whyte (eds), *Scottish Society, 1500–1800* (Cambridge, 1989). Illuminating discussions of the late-medieval domestic environment can be found in L. R. Poos, *A Rural Society after the Black Death: Essex, 1350–1525* (Cambridge, 1991), and M. Johnson, *The Archaeology of Capitalism* (Oxford, 1996). Women's work has been extensively researched in recent years. S. Mendelson and P. Crawford, *Women in Early Modern England, 1550–1720* (Oxford, 1998) provides a good general introduction, while excellent individual studies include M. Prior, 'Women in the Urban Economy: Oxford, 1500–1800', in M. Prior (ed.), *Women in English Society, 1500–1800* (1985), and the relevant sections of D. Woodward, *Men at Work: Labourers and Building Craftsmen in the Towns of Northern England, 1450–1750* (Cambridge, 1995), and L. Gowing, *Domestic Dangers: Women, Words and Sex in Early Modern London* (Oxford, 1996). For children's roles, see B. Hanawalt, 'Child-rearing among the Lower Classes of Late Medieval England', *Journal of Interdisciplinary History*, 8 (1977), and I. Krausman Ben-Amos, *Adolescence and Youth in Early Modern England* (New Haven and London, 1994).

Chapter 2: Household economies: priorities and strategies

Agriculture and farm incomes are particularly well discussed in Tawney, *The Agrarian Problem*; M. Overton, *Agricultural Revolution in England: The Transformation of the Agrarian Economy, 1500–1850* (Cambridge, 1996); and C. Howell, *Land, Family and Inheritance in Transition: Kibworth Harcourt, 1280–1700* (Cambridge, 1983). For urban wage-earners, see Woodward, *Men at Work*. The best short discussion of vulnerability to dearth and disease is P. Slack, 'Mortality Crises and Epidemic Disease in England, 1485–1610', in C. Webster (ed.), *Health, Medicine and Mortality in the Sixteenth Century* (Cambridge, 1979).

My discussion of economic attitudes is influenced by the arguments of J. C. Scott, *The Moral Economy of the Peasant: Rebellion and Subsistence in South-East Asia* (New Haven, 1979) and P. Musgrave, *Land and Economy in Baroque Italy: Valpolicella, 1630–1797* (Leicester, 1992), two studies which provide intriguing parallels with sixteenth-century England. For the proverbial wisdom of the period, see D. Rollison, *The Local Origins of Modern Society: Gloucestershire, 1500–1800* (1992), and A. Fox, *The Voice of the People: Oral and Literate Culture in Sixteenth- and Seventeenth-Century England* (Oxford, 2000).

On the 'putting forth' of children and their incorporation into other households, see Kussmaul, *Servants in Husbandry*, and Ben-Amos, *Adolescence and Youth*. The latter is also valuable on the subsequent careers of apprentices, as are Rappaport, *Worlds within Worlds*, Thrupp, *Merchant Class*, and Zell, *Industry in the Countryside*. Marriage is discussed in R. M. Smith, 'Marriage Processes in the English Past: Some Continuities', in L. Bonfield, R. M. Smith and K. Wrightson (eds), *The World We Have Gained: Histories of Population and Social Structure* (Oxford, 1986); P. Rushton, 'Property, Power and Family Networks: The Problem of Disputed Marriage in Early Modern England', *Journal of Family History*, XI (1986); M. Ingram, *Church Courts, Sex and Marriage in England, 1570–1640* (Oxford, 1987); D. O'Hara, *Courtship and Constraint: Rethinking the Making of Marriage in Tudor England* (Manchester, 2000). The question of inheritance is sharply introduced in R. Houlbrooke, *The English Family, 1450–1700* (1984), and is explored in detail by the contributors to J. Goody, J. Thirsk and E. P. Thompson (eds), *Family and Inheritance: Rural Society in Western Europe, 1200–1800* (Cambridge, 1976). For an illuminating recent discussion of family inheritance strategies, see J. Whittle, 'Individualism and the Family–Land Bond: A Reassessment of Land Transfer Patterns among the English Peasantry', *P&P*, 160 (1998). My discussion of authority and decision making is influenced by T. Harevan, 'The History of the Family and the Complexity of Social Change', *American Historical Review*, XCVI (1991), and P. Thompson, 'Women in the Fishing: The Roots of Power between the Sexes', *Comparative Studies in Society and History*, 27 (1985). In addition to the works on marital roles, service and apprenticeship already listed, conflict within the household and its resolution are discussed in P. Griffiths, *Youth and Authority: Formative Experiences in England, 1560–1640* (Oxford, 1996), and P. Rushton, ' "The Matter in Variance": Domestic Conflict in the Pre-Industrial Economy of North-East England', *Journal of Social History*, 25 (1992).

Chapter 3: Beyond the household: economic institutions and relationships

Good introductions to the complexities of lordship and tenures in England can be found in Youings, *Sixteenth-Century England*, and Overton, *Agricultural Revolution*. See also R. B. Smith, *Land and Politics in the England of Henry VIII: The West Riding of Yorkshire, 1530–46* (Oxford, 1970), and the introduction to E. Kerridge (ed.), *Surveys of the Manors of Philip, First Earl of Pembroke and Montgomery, 1631–1632*, Wiltshire Arch. & Hist. Soc., Records Branch, vol. 9 (Devizes, 1953). Welsh tenures are discussed in T. Jones Pierce,

'Landlords in Wales. A. The Nobility and Gentry', in *AgHEW, IV*, and those of Scotland in R. A. Dodgshon, *Land and Society in Early Scotland* (Oxford, 1981), and M. H. B. Sanderson, *Scottish Rural Society in the Sixteenth Century* (Edinburgh, 1982). The significance of custom has been much discussed. For particularly acute analyses, which are equally relevant to this period, see S. Reynolds, *Kingdoms and Communities in Western Europe, 900–1300* (Oxford, 1984), and E. P. Thompson, 'Custom, Law and Common Right', in his *Customs in Common* (1991).

The dominant values of late-medieval rural communities are examined in R. B. Goheen, 'Social Ideals and Social Structure: Rural Gloucestershire, 1450–1500', *Histoire Sociale–Social History*, 12 (1979). For good accounts of agriculture in open-field communities, see C. S. and C. S. Orwin, *The Open Fields*, 3rd edn (Oxford, 1967); W. G. Hoskins, *The Midland Peasant* (1957); and C. H. K. Oestmann, *Lordship and Community: The Lestrange Family and the Village of Hunstanton, Norfolk, in the First Half of the Sixteenth Century* (Woodbridge, 1994). Agricultural organisation in Scottish farming townships is discussed in the works by Dodgshon and Sanderson cited above. For estimates of the extent to which England was already enclosed in 1500, see J. R. Wordie, 'The Chronology of English Enclosure, 1500–1914', *EcHR*, 2nd Series, XXXVI (1983). J. M. Neeson, *Commoners: Common Right, Enclosure and Social Change in England, 1700–1820* (Cambridge, 1993) gives a vivid sense of the significance of common rights. For late-medieval parish 'communalism' and its expense, see B. Kumin, *The Shaping of a Community: The Rise and Reformation of the English Parish, c.1400–1560* (Aldershot, 1996), and for 'credit' see C. Muldrew, *The Economy of Obligation: The Culture of Credit and Social Relations in Early Modern England* (1998).

Most urban studies provide accounts of the social and institutional structures of particular towns. For a particularly lucid overview of the English situation, see K. Wilson, 'Political Organisation in the Sixteenth-Century Town', in *The Fabric of the Traditional Community*, Open University Course A322: English Urban History 1500–1780 (Milton Keynes, 1977), and for Scotland, Smout, *Scottish People*. The functions of the guilds and craft fellowships have been much discussed since the days of Ashley and Unwin. Important recent contributions include H. Swanson, 'Craft Guilds in Late Medieval English Towns', *P&P*, 121 (1988), and the relevant sections of C. Phythian-Adams, *Desolation of a City: Coventry and the Urban Crisis of the Late Middle Ages* (Cambridge, 1979), Rappaport, *Worlds within Worlds*, and Woodward, *Men at Work*.

Kinship in Scotland is examined in J. Wormald, 'Bloodfeud, Kindred and Government in Early Modern Scotland', *P&P*, 87 (1980), and R. A. Dodgshon, *From Chiefs to Landlords: Social and Economic Change in the Western Highlands and Islands, c.1493–1820* (Edinburgh, 1998). Discussions of the significance of kinship among English landowners and leading citizens can be found in A. J. Pollard, *North-Eastern England during the Wars of the Roses: Lay Society, War and Politics, 1450–1500* (Oxford, 1990), and in Phythian-Adams, *Desolation of a City*. For the situation in village society, see Z. Razi, 'The Myth of the Immutable English Family', *P&P*, 140 (1993), and the Postscript to K. Wrightson and D. Levine, *Poverty and Piety in an English Village: Terling, 1525–1700*, 2nd edn (Oxford, 1995). Hospitality and commensality in the local community are discussed in Heal, *Hospitality in Early Modern England*; J. M. Bennett, 'Conviviality and Charity in Medieval and Early Modern England', *P&P*, 134 (1992); and R. Hutton, *The Rise and Fall of Merry England: The Ritual Year, 1400–1700* (Oxford, 1994).

Chapter 4: Beyond the household: economic networks and dynamics

The farming regions of England and Wales and areas of rural industrial activity are described by J. Thirsk and F. Emery in *AgHEW, IV*. Those of Scotland are sketched in Lenman, *Economic History of Modern Scotland*, and I. D. Whyte, 'Proto-Industrialisation in Scotland', in P. Hudson (ed.), *Regions and Industries: A Perspective on the Industrial Revolution in Britain* (Cambridge, 1989). For recent attempts to reconceptualise local and regional variations, see A. Everitt, 'Country, County and Town: Patterns of Regional Evolution in England', *TRHS*, 5th Series, 29 (1979), and the introduction to C. Phythian-Adams (ed.), *Societies, Cultures and Kinship: Cultural Provinces and English Local History* (Leicester, 1993).

Markets and marketing are discussed in A. Everitt, 'The Marketing of Agricultural Produce' in *AgHEW, IV*. I have also drawn on the many studies of individual towns and their hinterlands, among which some of the most useful are J. Cornwall, 'English Country Towns in the Fifteen-Twenties', *EcHR*, 2nd Series, XV (1962); J. Patten, 'Village and Town: An Occupational Study', *Agricultural History Review*, 20 (1972); A. D. Dyer, *The City of Worcester in the Sixteenth Century* (Leicester, 1973); D. M. Palliser, *Tudor York* (Oxford, 1979); Pollard, *North-Eastern England*; J. Goodacre, *The Transformation of a Peasant Economy: Townspeople and Villagers in the Lutterworth Area, 1500–1700* (Aldershot, 1994). The English urban hierarchy is introduced in P. Clark and P. Slack, *English Towns in Transition* (Oxford, 1976). For recent research on Scottish towns, see M. Lynch (ed.), *The Early Modern Town in Scotland* (1987). For patterns of mobility and migration see for example the discussions in Poos, *Rural Society after the Black Death*; O'Hara, *Courtship and Constraint*; Palliser, *Tudor York*; Patten, *English Towns*; Ben-Amos, *Adolescence and Youth*; Rappaport, *Worlds within Worlds*. Market regulation is dealt with in Everitt, 'Marketing', and in A. J. S. Gibson and T. C. Smout, *Prices, Food and Wages in Scotland, 1550–1780* (Cambridge, 1995).

For the general context of economic and social trends in late-medieval England, see Britnell, *Commercialisation*, and S. H. Rigby, *English Society in the Later Middle Ages: Class, Status and Gender* (1995). The emergence of the yeomen has been frequently discussed. Particularly good studies are the later chapters of C. Dyer, *Lords and Peasants in a Changing Society: The Estates of the Bishopric of Worcester, 680–1540* (Cambridge, 1980), and P. Glennie, 'In

Search of Agrarian Capitalism: Manorial Land Markets and the Acquisition of Land in the Lea Valley, c.1450–c.1560', *Continuity and Change*, 3 (1988). Trends in Wales are discussed in G. Williams, *Renewal and Reformation*. Early enclosure is examined in context in I. Blanchard, 'Population Change, Enclosure and the Early Tudor Economy', *EcHR*, 2nd Series, XXIII (1970). Goodacre's *Transformation of a Peasant Economy* contains an illuminating study of the Leicestershire case. The development of rural industries is touched on in many local studies and discussed more generally in a classic article by J. Thirsk, 'Industries in the Countryside', in F. J. Fisher (ed.), *Essays in the Economic and Social History of Tudor and Stuart England* (Cambridge, 1961). An excellent discussion of the debate over the 'late-medieval urban crisis', with an extensive bibliography, is provided in A. D. Dyer, *Decline and Growth in English Towns, 1400–1640* (1991). For Wales, see M. Griffiths, 'Country and Town: Agrarian Change and Urban Fortunes', in Herbert and Jones (eds), *Tudor Wales*.

PART TWO: TRANSITIONS

Chapter 5: Prices and people, c.1520–c.1580

The most useful price indices for the period are E. H. Phelps-Brown and S. V. Hopkins, 'Seven Centuries of the Prices of Consumables Compared with Builders' Wage-Rates', *Economica* (1956), reprinted in E. M. Carus-Wilson (ed.), *Essays in Economic History*, vol. 2 (1962), P. Bowden, 'Statistical Appendix', in *AgHEW, IV*, and the London index in Rappaport, *Worlds within Worlds*, p. 131. The debate over the causes of inflation is lucidly reviewed in R. B. Outhwaite, *Inflation in Tudor and Early Stuart England*, 2nd edn (1983), and can be followed in the essays collected in P. H. Ramsey (ed.), *The Price Rise in Sixteenth-Century England* (1971). Debasement is discussed in J. D. Gould, *The Great Debasement* (1970). More recent contributions to the continuing debate include N. J. Mayhew, 'Population, Money Supply and the Velocity of Circulation in England, 1300–1700', *EcHR*, XLVIII (1995), and J. R. Wordie, 'Deflationary Factors in the Tudor Price Rise', *P&P*, 154 (1997). For inflation in Scotland, see Gibson and Smout, *Prices, Food and Wages*.

For estimates of the population of England in the 1520s, see J. Cornwall, 'English Population in the Early Sixteenth Century', *EcHR*, 2nd Series, XXIII (1970). The most important single work on demographic trends thereafter is E. A. Wrigley and R. S. Schofield, *The Population History of England, 1541–1871: A Reconstruction* (1981). For discussions of the vital period before the advent of parish registration, see J. Hatcher, *Plague, Population and the English Economy, 1348–1530* (1977), and M. Bailey, 'Demographic Decline in Late Medieval England: Some Thoughts on Recent Research', *EcHR*, XLIX (1996). Valuable local evidence is also provided in Slack, 'Mortality Crises and Epidemic Disease'; Dyer, *Lords and Peasants*; Poos, *Rural Society after the Black Death*; Zell, *Industry in the Countryside*. The details of demographic trends in

Scotland and Wales remain obscure for this period, though indirect evidence
indicates that the population was rising.

Chapter 6: Commodity and commonwealth, c.1520–c.1580

Tawney's *Agrarian Problem* remains an essential starting point for any student
of rural society in the period. The policies of landlords in England and Wales
are discussed in chapters by G. Batho and T. Jones Pierce in *AgHEW, IV*, which
also contains J. Thirsk's important essay on 'Enclosing and Engrossing'. For
examples of the fortunes of specific gentry families, see M. E. Finch, *The Wealth
of Five Northamptonshire Families, 1540–1640*, Northants Record Soc., 19
(Oxford, 1956), and A. Simpson, *The Wealth of the Gentry, 1540–1660: East
Anglian Studies* (Cambridge, 1961). Landlord–tenant relations also figure in
many of the local and regional studies listed below. For change in manorial land
markets in the early sixteenth century see Whittle, 'Individualism and the
Family–Land Bond' and her *The Development of Agrarian Capitalism: Land
and Labour in Norfolk, 1440–1580* (Oxford, 2000). The study of changing rural
living standards was pioneered by W. G. Hoskins in 'The Rebuilding of Rural
England, 1570–1640', *P&P*, 4 (1953), and his *Midland Peasant*, and is also
explored in other local studies.

The massive increase in the revenues of the English crown in the 1540s is identified in P. K. O'Brien and P. A. Hunt, 'The Rise of a Fiscal State in England,
1485–1815', *Historical Research*, LXVI (1993). The plundering of the church
and disposal of monastic lands which made that possible is discussed in J.
Youings, *The Dissolution of the Monasteries* (1971), and in chapters by Youings
on England and G. Williams on Wales in *AgHEW, IV*. See also Hoskins, *Age of
Plunder*, and many county studies of the changing patterns of gentry land-
holding. The effects of the dissolution in the towns have recently been illuminated by R. Tittler's *The Reformation and the Towns in England: Politics and
Political Culture, c.1540–1640* (Oxford, 1998). For the feuing movement in Scotland, see Sanderson, *Scottish Rural Society*, and Dodgshon, *Land and Society*.

The situation of wage-earners is discussed in Woodward, *Men at Work*, and
Rappaport, *Worlds within Worlds*. For the growing problem of poverty, see A.
L. Beier, *Masterless Men: The Vagrancy Problem in England, 1560–1640* (1985);
M. K. McIntosh, 'Local Responses to the Poor in Late Medieval and Tudor
England', *Continuity and Change*, 3 (1988), and P. Slack, *Poverty and Policy in
Tudor and Stuart England* (1988).

The moral protest of the English Commonwealthsmen is examined in
W. R. D. Jones, *The Tudor Commonwealth, 1529–1559* (London, 1970); Wood,
Foundations of Political Economy; and A. McRae, *God Speed the Plough: The
Representation of Agrarian England, 1500–1660* (Cambridge, 1996). For the
comparable Welsh and Scottish literatures of complaint, see Williams, *Renewal
and Reformation*, and Dodgshon, *Land and Society*. Resistance to enclosure is
surveyed in R. B. Manning, *Village Revolts: Social Protest and Popular Disturbances in England, 1509–1640* (Oxford, 1988). Good short accounts of the

revolts of 1536 and 1549 can be found in A. Fletcher and D. MacCulloch, *Tudor Rebellions*, 4th edn (1997). See also M. L. Bush, *The Pilgrimage of Grace: A Study of the Rebel Armies of October, 1536* (Manchester, 1996), and Part IV of D. MacCulloch, *Suffolk and the Tudors: Politics and Religion in an English County, 1500–1600* (Oxford, 1986).

The significance of Sir Thomas Smith's ideas is discussed in Wood, *Foundations of Political Economy*, and McRae, *God Speed the Plough*. The policy of William Cecil (Lord Burghley) is examined in detail in the second volume of Cunningham's *Growth of English Industry and Commerce*. For more recent assessments of mid-Tudor and early-Elizabethan economic and social policy, see Jones, *Tudor Commonwealth*; J. Thirsk, *Economic Policy and Projects: The Development of a Consumer Society in Early Modern England* (Oxford, 1978); P. Slack, *From Reformation to Improvement: Public Welfare in Early Modern England* (Oxford, 1999).

Chapter 7: Economic expansion, c.1580–c.1650

For trends in population and prices, see the works listed under chapter 5, and M. Flinn (ed.), *Scottish Population History: From the Seventeenth Century to the 1930s* (Cambridge, 1977).

Agricultural developments in England and Wales are discussed in *AgHEW*, IV, and in Overton, *Agricultural Revolution*. E. Kerridge, *The Agricultural Revolution* (1967) is valuable on changing techniques, though controversial in its overall interpretation. On change in the fenlands and forest areas, see K. Lindley, *Fenland Riots and the English Revolution* (1982); B. Sharp, *In Contempt of All Authority: Rural Artisans and Riot in the West of England, 1586–1660* (Berkeley, Los Angeles and London, 1980); V. Skipp, *Crisis and Development: An Ecological Case Study of the Forest of Arden, 1570–1674* (Cambridge, 1978). The renewal of the enclosure movement is examined in R. I. Hodgson, 'The Progress of Enclosure in County Durham, 1550–1870', in H. S. A. Fox and R. A. Butlin (eds), *Change in the Countryside* (1978); Wordie, 'Chronology of Enclosure'; R. C. Allen, *Enclosure and the Yeoman* (Oxford, 1992); Goodacre, *Transformation of a Peasant Economy*. For developments in the open fields, see M. A. Havinden, 'Agricultural Progress in Open-Field Oxfordshire', in W. E. Minchinton (ed.), *Essays in Agrarian History*, vol. I (Newton Abbot, 1968). The problem of estimating crop yields is discussed in essays by Allen, Glennie and Overton in B. M. S. Campbell and M. Overton (eds), *Land, Labour and Livestock: Historical Studies in European Agricultural Productivity* (Manchester, 1991).

The problems attending renewed urban growth are introduced in Clark and Slack, *English Towns in Transition*. For London, see R. Finlay, *Population and Metropolis: The Demography of London, 1580–1650* (Cambridge, 1981); A. L. Beier and R. Finlay (eds), *The Making of the Metropolis: London, 1500–1700* (1986); M. J. Power, 'The East London Working Community in the Seventeenth Century', in P. J. Corfield and D. Keene (eds), *Work in Towns,*

850–1850 (Leicester, 1990). The outstanding work on urban mortality and its economic and social consequences is P. Slack, *The Impact of Plague in Tudor and Stuart England* (1985). For rural–urban migration, see P. Clark, 'The Migrant in Kentish Towns, 1580–1640', in P. Clark and P. Slack (eds), *Crisis and Order in English Towns, 1500–1700* (1972).

Rural industry has been extensively studied. For woollen textiles, see for example G. D. Ramsay, *The Wiltshire Woollen Industry in the Sixteenth and Seventeenth Centuries* (Oxford, 1943); J. E. Pilgrim, 'The Rise of the "New Draperies" in Essex', *University of Birmingham Historical Journal*, VII (1959–60); D. C. Coleman, 'An Innovation and its Diffusion: The "New Draperies"', *EcHR*, 2nd Series, XXII (1969). P. Hudson (ed.), *Regions and Industries* includes informative essays on developments in Lancashire, the Weald and the west midlands. Import-substitution industries are discussed in Thirsk, *Policy and Projects*. For the metal trades, see C. W. Chalkin, *Seventeenth-Century Kent* (1965); P. Large, 'Urban Growth and Agricultural Change in the West Midlands during the Seventeenth and Eighteenth Centuries', in P. Clark (ed.), *The Transformation of English Provincial Towns, 1600–1800* (1984); R. Burt, 'The International Diffusion of Technology during the Early Modern Period: The Case of the British Non-Ferrous Mining Industry', *EcHR*, XLIV (1991); D. Hey, *The Fiery Blades of Hallamshire: Sheffield and its Neighbourhood, 1660–1740* (Leicester, 1991). The growth of the Derbyshire lead-mining industry is examined in its full social and political context in A. Wood, *The Politics of Social Conflict: The Peak Country, 1520–1770* (Cambridge, 1999). For the coal industry, see J. Hatcher, *The History of the British Coal Industry*, vol. I: *Before 1700: Towards the Age of Coal* (Oxford, 1993), though J. U. Nef's *The Rise of the British Coal Industry*, 2 vols (1932) also remains valuable. An intensive study of Tyneside developments is provided by D. Levine and K. Wrightson, *The Making of an Industrial Society: Whickham, 1560–1765* (Oxford, 1991).

The redistribution of population is documented in many local studies, and assessed more generally in Wrigley's 'Urban Growth and Agricultural Change'. For internal trade, see F. J. Fisher, 'The Development of the London Food Market, 1540–1640', in E. M. Carus-Wilson (ed.), *Essays in Economic History*, vol. I (1954); Everitt, 'Marketing', in *AgHEW, IV*; Chalkin, *Seventeenth-Century Kent*; A. Hassell Smith, *County and Court: Government and Politics in Norfolk, 1558–1603* (Oxford, 1974); Dyer, *City of Worcester*; Rollison, *Local Origins of Modern Society*. M. Spufford's *The Great Reclothing of Rural England* (1984) is an illuminating study of petty chapmen and their trade. For commercial litigation and its significance, see C. W. Brooks, *Pettyfoggers and Vipers of the Commonwealth: The 'Lower Branch' of the Legal Profession in Early Modern England* (Cambridge, 1986), and Muldrew, *Economy of Obligation*.

Developments in Scotland have been inferred more than depicted in detail for this period. However, valuable material can be found in Dodgshon, *Land and Society* and *From Chiefs to Landlords*; M. L. Parry and T. R. Slater (eds), *The Making of the Scottish Countryside* (1980); Lythe, *Economy of Scotland*;

Gibson and Smout's *Prices, Food and Wages*, and the same authors' 'Regional Prices and Market Regions: The Evolution of the Early Modern Scottish Grain Market', *EcHR*, XLVIII (1995).

For trends in English overseas trade, see R. Davis, *English Overseas Trade, 1500–1700* (1973); F. J. Fisher, 'Commercial Trends and Policy in Sixteenth-Century England', *EcHR*, X (1940); W. E. Minchinton (ed.), *The Growth of English Overseas Trade in the Seventeenth and Eighteenth Centuries* (1969); J. K. Federowicz, *England's Baltic Trade in the Early Seventeenth Century* (Cambridge, 1980); D. H. Sacks, *The Widening Gate: Bristol and the Atlantic Economy, 1450–1700* (Berkeley, Los Angeles and Oxford, 1991); R. Brenner, *Merchants and Revolution: Commercial Change, Political Conflict and London's Overseas Traders, 1550–1653* (Cambridge, 1993). For the new trading companies, see for example T. S. Willan, *The Early History of the Russia Company* (Manchester, 1956); R. W. K. Hinton, *The Eastland Trade and the Common Weal* (Cambridge, 1959); K. N. Chaudhuri, *The English East India Company* (1965).

Estimates of national income can be found in O'Brien and Hunt, 'Rise of a Fiscal State'.

Chapter 8: 'Tumbling up and down in the world'

The advent of the estate surveyor is discussed in McRae, *God Speed the Plough*. For the policies adopted to sustain and expand landed incomes, see *AgHEW, IV*, and the studies listed under chapter 6. A telling recent study is J. Broad, 'The Verneys as Enclosing Landlords, 1600–1800', in J. Chartres and D. Hey (eds), *English Rural Society, 1500–1800* (Cambridge, 1990). For conspicuous consumption among the landed elite, see F. J. Fisher, 'The Development of London as a Centre of Conspicuous Consumption in the Sixteenth and Seventeenth Centuries', *TRHS*, 4th Series, XXX (1948); L. Stone, *The Crisis of the Aristocracy, 1558–1641* (Oxford, 1965); L. Stone and J. C. Fawtier Stone, *An Open Elite? England, 1540–1880* (Oxford, 1984).

P. Bowden, 'Agricultural Prices, Farm Profits and Rents', in *AgHEW, IV*, discusses agricultural income and its distribution. For the prosperity of the yeomen, see M. Campbell, *The English Yeoman under Elizabeth and the Early Stuarts* (New Haven, 1942), and Johnson, *Archaeology of Capitalism*. The difficulties of husbandmen are discussed in many studies, of which the outstanding example is Part I of M. Spufford, *Contrasting Communities: English Villagers in the Sixteenth and Seventeenth Centuries* (Cambridge, 1974).

The mercantile community has been less fully researched. R. Grassby, *The Business Community of Seventeenth-Century England* (Cambridge, 1995) is a difficult but rewarding study, laced with imaginative insight. Other valuable studies of merchants and professional men include Sacks, *Widening Gate*; Brenner, *Merchants and Revolution*; Brooks, *Pettyfoggers and Vipers*; and W. Prest, *The Rise of the Barristers: A Social History of the English Bar, 1590–1640* (Oxford, 1986). On the changing structure of the guilds, see I. Archer, *The Pursuit of Stability: Social Relations in Elizabethan London* (Cambridge, 1991).

Urban wage-workers are discussed in Woodward, *Men at Work*. For rural industrial workers, see Hey, *Fiery Blades*, and the vivid depiction of the Stour Valley weaving communities in J. Walter, *Understanding Popular Violence in the English Revolution: The Colchester Plunderers* (Cambridge, 1999). The world of agricultural labourers is explored with great insight in A. Everitt, 'Farm Labourers', in *AgHEW, IV*, and in A. Hassell Smith, 'Labourers in Late Sixteenth-Century England', 2 parts, *Continuity and Change*, 4 (1989). For the structures of poverty, see Slack, *Poverty and Policy*. Scotland's vulnerability to famine is described in T. C. Smout, 'The Seventeenth Century', in Flinn (ed.), *Scottish Population History*. The English experience is analysed in J. Walter and R. Schofield, 'Famine, Disease and Crisis Mortality in Early Modern Society', and J. Walter, 'The Social Economy of Dearth in Early Modern England', both in J. Walter and R. Schofield (eds), *Famine, Disease and the Social Order in Early Modern Society* (Cambridge, 1989). The various dimensions of the traumatic economic crisis of the 1620s are examined in B. E. Supple, *Commercial Crisis and Change in England, 1600–1642* (Cambridge, 1959).

For perceptions of the changing structure of society, see K. Wrightson, ' "Sorts of People" in Tudor and Stuart England', in J. Barry and C. Brooks (eds), *The Middling Sort of People: Culture, Society and Politics in England, 1550–1800* (1994).

Chapter 9: Redefining the commonwealth

For the economic discourse of the period, see McRae, *God Speed the Plough*; Muldrew, *Economy of Obligation*; J. O. Appleby, *Economic Thought and Ideology in Seventeenth-Century England* (Princeton, 1978); J. McVeagh, *Tradeful Merchants: The Portrayal of the Capitalist in Literature* (1981); L. C. Stevenson, *Praise and Paradox: Merchants and Craftsmen in Elizabethan Popular Literature* (Cambridge, 1984). Changing attitudes towards usury are explored in N. Jones, *God and the Moneylenders: Usury and Law in Early Modern England* (Oxford, 1989). For changing policy on enclosure, see M. Beresford, 'Habitation versus Improvement: The Debate on Enclosure by Agreement', in F. J. Fisher (ed.), *Essays in the Economic and Social History of Tudor and Stuart England* (Cambridge, 1961); J. Thirsk, 'Enclosing and Engrossing', in *AgHEW, IV*; J. Thirsk, 'Changing Attitudes to Enclosure in the Seventeenth Century', in *The Festschrift for Professor Ju-Hwan Oh on the Occasion of his Sixtieth Birthday* (Taegu, Korea, 1991); McRae, *God Speed the Plough*; Goodacre, *Transformation of a Peasant Economy*. Change on the crown estates is illuminated in R. W. Hoyle (ed.), *The Estates of the English Crown, 1558–1640* (Cambridge, 1992), and early Stuart social and economic policy more generally in Slack, *Reformation to Improvement*.

The development of the poor laws is traced in Slack, *Poverty and Policy*, and A. L. Beier, 'Poverty and Progress in Early Modern England', in A. L. Beier, D. Cannadine and J. M. Rosenheim (eds), *The First Modern Society* (Cambridge, 1989). For emergency measures, see also P. Slack, 'Books of Orders: The Making of English Social Policy, 1575–1631', *TRHS*, 5th Series, XXX (1980); J. Walter and K. Wrightson, 'Dearth and the Social Order in Early Modern England', *P&P*, 71 (1976); R. B. Outhwaite, *Dearth, Public Policy and Social Disturbances in England, 1550–1800* (1991). The Scottish poor laws are examined by R. M. Mitchison in 'The Making of the Old Scottish Poor Law', *P&P*, 63 (1974), and her 'North and South: The Development of the Gulf in Poor Law Practice', in Houston and Whyte, *Scottish Society*. Among the best studies of the English poor laws in action are the essays by T. Wales and W. Newman Brown in R. M. Smith (ed.), *Land, Kinship and Life Cycle* (Cambridge, 1984), the relevant chapters of Archer, *The Pursuit of Stability*, and two recent essays by S. Hindle: 'Exclusion Crises: Poverty, Migration and Parochial Responsibility in English Rural Communities, c.1560–1660', *Rural History*, 7 (1996), and 'The Problem of Pauper Marriage in Seventeenth-Century England', *TRHS*, 6th Series, VIII (1998).

Demographic crises in early-seventeenth-century Scotland are examined in Smout, 'The Seventeenth Century', in Flinn (ed.), *Scottish Population History*. For Scottish migration, see I. D. Whyte, 'Population Mobility in Early Modern Scotland', in Houston and Whyte, *Scottish Society*, and D. Armitage, 'Making the Empire British: Scotland in the Atlantic World, 1542–1717', *P&P*, 155 (1997). English trends are detailed in Wrigley and Schofield, *Population History of England*. See also J. A. Goldstone, 'The Demographic Revolution in England: A Re-examination', *Population Studies*, 49 (1986). A British perspective on population dynamics is provided in R. A. Houston, *The Population History of Britain and Ireland, 1500–1750* (1992). Richard Napier's casebook is the subject of M. Macdonald's *Mystical Bedlam: Madness, Anxiety and Healing in Seventeenth-Century England* (Cambridge, 1981). For illegitimacy and the security of courtships in Elizabethan and early Stuart England, see the relevant essays in P. Laslett, K. Oosterveen and R. M. Smith (eds), *Bastardy and its Comparative History* (1980), and R. Adair, *Courtship, Illegitimacy and Marriage in Early Modern England* (Manchester and New York, 1996).

Chapter 10: Specialisation and integration, c.1650–c.1750

The new demographic context is depicted in Wrigley and Schofield, *Population History of England*, Flinn (ed.), *Scottish Population History*, and Houston, *Population History of Britain*. For mortality, see M. J. Dobson's illuminating *Contours of Death and Disease in Early Modern England* (Cambridge, 1997). Price trends are discussed in P. J. Bowden's 'Agricultural Prices, Wages, Farm Profits and Rents', in *AgHEW, V*, and detailed in his statistical appendix to the volume, which also includes real wage estimates. For real wages in the building trades, see Phelps-Brown and Hopkins, 'Seven Centuries', and Woodward's *Men at Work*. Scottish prices and wages are fully discussed in Gibson and Smout, *Prices, Food and Wages*.

For the emergence of greater regional economic specialisation, see

A. Kussmaul, *A General View of the Rural Economy of England, 1538–1840*
Cambridge, 1990). Patterns of agriculture and elements of agricultural change
in England and Wales are described in almost bewildering detail in the two-part
AgHEW, V. Overton, *Agricultural Revolution* provides a more structured inter-
pretation of the principal trends. For urbanisation see P. J. Corfield's excellent
The Impact of English Towns, 1700–1800 (Oxford, 1982), and the essays in
Clark (ed.), *Transformation of English Provincial Towns*, and P. Borsay (ed.),
The Eighteenth-Century Town: A Reader in English Urban History, 1688–1820
(London and New York, 1990). Borsay reprints E. A. Wrigley's 'Urban Growth
and Agricultural Change'. Also essential reading is Wrigley's 'A Simple Model
of London's Importance in Changing English Society and Economy, 1650–1750',
P&P, 37 (1967).

The European context of trade is sharply delineated in J. De Vries, *The
Economy of Europe in an Age of Crisis, 1600–1750* (Cambridge, 1976). Some
of the most important articles on trends in English trade are collected in W. E.
Minchinton (ed.), *The Growth of English Overseas Trade in the Seventeenth
and Eighteenth Centuries* (1969). Those by Ralph Davis are especially impor-
tant. Among more recent works, see Sacks, *The Widening Gate*; D. Ormrod,
'The Atlantic Economy and the "Protestant Capitalist International",
1651–1775', *Historical Research*, 160 (1993); N. Zahedieh, 'London and the
Colonial Consumer in the Late Seventeenth Century', *EcHR*, XLVII (1994);
C. J. French, ' "Crowded with Traders and a Great Commerce": London's Dom-
ination of English Overseas Trade, 1700–1775', *London Journal*, 17 (1992);
C. J. French, 'London's Overseas Trade with Europe, 1700–1775', *Journal of
European Economic History*, 23 (1994). The early volumes of the *Oxford
History of the British Empire* (*OHBE*) provide a vast amount of contextual
information, with guides to further reading. See in particular N. Zahedieh,
'Overseas Expansion and Trade in the Seventeenth Century', in N. Canny (ed.),
OHBE, vol. I: *The Origins of Empire* (Oxford, 1999), and D. Richardson, 'The
British Empire and the Atlantic Slave Trade, 1660–1807', in P. J. Marshall (ed.),
OHBE, vol. II: *The Eighteenth Century* (Oxford, 1999).

Domestic consumption is discussed in L. Weatherill, *Consumer Behaviour
and Material Culture in Britain, 1660–1760* (1988), Spufford, *The Great Reclothing*, and N. B. Harte, 'The Economics of Clothing in the Late Seventeenth
Century', *Textile History*, 22 (1991). Good recent studies of the manufacturing
industries of particular regions include M. B. Rowlands, *Masters and Men in
the West Midland Metalware Trades* (Manchester, 1975); L. Weatherill, 'The
Growth of the Pottery Industry in England, 1660–1815', *Post-Medieval Archaeo-
logy*, 17 (1983); J. Smail, *The Origins of Middle Class Culture: Halifax, York-
shire, 1660–1780* (Ithaca and London, 1994); Large, 'Urban Growth and
Agricultural Change'; Hey, *Fiery Blades of Hallamshire*; and the essays in
Hudson, *Regions and Industries*. For coal, see Hatcher, *History of the British
Coal Industry*, vol. I, M. W. Flinn and D. Stoker, *The History of the British Coal
Industry*, vol. II: *1700–1830: The Industrial Revolution* (Oxford, 1984), and
Levine and Wrightson, *Making of an Industrial Society*.

Internal trade and transportation are discussed by J. A. Chartres in *Internal Trade in England, 1500–1700* (1977) and in 'The Marketing of Agricultural Produce', in *AgHEW*, V. Other valuable contributions on these themes include M. Wanklyn, 'The Impact of Water Transport Facilities on English River Ports, c.1660–c.1760', *EcHR*, XLIX (1996); Rollison, *Local Origins of Modern Society*; Spufford, *Great Reclothing*; M. Carter, 'Town or Urban Society? St Ives in Huntingdonshire, 1630–1740', in Phythian-Adams (ed.), *Societies, Culture and Kinship*; N. Cox, 'The Distribution of Retailing Tradesmen in North Shropshire, 1660–1750', *Journal of Regional and Local History*, 13 (1993).

Chapter 11: The state and the Union

On public policy and 'mercantilism', Cunningham's *Growth of English Industry and Commerce* and Lipson's *Economic History of England* contain much information and many valuable insights. Among more recent works on these themes, see D. C. Coleman (ed.), *Revisions in Mercantilism* (1969); Appleby, *Economic Thought and Ideology*; J. Brewer, *The Sinews of Power: War, Money and the English State, 1688–1783* (1989); L. Davidson, T. Hitchcock, T. Keirn and R. B. Shoemaker (eds), *Stilling the Grumbling Hive: The Response to Social and Economic Problems in England, 1689–1750* (Stroud, 1992); J. Innes, 'The Domestic Face of the Military–Fiscal State: Government and Society in Eighteenth-Century Britain', in L. Stone (ed.), *An Imperial State at War: Britain from 1689 to 1815* (London and New York, 1989); P. O'Brien, T. Griffiths and P. Hunt, 'Political Components of the Industrial Revolution: Parliament and the English Cotton Textile Industry, 1660–1774', *EcHR*, XLIV (1991); J. Hoppit, 'Patterns of Parliamentary Legislation, 1660–1800', *Historical Journal*, 39 (1996).

P. G. M. Dickson's *The Financial Revolution in England, 1689–1756* (1967) is the most authoritative study of innovation in public finance at the turn of the eighteenth century. H. Roseveare, *The Financial Revolution, 1660–1720* (London and New York, 1991) is an excellent brief introduction to these complex matters. For the broader context of government finance in the period, see O'Brien and Hunt, 'Rise of a Fiscal State', and M. Braddick, *The Nerves of State: Taxation and the Financing of the English State, 1558–1714* (Manchester and New York, 1996). John Brewer's *Sinews of Power* introduced the concept of the 'fiscal–military state' and has been enormously influential. See also D. W. Jones, *War and Economy in the Age of William III and Marlborough* (Oxford, 1988), and P. K. O'Brien, *Power with Profit: The State and the Economy, 1688–1815* (1991).

The new historiography of economic and social change in Scotland really takes off from the later seventeenth century, partly as a result of the greater availability of records and partly because of the importance of establishing the state of the Scottish economy on the eve of union. For agriculture and rural society, see I. D. Whyte, *Agriculture and Society in Seventeenth-Century Scotland* (Edinburgh, 1979); T. M. Devine, *The Transformation of Rural Scotland: Social*

Change and the Agrarian Economy, 1660–1815 (Edinburgh, 1994); and the works of R. A. Dodgshon cited above. For prices, wages, nutrition and markets, see Gibson and Smout, *Prices, Food and Wages*. Industrial development is traced in Whyte, 'Proto-Industrialisation in Scotland', in Hudson (ed.), *Regions and Industries*; A. J. Durie, *The Scottish Linen Industry in the Eighteenth Century* (Edinburgh, 1979); C. A. Whatley, *The Scottish Salt Industry, 1570–1850* (Aberdeen, 1987); and the volumes of the *History of the British Coal Industry* by J. Hatcher and M. W. Flinn – though on coal, see also C. A. Whatley's corrective 'New Light on Nef's Numbers: Coal Mining and the First Phase of Scottish Industrialisation', in A. J. G. Cummings and T. M. Devine (eds), *Industry, Business and Society in Scotland since 1700* (Edinburgh, 1994). Urbanisation is discussed in M. Lynch, 'Urbanisation and Urban Networks in Seventeenth-Century Scotland', *Scottish Economic and Social History*, 12 (1992), and in T. M. Devine, 'Scottish Urbanisation', in his *Exploring the Scottish Past: Themes in the History of Scottish Society* (East Linton, 1995). For Edinburgh, see R. A. Houston, *Social Change in the Age of Enlightenment: Edinburgh, 1660–1760* (Oxford, 1994), and for Glasgow, G. Jackson, 'Glasgow in Transition, c.1660–1740', in T. M. Devine and G. Jackson (eds), *Glasgow. I: Beginnings to 1830* (Manchester, 1995). The principal study of Scottish trade in this period is T. C. Smout, *Scottish Trade on the Eve of Union, 1660–1707* (Edinburgh and London, 1963). For the Union and its impact, see the relevant chapters of Lenman, *Economic History of Modern Scotland*, and Whyte, *Scotland before the Industrial Revolution*, together with T. M. Devine's 'The Union of 1707 and Scottish Development', in *Exploring the Scottish Past*, and C. A. Whatley's *'Bought and Sold for English Gold?' Explaining the Union of 1707* (Glasgow, 1994).

For E. A. Wrigley's characterisation of the economy on the eve of the industrial revolution, see his *Continuity, Chance and Change: The Character of the Industrial Revolution in England* (Cambridge, 1988), and 'Society and the Economy in the Eighteenth Century', in Stone (ed.), *Imperial State at War*.

PART THREE: LIVING WITH THE MARKET, C.1660–C.1750

Gregory King's 'Scheme' and other extracts from his writings can be found in Thirsk and Cooper (eds), *Seventeenth-Century Economic Documents*. For comparison between King's estimates and the later tables of Joseph Massie, see P. Mathias, 'The Social Structure in the Eighteenth Century: A Calculation by Joseph Massie', *EcHR*, 2nd Series, X (1958).

Chapter 12: 'A nobleman, a gentleman, a yeoman': the landed interest

The structure of the 'landed interest' and the ethos of landed society are discussed in G. E. Mingay, *English Landed Society in the Eighteenth Century* (1963), in essays by Baugh, Habakkuk and Namier in D. Baugh (ed.), *Aristocratic Government and Society in Eighteenth-Century England: The Founda-*

tions of Stability (New York, 1975), and from a different perspective in E. P. Thompson, 'The Peculiarities of the English', in his *The Poverty of Theory and Other Essays* (1978). See also M. L. Bush, *The English Aristocracy: A Comparative Synthesis* (Manchester, 1984).

For the impact of the Civil Wars on landowners, see C. Clay, 'Landowners and Estate Management in England', in *AgHEW, V*, and two important articles by J. Thirsk: 'The Sales of Royalist Land during the Interregnum', *EcHR*, 2nd Series, V (1952–3), and 'The Restoration Land Settlement', *Journal of Modern History*, XXVI (1954). The sequestration system and its effects are also discussed in such county studies as J. S. Morrill, *Cheshire, 1630–1660: County Government and Society during the 'English Revolution'* (Oxford, 1974), and B. G. Blackwood, *The Lancashire Gentry and the Great Rebellion, 1640–60*, Chetham Society, 3rd Series, XXV (Manchester, 1978).

The strict settlement and the equity of redemption and their effects are examined in L. Bonfield, *Marriage Settlements, 1601–1740: The Adoption of the Strict Settlement* (Cambridge, 1983); R. Trumbach, *The Rise of the Egalitarian Family: Aristocratic Kinship and Domestic Roles in Eighteenth-Century England* (New York, San Francisco and London, 1978); L. Stone and J. C. Fawtier Stone, *An Open Elite?*, and H. J. Habakkuk's monumental *Marriage, Debt and the Estate System: English Landownership, 1650–1950* (Oxford, 1994).

The various dimensions of estate management have been very thoroughly studied. See for example Clay, 'Landowners and Estate Management in England', and D. W. Howell, 'Landowners and Estate Management in Wales', both in *AgHEW, V*; J. V. Beckett's *Coal and Tobacco: The Lowthers and the Economic Development of West Cumberland, 1660–1760* (Cambridge, 1981), and *The Aristocracy in England, 1660–1914* (Oxford, 1986); D. R. Hainsworth's excellent *Stewards, Lords and People: The Estate Steward and his World in Late Stuart England* (Cambridge, 1992). Tenant farmers and their fortunes have been less fully studied, but see Hainsworth, and also G. E. Mingay, 'The Agricultural Depression, 1730–1750', *EcHR*, 2nd Series, VIII (1956); P. Bowden, 'Agricultural Prices, Wages, Farm Profits and Rents', in *AgHEW, V*; R. C. Allen, *Enclosure and the Yeoman*; M. Spufford, 'The Limitations of the Probate inventory', in Chartres and Hey (eds), *English Rural Society*. For agricultural innovation, see A. H. John, 'The Course of Agricultural Change, 1660–1760', in Minchinton (ed.), *Essays in Agrarian History*, vol. I; J. Thirsk, 'Agricultural Innovations and their Diffusion', and F. Emery, 'Wales', both in *AgHEW, V*; and most recently Overton's *Agricultural Revolution*. Two good studies of change in Welsh landed society are P. Jenkins, *The Making of a Ruling Class: The Glamorgan Gentry, 1640–1790* (Cambridge, 1983), and M. Humphreys, *The Crisis of Community: Montgomeryshire, 1680–1815* (Cardiff, 1996). Knowledge of Scottish rural society in this period has been transformed in recent years by Whyte, *Agriculture and Society*, Dodgshon, *Land and Society*, Devine, *Transformation of Rural Scotland*, T. M. Devine, *Clanship to Crofter's War: The Social Transformation of the Scottish Highlands* (Manchester and New York, 1994), and Dodgshon, *From Chiefs to Landlords*.

Chapter 13: Capital and credit: the 'middle sort of people'

It is not easy to define the 'middle sort of people'. For the continuing effort
to conceptualise their place in society, see for example J.
Barry's intro-
duction to Barry and Brooks (eds), *The Middling Sort of People*; D. Wahrman,
'National Society, Communal Culture: An Argument about the Recent
Historiography of Eighteenth-Century Britain', *Social History*, 17 (1992);
J. Kent, 'The Rural "Middling Sort" in Early Modern England, c.1640–1740:
Some Economic, Political and Socio-Cultural Characteristics', *Rural History*, 10
(1999); H. R. French, 'Social Status, Localism, and the Middle Sort of People in
England, 1620–1750', *P&P*, 166 (2000). Nevertheless, this heterogeneous
grouping has inspired some first-rate studies in recent years. Studies touching on
most aspects of their economic and social worlds include: P. Earle, *The Making
of the English Middle Class: Business, Society and Family Life in London,
1660–1730* (1989); Grassby, *Business Community of Seventeenth Century
England*; Smail, *Origins of Middle Class Culture*; P. Corfield, *Power and the
Professions in Britain, 1700–1850* (1995); M. Hunt, *The Middling Sort:
Commerce, Gender and the Family in England, 1680–1780* (Berkeley, 1996);
Muldrew, *Economy of Obligation*; T. M. Devine, 'The Merchant Class of
Larger Scottish Towns in the Later Seventeenth and Early Eighteenth Centuries',
in his *Exploring the Scottish Past*; R. A. Houston, *Social Change in the Age of
Enlightenment*.

In addition, C. Brooks, 'Apprenticeship, Social Mobility, and the Middling
Sort, 1550–1800', in Barry and Brooks (eds), *The Middling Sort of People*, and
Ben Amos, *Adolescence and Youth*, examine entry and training. S. D'Cruze,
'The Middling Sort in Eighteenth-Century Colchester: Independence, Social
Relations and the Community Broker', and J. Barry, 'Bourgeois Collectivism?
Urban Association and the Middling Sort', both in Barry and Brooks (eds), *The
Middling Sort of People*, deal with patterns of association. Domestic ethos is
explored in M. Mascuch, 'Social Mobility and Middling Self-Identity: The Ethos
of British Autobiographers, 1600–1750', *Social History*, 20 (1995), and N.
Tadmor, *Family and Friends: Household, Kinship and Patronage in Eighteenth-
Century England* (Cambridge, 2000). On consumption and material culture, see
L. Weatherill, *Consumer Behaviour and Material Culture*; P. Borsay, *The English
Urban Renaissance: Culture and Society in the Provincial Town, 1660–1760*
(Oxford, 1989); the contributions to J. Brewer and R. Porter (eds), *Consump-
tion and the World of Goods* (London and New York, 1993); and Johnson,
Archaeology of Capitalism. Julian Hoppit's 'Attitudes to Credit in Britain,
1680–1790', *Historical Journal*, 33 (1990), contains much relevant discussion.
For social-mobility opportunities and aspirations, see, in addition to some of
the works cited above, L. Stone and J. C. Fawtier Stone, *An Open Elite?*; Beckett,
Aristocracy in England; M. Mascuch, 'Continuity and Change in a Patronage
Society: The Social Mobility of British Autobiographers, 1600–1750', *Journal
of Historical Sociology*, 7 (1994). The boatmen of Bridgnorth, including the
colourfully named members of the Head family, are described in M. Wanklyn,

'Urban Renewal in Early Modern England: Bridgnorth and the River Trade, 1660–1800', *Midland History*, XVIII (1993).

Chapter 14: Dependence and independence: labouring people

The world of labouring people in general is well introduced in R. W. Malcolmson, *Life and Labour in England, 1700–1780* (1981), and J. Rule, *The Experience of Labour in Eighteenth-Century Industry* (1981). An essential dimension of that world is examined in the latter's important essay 'The Property of Skill in the Period of Manufactures', in P. Joyce (ed.), *The Historical Meanings of Work* (Cambridge, 1987). For accounts of labour markets, conditions of work, wages and so on among particular groups and in particular local contexts, see Kussmaul, *Servants in Husbandry*; Rowlands, *Masters and Men*; M. Rediker, *Between the Devil and the Deep Blue Sea: Merchant Seamen, Pirates, and the Anglo-American Maritime World, 1700–1750* (Cambridge, 1987); Levine and Wrightson, *Making of an Industrial Society*; Woodward, *Men at Work*; Hey, *Fiery Blades of Hallamshire*; Wood, *Politics of Social Conflict*; J. D. Schwarz, *London in the Age of Industrialisation: Entrepreneurs, Labour Force and Living Conditions, 1700–1850* (Cambridge, 1992); J. Boulton, 'Wage Labour in Seventeenth-Century London', *EcHR*, XLIX (1996); Houston, *Social Change in the Age of Enlightenment*; C. Whatley, 'Labour in the Industrialising City, c.1660–1830', in Devine and Jackson, *Glasgow*; Devine, *Transformation of Rural Scotland*.

Rural–urban labour migration is discussed in D. Souden, 'Migrants and the Population Structure of Late Seventeenth-Century Provincial Cities and Market Towns', in Clark (ed.), *The Transformation of English Provincial Towns*. For good studies of women's work, see P. Earle, 'The Female Labour Market in London in the Late Seventeenth and Early Eighteenth Centuries', *EcHR*, 2nd Series, XLII (1989), and P. Sharpe, 'Literally Spinsters: A New Interpretation of Local Economy and Demography in Colyton in the Seventeenth and Eighteenth Centuries', *EcHR*, XLIV (1991). Children's work is discussed in M. Spufford, 'First Steps in Literacy: The Reading and Writing Experiences of the Humblest Seventeenth-Century Spiritual Autobiographers', *Social History*, 4 (1979), and H. Cunningham, 'The Employment and Underemployment of Children in England, c.1680–1851', *P&P*, 126 (1990). Broader discussions of wages can be found in Bowden, 'Agricultural Prices, Wages etc', in *AgHEW*, V, Woodward, *Men at Work*, and Gibson and Smout, *Prices, Food and Wages*. On the supplements provided by common rights, see Neeson, *Commoners*. Living standards and poverty are discussed, and vividly illustrated, in M. Spufford, *Poverty Portrayed: Gregory King and the Parish of Eccleshall* (Keele, 1995), the same author's 'Limitations of the Probate Inventory', and T. Arkell, 'The Incidence of Poverty in England in the Later Seventeenth Century', *Social History*, 12 (1987).

Attitudes to labour are dealt with in Appleby, *Economic Thought and Ideology*, and J. Hatcher, 'Labour, Leisure and Economic Thought before the

Nineteenth Century', *P&P*, 160 (1998). For attempts to instil greater labour discipline, see M. W. Flinn, *Men of Iron: The Crowleys in the Early Iron Industry* (Edinburgh, 1962); E. P. Thompson, 'Time, Work Discipline and Industrial Capitalism', *P&P*, 160 (1967); R. Houston, 'Coal, Class and Culture: Labour Relations in a Scottish Mining Community, 1650–1750', *Social History*, 8 (1983); E. P. Thompson, 'The Patricians and the Plebs', in his *Customs in Common* (1991); J. Rule, 'Employment and Authority: Masters and Men in Eighteenth-Century Manufacturing', in P. Griffiths, A. Fox and S. Hindle (eds), *The Experience of Authority in Early Modern England* (1996). The role of the poor laws is examined in Slack, *Poverty and Policy*; the essays by T. Wales and W. Newman Brown in Smith (ed.), *Land, Kinship and Life-Cycle*; B. Stapleton, 'Inherited Poverty and Life-Cycle Poverty: Odiham, Hants., 1650–1850', *Social History*, 18 (1993); T. Hitchcock, 'Paupers and Preachers: The SPCK and the Parochial Workhouse Movement', in Davidson, Hitchcock, Keirn and Shoemaker (eds), *Stilling the Grumbling Hive.*

Early forms of labour organisation, protest and industrial conflict have been researched since the time of Cunningham and Unwin. For a general introduction, see C. R. Dobson, *Masters and Journeymen: A Pre-History of Industrial Relations, 1717–1800* (1980). A number of important essays, including the enormously influential 'Moral Economy of the English Crowd', are collected in E. P. Thompson's *Customs in Common*. Among recent studies of industrial conflict in the period are J. Ellis, 'A Dynamic Society: Social Relations in Newcastle-upon-Tyne, 1660–1760', in Clark (ed.), *Transformation of English Provincial Towns*; Rediker, *Devil and the Deep Blue Sea*; Levine and Wrightson, *Making of an Industrial Society*; Rollison, *Local Origins of Modern Society*; Rule, 'Employment and Authority'; C. A. Whatley, ' "The Fettering Bonds of Brotherhood": Combinations and Labour Relations in the Scottish Coal-Mining Industry, c.1690–1775', *Social History*, 12 (1987), and 'How Tame were the Scottish Lowlanders during the Eighteenth Century?', in T. M. Devine (ed.), *Conflict and Stability in Scottish Society, 1700–1850* (Edinburgh, 1990).

LOCAL AND REGIONAL STUDIES

i. *Manors and parishes*

D. G. Hey, *An English Rural Community: Myddle [Shropshire] under the Tudors and Stuarts* (Leicester, 1974); W. G. Hoskins, *The Midland Peasant: The Economic and Social History of a Leicestershire Village [Wigston Magna]* (1957); C. Howell, *Land, Family and Inheritance in Transition: Kibworth Harcourt [Leicestershire], 1280–1700* (Cambridge, 1983); D. Levine and K. Wrightson, *The Making of an Industrial Society: Whickham [Co. Durham], 1560–1765* (Oxford, 1991); M. McIntosh, *A Community Transformed: The Manor and Liberty of Havering [Essex], 1500–1620* (Cambridge, 1991); G. Nair, *Highley [Shropshire]: The Development of a Community, 1550–1850* (Oxford, 1988); C. H. K. Oestmann, *Lordship and Community: The Lestrange Family and the Village of*

Hunstanton, Norfolk, in the First Half of the Sixteenth Century (Woodbridge, 1994); C. S. and C. S. Orwin, *The Open Fields [Laxton, Nottinghamshire]*, 3rd edn (Oxford, 1967); M. Spufford, *Poverty Portrayed. Gregory King and the Parish of Eccleshall [Staffordshire]* (Keele, 1995); K. Wrightson and D. Levine, *Poverty and Piety in an English Village: Terling [Essex], 1525–1700* (New York, San Francisco and London, 1979; 2nd edn, Oxford, 1995).

ii. Towns and cities

I. W. Archer, *The Pursuit of Stability: Social Relations in Elizabethan London* (Cambridge, 1991); J. Boulton, *Neighbourhood and Society: A London Suburb [Southwark] in the Seventeenth Century* (Cambridge, 1987); T. M. Devine and G. Jackson (eds), *Glasgow*, vol. I: *Beginnings to 1830* (Manchester, 1995); A. D. Dyer, *The City of Worcester in the Sixteenth Century* (1973); P. Earle, *The Making of the English Middle Class: Business, Society and Family Life in London, 1660–1730* (1989); R. Finlay, *Population and Metropolis: The Demography of London, 1580–1650* (Cambridge, 1981); R. A. Houston, *Social Change in the Age of Enlightenment: Edinburgh, 1660–1760* (Oxford, 1994); W. T. MacCaffrey, *Exeter, 1540–1640: The Growth of an English County Town* (Cambridge, Mass., 1958); D. Marcombe, *English Small Town Life: Retford [Nottinghamshire] 1520–1642* (Nottingham, 1993); D. M. Palliser, *Tudor York* (Oxford, 1979); C. Phythian-Adams, *Desolation of a City: Coventry and the Urban Crisis of the Later Middle Ages* (Cambridge, 1979); S. Rappaport, *Worlds within Worlds: Structures of Life in Sixteenth-Century London* (Cambridge, 1989); D. H. Sacks, *The Widening Gate: Bristol and the Atlantic Economy, 1450–1700* (Berkeley, Los Angeles and London, 1991); L. D. Schwarz, *London in the Age of Industrialisation: Entrepreneurs, Labour Force and Living Standards, 1700–1850* (Cambridge, 1992); J. Smail, *The Origins of Middle Class Culture: Halifax, Yorkshire, 1660–1780* (Ithaca and London, 1994); S. Thrupp, *The Merchant Class of Medieval London* (Chicago, 1948); T. S. Willan, *Elizabethan Manchester*, Chetham Society, 3rd Series, XXVII (Manchester, 1980).

iii. Counties and regions

S. D. Amussen, *An Ordered Society: Gender and Class in Early Modern England [East Anglia]* (Oxford, 1988); A. B. Appleby, *Famine in Tudor and Stuart England [Cumbria]* (Stanford and Liverpool, 1978); B. G. Blackwood, *The Lancashire Gentry and the Great Rebellion, 1640–60*, Chetham Society, 3rd Series, XXV (Manchester, 1978); C. W. Chalkin, *Seventeenth-Century Kent: A Social and Economic History* (1965); J. T. Cliffe, *The Yorkshire Gentry: From the Reformation to the Civil War* (1969); C. Dyer, *Lords and Peasants in a Changing Society: The Estates of the Bishopric of Worcester, 680–1540* (Cambridge, 1980); A. Fletcher, *A County Community in Peace and War: Sussex, 1600–1660* (1975); P. J. P. Goldberg, *Women, Work and Life-Cycle in a Medieval Community: Women in York and Yorkshire, c.1300–1520* (Oxford, 1992); J. Goodacre,

The Transformation of a Peasant Economy: Townspeople and Villagers in the Lutterworth Area [Leicestershire], 1500–1700 (Aldershot, 1994); A. Hassell Smith, County and Court: Government and Politics in Norfolk, 1558–1603 (Oxford, 1974); D. Hey, The Fiery Blades of Hallamshire: Sheffield and its Neighbourhood, 1660–1740 (Leicester, London and New York, 1993); G. A. J. Hodgett, Tudor Lincolnshire (Lincoln, 1975); C. Holmes, Seventeenth-Century Lincolnshire (Lincoln, 1980); M. Humphreys, The Crisis of Community: Montgomeryshire, 1680–1815 (Cardiff, 1996); M. E. James, Family, Lineage and Civil Society: A Study of Society, Politics and Mentality in the Durham Region, 1500–1640 (Oxford, 1974); P. Jenkins, The Making of a Ruling Class: The Glamorgan Gentry, 1640–1790 (Cambridge, 1983); N. Lowe, The Lancashire Textile Industry in the Sixteenth Century, Chetham Society, 3rd Series, 20 (Manchester, 1972); D. MacCulloch, Suffolk and the Tudors: Politics and Religion in an English County, 1500–1600 (Oxford, 1986); A. F. Pollard, North-Eastern England during the Wars of the Roses: Lay Society, War and Politics, 1450–1500 (Oxford, 1990); L. R. Poos, A Rural Society after the Black Death: Essex, 1350–1525 (Cambridge, 1991); G. D. Ramsay, The Wiltshire Woollen Industry in the Sixteenth and Seventeenth Centuries (Oxford, 1943); D. Rollison, The Local Origins of Modern Society: Gloucestershire, 1500–1800 (London and New York, 1992); M. B. Rowlands, Masters and Men in the West Midlands Metalware Trades before the Industrial Revolution (Manchester, 1975); R. B. Smith, Land and Politics in the England of Henry VIII: The West Riding of Yorkshire, 1530–46 (Oxford, 1970); V. Skipp, Crisis and Development: An Ecological Case-Study of the Forest of Arden [Warwickshire], 1570–1674 (Cambridge, 1978); M. Spufford, Contrasting Communities: English Villagers in the Sixteenth and Seventeenth Centuries [Cambridgeshire] (Cambridge, 1974); J. Thirsk, English Peasant Farming: The Agrarian History of Lincolnshire from Tudor to Recent Times (1957); G. H. Tupling, The Economic History of Rossendale [Lancashire], Chetham Society, New Series, LXXXVI (Manchester, 1927); S. J. and S. J. Watts, From Border to Middle Shire: Northumberland, 1586–1625 (Leicester, 1975); L. Weatherill, The Pottery Trade and North Staffordshire, 1660–1760 (Manchester, 1971); A. Wood, The Politics of Social Conflict: The Peak Country [Derbyshire], 1520–1770 (Cambridge, 1999); M. Zell, Industry in the Countryside: Wealden Society [Kent] in the Sixteenth Century (Cambridge, 1994). See also the essays on economic and social development in the various volumes of the Victoria History of the Counties of England.

UNPUBLISHED DISSERTATIONS

J. Cooper, 'Nayland: Prosperity and Decline in a Suffolk Cloth Town, 1650–1800' (University of Essex MA in Local and Regional History, 1996); N. A. J. Davie, 'Custom and Conflict in a Wealden Village: Pluckley, 1550–1700' (University of Oxford DPhil., 1987); R. A. Davies, 'Community, Parish and Poverty: Old Swinford, 1660–1730' (Leicester University PhD, 1987); H. R. French, 'Chief Inhabitants and their Areas of Influence: Local Ruling Groups in

Essex and Suffolk Parishes, 1630–1720' (University of Cambridge PhD, 1993); F. Hull, 'Agriculture and Rural Society in Essex, 1560–1640' (University of London PhD, 1950); A. D. Mackinnon, ' "According to the Custom of the Place I Now Live In": Life and Land in Seventeenth-Century Earls Colne, Essex' (Melbourne University PhD, 1994); M. J. Mascuch, 'Social Mobility in English Autobiography, 1600–1750' (University of Cambridge PhD, 1989); F. A. C. Newall, 'Socio-economic Influences in the Demography of Aldenham: An Exploration of the Techniques and Application of Family Reconstitution' (University of Cambridge PhD, 1985); S. Pennell, 'The Material Culture of Food in Early Modern England, c.1650–1750' (University of Oxford DPhil., 1997); L. Shaw-Taylor, 'Proletarianisation, Parliamentary Enclosure, and the Household Economy of the Labouring Poor, 1750–1850' (University of Cambridge PhD, 1999).

Index